S0-ESG-982

*Person to Person*
Revised

This book is dedicated
in memory of my Dad
**WILLIAM T. RICHARDS**
August 22, 1921—March 13, 1975

# Person to Person
## Revised

**Connie R. Sasse**
Former Editor,
*Tips and Topics,*
Texas Tech University
Lubbock, Texas

**GLENCOE PUBLISHING COMPANY**
BENNETT & McKNIGHT DIVISION

Copyright © 1981 by Connie Sasse

Published by Glencoe Publishing Company, a division of Macmillan, Inc.

All rights reserved. No part of this text shall be reproduced or transmitted in any form or by any means, electronic or mechanical, including photocopying, recording, or by any information storage and retrieval system, without written permission from the Publisher.

Send all inquiries to:
Glencoe Publishing Company
15319 Chatsworth Street
Mission Hills, California 91345

Printed in the United States of America

**ISBN 0-02-665320-6 (Student Text)**
ISBN 0-02-665340-0 (Student Guide)
ISBN 0-02-665330-3 (Teacher's Guide)

6 7 8 9 10  91 90 89 88 87

# Preface

Relationships with others are an inescapable part of everyday life. People have relationships with family members, peers, employers, friends, colleagues, and authority figures. Satisfaction with life often depends on the quality of a person's relationships with others. Frequently, people tolerate situations which could be changed and improved with some skill and knowledge in the art of relating to others.

People can be taught to improve their relationships. This happens when people are able to learn about themselves and others and to understand how person-to-person relationships can be built.

This book was written to help students learn to relate to the people who make up their worlds. It begins with a brief survey of what happens to relationships in a changing world. The second unit was designed to help students understand themselves better, because learning relationship skills begins with learning about the self. Self-concept and self-acceptance are discussed as well as the basic needs which all people have. The process of decision making based on values is explored and then applied to the areas of drug use and premarital sex. Students will find that when they understand themselves—what they are, what they can do, and what they value—they have a better basis for understanding and relating to others.

The third unit in this book explores how people relate to others. There are certain common relationships traits that apply when people build relationships in any setting. Important aspects of relating to others included in this unit are communication, roles, and conflict between people.

In the unit on family relationships, the material concerning how people relate to others is applied to the family. Students will study aspects of living in families as well as the process of forming their own families. Family breakdown and changing life styles are also explored.

Finally, relationships develop between students and the larger world as they join groups and become members of the world of work. The final unit in this book explores students' relationships with that world.

Accompanying the text is a series of "Experiences in Human Relations." The "Experiences" were designed to give students an opportunity to interact with each other or to confront themselves and what they believe. "Experiences" should help increase student self-awareness, promote individual thought and self-assessment, and stimulate values clarification.

Learning facts and figures about human relationships can be important in understanding others. However, a knowledge of such facts rarely changes behavior. Students' affective responses are more important in behavioral change than their cognitive ones.

This book is a blend of the cognitive and the affective, designed to teach students skills and processes. Faced with a changing world and a bewildering array of options, they will be able to use these skills and processes as tools in making rational, intelligent choices about their lives and relationships.

## Acknowledgments

This book could not have been written without the help of the following people:

    Chuck and Lisa Sasse, who showed patient tolerance for a disrupted household, a preoccupied wife and mother, and the ups and downs of living with an author;

    Helen Kowtaluk, who used her considerable editorial prowess to strengthen and improve the manuscript;

    Cheryl Wormley and Dr. Joyce Nies, who reviewed the manuscript, making many useful suggestions and comments; and

    Drs. Joan Kelly and Valerie Chamberlain, who convinced me that I had the capabilities needed to undertake such a project.

CRS

**Drawings: Mary Lou Myers and Darcy Sternitzky**

**Production Manager: Gordon Guderjan**

**Cover Design: Judy Constantino**

# Table of Contents

**PREFACE, 5**

**ACKNOWLEDGMENTS, 6**

**UNIT ONE: RELATIONSHIPS, 11**

### Chapter 1: Relationships in a Changing World, 12
The Fast Pace of Change, 12
A New Stress On Relationships, 18
Learning New Relationship Skills, 20

**UNIT TWO: RELATIONSHIPS BEGIN WITH YOU, 23**

### Chapter 2: Discovering Who You Are, 24
How Selves Differ, 24
Development of the Self, 26
Self-Concept, 29
Learning Self-Acceptance, 40

### Chapter 3: Making the Most of Yourself, 44
Meeting Your Needs, 45
Self-Actualizing People, 52

### Chapter 4: Decision Making and Values, 60
The Process of Decision Making, 60
What Are Values?, 65
Sources of Values, 69
The Valuing Process, 72
Exploring Your Values, 76

### Chapter 5: Personal Decisions, 80

Drug Definitions, 80
Kinds of Drugs, 84
Why People Use Drugs, 94
Decision Making About Drugs, 96
Patterns of Premarital Sexual Behavior, 99
Sexual Responsibilities, 101
Decision Making About Sex, 103

## UNIT THREE: RELATING TO OTHERS, 107

### Chapter 6: Building Relationships, 108

Kinds of Relationships, 108
Purposes of Relationships, 111
Developing Relationships, 115
Characteristics of Relationships, 121
Relating Person-to-Person, 131

### Chapter 7: Communicating with Others, 136

Communication is Important, 136
Levels of Verbal Communication, 139
Patterns of Communication, 144
Learning Communication Skills, 148
Nonverbal Communication, 157
Communication Risks and Benefits, 163

### Chapter 8: Role Relationships, 165

What are Roles?, 165
How Roles Work, 170
Role Conflict, 175
Sex Roles, 177
Beyond Roles, 187

### Chapter 9: Conflict in Relationships, 189

What is Conflict?, 189
Handling Conflict, 194

## UNIT FOUR: FAMILY RELATIONSHIPS, 209

### Chapter 10: Living in Families, 210

Functions of Families, 212
The Family Style, 219
Relationships in the Family, 224
Family Crisis, 230

### Chapter 11: Forming Your Own Family, 236

Love, 237
Forming Your Family, 245

### Chapter 12: Changing Life Styles, 258

Singlehood, 260
Single Parents, 263
Changing Marriage Styles, 266
Living Together, 278
Communal Living, 279

### Chapter 13: Family Breakdown—Death and Divorce, 286

Death, 286
Divorce, 298

## UNIT FIVE: RELATING TO THE LARGER WORLD, 313

### Chapter 14: Relationships in Groups, 314

Meeting Needs Through Groups, 316
Roles in Groups, 319
Group Norms, 329
Group Communication, 332
Growing Through Group Membership, 335

**Chapter 15: Entering the World of Work, 338**
　Why Work?, 340
　Work Roles, 344
　Relationships on the Job, 347
　Job Expectations, 352

**Chapter 16: Careers in Working with Others, 361**
　Choosing a Career, 361
　Career Clusters and Ladders, 363
　Careers in Service Industries, 367
　Planning for the Future, 384

# UNIT ONE
## *Relationships*

**Chapter 1. Relationships in a Changing World, 12**

# CHAPTER 1
## Relationships in a Changing World

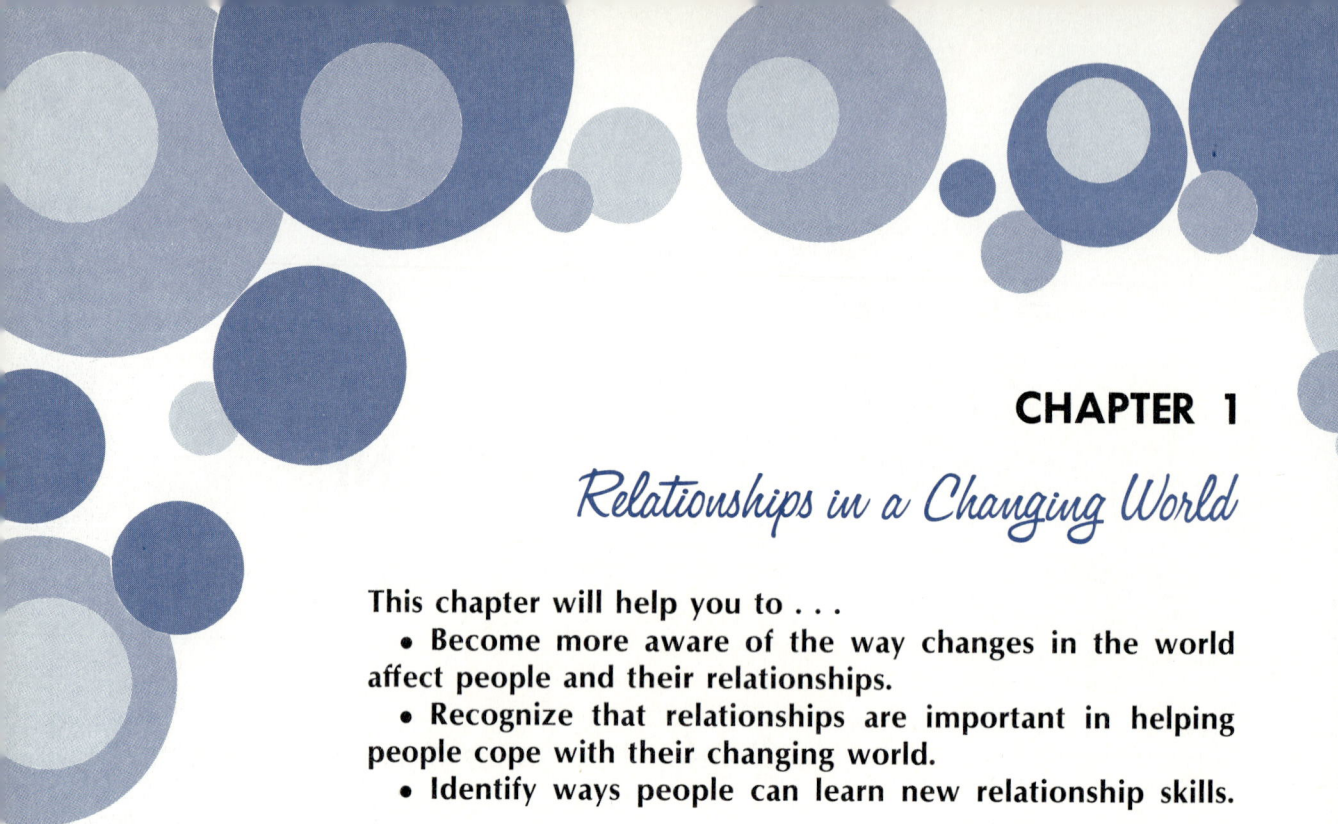

This chapter will help you to . . .
- Become more aware of the way changes in the world affect people and their relationships.
- Recognize that relationships are important in helping people cope with their changing world.
- Identify ways people can learn new relationship skills.

People are always faced with the problem of building relationships with others. You first faced this issue as a child, when you tried to get along with people you knew. The need to get along with others is part of your life as a teenager and will continue throughout your adult years.

Building good relationships with other people is one way to find joy and satisfaction throughout life. Yet your ability to build such relationships is influenced by the fast pace of change.

### THE FAST PACE OF CHANGE

Almost every day, scientists announce new discoveries and breakthroughs. Often, these discoveries are quickly put to practical use in ways that change lives. For example, about thirty-five years ago television became available to the public. Since then, people's use of leisure time has changed. Instead of playing games, reading, or making music together, families are apt to center their recreation around the television.

The pioneering spirit of the people in the United States created a nation of change. As a result, you now live in an age in which technology changes at a rapid pace. This is because change breeds on change. New technology leads to new discoveries, which lead to new technology. Thus change spirals upward at an ever-faster pace. It affects people's abilities to relate to each other.

What are some of the fast-moving changes occurring today? How do such changes affect relationships?

### Changes at Home

In the past, most people lived their entire lives in one community. Today, 20 percent of the people in the United States move each year. Most of these moves mean leaving

**Ch. 1: Relationships in a Changing World**

*Scientists have helped increase the rate of change through discoveries and breakthroughs.*

## Unit 1: Relationships

friends, neighbors, schools, and communities. Families who move are faced with building new relationships.

Karen Monroe describes how moving has influenced her family. She says, "My dad changes jobs pretty often and that means we've moved a lot. This is the third high school I've attended. You'd think by now I'd be used to going to schools where I don't know anyone. Instead, I think it's harder each time I have to leave my friends and start again. When my family moves, it's more than just a new apartment or house. It's new neighbors, new teachers, new classmates, and new friends."

New consumer products can also create changes in the home. Microwave ovens, quadrophonic sound, intercom systems, and special television equipment are just a few products available through the new technology.

Such changes are apt to continue. Soon automatic cleaning systems for homes will be available. These will remove dirt and dust with a flick of the switch. Within your lifetime, most homes are expected to have a computer terminal. Shopping will be one of many activities done through the computer.

These new products can influence relationships in the home in many ways. Sometimes such products can cause conflict. When the Andrews family bought a new component stereo system, no one could agree on what kind of music to play. Mr. Andrews wanted to play classical music. Country music was Mrs. Andrews' favorite. The two Andrews teenagers liked to play rock music. Each evening, they began to quarrel as soon as the stereo system was turned on. Thus, in the Andrews family, the new stereo system created conflict rather than harmony.

Mrs. Platt dreaded coming home from work each day because she hated to cook. Knowing she had to fix supper for her family made her cross and short tempered. At the end of the year, she received a bonus for outstanding performance on the job. She spent the bonus on a microwave oven. The new oven made supper preparation an easy chore. Mrs. Platt found she was happier and more pleasant toward her family after work. Her good humor at suppertime helped improve the relationships in the family. The microwave oven led to better human relations in the Platt home.

## CHANGES IN EDUCATION

Changes in education affect how people live and learn. It is estimated that knowledge, the total of what people know, doubles every ten years. Teaching this greater volume of knowledge has led to changes in education.

The school which Jeff Lawrence attends uses modular scheduling. He goes to classes for varying lengths of time each day, depending on the kind of instruction planned. The flexible time plan lets Jeff meet and get to know many students. He has more friends than he had in his previous school.

Cleo Walls attends a school which uses individualized instruction so students can learn at their own pace. Computers teach many subjects at Cleo's school. Cleo finds that she has little time to be with her friends. When all students work at their own speed, they aren't free to get together to talk between classes, over lunch, or after school. Cleo often goes home from school without having had a chance to see her best friend or her dating partner. When Cleo works with the computer, she misses having contact with teachers. Computer learning in Cleo's school eliminates the chance for strong student-teacher relationships.

In the future, a computer terminal in each home may be the source of education for all

## Ch. 1: Relationships in a Changing World

family members. The computer will assign lessons by the knowledge level of each learner. When this occurs, most students will have little daily contact with others. They may join clubs or other groups to have a chance to be with their friends.

Parents as well as children will have lessons on the computer. Family members may do homework together. Thus the common experience of being students could help draw families closer together.

### CHANGES AT WORK

Many of the students in the future will be adults who are taking job retraining. The use of technology in business has cut out many unskilled jobs. This trend is expected to continue into the future. New careers and jobs are being developed all the time. As a result, workers may need retraining several times in their lives as the job market changes and their job skills become outdated.

People will need to learn new ways of relating to others during retraining and on new jobs. Mr. Jacobs had supervised ten people in a factory. He expected the workers in his department to obey his orders without question. When the company bought machines to replace the workers, it paid for their retraining. Mr. Jacobs found it frustrating to be a student again. The other students would not help or obey him when he "ordered" them to do something. Mr. Jacobs found that he had to learn to relate to the other students as equals. He discovered that he could not use his former position as the boss to make others do as he wished.

Some workers find it hard to adjust to new work situations. Alice Graber sold insurance and spent most of her days out of the office with customers. Promoted to a full-time position in the office, she found it hard to work with the same people day after day. Her methods of relating to customers did not always work with co-workers in the office. Many people like Alice find that they need different relationship skills on each of the jobs they hold during their working lifetime.

### CHANGES IN SOCIETY

Changes also take place in society as a whole. New sources of energy must be developed as people use up supplies of coal, oil, and natural gas. Solar and nuclear energy may bring changes in housing and transportation.

Because people move frequently, many live far from parents, grandparents, aunts, uncles, and cousins. As energy to power cars, trains, or airplanes becomes more expensive and less available, many people will be unable to make trips to see relatives. John and Grace Ladd have not seen their grandparents for two years. The trip from their home in Montana to their grandparents' home in Florida is too expensive for the Ladd family to afford.

Space exploration continues to bring scientific knowledge and progress. Probes to other planets and trips to the moon may be commonplace in the future. Such long space voyages may cause family members to be separated for months at a time. Children left behind may not recognize their parents when they return to earth. Thus family relationships may be weakened by such travel. Privacy and room will be limited on journeys into space. Thus space travelers will have to learn to get along with others under stressful, difficult conditions.

The world is becoming more mechanized and computerized. Computers bill and collect accounts for credit card firms. People are no longer asked to identify themselves by name. Instead, they are asked to supply their Social Security number or their driver's license number. Banking, tax, and medical records are often filed by numbers rather than

15

**Unit 1: Relationships**

name. Groups to which people belong often use computerized mailings.

Walter Harris often wonders if his identification numbers are somehow more important than he is. When he goes to the bank, the tellers identify him as account number 45-95175 rather than by his name. This makes Walter feel that the tellers don't see or relate to him as a person, but simply as a number. He believes that being known by numbers lessens him as a person.

*In an impersonal world, people are often identified by number rather than name.*

## experiences in human relations

### WHAT'S YOUR NUMBER?

Computers have taken over much of the record keeping in this country. As a result, numbers are often more important than names. This experience will help you explore some of the ways people are "numbered."

Think about the numbers that you have. Do you have a Social Security number? A driver's license number? A work identification number? Credit cards? Insurance numbers? Bank account numbers? A check through your personal papers may show that you have more identifying numbers than you realized. Count the numbers you have.

Talk to some adults who are no longer students. Ask them to count how many identifying numbers they have. They may have many of the same numbers as you do, but they may also have others, such as union or professional group membership numbers and tax or loan numbers.

Share your findings with your classmates. Listen as they tell what they discovered about numbers. Did you have more or fewer numbers than most of your classmates? What was the highest total of numbers that any one person had? The lowest? What do all these numbers tell you about your world?

• • • • • • • • • • • • • • • • • • • •

The widespread use of credit has changed the way people shop and live. Vicky Martinez uses her credit cards to purchase items ranging from medicines to vacation trips. Such use of credit and credit cards can influence

### Ch. 1: Relationships in a Changing World

family relationships. Clare and Duane Evans applied for and received several credit cards after their marriage. They enjoyed the freedom of buying items for which they could not pay cash. However, when the bills started coming in, their relationship suffered. They discovered that the interest on the money they owed each month was about one-half of Clare's salary. Arguments soon raged about whose fault it was that they were having financial problems. They were close to divorce over the use of credit when they went to a marriage counselor. The counselor helped them make a plan for getting out of debt. Clare and Duane did not get a divorce, but they learned that relationships can be affected by conflict over money and credit.

Some people predict that in the future, Americans will live in a cashless world. Instead of paying cash for goods, people will carry special money cards. When placed in the computer terminals at stores, these cards will transfer funds from the shopper's account to the store's. Such a system may help families make better use of their money. On the other hand, such a system could also increase family disagreement over the use of money.

The changes which occur in society bring exciting new choices to people. They open up new fast-paced and stimulating ways of living. Although these changes may bring personal satisfaction, they may not help people understand each other better. In fact, changes often seem to increase the distance between people.

A television set brings entertainment right into the home. Mr. Cravens, a devoted sports fan, spends his weekends watching ball games and other athletic contests. He makes no time for conversation or even a game of catch with his children. While Mr. Cravens' interest in televised sports bring him much

## Unit 1: Relationships

pleasure, it also leads to poor relationships with his children.

When a situation changes, people need to change, too. If they don't, they are less able to relate to others around them. They have more difficulty understanding themselves, their families, their neighbors, their co-workers, or people of other nations. Thus changes at home, at work, in education, and in society bring about a new emphasis on relating to others.

## experiences in human relations

### YOUR CHANGING WORLD

The world is constantly changing. Some changes affect most people. Others influence only a few. This experience will help you think about some of the changes that have influenced you.

On a separate piece of paper, list ten changes that you have experienced in your lifetime. These changes may have taken place at home, school, or work or in your family, neighborhood, religious group, or community. When you have completed your list, think about what influence these changes had on you. Did any of these events cause much direct change in your personal life? Did they influence your family or others?

Were most of the changes concerned with technology or with relationships? What did you do about each change? How did you feel about the changes you listed? Did you see them as exciting opportunities? Or were they unpleasant or unhappy events?

What kind of changes do you foresee in your future? List some technological changes that you expect to occur. What changes in relationships might occur in your future?

• • • • • • • • • • • • • • • • • • •

### A NEW STRESS ON RELATIONSHIPS

Many of the changes discussed in this chapter bring loneliness to people. Computerization, frequent family moves, new jobs, and changes in life style affect relationships. Changes often occur so rapidly that people have little time to adjust to them. This leaves individuals with even less time to give to their relationships with others.

In the past, many people believed that material possessions could help protect them from the changing world. They were absorbed in earning money for more clothing, better housing, or recreational equipment. Today change occurs so rapidly that many people find that material goods don't bring the happiness they expected.

Maria Barton had always been lonely as she grew up. Her family moved many times and Maria made few friends. Maria's dream was to have a home of her own someday. A home, she believed, would keep her from being so lonesome. Maria describes what happened after she and her husband finally were able to buy a small house. "At first, it was like my dream," she says. "But after a while I realized that I was just as lonely in my house as I had been before. After all, a house is only four walls and a roof. Somehow, I had gotten so I believed that I would automatically have many friends if I just had a house. I still love my house dearly, but I realize now that I have to make my own friends—the house can't do that for me."

## Ch. 1: Relationships in a Changing World

In the past, people who lived in the same community all their lives had strong, deep relationships with the people they knew. Now, in a world where families move an average of every five years, there is no time to build such strong ties to others.

Glen Davis is in the Air Force. He says, "In the Air Force, you just expect to be transferred every 18 months or so. You have to learn to meet people easily and to work and have fun with people who are strangers. My parents have lived in the same place for over 30 years. They don't like to associate with people they don't know. That kind of attitude may be fine for their situation, but it would be a disaster in my life. I go to a new duty station, meet many people, build a few fairly close relationships, and then move on. I can't allow myself to be upset because I'm leaving friends behind. I know I'll make new ones at my next job."

People who enter new schools or new jobs can't wait for others to make the first move. They have to be friendly, outgoing, and willing to put forth some effort to meet and learn about others. Those who do not know how to do this are apt to be lonely and friendless as they move from one place to another.

Because people are apt to move, change jobs, or divorce, relationships today are less permanent. It makes sense to build relationships with many people, rather than with only a few. A person with a few close ties may find loneliness if friends move.

Sonja and Louise were best friends who worked in the same office. Because of their friendship, they ignored the others who worked with them. When Louise was transferred to another department, Sonja was lonely and miserable without her friend. She barely knew the names of the others in her office. They had been ignored so long that they weren't willing to be friendly with her. It took a long time before Sonja was able to make friends with the others. When she did, she was careful not to become too friendly with any one of them. She had discovered that having many office friendships protected her from loneliness if someone was transferred or left the job.

Skill in communicating with others is necessary in a changing world. People must be able to understand changes and explain them to others. Being able to send and receive information requires skill in speaking, writing, and listening.

Eddie's school began using a new system of course registration during his junior year. The new system was not hard, but it was very different from the old one. Many students were unable to figure out how they were supposed to sign up for the courses they wanted for the next fall. Eddie listened carefully as the counselor explained the new system. He read the pamphlet explaining the new system from cover to cover. When he didn't understand the directions on the cards and charts, he asked intelligent questions. Because Eddie used his communication skills, he was able to understand the change in registration procedure. Other students with fewer skills had problems in handling the new system.

Changes in ways of living can be handled through good communication. Marion's career as a teacher was very important to her. Therefore, after the birth of her first baby, she continued teaching school. The baby was left with a sitter each day. Marion and her husband, Doug, shared the housework and the child care in the evenings and on weekends. Both Marion and Doug's parents disapproved of their life style. The parents felt that Marion should stay home with the baby and that

Unit 1: Relationships

Doug should not have to help at home so much. By talking things over with their parents, Marion and Doug were able to explain why they felt that their life-style was right for them. Their communication skills helped their parents begin to understand and accept the differences between their lives and their children's lives.

As the population of the United States grows, there is less space for each person. The crowding together that occurs often causes conflict. People of different races or ethnic groups may not understand each other's customs and habits. New relationship skills are needed so that people can learn to live peacefully with others who are different from themselves.

Change often creates a need to be able to resolve conflict successfully on a personal level. After Mr. and Mrs. Greystone divorced, Bobby Greystone lived with his mother. Mr. Greystone had usually served as a peacemaker when Bobby and Mrs. Greystone disagreed or had fights. After the divorce, there was no one to help them solve their differences. Their fights usually ended up with the situation still unsolved. Mrs. Greystone and Bobby needed to learn new ways to settle conflict in order to live together without constant friction.

Many of today's changes involve attitudes, beliefs, and values. There are wide differences and variations in what people believe about any one issue. These differences make it important that people learn to accept and tolerate others with different ideas. No one way of life, thinking, or believing can be suitable for everyone. You will need the skills to build your life according to your own ideals and beliefs. At the same time, you will need to accept the way others choose to build their lives, even though their life styles may differ greatly from yours.

## LEARNING NEW RELATIONSHIP SKILLS

In a changing world, people need all the skills they can get to find satisfaction in their relationships. However, skills in relating to others don't come naturally. Some people have learned these skills in their family or from others with whom they interact. Most people, however, have a very limited number of relationship skills. While they may long to have good relationships, they do not understand other people. They also don't act in ways that help others understand them. Thus they remain lonely strangers. Most people need help to learn better ways of relating to others.

One way people can learn to understand themselves and others is through courses in human relationships. High schools and colleges offer classes which can help students learn more about themselves, others, and relationships. Richard took a one-semester course called "Personal Living" during his senior year in high school. The content of the course helped Richard discover ways that he could improve his relationships with family and friends.

Many classes in relationships and related topics are offered by religious groups, YMCA's and YWCA's, Cooperative Extension Service, and other groups. Mr. and Mrs. Colburn took a four-week course in parent education at their temple last winter. They learned some new ways of disciplining and communicating with their children.

Some people learn about relating to others through counseling or therapy. Marriage counselors help husbands and wives learn to relate better to each other. Psychologists and psychiatrists work to help troubled people understand themselves and their relationships to others in a changing world. Many students with problems talk to counselors to help them through unhappy times.

*Ch. 1: Relationships in a Changing World*

Joe was always in trouble in Mr. Maple's history class. After being asked to leave the class two weeks in a row, Joe began visiting the counselor, Mrs. Thomas. Through counseling, Mrs. Thomas helped Joe begin to understand why he had so much trouble in his relationship with Mr. Maple.

Finally, many people learn about relationship skills through reading books and newspaper and magazine articles. There are many available publications concerned with relating to others. Reading alone, however, will not improve a person's skill in getting along with others. You have to be willing to try to put into practice the ideas about which you have read. Relationship skills need to be practiced and used to be effective.

You can learn new skills in relating to other people. Most relationships can be improved even if they are satisfactory to begin with. If you learn the ability to get along at home, at school, on the job, and during your leisure time, you will be better prepared for the future.

*Many organizations offer courses which help parents learn to enjoy working and playing with their children.*

Unit 1: Relationships

## experiences in human relations

### LOOKING AT THE FUTURE

Pretend that you have a magic crystal ball which can foretell your future. Look into the ball and list five events which you see for yourself in the future. Write these five events on a sheet of paper. Estimate when these events will happen.

Look over your list. How many of these events can you do completely alone? Which of them involve other people? Below your list of events, list the other people who will be involved in these events in your future. These may include friends, family members, teachers, employers, dating partners, a spouse, children, or others.

What kind of skills in relating to others do you think your future will require? Do you possess the necessary skills to have good relationships with all the people in your future? How do you expect to learn the skills that you will need?

### TO SUM UP...

1. Explain the statement, "Change breeds on change."
2. What are some of the changes that have occurred at home, school, and work and in society?
3. Describe some of the relationship skills needed by families who move frequently.
4. Why are relationships today less permanent than in the past?
5. List some ways people can learn new skills in relating to others.

# UNIT TWO

## Relationships Begin with You

**Chapter 2. Discovering Who You Are, 24**
**Chapter 3. Making the Most of Yourself, 44**
**Chapter 4. Decision Making and Values, 60**
**Chapter 5. Personal Decisions, 80**

# CHAPTER 2

## Discovering Who You Are

This chapter will help you to . . .
- Describe ways in which people's selves differ.
- List influences which can direct or change the development of a child's self.
- Understand what self-concepts are, how they develop, and how and why people protect them.
- Describe the characteristics of a self-accepting person.

Each person is unique in appearance, experiences, goals, thoughts, and ideas. You have a combination of qualities unlike that of any other person. These qualities make up your basic worth as a person and as a human being. This unique core of your personality is a center of strength and growth which is called your *self*. It belongs only to you—no one else on earth is the same as you are. Even identical twins, who look alike, have different personality traits.

### HOW SELVES DIFFER

Your unique self stems from the ways you differ from other people. These differences are physical, intellectual, emotional, and social.

#### Physical Differences

As soon as a group of people get together, physical differences are apparent. John is short and rather plump while May is tall and willowy. Pete, with black curly hair and brown eyes, differs from Andy, who has red hair and blue eyes. Sue has brown skin and Tanya's skin has a yellow hue.

These obvious physical contrasts cover a number of more subtle differences. Each person has unique fingerprints and voice patterns. Some people need eight or nine hours of sleep daily to stay in good health. Others thrive on lots of activity and little rest. People also differ in the amounts of food they require.

#### Intellectual Differences

All people have their own sets of intellectual capabilities. Some people are more intelligent than others while some have abilities in special areas.

For example, Tom has always had a hard time making good grades in school, yet few

**Ch. 2: Discovering Who You Are**

"I've Got To Be Me!"

teenagers can repair an engine any better or faster. Reba doesn't know a spark plug from an oil dipstick, but she can memorize easily and loves learning new languages. Earl's creative intelligence shows in his paintings and drawings.

**EMOTIONAL DIFFERENCES**

People differ in how they feel and experience emotions, such as anger, joy, love, and hate.

Sam has a very hot temper and can become angry in a moment if provoked. On the other hand, Will is very placid and rarely gets upset and angry.

Every week or two Tina falls madly in love. The exuberant highs and depressing lows of her strong emotions color her short-lived romances. Maria is more reserved in her romantic interests. Her attachments to men are usually less stormy but longer and with more depth than those of Tina.

**SOCIAL DIFFERENCES**

People differ in their ability to relate to others. Everyone likes Carlos, who makes friends easily but doesn't have any close friends. When Beryl becomes friends with someone, she usually forms a very strong relationship with them even though she does not make friends easily.

Vern does not get along well with his family and intends to move away from home as soon as he graduates from high school. In contrast, Tim's relationship with his family is very close.

Rosa doesn't seem to know how to make friends of her own age, yet she relates well to

### Unit 2: Relationships Begin with You

her teachers and her parents' friends. She is just the opposite of Claude, who has many friends his own age but cannot seem to get along well with teachers and other older people.

In summary, each person has physical, intellectual, emotional, and social characteristics which are unique. These differences blend together to make the *self* of each person different from that of anyone else on earth. Each person is an original creation with unique individuality—a self.

## experiences in human relations

### DIFFERENT PREFERENCES

What kinds of likes and dislikes express your self? To begin to see how people are different in their preferences, try the following experience.

Note three areas in the room: a middle neutral area and two side position areas. Have one class member or your teacher read the following list of items. If you identify with the first item in the pair, go to one position area. If you identify with the second item in the pair, go to the second position area. Go to the neutral middle area if you do not identify with either word in the pair. Do this with each set of paired words in the list.

Red—Green
Happy—Unhappy
Volkswagen—Cadillac
Dog—Cat
Bicycle—Motorcycle
Hamburger—Pizza
Mathematics—English

Work—Play
Rock Concert—String Quartet
Television—Books
Privacy—Being With People

If you wish, add other paired words to this list. Did any of your choices surprise you? Were you ever alone at a position? Did you feel uncomfortable when your choice was a minority one? Did you feel better if many people made the same choice that you did? How did you feel about publicly stating your preferences?

### TO SUM UP...

1. What is a person's self?
2. List four general ways in which you are unique and different from others.
3. Describe some of the different "kinds" of intelligence.
4. What are some ways that people are emotionally different from each other?

### DEVELOPMENT OF THE SELF

Where do people's selves come from? How do they develop? The self develops as an individual has contact with and relates to others. Children coming into the world have no way to judge their self-worth. Thus the most important influence on the development of a child's self is the family.

#### INFLUENCE OF THE FAMILY

The family usually has the longest period of influence on the child. The family affects the baby during early years, when the child's self is "plastic" or unformed. Repeated experi-

*The family is the most important influence in forming a child's self.*

ences in family life begin to form and mold the baby's "plastic" self. As a result of these experiences with their families, children discover their worth.

Obviously, there is a wide variety of family patterns into which babies are born. A baby who lives with both parents will have different experiences than a baby who lives with one parent, a guardian, or a grandparent. A "stay-at-home" family will influence a child's development differently than will a family that is "on-the-go." A quiet family will have a different effect than a noisy one.

For example, Bobby came home from the hospital with his newly divorced mother. Since his mother has to work to support the two of them, Bobby stays with an older woman who babysits during the day. Bobby's mother dates frequently so at night he often stays with his grandmother, who plays with him and gives him a great deal of love and cuddling. Life is calm and peaceful both at the babysitter's and at his Grandma's, so Bobby is not used to noise or activity.

Freda was born into a very different kind of situation. Her family consists of her parents plus two brothers and two sisters. This family is lively and active, with lots of noise and frequent fights among the children. Freda's mother loves her dearly. However, with four other children to care for, she has little time to cuddle and play with Freda.

Because Bobby and Freda are growing up in different kinds of families, their everyday ex-

## Unit 2: Relationships Begin with You

periences are quite different. These different experiences will have an effect on how their selves develop.

It is likely that Bobby will grow up to be quiet and shy. He probably will not enjoy being in crowds of people, but may instead prefer being in small groups with friends. He may learn to expect others to look after him and provide entertainment for him.

Freda probably will become independent and outgoing. She will likely enjoy being with others as she participates in many activities.

It is very hard to predict just how a certain family situation will affect people. It is possible that Bobby could reject the quiet life of his early years to become outgoing and active. Freda may find the noise and activity at home overpowering. As a result, she could easily become shy and bashful. Whatever the outcome, the particular family in which a child grows up influences what the child becomes.

The status of the family in the community can also affect the selves of family members. Unjust or not, many people have a different opinion of a family on welfare than they do of the family of a bank president. Children learn to see and feel these differences early, which may affect their development.

Thus the experiences in the family are crucial in the growth of the self. A child's self grows as it receives the messages of worth and the feelings and attitudes held by other family members.

By the time children begin to meet and relate to others who are not family members, they already have basic patterns for their behavior. Bobby meets others quietly and shyly. "Loud and friendly" describes Freda's way of relating to others. However, the patterns that develop in the family can be changed by others.

### INFLUENCE OF OTHERS

Other than their families, the most important influence on children is friends of about the same age, known as *peers*. Meeting and playing with peers can change the developing self of the child.

When five-year-old Martha started school, she was the apple of her parents' eyes. She did anything she wanted at home and expected people to do what she said. However, her classmates did not like to be "bossed" around and soon showed their dislike by avoiding her. This was Martha's first experience with people who didn't like her. She was quite unhappy for a while until she learned to control her habit of giving orders. By changing the behavior patterns she had

*When a child enters school, the peer group becomes important to the child's developing self.*

Ch. 2: Discovering Who You Are

learned at home, she was able to get along with the others.

Fifteen-year-old Tony found that his peer group was pressuring him to begin smoking. Tony did not particularly want to smoke, but he felt that he needed to be accepted. Responding to the pressure of his friends, Tony now smokes with them.

The influence of non-family members can be obvious when a child first goes to school or to a group child care center. In many cases, "Teacher" becomes very important to the child and may be in a position to change the child's developing self.

Others can affect the development of children and teenagers. A music teacher, drama coach, or Little League coach can be important. A neighborhood teenager can have a strong effect on a child's growing self.

In addition, it is a normal human trait to adopt some ideas from those who have authority over you. Workers often take on some of the attitudes of their bosses or employers. Worshipers follow their religious leaders.

Each person's self continues to grow and change as it relates to family, peers, teachers, authority figures, and others. Influences merging in the self help make each person special and unique.

## experiences in human relations

### DEVELOPMENT OF THE SELF

How do your interactions with others affect your developing self? The following experience can show how your experiences affect the way you feel about who you are.

Make six paper strips, each with a different label as follows: *Ask Me, Defend Me, Praise Me, Ridicule Me, Pamper Me, Ignore Me*. With five other classmates, sit around a small table. Have another class member place one strip of paper around each person's head without letting any of you know what your own paper strip says.

Using children's building blocks, pretend you are all six-year-olds building a bridge. You are to do the best job you can building the bridge, relating to each other according to the labels you see on the others' foreheads.

When you have finished building the bridge, guess what your label says. How did you feel during this experience? Compare and contrast the feelings of those who wore "positive" labels with who wore "negative" ones. How would children who received one of these treatments day after day, year after year, come to feel about themselves?

### TO SUM UP...
1. How does the self develop?
2. Why is the family the most important influence on the child's developing self?
3. What are peers?
4. At what age do peers become important in influencing a person's self?
5. Name as many people as you can who might have an effect on a school-age child's developing self.

### SELF-CONCEPT

The good and bad experiences which each person has had result in a unique and individual self. What you think about the unique self you have is called your *self-concept*. Your

29

**Unit 2: Relationships Begin with You**

*All experiences help build self-concept.*

ideas about your worth as a person, your strengths and weaknesses, and your special abilities are all part of your self-concept.

## Positive and Negative Self-Concepts

Some people have *positive self-concepts*. Jim sees himself as a capable, competent person. Because he is old enough and has shown himself to be responsible, his parents allow him a great deal of freedom. An average student, he is planning to go to college. His after-school job in a local restaurant as a busboy is interesting, and he knows his boss is pleased with his work. He enjoys his friends, who like having him around. While Jim knows his life wouldn't suit everyone, he is comfortable with it. He gets a lot of satisfaction from what he does.

Other people have *negative self-concepts*. They lack confidence in their ability to handle their lives. Outwardly, Rick is very much like Jim. He does moderately well in school, but he feels that his best is never good enough. Frequently he becomes upset because he hasn't done as well as he wanted. He, too, holds an after-school job, but he is always worried about being fired since he is never certain he is doing what his boss wants. Even with his friends, Rick is often uncomfortable because he isn't sure why they let him join the group. He finds it hard to believe that they could like him for himself, which they do. He is afraid that if he does something wrong, he will be dropped from the group.

## Ch. 2: Discovering Who You Are

Therefore he is always careful to do exactly what everyone else does, whether he really wants to or not.

Jim and Rick appear to lead similar lives. The one important difference is how they see themselves. Jim likes what he sees about himself—his abilities as a student, a worker, and a friend. He feels he can take care of anything that comes his way. Rick doesn't like what he sees in himself. He feels as if he has never done enough—has not received high enough grades, done his work well, or contributed to his friends' activities. Rick is always afraid he can't handle what might come his way.

Most people have some positive and some negative feelings about themselves. People with negative self-concepts have mostly negative feelings about themselves, while people with positive self-concepts have mostly positive feelings about themselves. Even people with good self-concepts, like Jim, have areas where they have some negative feelings. Jim is uncomfortable with girls. He can relate to them in a group with his friends, but is uneasy and doesn't know what to say when he and a girl are alone. Rick, on the other hand, has one area where he has good feelings about himself and his accomplishments. He enjoys making small wooden carvings of animals and birds. While he worries and feels inadequate in many areas of his life, he knows his carvings are good.

### experiences in human relations

#### SELF-CONCEPT

How do you feel about your self? Are you "in touch" with your self? Can you identify some of the components which make up your self? The more people are aware of the facts about themselves, the better able they are to form realistic self-concepts. This helps them use their abilities effectively. The following experiences can help you identify some aspects of your self-concept.

- Find a picture that seems meaningful to you or that you feel represents you in some way. Mount it on heavy paper and cut it into jigsaw pieces. On the back of each piece write a word which you feel is a characteristic you have. Some examples might be: outgoing, skinny, withdrawn, clumsy, intelligent, athletic, or vivacious. Put your puzzle together for other class members, explaining why you feel the words you chose describe you.

- One simple experience to help you understand how you see yourself is to think of yourself as an animal. The animal you choose may reflect the characteristics which you see in yourself.

- Choose a famous person, dead or alive, whom you admire. Role play that person. What qualities do you admire in that person? How can you express those qualities in your role playing? Do you feel that you have any of the same characteristics? Do you try to act as if you have some of the famous person's characteristics?

### How Self-Concepts Develop

How do people develop either positive or negative self-concepts? As discussed earlier, the family has the most influence on the development of the self. The quality and type of experiences that a person has in the family determine self-concept. A family can promote a positive self-concept or it can promote a negative self-concept.

**Unit 2: Relationships Begin with You**

Rewarding experiences help build a positive self-concept. A family that treats children with respect and love helps them to feel that they are lovable and accepted.

Defeating experiences in the family help build a negative self-concept. When parents call their children names, ridicule them, or ignore them, the children come to feel worthless and unimportant. It is easy for children in such a family to feel that they are not loved or liked and are inadequate.

The early family experiences of the child are very important in building the child's self-concept. As the child then comes in contact with teachers, youth leaders, and peers, the original self-concept becomes weakened or strengthened by the new experiences.

Marilyn had a happy home life as a baby and a toddler. Her parents loved her and gave her many chances to grow and develop as a person. When she entered school, her self-concept was positive. She enjoys school and is able to do her work well, which strengthens her positive self-concept.

Harold also had a good self-concept when he entered school. However, he is unable to learn easily and is usually in trouble with his teacher. His classmates do not seem to like him, and he is quite unhappy in school. His originally high self-concept has become somewhat negative as he seems unable to cope with the demands of school.

Ken had a rather unhappy home life because his mother wanted to work but his father forebade her. She took out many of her frustrations on Ken. When he got to school, he found schoolwork easy and interesting. In addition, he made many friends whom he enjoys. His low self-concept rose rapidly with his many successful school experiences.

Robert's early experiences were unhappy and he did not learn to adjust well to school. His original poor self-concept has been reinforced by his school experiences.

These examples have focused on what happens when children enter school. However, almost any contact with new acquaintances, such as teachers and peers, can influence a person's self-concept.

## Aspects of Self-Concept

There are three basic aspects of self-concept:
- How you see yourself.
- How others see you.
- How you respond to others' judgments.

These three factors are important in determining how a person's self-concept changes and grows during everyday living. For example, take the case of Nancy, who has many friends and is the star of the girl's basketball team. Overall, Nancy has a good self-concept. However, she does very poorly in her school work and often feels inadequate in school. Usually, she feels able to cope well with her world. She enjoys life and sees a worthwhile place for herself. This is how Nancy sees herself.

There is more to Nancy's self-concept than just what she thinks of herself. The second aspect of self-concept is how others see a person. Nancy is seen in a variety of ways by the people she knows and interacts with. Mr. Marks, her English teacher, despairs of Nancy's themes. He is forever telling her that a mind that can figure basketball strategy so well should be able to do something as simple as writing a good theme. Nancy's basketball coach values her star player. She makes Nancy work hard, but knows that Nancy will perform to the best of her ability in each game. Nancy's teammates know they can depend on her, and she is the undisputed leader of the squad. Nancy's friends enjoy her status

**Ch. 2: Discovering Who You Are**

*A person's self-concept is influenced and changed by these three factors.*

as a basketball star, but appreciate her wit and good humor more than her athletic ability. Her parents are proud of their daughter and generally help her do whatever she is interested in. They learned long ago that it doesn't pay to nag Nancy about her poor grades.

These views of Nancy, held by the various people that she relates to, have an effect on her. When Mr. Marks, the English teacher, returns a paper with a low grade on it, Nancy pays little attention to it. She merely thinks, "Well, I always knew I was pretty stupid." Thus her negative self-concept in the intellectual area is strengthened each time she receives a poor grade and a lecture from one of her teachers.

On the other hand, her positive self-concept is reinforced by the support of her basketball coach, the following of her teammates, and the love of her family and friends. Nancy feels she can handle many aspects of her life well, and her experiences with these people tell her that she is right. Thus, her overall positive self-concept continues to grow and be strengthened.

In the same way, a negative self-concept can become more negative with experiences that are defeating and discouraging. Ken sees himself as a worthless person with few strengths. He often disrupts classes, which causes his teachers to dislike having him as a student. He has a few friends, but most of his classmates avoid him. As Ken interacts with

**Unit 2: Relationships Begin with You**

his teachers and peers, he realizes that they don't like him, which causes him to feel even worse about himself. Unhappy experiences with others have reinforced Ken's negative self-concept.

People constantly make adjustments in their self-concepts, as Nancy and Ken do. Children and adults alike find that their self-concepts improve with positive, happy, successful, and rewarding experiences. Defeating, failing, and unpleasant experiences can have a negative effect on the self-concepts of children and adults. Your self-concept is always changing and adapting to the experiences you have as you interact and relate to others.

## experiences in human relations

### ASPECTS OF SELF-CONCEPT

Your self-concept is how you feel about yourself. However, how do others see you? How do you react to what others see? The following experience may help you gain some insight into these questions.

Paper-clip your name to an envelope. Place your envelope in a central location with the envelopes of other class members. Without using any names, write one positive characteristic and one negative characteristic which describe each student in the experience. Write these descriptions on small separate slips of paper, which you place anonymously in the envelope of the appropriate person. Then remove the names from each envelope and thoroughly mix the envelopes. This way, you cannot identify your own envelope. Then attempt to find your envelope by reading the descriptions in the envelopes and deciding which one fits you.

It is interesting to see what happens when you try to find your envelope. Did you find an envelope which you felt described you? How did you feel about the descriptions of yourself? Did you agree with them? Did you accept or reject them? Do others see you the same way you see yourself?

• • • • • • • • • • • • • • • • • • • • • • •

### PROTECTING YOUR SELF-CONCEPT

All people have a combination of strengths and weaknesses. A *strength* is any skill, talent, ability, or personal trait which helps you function well as a person. On the other hand, a *weakness* is a lack of ability or skill which keeps you from functioning well.

## experiences in human relations

### HIDDEN ASPECTS OF THE SELF

People freely show many parts of their selves to others, but some aspects they keep hidden. Can you identify some of your characteristics that you feel others are not aware of?

Using old magazines, select and cut out words, pictures, and phrases that you feel express your self—both the inner hidden and outer aspects of what you are. On the outside of a brown paper bag, paste the clippings which you feel represent your unhidden or outer self. On the inside of the bag place those clippings which you feel represent hidden or unknown aspects of your self. Staple the bag shut.

Ch. 2: Discovering Who You Are

*Masks can hide people's inner feelings and thoughts from others.*

Place the bags on display around the room. Do they illustrate how different and unique the people who made them are? Can you identify the bags' owners by the pictures and words on the outside of the bags?

If you feel comfortable doing so, share the items that you placed inside your bag with others.

● ● ● ● ● ● ● ● ● ● ● ● ● ● ● ● ● ● ●

People with positive self-concepts are apt to think more about their strengths. Those who have negative self-concepts are likely to be most concerned with their weaknesses.

People are open to hurt or attack in some part of their inner self. Because of the way they were taught as they grew up, they are embarrassed by their areas of weakness. To protect their self-concepts, they try to keep others from knowing about these weaknesses. How do they accomplish this? They do it by wearing masks, building self-defenses, or trying to draw attention away from themselves.

### Masks People Wear

One way that people often use to hide their weaknesses is the wearing of *masks*. They position their facial muscles to hide

35

## Unit 2: Relationships Begin with You

what they don't want others to know. These masks disguise them just as Halloween masks do.

People wear these masks to protect those parts of themselves that they consider weaknesses. However, they also wear masks to keep others from rejecting them when they discover their weaknesses.

Joe's mother taught him that anger was a "bad" emotion and that he should learn to control it. Whenever Joe begins to have angry feelings, he puts on a smiling mask to hide his anger from others. Tansy's father was a serious, solemn man who detested giggling and laughing. Thus Tansy learned at an early age to hide her sense of humor. Now, whenever something strikes her as funny, she frowns as she struggles to keep from laughing.

Many men have been taught that it is unmasculine to be tender and caring. They put on a tough, hard, "manly" mask to show that they are men. In the same way, women often put on feminine, helpless masks because they feel that this is what is expected of them as females.

Often the people you are trying to please don't share the same ideas about weaknesses that you do. Many men find that women admire and appreciate them more when they are able to show their tender feelings. Joe's friends often wish he would show his anger. They find it very strange to see Joe smiling when they know he is angry.

Karen often told her friends that her grades were better than theirs. She felt that if they knew how "stupid" she was, they would not want to be her friends anymore. Therefore by hiding what she felt was her stupidness, she was protecting herself from rejection by her friends. What Karen didn't realize was that her friends didn't really care about her grades but accepted and liked her for herself.

## experiences in human relations

### MASKS

Recognizing the masks that you and others wear often is difficult. People become used to wearing masks and seeing others wear them. They often find it hard to realize that "real" people are hiding behind the masks. Keep a record of the people you observe for a few days and see if you can recognize masks. The following suggestions may help you in mask identification.

- One place where a "charming" mask is often obvious is on the faces of television talk show stars. Their job is to be nice to their television guests. Thus their faces often seem to have a fixed expression with little emotion showing. An unexpected return after a commercial break may catch the program's star without a mask. How many masks can you identify on television personalities?

- Become conscious of the masks you wear. Look at yourself in the mirror. Are you wearing a mask to impress others with your interest in them? Do you wear a mask in the classroom to impress the teacher? Do you try to be sophisticated? Bored? Do your "inside" feelings match your "outside" mask?

- Observe when people drop their masks. Many people do not wear their masks when driving. Somehow they feel that in their automobile no one knows who they are. This gives them a chance to act as they want. Do you act differently when you drive? Are you more aggressive and quicker to take offense when someone cuts you off in a car than if you were on foot or on a bicycle?

- Observe people on busses or subways, if you have the opportunity. Faces will be especially revealing during evening rush hour. People are likely to be tired and allow their masks to slip. It is interesting to note how fast people put their masks back on if they see someone they know.

• People usually do not wear masks when they interact with family members. Watch parents interact with their children and others. Do they drop their masks when talking with their children and put them on when talking with other adults? Observe whether people use a "voice mask" when talking on the telephone.

● ● ● ● ● ● ● ● ● ● ● ● ● ● ● ● ● ●

## Defending the Self

Another way people protect their self-concepts is by putting up *defenses* around the self. If they feel that their selves are unlovable, or are not worthy of respect, they develop defenses to keep others from knowing these things. People use a great deal of energy building and maintaining defenses to prove to themselves and others that they are worthwhile.

What are some of these defenses that people use when they feel that the weaknesses of their selves are going to be discovered? One defense is changing the subject. Ralph's friends recently became interested in tennis, which Ralph doesn't know anything about. Whenever the group begins to talk about the subject—the pro tennis tour or the high school tennis team's schedule—Ralph attempts to turn the talk to baseball. He is afraid that his friends will laugh at him for not knowing anything about tennis, so he tries to turn the conversation to something with which he is familiar.

Althea often uses the defense of silence. When feeling anxious or afraid, she becomes very silent and hopes that no one will notice her. She very rarely talks in classes, hoping that her teachers will not call on her. Often, she knows the answers or has ideas about the discussion. However, she is afraid that if she does participate, she may be called on sometimes when she does not have anything to contribute.

Charlotte often uses another kind of defense—perfectionism. She is so afraid that she won't perform well enough that she expects everything to be perfect. She makes the other members of her cheerleading squad miserable with her demands that they have perfect coordination and routines.

Another defense that some people use is criticism of others. Have you ever known anyone who seemed to do nothing but run down other people? Martin always criticizes people: His teachers are terrible; Abe is really bad at basketball; Terri is a flirt who leads men on; Les is a skirt-chaser; his parents are mean and stingy. No one ever did anything that pleased Martin. What is not so obvious is that Martin criticizes others to make himself feel better because he has a very negative self-concept. To keep people from realizing how inadequate he feels, he tries to draw attention to other people's weaknesses.

Bragging is Nelly's way of protecting herself. She has a large allowance and spends her money on clothes, makeup, records, and tapes. She always brags to her friends about her possessions. This is her way to hide what she feels are her weaknesses.

There is one problem with building defenses such as silence, perfectionism, criticism, or bragging. The defenses are often more offensive to other people than the weaknesses you try to protect. Often a person who brags or criticizes others finds that these defenses drive people away rather than attract them.

**Unit 2: Relationships Begin with You**

While everyone has and needs defenses, you can learn to use them so they won't drive away the people with whom you are trying to get along.

**Positive Ways To Protect the Self**

What are the positive methods you can use to protect your self? One way is to seek out those experiences which you are able to handle and which will help you gain some kind of reward for yourself. You can seek out those people and activities that help you feel confident and competent. You might want to avoid those people and activities that make you feel anxious and inadequate.

## experiences in human relations

### DEVELOPING STRENGTHS

One way of developing self-acceptance involves knowing your strengths. A strength is any skill, talent, ability, or personal trait which helps you function productively. The following experiences will help you concentrate upon identifying your strengths. How does identifying your strengths make you feel about yourself?

• Think of all the things that you do well, all the things which you are proud of having done, and all the things for which you feel a sense of accomplishment. List all of your accomplishments and successes.

• Share your accomplishments and successes with a partner. What strengths helped you achieve these accomplishments and successes?

• What other strengths do you feel that you have? Are you able to use all these strengths?

What might be keeping you from using your strengths? How can your strengths help you in developing further self-acceptance?

• • • • • • • • • • • • • • • • • • • • • • •

Charlie puts all his efforts and energy into motorcycle racing. He gets much satisfaction from winning races and in knowing that his cycle is a good one that he can handle. However, he avoids events where there will be dancing because he feels awkward and clumsy when he tries to dance.

Ian selects his activities on the same basis as Charlie, but his choices are different. His favorites are reading, learning, and school. He gets many rewards from his parents and teachers for doing well. Because he does poorly in physical activities, however, he avoids sports and athletics.

Louise gets her rewards from music. An outstanding pianist, she also plays several other instruments. She practices at least four hours a day but feels that it is worth it because of the satisfaction she receives.

Janelle gains a great deal of satisfaction in social relationships. Being with her group, talking, laughing, and sharing ideas make her happy. Usually, she avoids activities that she must do alone because she doesn't find these nearly as rewarding as those she can do with her friends.

Thus one way to positively protect your self is to select those activities and acquaintances that preserve or enhance your self. Activities they can do well and that give them satisfaction help people to accept themselves. People also tend to seek out friends who will appreciate and enjoy them for the traits they have. It is much more comfortable being with someone who accepts you as you are than with someone who tries to change you.

*Participating in activities that you do well is one way to promote a positive self-concept.*

## experiences in human relations

### CAREER CHOICES

One protection for your self is to choose activities that make you feel confident and comfortable. In this way, you can feel good about your self. What kind of implications does this have for planning careers? Can you provide protection for your self by choosing a career or job that you like or that will make you feel comfortable or competent?

Think about the job or career you have been considering for yourself. Will it allow you to feel good about yourself? Will you have to do anything that makes you feel unworthy or incompetent? Based on how you feel about yourself and what you consider your personal strengths to be, do you think your chosen career or job will be a good one for you?

Another kind of positive protection people can give to their selves is to deliberately work to strengthen their weaknesses. People often build defenses to hide a weakness that could be easily eliminated. Laurie always felt inadequate when her friends played volleyball together. Whenever a game was planned, she used to make excuses to be busy. Then she began to practice, serving the ball in her backyard until she could do it reasonably well. Her practice allows her to enjoy playing with her friends since she now feels she can contribute to the game.

Henry always felt left out when his friends started to talk about electronic recording equipment. He listened, learned, and read until he could talk about stereo components with them.

Julie was uneasy with strangers and always felt she made a bad impression. Determined to improve, she read about conversational arts and learned a few key questions which she uses when she meets someone new. She

## Unit 2: Relationships Begin with You

has learned to feel more comfortable with strangers, which helps her feel better about herself.

Often it isn't as easy to work on your weaknesses as it was for Laurie, Henry, or Julie. However, if there is an area where you feel uncomfortable and incompetent, a little effort may be your best defense to help you learn to feel more adequate and worthy.

### TO SUM UP...

1. What is a self-concept? A positive self-concept? A negative self-concept?
2. How are people's self-concepts developed?
3. What influence does success or failure have on a person's self-concept?
4. What are the three aspects of self-concept? Explain what each aspect means in terms of a person's total self-concept.
5. Why do people feel they need protection for themselves?
6. What kind of self-protection does the wearing of masks provide?
7. What are some defenses that people use in protecting themselves?
8. Why is participating in activities that you do well considered a positive protection for your self?

### LEARNING SELF-ACCEPTANCE

People act in many ways to protect themselves. They wear masks, put up defenses, or act to emphasize their strengths. All of these avoid what is perhaps the most important aspect of self-concept. This is *self-acceptance*—the ability to like yourself as you are.

The teenage years are perhaps the most important years of all in the search for self-acceptance. This is a time when young people learn who they are and what they really feel. They can recognize strengths and weaknesses and learn that all people have both. Adolescence is the time to discover the real self within and accept it for what it is—a combination of positive and negative traits that make each person unique.

People can learn to live with and within their own limitations. Weaknesses are nothing to be ashamed of. A healthy acceptance of weaknesses can keep you from blocking the use of your strengths. If you spend all your time hiding your weaknesses from others, you have little time left to use your strengths. Accepting your weaknesses means not wasting energy defending them. It means being realistic about seeing them, and then going beyond them to make a life which is satisfying to your self.

Darryl loved sports and hoped to be a college and professional football player some day. Although he was a good athlete, he was not outstanding. In fact, he had very little chance of playing either college or professional ball. When he realized that his ability was not sufficient, he seemed to hate himself and became very depressed and irritable. Darryl finally realized that he was not a failure as an athlete and that he could still use and enjoy his athletic skills in other ways. At that point, he began to like himself again. He now plays intermural ball at his college and is studying to be a football coach.

Tracy learned self-acceptance in a very different area of life. She was tall—taller than all the girls she knew and taller than most of the boys. Because she disliked being tall and conspicuous, she slouched to try to appear shorter. She avoided wearing attractive clothes and makeup because, as she said,

*Hiding weaknesses from others often takes energy which could be used in building your strengths.*

"They're wasted on a freak like me." Self-acceptance came to Tracy when she realized that her height wasn't really the overwhelming problem she had thought. She became aware that she could be liked and accepted for other characteristics. Tracy is usually found now in a circle of friends who enjoy her lively humor and ideas for having a good time. She says, "Being tall really is just an inconvenience, not a tragedy."

*Self-accepting individuals can look forward to a full and rewarding life.*

Unit 2: Relationships Begin with You

# experiences in human relations

## ACCEPTANCE FROM OTHERS

Self-acceptance is an important step in learning to relate to others. In addition to self-acceptance, people often spend a great deal of time and energy trying to gain the acceptance of others. How does lack of acceptance—whether it is the lack of self-acceptance or the acceptance of others—feel? The following experience gives you an opportunity to feel lack of acceptance.

With other class members, form a tight circle by locking arms and pressing close to each others' sides. In turn, members of the circle volunteer to be the outsider. When you are the outsider, try to break into the group by forcing your way to the center of the circle. Those in the circle try to keep the outsider from breaking in. This experiment can become quite active, so be careful not to hurt anyone by becoming too rough.

After everyone who wishes has been an outsider, discuss the feelings that this experience aroused in you. How did you react to being an outsider? How did you react to trying to keep the outsiders from getting into the center of the circle? Describe the ways people tried to break into the circle. What did you learn about yourself from the experience?

• • • • • • • • • • • • • • • • • • • • • • •

## THE SELF-ACCEPTING INDIVIDUAL

What is a self-accepting person like? What kinds of characteristics does the self-accepting person have?

Self-accepting people believe strongly in certain values and principles. They are willing to defend them even when others hold opposite ideas. However, when evidence shows they are in error, they are willing to change their opinions. They are capable of acting on their own judgment. If others disapprove, they don't feel guilty or regret their actions.

Andrew does not believe in drinking beer until he is legally old enough, even though many of his friends tease and make fun of him. He has enough confidence in himself to ignore their teasing and do what he feels is right.

Self-accepting people don't spend a lot of time worrying about what is coming in the future or what has happened in the past. They feel confident that they can handle what comes to them. Even when they fail or have setbacks, they have confidence in their ability to deal with problems.

Jana plays tuba in the band. At the last try-out for first chair, she had some difficulties. She didn't achieve her goal of being assigned first chair, but she isn't worrying about it. She's practicing now for the next try-out.

Self-accepting people feel equal to others as people. In spite of differences in abilities, family backgrounds, or the attitudes of others, they do not feel superior or inferior. They take for granted that they are persons of interest and value to others, at least to those with whom they choose to be.

Katrina's family has very little money. Her older brother is in jail for writing bad checks. Katrina wishes her life were different, but she knows that circumstances have no bearing on her worth as a person. She does not waste time feeling inferior for actions she didn't do or events over which she has no control.

Self-accepting people can receive praise and compliments without feeling guilty or falsely modest. They are able to accept and admit to others the wide range of impulses and desires they feel. Anger, love, sadness, resentment, and acceptance are seen by them as normal, natural feelings. They are able to enjoy themselves in many ways through play, work, companionship, solitude, and loafing. Aware of the needs of people, they do not enjoy themselves at the expense of others.

## Accepting Your Self

Your future happiness and growth depend on your being able to work through and form a clear self-concept. People need to discover who they are, what they believe in, how they will translate these beliefs into action, and how they will value what they are. The ability to develop a clear picture of who they are is important for any person's future. For if people deny their essential selves, they will be emotionally distressed. Often they are bored with the self they allow others to see.

Another result of denying the "real" self is loneliness. If you don't allow people to see and interact with your real self, you never feel that they know you. It is only as you allow people to know you as you really are that you escape loneliness.

On the other hand, some people have discovered and explored their selves. They have come to accept and like who they are. Thus they can look forward to the future with zest for life and a real interest in what they are doing. Their positive outlook on life helps others relate to them as real people.

The choice is yours. Who are you? What kind of person have you been in the past? What kind of person are you right now? What kind of person would you like to be in the future? How can you accept what you have been and who you are now? What can you do to work and grow to be the kind of person you want to be?

### Ch. 2: Discovering Who You Are

The following poem describes the choice that faces everyone.

INSIDE YOUR SELF*
You have within you a self.
This stable core of strength
and growth is the essential you—
who you really are,
what you really want. If you
deny your self, you are doomed
to a life of pain and dissatisfaction.
But if you find your self
and act in accord with it,
you will be self-accepting and at peace.

People in touch with their inner selves feel self-acceptance, which can be joyful and exalted. They have a full range of emotions and desires. They can understand who they are and how they want to lead their lives.

## TO SUM UP...

1. What is self-acceptance?
2. What time in a person's life is perhaps most important in developing self-acceptance?
3. How can hiding your weaknesses prevent you from using your strengths?
4. What are some characteristics of self-accepting people?
5. Why is it important for your future to work toward becoming self-accepting?

*From *Growth Games*, copyright © 1970 by Howard R. Lewis and Harold S. Streitfeld. Reprinted by permission of Harcourt Brace Jovanovich, Inc.

# CHAPTER 3

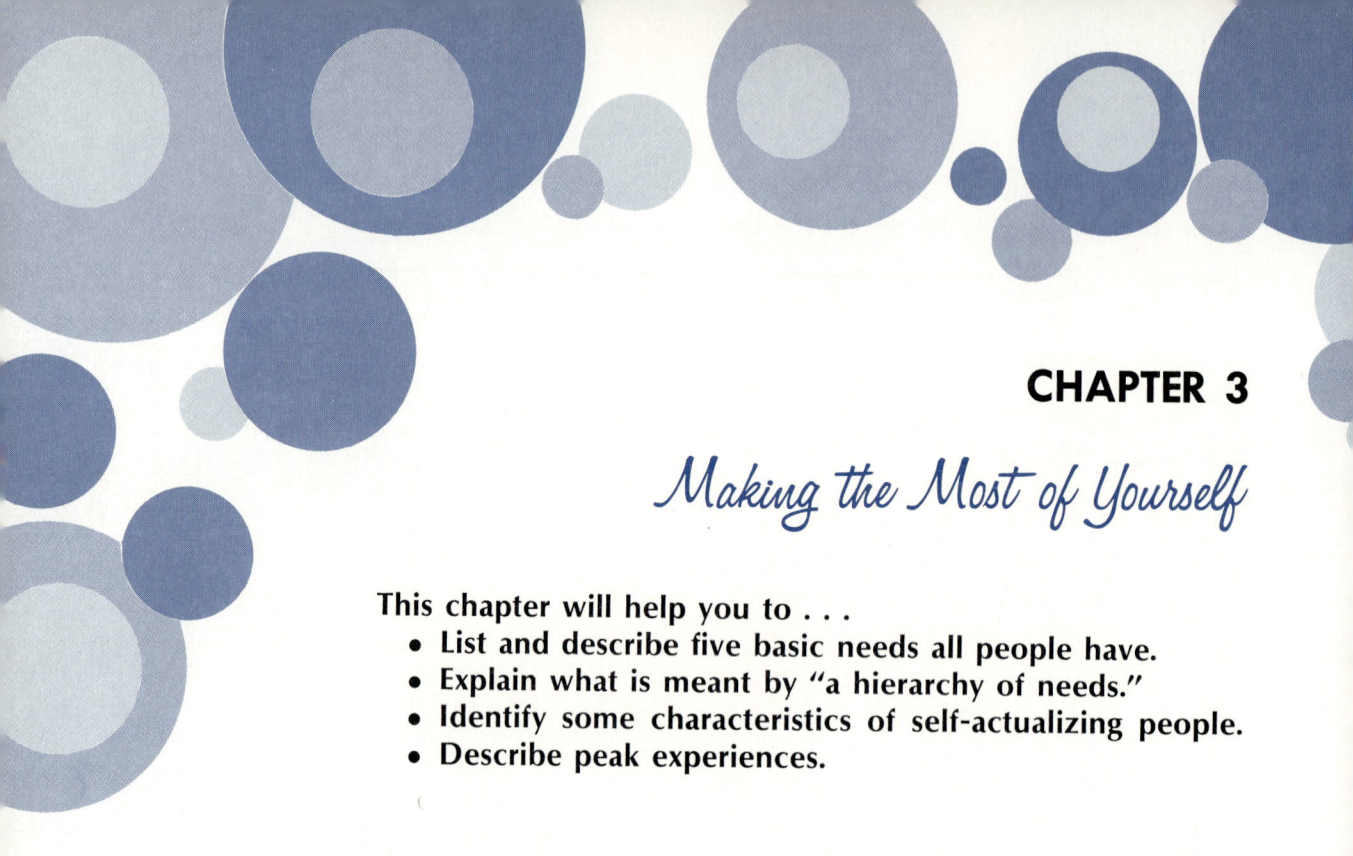

## Making the Most of Yourself

**This chapter will help you to . . .**
- **List and describe five basic needs all people have.**
- **Explain what is meant by "a hierarchy of needs."**
- **Identify some characteristics of self-actualizing people.**
- **Describe peak experiences.**

People have skills or talents which they can use in many ways. James has talent in relating to others. Paula's skill involves repairing television sets. Painting pictures is how Lorna uses her artistic talent. Gus earns high grades through the use of his intelligence. However, all of these people are using only a fraction of their possible abilities.

Most people have hidden talents or abilities that they have never used, developed, or perhaps even discovered. It may be that James' skill in getting along with other people could be used in acting. However, James has never been in a play and has no idea whether or not he has theatrical talent. Paula's skills in repairing television sets might also be used in designing electronic circuitry. Since Paula did not go to college, she does not have the schooling that would allow her to use her talent fully.

The creativity that Lorna shows in her paintings might be used in drawing cartoons. Because of her focus on painting, she has not tried to use her talent in other ways. Gus could use his intelligence to become a master bridge player. But since he has no interest in playing cards, his possible talent in that area has never been discovered.

Around 1900 it was thought that people used only about ten percent of their abilities or potential. Now, scientists who study how humans use their talents estimate that people use only four to six percent of their possible abilities. This figure has been lowered over the years because researchers have found that people have many more powers, resources, and abilities than were ever suspected before. People just do not use the enormous capacities that they have—to love, to feel, to take risks, to accomplish things.

Ch. 3: Making the Most of Yourself

Why aren't people able to use their abilities more fully? What keeps you from using your talents? How can you make the most of yourself?

## experiences in human relations

### TALENT INVENTORY

All people have a variety of talents, skills, abilities, and aptitudes. They use their talents in many ways. Some people use a very large percentage of their abilities. Others use only a few skills, even though they realize that they have other talents which could be developed. And finally, some people have abilities of which they are unaware. Most people have a few talents they have worked on, some undeveloped talents, and many undiscovered talents.

This experience is to help you survey or inventory the talents, abilities, and skills which you have. First, think about the things you do well. Can you drive a car well? Are you patient with others? Do you have good physical endurance? Are you cheerful and smiling toward others? All these traits are skills which can make your life easier and more satisfying. Think of all the talents which you have, whether they are large or small. Make a list of all your developed or used talents.

Now, think about those talents which you have not worked on. These are the abilities that you know are within you, but which you have neglected. Could you get better grades with more studying? Could you learn to play a new musical instrument? Excell in a new sport? Could you improve your relationships with others with some effort? You will probably be able to list several areas where you feel you have some undeveloped talent.

Finally, try to imagine areas where you have undiscovered talent. List all the abilities that it might be possible for you to have. Why don't you know if you have talent in these areas? Have you ever tried doing any of these things? How could you work to uncover hidden potential in yourself?

Look over your lists and think about what you have written. Were you surprised at the number of developed talents that you have? Are there many talent areas that you have ignored? In other words, have you focused your work on a few areas rather than trying to develop many skills? How did thinking about hidden talents make you feel? How could you use your developed, ignored, and undiscovered talents to make the most of yourself?

● ● ● ● ● ● ● ● ● ● ● ● ●

## MEETING YOUR NEEDS

Psychologist Abraham Maslow suggests that people are not able to fully use their talents because they must spend time and energy meeting their needs. He says that all people have five basic needs. These are physical needs, safety needs, love needs, esteem needs, and self-actualization needs.

### Physical Needs

Physical needs are simply those which your body must have in order to work properly. Your body needs food, water, sleep, exercise, and protection from illness. It needs to eliminate wastes and to be sheltered from the weather. If any of these needs are not met, nothing else seems important.

When the regular worker became sick one Wednesday night, Alvin worked the 10:00 p.m. to 2:00 a.m. shift at the laundromat. The next day in school, Alvin could not concen-

## Unit 2: Relationships Begin with You

trate in class. He tried to listen to what his teachers were saying, but all he could think about was how sleepy he was. Because his physical need for sleep had not been met, Alvin was unable to pay attention to what was going on around him.

Vicky was an enthusiastic football fan. She attended all the games her high school team played. She was especially looking forward to the game which would decide the conference championship. That Friday night was not very cold so Vicky did not wear her warmest clothes to the game. In the second quarter of the game, the temperature suddenly dropped and it began to snow. Stiff with cold and covered with snow, Vicky left the game after the third quarter. Her need for warmth and shelter from the cold proved stronger than her interest in the football game.

### SAFETY NEEDS

People have the need to feel safe from harm. You need to feel safe from crime, from violence, or from being punished or hurt because of something you did. When your safety needs are met, you feel protected and comfortable. When you do not feel safe, you are likely to worry about what you can do to make your life more secure.

Mrs. Rivers lived by herself in a neighborhood which had a high crime rate. As more and more people were robbed or beaten, she became afraid to go outside of her apartment. She bought several locks and bolts for her door and windows. She has become so afraid for her safety that she only goes outside her rooms to go to work or to the grocery store. Her one thought is to stay behind her locked door and be safe.

Mr. Williams had worked in the shoe factory for many years. In fact, he had more seniority than any of the other supervisors. Sometimes he wished for a more exciting, challenging job. But as he said, "The reason I like my job is that it's secure. I know I won't be laid off because of my seniority. It makes me feel safe to know that I can work at the factory a few more years and then retire on my pension. Who knows what would happen if I took another job. That's a risk I'm just not ready to take." Keeping his job as a factory foreman helps Mr. Williams meet his safety needs.

*All people share these five basic needs.*

*Teenagers begin to look to the opposite sex to meet their love needs.*

## LOVE NEEDS

Another need which all people have is the need for love, affection, and belonging. You need friendships and to belong to a group such as a family, a community, or a friendship group. You need to be accepted and loved for the unique person that you are.

Everyone wants to be accepted and loved by others. Three-year-old Jocelyn is crushed when she is scolded by her parents. She feels that because they have punished her, they don't love her. For Jocelyn and other children, the need for love from parents and family is very strong.

As children grow older, they become less concerned about love from family members, although it is still important to them. They turn most of their energies toward being accepted by their peers. They often feel the need to belong to a group or to have a special friend or buddy.

Kevin, a ten-year-old, was on top of the world the day a group of boys, who called themselves "The Champions," asked him to become a member of their club. The Champions usually went to each others' houses after school and did many activities together. Kevin's need to belong was filled through membership in The Champions.

Most teenagers begin to fill their love needs by dating members of the opposite sex, even though family love and friendships are still important. However, love needs usually focus on dating partners. The need to love and to be loved usually leads to engagement and marriage.

47

## Unit 2: Relationships Begin with You

Orlando and Sandi were engaged last Christmas and are planning their wedding. When they are together, their happiness seems to shine from their faces, showing that their relationship is meeting their love needs.

### ESTEEM NEEDS

The need for esteem is the need to feel important and worthwhile. You need to feel respected and approved of, for by receiving approval or esteem from others, you come to feel esteem and respect for yourself.

A person's self-concept is directly related to the need for esteem. The more you feel important and worthwhile, the more positive is your self-concept. People who have their esteem needs met are more likely to accept themselves.

People can get their esteem needs met in many ways. Charlie feels worthwhile when he scores well on the basketball team. Being on the honor roll makes Marcia feel she is really respected. Craig gets good feelings when he gives a successful party for his friends. David's work at the rehabilitation center makes him feel that he has a contribution to make. Being a member of the pit crew for the winning entry at the stock car races makes Caroline feel important. In these and other ways, people make their special contributions which earn the respect and esteem of others.

## experiences in human relations

### BUILDING SELF-ESTEEM

The need for esteem includes both esteem from others and esteem from yourself. The following experiences highlight some ways that you can work to build self-esteem.

• One way to build self-confidence is to use imagination to forecast your own success. Think of some real-life situation that is coming to you soon but is not here yet. Imagine yourself in the situation and think about what you will do. Instead of thinking of all the bad events which could happen to you, concentrate on the good possibilities. Imagine yourself carrying out your responsibilities well. Think of yourself capably doing your job successfully. Imagine the rewards which will be yours for doing well. If you believe that you can do well, you *will* be able to handle the situation in a successful way.

• Many people live their lives very well without ever getting much praise for their efforts. There are many times when you know you have done a good job. However, you don't receive any recognition for your work. A way to help build self-esteem is to "recognize" yourself when you know you have done something well. You can give yourself a verbal compliment or you can give yourself a present of some kind. If you give yourself something that is meaningful or important to you, the gift will make your good feelings about your work even stronger. This will, of course, help increase your self-esteem.

• Keeping a "Success Record" for several weeks or months is another way to build self-respect. In a separate notebook or journal, write down the successes that you have had or items you have done well. You might want to include successes in projects, in making other people happy, in school work, on the job, or in other areas important to you. Over the weeks, you will find that you have included many successes. Your Success Record is likely to show that you have many more successes than you probably imagined you could have.

• • • • • • • • • • • • • • • • • • • • • • •

## Self-Actualization Needs

Self-actualization is the need people have to become everything that they can become. Self-actualization means using all the talents that you have in order to fulfill your potential. Making the most of yourself is another way to describe what self-actualization means.

The need for self-actualization means that people feel some kind of urge to use their skills and talents. People with athletic ability have the need to use their muscles. Others with intelligence must use it. Those with special skill in relating to others feel the need to build many kinds of relationships. It is through the use of their talents that people feel satisfied and fulfilled.

Many people seem to feel that self-actualization is for the special few who are very talented or intelligent. However, all people can become the best that they can be. You are born with a certain range of potential, which you may develop and use. The closer you come to the upper limit of your potential range, the more self-actualized you will be. Whether you plan to be a salesperson, an accountant, an assembly line worker, or an astronaut, you have the ability to be the best you can be. No matter what your job or role, you can work to live up to your potential through self-actualization.

Self-actualization is most likely to occur when people are involved in something beyond themselves. The more you are committed to a project or problem, the more you give of yourself in working on it. Self-actualization is one result of giving yourself to something you consider worthwhile.

People have the drive or urge to give the best expression of themselves in life. Barbara is a talented musician who practices the violin a great deal. She wants to use her musical talents to bring pleasure to others. She knows that it is only through work and practice that she can do this.

Vernon's special talent is relating to people. He donates much of his spare time to volunteer work in a Senior Citizen's center. He tries hard to become acquainted with people who come to the center and to help them in the best way he can. Vernon feels that he is putting his talent to use in a way that is satisfying and rewarding.

Working with children is Maria's love so she hopes to marry and have a family someday. However, she feels that she has enough love to share with more than just her future children. She works in a children's home where there are children who need the love she has to give.

## The Hierarchy of Needs

Abraham Maslow organizes the five basic needs described above into what he calls a *hierarchy of needs*. This means that certain needs come before others and that the needs must be met in a certain order. A hierarchy can be compared to a ladder. Just as you climb one rung to reach the next on a ladder, you meet one need before you go on to meet the next.

The lowest needs are the physical needs. When you have food, shelter, and a healthy body, you are able to go to the next level on the hierarchy, which is safety. As you come to feel secure and safe in your surroundings, you are free to work on meeting your love needs.

Again, when love needs are fulfilled you can proceed toward meeting your esteem needs. Finally, when esteem needs are met you can move to the highest need, that of self-actualization.

The lower needs are stronger and more pressing than the higher needs. Safety is a stronger, more vital need than love, for in-

**Unit 2: Relationships Begin with You**

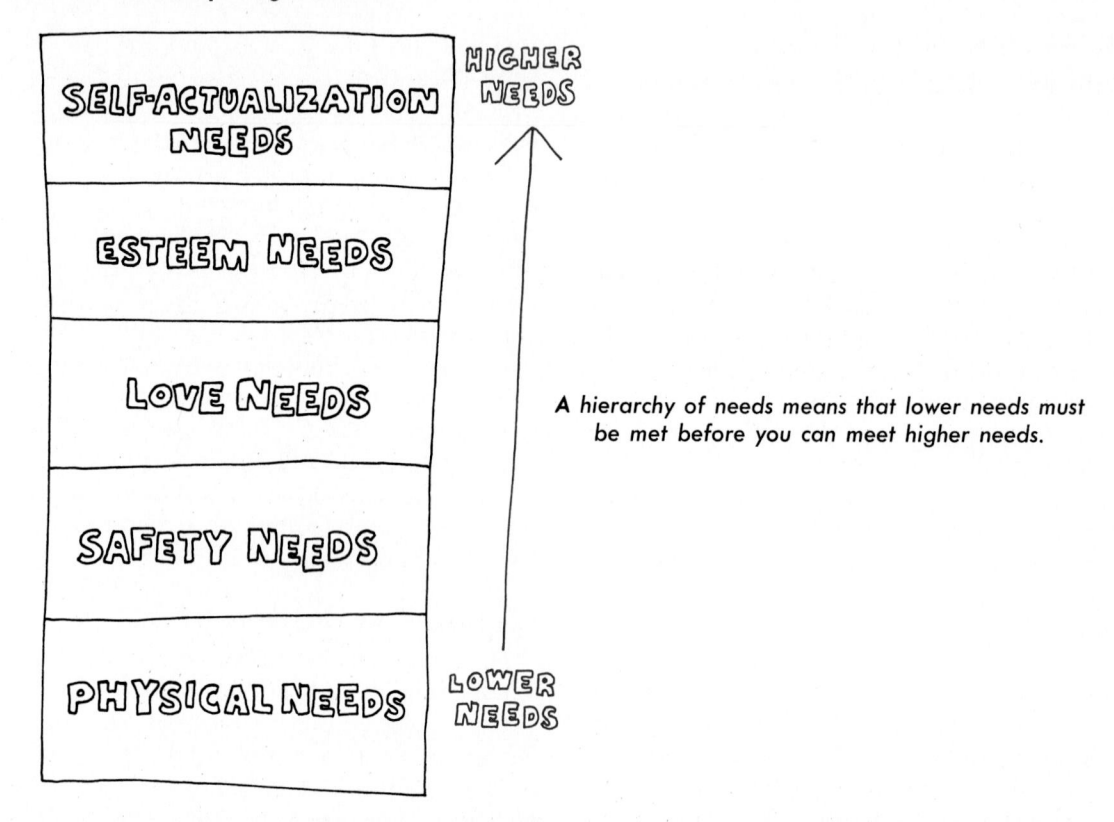

- SELF-ACTUALIZATION NEEDS
- ESTEEM NEEDS
- LOVE NEEDS
- SAFETY NEEDS
- PHYSICAL NEEDS

HIGHER NEEDS ↑ LOWER NEEDS

*A hierarchy of needs means that lower needs must be met before you can meet higher needs.*

stance. The need for food is usually stronger than either. People who are starving because of lack of food are not interested in love or esteem from others. Instead, their entire energies are focused on finding something to eat.

It is only as lower needs are met that higher ones emerge. In other words, people are not even aware of their higher needs until their lower needs are met. Thus a person who struggles to meet physical and safety needs would feel no urge to fill needs for esteem and self-actualization.

In moving through the hierarchy, people concentrate on one level at a time. Reba is working on meeting her love needs by dating several different males, but she can't seem to find anyone special who cares for her. Because she is intent on having her love needs met, she does not think about the next step, esteem needs. Only when she finds someone to love will she be in a position to begin thinking about earning respect and approval from others.

Bonnie was becoming more worried each day because Rex, whom she had dated for two years, had started to sell drugs to other students. Bonnie spent a great deal of time with Rex, but she didn't use or sell the drugs. However, she was afraid that if Rex were found out, she would be accused, too. If that happened, she would be suspended from school, fined heavily, and perhaps receive a jail sentence.

Bonnie's problem was that she cared for Rex very much and really didn't want to break

## Ch. 3: Making the Most of Yourself

up with him. Finally, when her concern for her own safety became too great, she broke off the relationship and started dating others. Her need for safety was so strong that she gave up a relationship that meant a great deal to her. Thus Bonnie moved down the hierarchy to meet a lower, stronger need.

At first glance, it would appear that people move one step at a time up through the hierarchy of needs. Instead, like Bonnie, people move up and down depending on which needs are most urgent. Moving through the hierarchy is a *process* of discovery and growth of your self.

Phyllis has been absorbed in creating a beautiful picture. Sooner or later, she becomes hungry and stops to fill her physical need. Bill is a computer programmer who has been successfully figuring out a difficult project. After working a while, he feels lonely and seeks out his family for some love and affection.

In these examples, Phyllis and Bill briefly reach self-actualization in their work. Then other needs arise and they seek to meet them. When these lower needs are met, Phyllis and Bill may again work toward self-actualization. Thus people never actually reach and stay at self-actualization. They may work toward self-actualization, achieve it for a while, and then begin again at some lower level.

Some people feel that happiness is one of their basic needs. Very often you will hear people say, "I would be happy if only . . . ," and a new dress, a good grade, or a date with a special person may be what they want. Happiness, however, is not really a need but a by-product which occurs as people work to meet their needs. Happiness cannot be sought directly. People who do things "because they will make me happy" are rarely happy. Happiness comes when people give themselves wholeheartedly to whatever they are involved in. They work at their jobs, their relationships, their activities, and toward self-actualization. By using their abilities in a satisfying way, they find happiness.

Other people feel that material objects such as money, clothes, and possessions will satisfy their needs. It is true that certain amounts of money and possessions are necessary in order to meet physical and possibly safety needs. Once these lower needs are met, however, possessions and money cannot help people obtain love, esteem, and self-actualization. People have higher needs which they are not able to meet through material goods.

## experiences in human relations

### MEETING YOUR NEEDS

All people have the five basic needs as outlined by Maslow. You are at some level of the hierarchy now, working to meet the needs that are presently most important to you. As these needs are met, you can then go on to meeting higher needs.

In this experience, you will try to discover how the needs that you work to meet fit on Maslow's hierarchy of needs. Take five sheets of paper and at the top of each write one of the five basic needs. One sheet will be labeled "Physical Needs," another "Safety Needs," another "Love Needs," the fourth "Esteem Needs," and the fifth, "Self-actualization Needs."

Think about your behavior and actions over the past few days. Which actions helped meet which needs? It is easy to see that eating lunch and going to the restroom meet physical needs. But why did you wear that attractive shirt this

### Unit 2: Relationships Begin with You

morning? Did you hope to impress your dating partner? If so, you were working to meet your love needs. Perhaps you thought that it would make you appear important and "special." In that case, perhaps you selected your outfit because you were trying to meet esteem needs.

You may need to work on filling out these sheets over the course of several days. It is hard to identify needs and how you fill them. It is especially hard to do it quickly or without some thought.

When you have identified as many needs as you can think of, analyze your lists. Under which needs did you have the most entries? Which needs are you working on the hardest? How far up the needs hierarchy have you gone? Most teenagers have few entries in the top two need levels. Usually, most of their entries are focused on meeting physical, safety, or love needs. Was this true for you?

If you feel comfortable doing so, share some of the items on your lists with your classmates. Did you seem to mention the same kinds of items? Did listening to their lists help you think of things you might have missed? How do you think this experience could help you work toward living up to your potential?

### TO SUM UP...

1. According to scientists, what percentage of their potential do most people use?
2. What explanation does Maslow give about why people don't reach their potential?
3. List the five basic needs.
4. Describe various kinds of physical needs.
5. What is the need for safety?
6. At what age is love from family members most important? Least important?
7. How do people have their esteem needs met?
8. What is self-actualization?
9. List the order of needs in the hierarchy of needs.
10. Describe how people move through the hierarchy to meet their needs.

### SELF-ACTUALIZING PEOPLE

In the introduction to this chapter, it was noted that scientists believe that people are using only four to six percent of their potential. Since using potential is one aspect of self-actualization, it would seem that not many people have reached this level.

What are those people like who have achieved moments of self-actualization? What traits do they have? How have their characteristics helped them grow to be self-actualizing? What traits would help you work toward self-actualization?

#### ACCEPTANCE

Acceptance plays an important role in self-actualization. Self-actualizing people have learned self-acceptance as well as acceptance of others. The importance of self-acceptance was discussed in Chapter 2. Self-actualizing people have learned to know and accept themselves. They function in terms of their own talents, traits, and choices.

In addition to accepting themselves, self-actualizing people are able to accept others. They have a warm regard for other people in spite of conditions, behavior, or feelings. They can allow others to be themselves without judging them in any way. They accept

*Acceptance of themselves and others is an important trait of self-actualizing people.*

### Ch. 3: Making the Most of Yourself

have different musical tastes. Joyce is allowing Ted more freedom to be himself.

Learning to accept others as they are helps others come to accept you in the same way. This can be important as you work to meet your love needs. When you are accepted, not judged, as a person, you are comfortable in the relationship. Through relationships such as these, you feel free to show your real self. You know that your self will be accepted. An accepting kind of love relationship gives you the freedom to come to grips with yourself. You are able to face what you are. You can decide what to do to make the most of what you have and are.

## experiences in human relations

### INVITATION TO TALK

Telling others about yourself is one way to learn more about what you think and feel. Somehow, the act of putting your thoughts into words helps you clarify your ideas and discover exactly how you feel about them. In addition, being open about yourself works like a spiral. If you freely disclose yourself, your partner will be more likely to disclose also. This in turn will help you feel more free to talk about yourself. This spiral helps both you and your partner come to know yourselves and each other better. This makes it easier for you both to accept yourselves and each other.

For this experience, you need to prepare a series of cards. Each card has a question on it that would require your partner to tell something about the self. The rule for preparing questions is that you can ask anything that you would be willing to answer. Choose a partner

others simply because they are human and, as humans, are valuable for themselves.

The one area of conflict between Ted and Joyce, long-time dating partners, has been Joyce's interest in classical music. She has spent many hours trying in vain to interest Ted, a popular-music fan, in other kinds of music. Joyce often thought that Ted was a bit "stupid" since he refused to see how thrilling classical music could be. Lately, however, Joyce has come to see that Ted does not have to share her musical interests. She can care for him and accept him even though they

## Unit 2: Relationships Begin with You

with whom you feel comfortable. Your partner should also prepare a set of cards. Shuffle the two sets of cards together.

Begin by sitting opposite your partner with the cards face down on the table between you. If you are to go first, pick up a card and look at the question. If you would be willing to answer the question, ask it of your partner. If you would not be willing to answer the question, replace it and turn over a new card. When you ask the question, your partner can either answer it or choose to pass. At no time should either you or your partner answer a question that you don't wish to. After your partner has either answered or passed, replace the card. Then it is your partner's turn to choose a card and ask you a question.

When you have asked questions for a set period of time (such as fifteen minutes), talk over the experience with your partner. How did asking the questions make you feel? Answering them? What kinds of questions were easiest to answer? Hardest? How did this experience make you feel about yourself? How did it make you feel about your partner? What is the relationship between knowledge and acceptance?

• • • • • • • • • • • • • • • • • • • • • • •

### Balancing Your Self and the World

Once you have learned to accept the self that you are, you have the job of relating that self to the world around you. Your self has needs, but so does the environment around you. Your self makes demands, but other demands come from the outside world. Learning to balance the needs and demands of both your self and the world is important in growing toward self-actualization.

A person who has learned to listen to the needs of the self feels comfortable in making decisions about the self. Sherry says, "My feelings can be trusted. Therefore, what I want is what I do."

Robby expresses his idea another way, "Whatever I decide, I'm responsible for it. If I'm wrong, it will be my mistake and no one else's. If I'm right, it will be my win."

While it is rewarding to do what you feel is right for you, it can also be selfish and inconsiderate. Carol prided herself on "being in touch with my feelings." She often commented that "this feels so right for me." Because Carol was so convinced of her rightness, she often was insensitive to the rights of others. She ignored the feelings of her friends, who felt pushed around. She acted as if what was right for her was automatically right for the others, too.

On the other hand, some people are so cut off from their own feelings that they always try to do what others suggest. Peter allowed the others in his group of friends to use him. He ran errands and did chores for the others. He was so afraid that if he didn't do what his friends asked, he would be excluded. Therefore he ignored his feelings of resentment and did what the others asked.

Somewhere there is a balance between the two positions, and self-actualizing people have found it. In order to grow, you need to know what you feel and be able to act on those feelings. On the other hand, you can be so wrapped up in your own feelings that you ignore the feelings and needs of others. Finding the balance that is right for you will promote your best growth.

Margo has learned to balance the needs of her self and the needs of others. She is sensitive to other people's approval, affection, and good will. However, the major source of her actions comes from a sense of their being right for her. She says, "I check with the people who love me and then make my own

*Self-actualizing people have learned to balance the needs and demands of their self with those of their world.*

decisions. I am free from their pressure, but I am still interested in what they think."

## experiences in human relations

### MAKING DECISIONS

Self-actualizing people are able to know who they are and what they feel. They use this self-knowledge to make decisions about their own lives. Yet at the same time, they consider the effects of their choices on others around them.

This experience will help you begin to think about how you balance your needs with the needs of others when you make decisions. On a separate sheet of paper, list ten choices that you made recently. Some of your choices may be important, such as where to go to vocational school after graduation. On the other hand, everyone makes routine decisions each day.

## Unit 2: Relationships Begin with You

Examples of routine decisions may be choosing what to wear in the morning or what you want to eat from the cafeteria offerings.

Think about your decisions. Whose needs influenced your choices? How did you balance your needs with those of others around you? What effect did your decisions have on others?

Now code each decision that you made with the following key:

1. The decision was made on the basis of only my own desires.
2. The decision was my own, but I did consider what the effect on others would be.
3. My decision was a compromise between what I wanted and what others wanted.
4. I made my decision to please others, but I thought about what I would like.
5. My decision was made on the basis of someone else's wishes and desires.

What kind of pattern did your codings form? Do you seem to make your decisions one basic way? Do you use a variety of patterns when decision making? How good does your balance between self and others seem to be?

● ● ● ● ● ● ● ● ● ● ● ● ● ● ● ● ● ● ●

### SEEKING NEW EXPERIENCES

People who are self-actualizing constantly seek new ideas and experiences. They are actors rather than re-actors. They are the ones with the ideas of what to do, where to go, what's happening, and how they can be involved. They grow and develop new abilities and talents through the experiences they have.

Ruthie is the one in her circle of friends who has ideas about what to do. She always knows of a good movie playing close by. She is the one who encouraged the group to take up square dancing, even though everyone laughed when she first suggested it. Parties at Ruthie's house are always great fun because she knows party games and tricks that entertain everyone. Ruthie says that seeking out new experiences and trying new things always make her feel as though she's changing and growing.

Another way that self-actualizers seek new experiences is through creative use of habits and set patterns of behavior. Most people have a variety of habits. Some people routinely turn on the radio or television when they enter their house. Others may brush their teeth the same way at the same time each day. Habits can be as trivial as the motions people use to wash themselves. They can be as important as always relating to people in the same way.

Some people set up routines and habits so that they can concentrate their efforts on more important activities. Alma Elliott is a school teacher. She likes to think about and plan for the upcoming day each morning. She has developed a morning routine which has become a habit. Thus as she showers, breakfasts, and dresses, she can think about the activities of her day at school.

On the other hand, habits can keep people from trying new experiences. Habits can thus be a block to growing toward self-actualization. Danny had fallen into the habit of going to Funland every Friday night. He enjoyed playing the various electronic games and usually saw many of his friends. One night, however, he realized that he hadn't done anything different for a long time. So he deliberately set out to try some new activities. One Friday night he went to a choral concert. Another time, he saw a play. Next, he tried a wrestling meet. He went to a tennis match, a stock car race, and a chamber music concert over the next few weeks. He found he didn't enjoy some of the new activities he tried. However, he did find it exciting to search for and try new experiences.

Ch. 3: Making the Most of Yourself

## Peak Experiences

People who have reached moments of self-actualization do so through peak experiences. Peak experiences, or the "high points" of life, occur when people have been working and growing to the best of their ability. Peak experiences are the most wonderful moments in life.

Self-actualizing people feel that they are at the peak of their powers during their high points. They seem to function effortlessly and easily during peak experiences. Jane was taking a solid geometry course. One evening she had been having some trouble figuring out a set of problems. Then suddenly, everything seemed to click. All at once she saw how to get the solutions to the problems. Her brain seemed alive and full of answers. She was excited and brimming with energy. Jane felt as if she were using every bit of mathematical knowledge that she had. Instead of the boredom she often felt when doing her geometry problems, she was stimulated to do her best as she worked them.

People in peak experiences feel that they are truly themselves. Somehow, as their high points happen, they feel whole and unified. They usually feel more open and natural than otherwise, without the need for masks or other defenses of their selves. They feel lucky and fortunate during and after a peak experience.

When Art won the mile race in the state track meet finals, he was on top of the world. Somehow, he felt more like himself. At the same time, he had a feeling that he was parts of all the other athletes rolled into one person. He was happy and excited afterwards, telling his friends about his victory, being open about how happy he was to have won. He said, "You know, sometimes I feel like I didn't deserve to win. At the same time, though, it was just right. I had a good plan for

*The world seems at its brightest and best during a peak experience.*

the race and somehow my body just worked perfectly. It's hard to believe I could be so lucky! It was some experience!"

Maxine worked with retarded children through a Future Homemakers of America

## Unit 2: Relationships Begin with You

service project. It was often slow and frustrating work. She especially spent a lot of time trying to teach Bertha to tie her shoes. After weeks of patient help, Bertha tied a bow for the first time. Maxine was so excited she could hardly restrain herself. Helping Bertha achieve this step was tremendously important to her. This high point in Maxine's life made her feel both proud and humble. She felt it was one of the most important things she had ever done.

Peak experiences do not have to be earth-shaking discoveries or happenings. They occur when something important happens to you or when you make something important happen. Peak experiences make life really rewarding and worthwhile. They are most likely to happen when you are using your abilities to their fullest, when you stretch yourself to grow to be the best you can. Through peak experiences and self-actualization, you will be able to make the most of yourself.

## experiences in human relations

### HIGH POINTS

The peak experiences which come to self-actualizing people can be called "high points." They are the experiences that make life worth living. All people experience high points which make them happy, satisfied, or fulfilled. The following experience will help you identify the high points of your life.

Take a standard size sheet of paper and fold it into fourths. At the top of the first quarter, write what you were doing one week ago. Then, after thinking about what happened since that time, list eight or nine high points of your week. List those things which really gave you a sense of pleasure, accomplishment, or happiness. Then star your two highest high points of the week.

Now think about those people that you saw and worked with this week. In the second quarter of your paper, list the names of those people who were involved in your high points (if any). Did they add to or take away from your high points? Was there one other person who was involved in several of your high points?

In the third quarter, list the plans that you made for the future this week. Did you check books out of the library? Buy yarn to knit a scarf? Make plans for a party? Take film to be developed? List as many items as you can remember that will involve future action.

In the fourth quarter of your paper write five or six items that could have made the week better for you. What could have made your high points higher? What could have given you more high points?

Now look at your sheet and think about what you have written. Did your week bring you several important high points? Do you think that the plans you made for the future are likely to help you have more high points? Did most of your high points involve only yourself or you and others? Do some people seem to be especially good at helping you grow through high points? Could you have done anything to have made your week better? Were most of the ways the week could have been improved beyond your control?

High point charts should be kept each week for six weeks. You will probably find, after keeping the charts for about three weeks, that you will begin to try to get more high points. You will arrange to be around those people who help you reach the high points. You will learn to make your high points higher and more frequent. High points are worth working for—after all, they are what life is all about!

### Ch. 3: Making the Most of Yourself

**TO SUM UP...**

1. How does accepting others as people in their own right help you work toward self-actualization?
2. Explain what is meant by "balancing your self and the world."
3. Why do self-actualizing people seek new experiences?
4. What are peak experiences?
5. How do peak experiences occur?
6. Describe how people who have peak experiences feel.

# CHAPTER 4

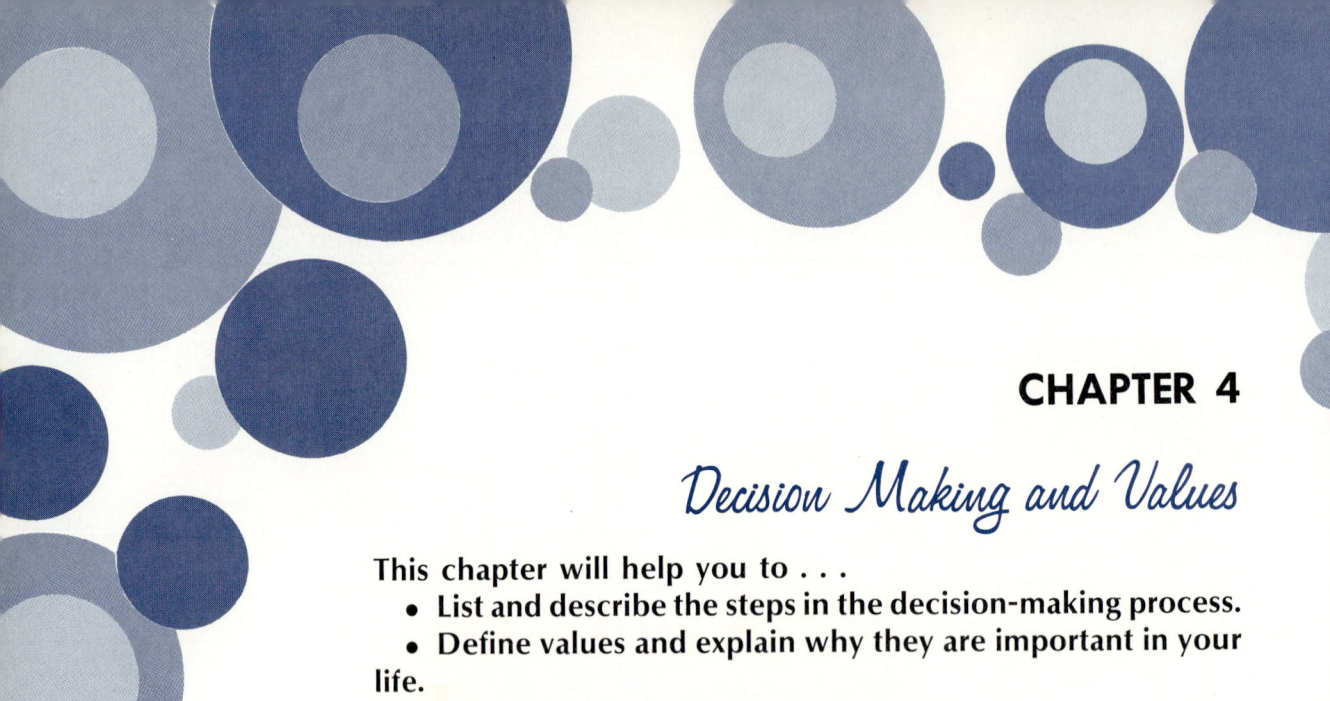

## Decision Making and Values

This chapter will help you to . . .
- List and describe the steps in the decision-making process.
- Define values and explain why they are important in your life.
- Identify some sources of values.
- Discuss the process of developing a value.
- Describe ways to explore which values are important to you.

Each day, you make choices about your life and how you live. Many of these decisions call for thought, opinions, and actions. Some of the decisions which you make are about familiar matters, others are about new situations. You make choices about casual as well as important experiences.

### THE PROCESS OF DECISION MAKING

Many of the decisions that you make seem to take little time or thought. After a brief look at the menu, for instance, you order what you like to eat. You may decide automatically to walk a certain route to school. You glance at the money in your purse or pocket and decide that you can afford to put only $2.00 worth of gas in your parents' car.

On the other hand, some decisions call for more time and thought. A long look at your feelings and future plans convinces you that you are not ready to be married. Another important choice is the one you will make concerning your career. You consider carefully what additional education you will need after you graduate.

On the surface, these two types of decisions appear to be quite different. One is concerned with minor aspects of your life. Choosing usually involves little time or thought. The major decisions are important in charting how your life will develop. These require much thought and consideration.

Both of these choices are made through the process of decision making. Decision making involves several steps. These are: identifying your problem; listing your options; thinking about these options; making your decision; and being responsible for your choice.

*The process of decision making gives answers to the many questions people face each day.*

## What Is Your Problem?

The first step in decision making is to determine exactly what you want to decide. What is the problem you face? Is it which salad to choose in the cafeteria line? Do you need to buy some new clothes? Are you trying to decide whether to spend your savings on a car of your own or keep them for future education? Choosing a job or a career is an important decision in every teenager's life. The first step in decision making involves identifying the exact problem for which you are to make a choice.

Joe had recently found an after-school job. His problem was that he had no transportation from school to work. He didn't have time to walk to work after school was out. Therefore Joe's problem or decision was how he would get to work each day.

## What Are Your Choices?

After you have decided on the problem, you need to consider your choices. What options do you have? If you are planning to go to vocational school, what schools might you attend? What courses could you choose to include in your senior schedule? The various makes and models give you many options when you go shopping for a new motorcycle.

Lorraine had saved $60 from her summer job to buy some new clothes for school. Her possible choices were wide. She could buy jeans and tops or matching pant suits. Dresses were another option. She also considered buying a long formal dress or a coat with her savings.

## Thinking about Your Choices

The next step in the decision-making process involves thinking about the options you have. What would be the results of the choices you are considering? What are the advantages and disadvantages of each? How would each option affect your relationships with others? Would there be different financial costs with each choice? What is important to you?

Thomas was trying to reach a decision about smoking marijuana. Since many of his friends smoked it, he felt that he would be more a part of the group if he also smoked.

61

Unit 2: Relationships Begin with You

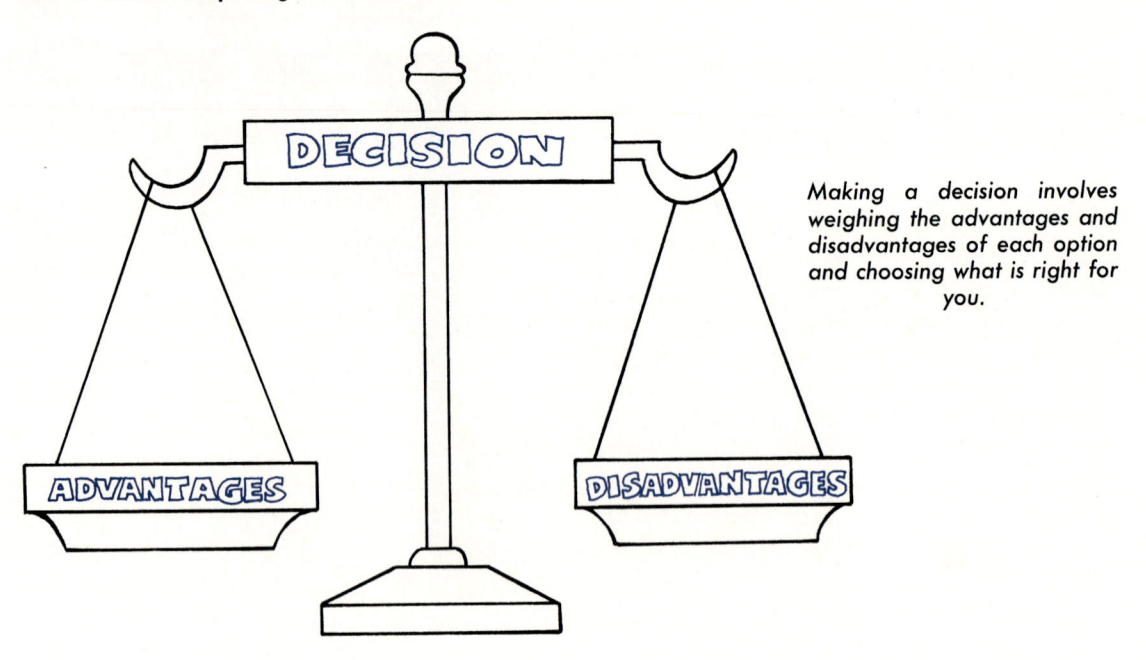

**DECISION**

**ADVANTAGES**  **DISADVANTAGES**

*Making a decision involves weighing the advantages and disadvantages of each option and choosing what is right for you.*

However, he knew that his parents would be very upset and hurt if he started using marijuana. In addition, his boss had commented that he wouldn't employ people who used marijuana. Therefore Thomas knew that if his boss found out that he had smoked he would lose his job.

Thomas wasn't too worried about the physical effects of marijuana, although he didn't want to become mentally dependent upon it. Thomas lived in a state where the legal penalties for marijuana use were quite severe. If he were convicted, he would never be allowed to hold a government job. In addition, he thought he might like to go to law school after college. A marijuana conviction would prevent his entry into law school. Finally, Thomas considered the cost of smoking marijuana. He was saving all his money for college and didn't want to start a habit which could turn out to be expensive.

## Make Your Choice

After thinking through the possible results of the options you have, you make your choice. Choosing involves thinking about what is most important to you. Which option has the most reward for you in terms of satisfaction and growth? Which possibility has the most negative results? Which choice will help you become the best person you can be? On the basis of questions such as these, you pick the choice which seems best for you.

Reba was trying to decide whether she wanted to become engaged to Mark at her graduation. They had dated steadily for almost two years. She was sure that their love was strong enough to make a good marriage. They both wanted to have some kind of symbol which told others that they belonged together.

At the same time, Reba had some doubts. For years she had planned to learn to fly a plane and become a pilot. She had been accepted at a technical school where she would learn airplane mechanics while she earned her pilot's license. She knew that she would always be disappointed if she didn't have a chance to attend the school. Yet Mark wanted her to take a job in the town where he attended college. He was hoping that they could be married the next Christmas after Reba had saved some money. Becoming engaged to Mark on his terms meant giving up her own dreams.

Reba considered all the advantages and disadvantages of becoming engaged. After much thought she decided that her year of school was too important to give up to become engaged. She assured Mark that she would be happy to become engaged in another year. For the present, she wanted to be free to carry out her own plans.

## Taking Responsibility for Your Decision

The last step in the decision-making process is to be responsible for the choice that you made. Too often, choices are made with little or no thought for the consequences. Then, when unpleasantness results, the person makes all sorts of excuses.

Gary convinced his father that the used car he wanted to buy was in top-notch shape. He repeated the salesperson's comments and added enthusiastic remarks of his own. Finally, his father gave his consent. Gary proudly drove his car for two weeks before he had a flat tire and found the spare unusable. Gary returned to the auto agency, requesting they give him a good spare tire. The salesperson told him that all used cars were sold "as is" with no repairs or replacements for breakdowns. Gary used most of one month's salary to pay for newer tires for the car. Shortly afterwards, the muffler on the car gave out. By this time, Gary realized that his decision to buy the car was not a good one. However, he was forced to be responsible for the cost of keeping the car in running order.

Another aspect of being responsible for your decisions involves knowing whether your choice was a good one. When the results of a decision are not satisfactory, you may need to rethink your decision. In some situations you can go back and make a new choice which is more satisfactory. In others, you may have to decide how you can best live with the unpleasantness of the first decision.

Della decided to enter the Air Force after high school graduation. The chance to travel attracted her. She also wanted to attend college, but didn't have the money. She planned on taking courses while in the service, then finishing college later on the GI Bill. However, Della found that she was unhappy and homesick in the Air Force. She tried to get out of the military but learned that she had to stay in for her enlistment time. Although it was hard, Della found that she was mature enough to take the responsibility for having made a poor choice. She decided to see how she could improve her situation. A transfer to a new company and schooling in the area of personnel work helped make her happier.

Other decisions are easier to reverse. Sam went shopping for a jacket to match a pair of plaid slacks. He found a jacket that seemed to match well. In addition, it cost less than he had expected to pay. However, when he wore the jacket out in the sunlight, he found that the red of the jacket did not match that in the pants. The artificial light in the store had distorted the colors. In addition, in the stronger light, he could see that the jacket was poorly made. Sam was quick to realize that he had made a poor selection. Luckily, he was able to

## Unit 2: Relationships Begin with You

return it to the store, get his money back, and look for another more suitable jacket.

In many cases, you may decide that your decisions were good ones. When similar circumstances come up, you may find yourself automatically making the same choice again. Many of the choices which you make without thought are the result of your judgment that a previous choice was a good one.

Karen always ordered a tenderloin sandwich when she ate at the E-Z Drive Inn. She didn't like the hamburgers there and had found the tenderloin to be quite good. Therefore, when she placed her order, she was repeating past successful choices.

When Clyde first took the job at the dairy plant, he drove his car to work each day. One day when his car was being repaired, he took the bus. He found that it was much simpler and cheaper to ride the bus. Riding the bus became a habit because Clyde recognized that it was a good choice for him.

The entire decision-making process is based on what is important to you or your values. Everything you do—every decision you make and every action you take—is based on your values. Your values influence the problems that you face, the options that you consider, and the choices that you make. Thus your decisions are bound up with the values that you hold.

### experiences in human relations

#### MAKING A DECISION

Most people are not aware of the steps they follow in making decisions. They may have never heard of the decision-making process, even though they follow it when making choices. As people become more aware of how to make decisions, they tend to become happier with the results of their choices. In other words, making conscious use of the steps in the decision-making process can help you make better choices. This experience will help you use the decision-making process.

First, consider some problem that you are facing or will face in the next few months. On a separate piece of paper, write down the decision you must make.

Now list all the possible options you could consider in solving your problem. Some may seem ridiculous or impractical to you, but list everything you can. Now think about each of these possibilities. What are the advantages of each choice? The disadvantages? Which options would actually be possible for you to do? Are some impossible for you? Consider the results of each choice. How would these choices influence you, your friends, your family, or others? Write your thoughts about each choice on the paper.

Based on the list you have made, make your decision. Try to put that decision into action. After you have done so, think about whether your choice was a good one. How have you taken the responsibility for your decision? Do you think doing this experience led you to a different choice than you might have otherwise made? If so, do you feel that was good or bad? How can you use the decision-making process in your everyday life?

### TO SUM UP...

1. What is the first step in the decision-making process?

2. What advantages can you see in making a long list of possible choices before reaching a decision?

**Ch. 4: Decision Making and Values**

3. List several effects that you might consider in thinking about your choices.

4. Describe what is involved in being responsible for your decisions.

5. Explain the relationship between decision making and values.

## WHAT ARE VALUES?

*Values* are standards you have developed which guide your actions, attitudes, comparisons, and judgments. Values define something of worth which you prize and believe to be beneficial or good. You may value physical fitness, companionship, honesty, or good looks.

Because people are different, not everyone has the same values. John values the friendship of his group. A savings account and tape collection are prized by Martin. Good grades are important to Betty while Julie works hard to become a good musician. Loyalty to those he loves guides many of Denny's actions. Teresa enjoys being a leader in many school clubs. Of course, all of these people also have other values, just as you have many values.

*The ability to express himself through painting is an important value for this teenager.*

Unit 2: Relationships Begin with You

## experiences in human relations

### WHAT DO YOU VALUE?

Your values are those things that are important to you. Have you ever thought about what you value? This experience will help you begin to think about what is important to you.

Write the following items on index cards, one item to each card:
  Time to be alone
  Watching your favorite television program
  A car of your own
  Being with your friends
  Education beyond high school (vocational training or college)
  A wardrobe of the latest fashions
  A dating partner who loves you
  Doing your favorite sports activity
  Lots of money
  Recognition from others
  A steady supply of alcohol or cigarettes
  A savings account
  Having a good time on Saturday nights
  Going to X-rated movies
  Earning praise from others
  Having a closely knit family

Take your packet of cards and arrange them in order of their importance to you. Place the card first that lists the item that is most important to you. Place the card second that is next in importance for you, continuing until you have arranged all 16 cards. Make a list of your order. Now arrange the cards as you think your best friend would. Compare this order to your list. How similar or different are the two lists?

Arrange the cards as you think one of your parents might. How is that list different from your list? Are your values more similar to your friend's or your parent's?

Now think about the items on the cards. What things are important to you that were not included? What items were included that you felt were very unimportant? Make up a new set of cards that contain 16 items that are very important to you. Arrange them in order of importance. Do you actually live your life according to what you feel is important?

• • • • • • • • • • • • • • • • • • • • • •

### INTRINSIC AND EXTRINSIC VALUES

Some qualities or objects are valued as ends in themselves. An old proverb states that "Honesty is its own reward." *Intrinsic values*, like the honesty in the saying, are those qualities or objects which you find rewarding for themselves. Intrinsic values are worthwhile because they are ends, not means to other ends.

Toby values learning, which he finds exciting and stimulating. Instead of working for high grades, Toby studies because he likes learning new ideas.

Laura, a member of the track squad, likes to run to keep her body in shape. She enjoys the sensation of gliding through the air, hair flowing, with all her body parts working together. Laura runs for the good feelings that running gives her, not because she values the ribbons that she wins in track meets.

The warmth and companionship of friendship is an important intrinsic value to Kenneth. Much of the time, Kenneth can be found with his group of friends, whose company gives him pleasure. He does not consider whether his friends will be able to do things for him or whether he will be seen as important by others because of his group membership.

Christine saved her allowance and babysitting money for a tape deck and speakers for her room. She enjoys owning the equipment, which produces excellent sound. Owning good sound equipment is an intrinsic value for her because she loves the musical results.

*Extrinsic values* are means to an end. These qualities or objects are important as a way to gain other desired results. Their value does not come from their own nature.

Calvin always has a date for Saturday night, usually with a different girl each week. He dates not so much because he enjoys the companionship of his partners, but because he feels it is important to be seen with a variety of girls.

Marjorie's mother likes Marjorie to keep her room neat and clean. Marjorie would rather take time to keep her room orderly than listen to her mother's nagging about how messy it is. Marjorie doesn't particularly value neatness, but keeps her room clean because she values harmony at home.

Joline spends a lot of money on new clothes. She feels that her wardrobe is important in earning the admiration of her friends. Her clothes are valued for their ability to impress others rather than because she likes them or enjoys wearing them.

Some qualities or objects may be both ends in themselves and means to other ends. Thus the same value can be both extrinsic and intrinsic. Tammy finds intrinsic value in acting in plays and dramas. She finds taking on the role of someone else enjoyable and challenging for itself. In addition, she also likes the praise and public acknowledgment she gets when she performs her part well. The praise and recognition give extrinsic value to her acting.

David enjoys being Carla's steady date for two reasons. He likes her lively sense of humor and the feeling he has of being at ease when he is with her. This is the intrinsic value of dating Carla. However, he also likes the fact that Carla was elected Homecoming Queen and was a runner-up in their city's Miss Teenager Contest. He feels important when he is seen with Carla on a date. These feelings are the extrinsic value he receives from being with Carla.

## experiences in human relations

### THREE WISHES

The things that you wish for indicate what you value. Suppose you had a magic genie who could grant you three wishes. What three things would you wish for? What would be important enough to you to spend your wishes on? Would your wishes be for intrinsic or extrinsic values? Would your wishes be about items or ideas? Would they be for you only or would you wish for something for others?

When you have decided what you would like from your magic genie, think about what the genie might bring your best friend. Your family.

What have you been doing or what could you do to get the things you wished for? If you feel comfortable doing so, tell your classmates about your three wishes.

• • • • • • • • • • • • • • • • • • • •

### THE INFLUENCE OF VALUES

Values are important in life because they cover the whole range of people's feelings, thoughts, and actions. The choices people make in the use of their time, money, energy, and affection are all influenced by the values they hold.

Unit 2: Relationships Begin with You

*This teenager's values are shown in the products she has chosen to buy with her money.*

Sally volunteers her time to answer the telephone on Saturday at the county Democratic Headquarters. This work is a result of her value that each person should participate in the political process. She chose to work for the Democratic party because her beliefs are similar to those of other Democrats.

How people use their money is an important indicator of what they value. Carol uses her spending money to buy the latest hit records and tapes. Spike spends his salary on upkeep and new accessories for his car. Having the latest fashion in clothing is important to Delorise. Andrew buys books or saves his money for college. In these and other ways, people spend or save their money in terms of what they value.

Values can be important in people's relationships, too. Tony values the company of other people and works to have good relationships with others. He is always willing to help his family and friends with their problems or work. He gets much satisfaction from the companionship he shares with others.

Beth values her relationships with her friends from school. She spends a lot of time and effort to keep her friendships running smoothly. However, she is ill at ease with her parents, teachers, and other adults. She makes very little effort to have good relationships with them. Beth values various kinds of relationships differently.

Norajean spends much of her time and energy working. Her job at the discount store, her babysitting, and an occasional sewing or cleaning job keep her busy. She only goes out with her friends when she can't find a job to earn extra money. For Norajean, earning money is more important than her relationships with others.

In summary, your values are extremely important in how you build your life. Your values, or what is important to you, are personal and individual. Your ideas, your feelings, and your actions are all influenced by the values you hold.

## experiences in human relations

### AFTER-SCHOOL PATTERN SEARCH

How you spend your time tells a great deal about what you value. It may even tell more about what you value than what you say.

Think about what you have done every night after school for the past week. Write down what you did each day from the time school was dismissed until bedtime. Now, look over your list. Do you see any patterns in your activities? Do you like what you see? What values does your time record reveal? Are you spending your time on activities that are important to you? What other ways could you be spending this time?

Think about how you spend your time on Saturday nights, on Sundays, during study periods at school. What patterns can you discover in how you spend these times? Are you living your values? If not, what can you do to bring the way you spend your time and your values closer together?

## TO SUM UP...

1. What are values?
2. Why don't all people value the same things?
3. Define intrinsic and extrinsic values. Give an example of each.
4. List several aspects of life that are influenced by values.

## SOURCES OF VALUES

Where do values come from? Values don't just appear full and strong to influence people's lives. They are developed through experiences with the family, the peer group, and others.

### VALUES FROM THE FAMILY

A baby has no conscious values. On some unconscious level, a baby values food, sleep, dry diapers, and love. As the child grows, it begins to learn what others in its family value.

Three-year-old Ricky is beginning to learn about the things that are important to his family. He lives with his mother, his grandmother, and his aunts and uncles. Although he is too young to reason and understand, he knows that money is important. His mother often tells him that when she finishes school and gets a job, they won't have to worry so much about having enough money. Loving, hugging, and kissing are important in Ricky's family. He gets and gives much love and affection. Ricky also knows that his grandmother does not value what she calls

*People learn values from their experiences with others who are important in their lives.*

## Unit 2: Relationships Begin with You

"drunks." He doesn't know how people get to be drunks, but his grandmother calls them sinful, wasteful, and godless. So Ricky knows that drunks are bad. Ricky's family has not tried to deliberately teach him to value money, family love, and sobriety. Instead, he has learned these values from their words and actions.

Other families teach other values. Joan's mother and father are college students, so Joan often sees them studying or writing papers. Through their actions, she is learning to value reading, writing, and education. Her favorite game is called "going to class." In it, she uses books and papers to act out what she sees her parents doing. Joan's parents usually spend Saturday nights playing cards and drinking beer with other students. Through her parents' actions, Joan learns that playing cards and drinking beer is a way to have fun and enjoy life.

### VALUES FROM PEERS

The family is the main source of values until the child enters school or begins attending a child care center. Then the peer group, or other children of about the same age, becomes an important source of values. Some of the values which children learn from each other are similar to those they learn at home. Other values may be quite different.

Barbara's parents taught her to value education and to work to do well in school. Barbara's friends at school all value education, too, so they work together to do their best on their lessons.

Nat's parents have never allowed him to have toy guns or to watch television shows that contain violence. They have also taught Nat not to fight with other children, that there are better ways of handling conflict. However, Nat's school friends are a group of boys to whom violence is important. They fight among themselves and they often fight with other children. They watch all the police and detective television programs and imitate their heros. Nat has had several conflicts with his parents over the values he has learned from his friends.

## experiences in human relations

### WHERE DO YOUR VALUES COME FROM?

People learn their values from many places. They see values shown on television, or they read about them in newspapers, magazines, and books. They learn values from their families, friends, teachers, and other people. This experience is to help you recognize the people who influence your values and to what extent they are able to influence you.

Take two sheets of paper and fold them in fourths. At the top of each fourth, write one of the names of the following people (identify real people): your parent or guardian, the leader of your group of friends, a favorite relative, your best friend, a teacher who is important to you, the person you are in love with, an important neighbor, and your name.

Below each name, list four or five things that each of these people want you to value. Leave the quarter below your name blank. What do they count on you for? What do they want you to be, to think, or to do? What do they want to be important to you?

Look at the list you have made. How similar or different are the things that the people in your life want from or for you? Under your name, make a list of those values that you are willing to accept for yourself. Are you willing to accept most of the values others wish for you?

Are there many values that you don't want? Can you see how differing values can be a source of conflict in relationships with others?

● ● ● ● ● ● ● ● ● ● ● ● ● ● ● ● ● ● ●

**VALUES FROM OTHERS**

The school and teachers are another source of values. Some teachers have a great deal of influence on their students' values while others have very little. Neighbors, community members, and spiritual teachings can influence the values of children. Television programs, magazines, and books are also important sources of values.

With all of these possible sources of values, it is no wonder that most people reach their teen years and even adulthood with little clear idea of what their values are. You are faced with many choices, with many alternatives. As the number of value choices increases, it is harder to know what is really important to you.

People with few values often drift, not knowing what they believe or feel. The less people know about their values, the more confused they are. Too often their decisions are made on the basis of pressure from peers, by giving in to authority, or on the power of advertising. It is only as people come to understand their values that they are able to make good choices and take appropriate action.

### experiences in human relations

**A VALUES SURVEY**

The values that you hold are influenced by the values of others. You are probably unaware of how often you hear others express or see them act out their values. This experience is to help you become more aware of how often people make value statements. It will also help you become more aware of the different views which people hold about a particular value.

Select an item from the following list or choose another item in which you are interested:

| | |
|---|---|
| Good grades | Good looks |
| Political reform | Having children |
| Communicating with others | Popular music |
| | Going to college |
| Making decisions | Teenage marriages |
| Violence on television | |

Over the course of a week observe, listen, or ask questions to discover what people think about your topic. Write their statements in a notebook along with a brief description of the person who made it. You may wish to include sex, occupation, or approximate age in your description. You may want to talk to people other than your own friends or family to get a variety of responses.

Summarize your findings in a report. Did people of the same age, sex, or occupation tend to hold the same values about your topic? Were there differences between sexes, workers and students, old and young people? Were your values influenced by what you heard?

### TO SUM UP...

1. How are values developed?
2. Why do children first learn values from their families?
3. When do children begin learning values from non-family members?
4. List at least five people who influence your values. What are their relationships to you?

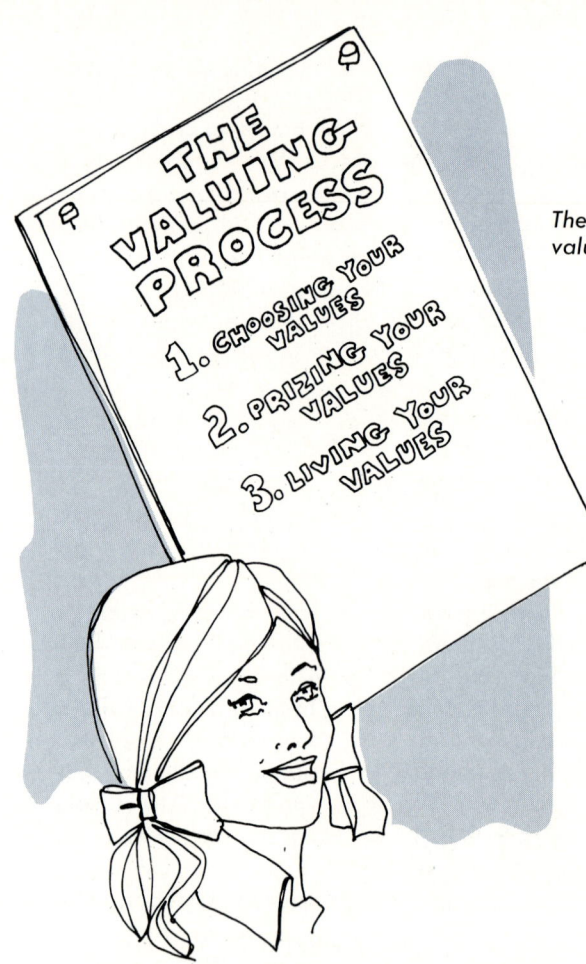

*The most important influences on your life are those values that have been developed through the valuing process.*

## THE VALUING PROCESS

How do people learn to identify and understand their values? How do they know what they value? The *valuing process* is an ongoing series of actions through which a person determines the worth of an idea or activity. The process of valuing centers on choosing, prizing, and living your values.

### CHOOSING VALUES

Choosing values and decision making are closely related. Decisions are made on the basis of what you value or consider important. On the other hand, choosing values involves making decisions about what it is that you feel is worthwhile.

When Mariana was hunting for after-school work, she had two job offers. One job was to work as a nurses' aide in the neighborhood hospital. The pay was quite good, but the work itself did not appeal to her. Her best friend also worked as a nurses' aide at the hospital so they would be working together. The other job involved monitoring electronic gauges at the water treatment plant. If the gauges registered incorrect figures, she would alert a supervisor. Once an hour she would take and test several water samples. The pay was low, but she would have free time to read or study. She would be alone in the lab during working hours.

Mariana's job decision basically involved choosing her values—what was really important to her. Did she value the amount of money earned? The chance to be with her friend? Time to study? After much thought Mariana decided that money and friendship were more important than an easy job and study time. Once she had chosen these values, her decision as to which job to take was easy to make.

Before you can choose a value, you must have at least two possibilities from which you can select. You cannot choose a value if there is only one available to you. In much the

Ch. 4: Decision Making and Values

same way, you need not make any decision if there is only one option open to you.

It makes no sense for Peter to say that he values eating because he must eat to live—he has no choice. Peter does have value choices in what foods he eats, however. He can choose nutritious foods which help meet his body's needs for nourishment and good health. Peter may choose to eat junk foods which contain calories with few if any nutrients. If he chooses junk food, he shows that he values the taste of such foods more than their nutritional content.

For a value to guide your life meaningfully, it must be chosen after careful thought and deliberation. Juan did not particularly enjoy school even though he earned good grades. He spent a long time thinking about whether he wanted to attend college. He finally decided that a college degree would increase his chances of getting a well-paid, interesting job. When he entered college, he was prepared to study hard even when he didn't enjoy it. His careful thought about the value of a college education helped him do well even though he didn't always enjoy his schooling.

If a value is a guide for your life, it must be chosen freely. If it has been imposed by someone else, it may guide your actions only when that other person is watching.

Quinn says that he has the value of "honesty is the best policy." His parents and teachers have certainly told him to be honest. However, Quinn has not as yet come to see for himself that honesty is a worthwhile value. Therefore he is honest only when he knows others are watching. If he thinks he can run a stop sign, shoplift, or cheat on a test without being caught, he stops being honest. Because Quinn has not freely chosen the value of honesty, it is not really a value for him, even though he claims it is.

## experiences in human relations

### MAKING CHOICES

When was the last time you made a choice from more than three alternatives? Too often people make decisions and live their lives without looking at all the possible alternatives open to them. Looking for alternatives is an important step in the process of valuing.

With a partner, spend three to five minutes talking about all the possible alternatives to one of the following problems:
Activities to do on a Saturday night date
Ways to earn money
Ways to make new friends
How to give a great party
How to use your leisure time
Ways to have fun without spending money

When you have listed as many possibilities as you can, choose the three alternatives that you and your partner like best. Read your list of alternatives to your classmates. Do they agree with your "top three"?

Do you spend much time thinking about all the possibilities open to you when you make decisions? What would your life be like if you tried one new alternative each day?

• • • • • • • • • • • • • • • • • • • •

### PRIZING VALUES

Prizing and cherishing your values means that they have a positive quality for you. You hold your values dear, you respect and esteem them, and you are happy with them.

Althea and Bart have become engaged. Bart has suggested that they have premarital sex. However, Althea believes that it is important for a girl to be a virgin on her wedding night. As Althea says, "It was really hard for me to

**Unit 2: Relationships Begin with You**

*Telling others about what is important to you is one step in the valuing process.*

say no to Bart at first. After all, I love him and want to please him. But my value of virginity is really important to me. I'm not ashamed to value it even though Bart sometimes tries to convince me that my values are old-fashioned. But old-fashioned or not, I think you have to stand by what you believe in."

If you have thoughtfully chosen a value and feel it is important to you, you are willing to tell others about how you feel. When you are ashamed of a choice you have made, or are unwilling to tell others how you feel, it is likely that you do not value your choice or feelings.

Loren was one of the few members of his group of friends who did not smoke. Usually, Loren did not talk about smoking, but one night when the group was talking about being healthy, Loren spoke up. He said, "Well, you know, that's why I don't smoke. I really thought about it when most of you began smoking, and I just decided that I didn't want that tar and stuff in my lungs. Sometimes it's hard when you're all smoking, but it is something that I feel is important. I want my lungs to be healthy and to stay healthy."

## experiences in human relations

### A SACKFUL OF VALUES

One step in the valuing process involves talking about your values with others. This experience allows you to tell others about some values that are important to you.

Bring to class a paper sack containing five objects which are important to you. The five items may be actual objects, replicas, or pictures of items you value.

Show your sackful of values to your classmates. Explain why these are values for you. Listen as others tell you about items that are important to them.

When all the students have talked about their sack of values, discuss what people shared. Were there some objects that several people valued? Did some people have values that weren't mentioned by any others? How did the values mentioned seem to be alike or different? Why would there be similarities and differences in the values that were discussed? How did you feel about hearing other peoples' values? Telling about your own?

●●●●●●●●●●●●●●●●●●●●

## LIVING YOUR VALUES

For your values to be guides in your life, you need to act on them. Unless you live or act upon your values, they are meaningless, no matter how much you believe them or talk about them.

People act on their values in many ways. They read about their values, they spend money on them, and they relate to others on the basis of their values. In other words, your life is influenced when you live your values.

Rosa not only talks about the drug problem in her high school, but she also does something about it. She feels that drugs can easily ruin a teenager's life so she works to help others avoid involvement with drugs. A member of the student council, she formed a committee which sponsored an assembly program on the physical results of drug use. The committee also raised money to purchase a set of posters about drug abuse, which they displayed in the school halls. Rosa wrote a series of articles for the school newspaper on drug use.

The final aspect of the valuing process is that a value becomes a part of the pattern of your life. The values that you hold are shown many times in a variety of situations. Values are persistent and reoccur on many occasions in your life.

Sidney believes that it is important to treat others as he wants to be treated. He works very hard at listening to others and trying to understand what they are saying. Sidney doesn't just listen to his friends. He listens to those with whom he has conflict, as well as to his family members. He listens to old Mrs. Barker and to his five-year-old neighbor, Errin. Sidney's respect for others is shown in all his relationships. He doesn't just talk about his values, he lives them every day.

## VALUE INDICATORS

A *value indicator* shows that a value is in the process of being formed. You may have some idea of a value that seems important to you, such as doing something for others in your leisure time. If you do not act on the idea, it is not a value for you. Instead, it is a value indicator.

Julian is studying child discipline in his child development course. He has learned that physical punishment, such as spankings, rarely change children's behavior. He has also learned about the power of rewarding children for the good things they do. Julian is very enthusiastic about the new discipline methods he has learned. However, in the play school, he frequently slaps the children's hands when they do something wrong. Julian is in the process of forming a value about disciplining children, but he has not yet learned to act on his value repeatedly.

Value indicators can be important in a person's life because they give some clue to the values that are in the process of forming. But, the most important standards in guiding behavior are those that have already been formed through the valuing process.

Unit 2: Relationships Begin with You

## experiences in human relations

### CHARTING YOUR VALUES

How many of the ideas that are important to you are actually values? Have they been taken through all three steps in the valuing process?

On a separate piece of paper, prepare a chart. At the top left, write the words, "Important Values." At the top right, number across from 1 to 3. These numbers stand for the steps in the valuing process:

1. Have you chosen thoughtfully and freely from alternatives?
2. Do you cherish your value and share it with others?
3. Are you acting on your value so that it is a part of your life?

Think about some items that are important to you. Write at least five items under the heading "Important Values." Think about these five items. How many steps of the valuing process have you done for each? Place a check under the number that stands for the step (or steps) which you have completed.

For example, if you think that racial equality is important, you could list it under "Important Values." Did you choose it freely and thoughtfully from alternatives? Is it important to you and are you willing to tell others how you feel? Have you ever done anything about racial equality? If so, have you made your actions a part of your life pattern? Place a check mark under the numbers which represent the questions which you answered yes.

How many of your important items actually turned out to be values? Where is your weak area? Action? Sharing? How could you work to turn your value indicators into values?

### TO SUM UP...

1. What is the valuing process?
2. Describe the three parts of the valuing process.
3. Give an example which shows why being thoughtful about choosing a value is important.
4. What is likely to be the result of people not freely choosing their own values?
5. Why is telling others what you believe important in the valuing process?
6. How can values become a part of your life pattern?
7. What is a value indicator?

### EXPLORING YOUR VALUES

Many people are confused about their values. They are not too sure how they feel about politics, leisure time, love, death, or authority. How do you know what you believe? How can you find out what you actually value? As you listen to what your parents, teachers, and friends say and see what they do, it is hard to know just what is right for you.

When you explore your values, you weigh the choices you have and decide just what is important to you. To do this, you need an open mind and a questioning approach to your experiences. As you participate in an activity, think about whether you believe in what you are doing. Do your words and actions represent what you really feel or are you just doing what someone else told you was right?

Roger was getting ready to vote in his first election after turning 18. His parents always voted a straight Democratic ticket so, at first,

**Ch. 4: Decision Making and Values**

Roger planned to do the same. He read all he could about the candidates and what they stood for. Soon he found that his ideas were more similar to some of the Republican candidates. Roger decided that he was more interested in what specific people stood for rather than supporting a particular party, so he ended up voting a split ticket.

Another way to become more aware of what you value is to weigh the pros and cons and think about the consequences of your actions.

Sue was considering taking an after-school job since she was always short of money. She thought about what would happen if she did take a job. She would have to give up her after-school participation in the mixed chorus and her volunteer work at the community center. Because her mother didn't get off work until 6:30, Sue always fixed supper at home. An after-school job would keep her from doing the evening cooking. Sue talked it over with her mother and thought about what would happen if she did or didn't take the job. She decided that the money from a job was less important to her than her other activities, so she did not look for work.

Another way to think about what you value is to compare what you believe with what you do. Do your actions match your beliefs? If not, why? What can you do to act on what you believe is important?

*Working to discover what is truly important can be difficult. Yet it can help you be more enthusiastic and confident about your life.*

Unit 2: Relationships Begin with You

## experiences in human relations

### A DOZEN FAVORITES

Exploring your values means that you look at the way you live your life and think about whether your life reflects what is really important to you. The following experience will help you think about whether you are really getting what you want out of life.

Take a piece of paper and number from 1 to 12 down the center of the sheet. Beside each number, write down one activity in life that you love to do. Your dozen favorites can be big or little, just as long as you list those you love to do.

When your list is complete, use the left-hand side of your paper to code your favorite activities in the following way:

- Think about which five activities are most important to you. Label these items 1 through 5 with the most important activity labeled 1, the second 2, and so on.
- Place the letter A beside those activities that you prefer to do alone. Use the letter O to code those that you like to do with others. An A-O can be used to mark those that you enjoy doing either with others or alone.
- Write a $ beside those activities that cost more than $5.00.
- Place a W beside those activities that you would like to do at least once a week.
- Beside each item, write approximately how many days, weeks, or months it has been since you last did each activity.
- Place an MT beside those activities that you would like to spend more time on in the future.
- Place the letters CH next to those you hope your own children will have on their lists some day.
- Label with an I three activities which you would like to improve.

When you have finished coding the list of your dozen favorite activities, think about what you have written. Do you actually spend much of your time doing your dozen favorites? If not, why? Are most of your favorite activities done alone or with others? What does this tell you about your relationships with others? Did you find it hard or easy to identify those activities that you would like to do weekly, would like to do better, and would like to pass on to your children? How does money relate to your favorite activities? What have you learned about yourself in thinking about your dozen favorites?

• • • • • • • • • • • • • • • • • • •

Jeff often let Lita copy his algebra papers when she didn't get hers done. He knew that it was wrong, but when she smiled at him and asked for the loan of his papers, he couldn't refuse. Finally Jeff realized that he was not living up to what he believed. The next time Lita asked to copy his paper, he refused to let her have it.

By learning what you value, you can take an important step in building a strong self-concept. If you know what is important to you, you will be more confident that you can make the right decisions for you. This confidence helps you feel better about yourself.

Will had a poor self-concept and usually did what his parents wanted. As graduation came closer, Will knew that he had to decide what he was going to do. His parents were pressuring him to go to college. After thinking a great deal about the situation, he decided that he didn't want to go to college, that he wanted to take a job.

Will explained to his parents how he felt. "I know you are disappointed. But I just couldn't go to college because *you* felt it was important. I might still want to go in a year or so, but right now, I want to earn some money. I want to know that I can handle a job, can be responsible for myself." When Will had made his decision, he felt much better about himself. He was sure that he was right and as a result, he developed a more positive self-concept.

By learning to discover what you value, you will develop a skill that will be useful all through your life. Most values are relatively stable, but your emphasis on what is important to you may change as you experience life. If you have learned to question and think about what you value, you are more likely to know when your values change. This can help you keep your actions in line with your changing values.

When Vera and Doug were first married, they enjoyed going out a great deal. They saw the latest movies and went to nightclubs and discotheques. Their social life was very important to them.

Later, when they had children, Vera and Doug discovered that going out became less important. Much of their leisure time was spent in activities with their children. They felt it was important to be with the children, enjoying the times they shared together.

As the children grew up, Vera and Doug's spare time slowly began to center around activities for their synagogue. They were gone from home a great deal, working on projects which their synagogue sponsored and attending related social affairs. Thus, through the years Vera and Doug's changing values influenced how they spent their leisure time.

When people know what they value, they are more critical in their thinking about what is right for them. They are able to make and follow through on choices about how they live. People who have found out what they value and who live by what is important to them are excited and enthusiastic about life. By learning to explore your values, you can be better equipped to face the world with eagerness and confidence.

## experiences in human relations

### ONE PERFECT DAY

Imagine yourself in the future, any time from tomorrow to several years from now. Think about one day that would be perfect for you. Imagine 24 hours of ideal bliss. What would you be doing? Where would you be? With whom would you spend your time?

Write about your perfect day. Try to describe exactly what you would be doing for those 24 hours. You may wish to include the smells, sounds, and weather of your day.

Are you doing anything to help you achieve your perfect day? How could you work to have a perfect day? How could you introduce the values of your perfect day into your everyday life?

## TO SUM UP...

1. What does exploring your values mean?
2. How can thinking about the consequences of your actions help you discover your values?
3. Describe characteristics of people who are clear about what they value.

# CHAPTER 5

## *Personal Decisions*

This chapter will help you to . . .
- Recognize the importance of decisions about drug use and premarital sex.
- Define terms associated with drugs and their use.
- Summarize the effects and dangers of the use of various kinds of drugs.
- Explain some reasons why people use drugs.
- List different patterns of premarital sexual behavior.
- Understand the responsibilities of sexual behavior.

Sexual activity and the use of drugs such as alcohol or nicotine have long been considered adult privileges. As teenagers mature into adulthood, they face choices about drug use and premarital sex.

Many teens are eager to experiment with drugs or sex to bring about their entry into the adult world. Others are willing to go along with peer group pressure and conform to the accepted behavior of the group. However, some teenagers realize that drug use and premarital sex are not matters to be taken lightly. Your decisions about drugs and sex are likely to have a long-lasting effect on your future.

Too many people casually choose to use drugs or participate in sex. They have not seriously weighed the advantages and disadvantages of their actions. Often, they ignore the possible results of their behavior. Thus many people find unhappiness and even tragedy because of thoughtless choices.

In contrast, some people have carefully considered all aspects of their possible choices. They tend to be more satisfied with the results of their decisions. Premarital sexual behavior and drug use are areas which are highly influenced by your values. You need to consider carefully your values and the choices you make based on those values. When you do this, you are more apt to make mature choices about drug use and sexual behavior.

## DRUG DEFINITIONS

Throughout history, human beings have been drug users. Different areas of the globe used different drugs. Tobacco was commonly used in North America. People who lived in the Orient smoked opium. Alcohol was the

**Ch. 5: Personal Decisions**

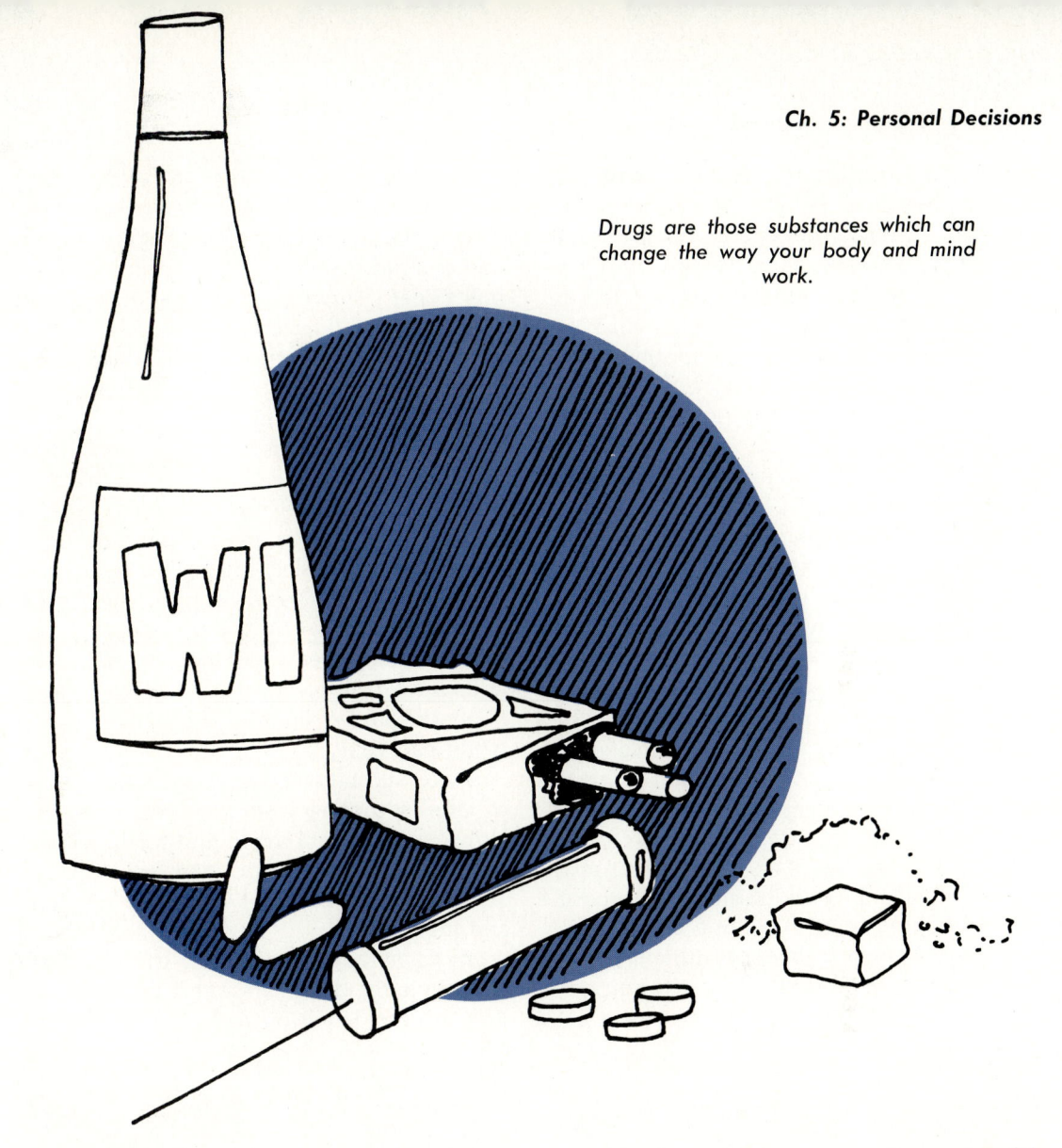

*Drugs are those substances which can change the way your body and mind work.*

drug used by Europeans. The people of Central America and what is now the southwestern United States used peyote to induce trances and drug highs. Cocaine was found in large areas of South America. Caffeine was common in many parts of the world. It has been noted that every culture throughout history has used drugs except the Eskimos. Since they could grow nothing, they had to wait for the white man to bring them alcohol.

Drugs have been a part of people's life styles for many thousands of years. Today, people are familiar with drugs from all over the world. Yet, despite centuries of experience with drugs, there is still controversy over their control and use.

A *drug* is a chemical substance, other than food, which causes changes in the way the body and mind function. Drugs can be either beneficial or harmful. You may be alive today

81

## Unit 2: Relationships Begin with You

because of the use of drugs. Barnaby has diabetes, which is controlled by the use of the drug insulin. The chemotherapy treatments that Mr. Dana takes weekly are helping insure that his cancer will not return. Digitalis and nitroglycerin tablets help keep Mrs. Wong's heart pumping smoothly.

Many people also experience the harmful effects of drugs. Terry was drunk the night he hit another car broadside, killing the other driver. The accident also injured several of his friends who were riding with him. The drug nicotine in the cigarettes which Mr. Tibbitts smoked over the years led to lung cancer. Jennifer experienced a severe allergic reaction to the penicillin she was given when she had pneumonia.

People may react differently to the same drug. For instance, you may be cured by the same drug that gives someone else an allergic reaction. A drug that is life-saving in small doses may be very dangerous in larger amounts.

The U. S. government describes *drug use* as the "taking of a drug for its intended purpose, in the appropriate amount, frequency, strength, and manner." It says *drug misuse* is "taking a substance for its intended purpose, but not in the appropriate amount, frequency, strength, or manner." Finally, *drug abuse* is "deliberately taking a substance for other than its intended purpose, and in a manner that can result in damage to the person's health or ability to function."

For example, Jeff's father died suddenly. The doctor gave Jeff some pills to keep him calm and to help him sleep. He was to take the tablets whenever he felt particularly upset, but no more than three times a day. A fourth tablet was to be taken at bedtime. By following the doctor's directions, Jeff was meeting the definition of drug use. Jeff soon discovered that he could block out many of the events that upset him by taking six or eight tablets a day. He was then misusing the drug. He was still taking it to help him sleep and to relieve the upset and pain of his father's death. However, he was not taking it in the way the doctor directed. Finally, Jeff would have abused the drug if he had deliberately taken enough of the tablets to make himself "drunk" on the drug.

People can very easily become dependent on the drugs they take. Marilyn doesn't feel that her day can begin until she has at least two cups of coffee in the morning. Mrs. Thomas relies on sleeping pills to get a good night's sleep. Without the pills, she tosses, turns, and sleeps very little. A cigarette between classes seems to help Phil stay calm and ready to listen to his next teacher. Tony depends on heroin to help him face the world each day.

The term drug addiction is most often used to label someone who uses drugs illegally. However, *drug addiction* describes a habit brought about by the continued use of drugs. There are two kinds of addiction, physical and mental.

*Physical addiction* involves chemical changes in the body. These changes cause the user to need larger doses of the drug to get the same effect. This is called *tolerance* for a drug. True physical dependence only occurs with heroin and other opiate drugs, alcohol, barbiturates, and, in some cases, nicotine. With these drugs, stopping the drug brings on certain physical complaints called *withdrawal symptoms* such as dizziness, nausea, or headaches. Each drug has characteristic withdrawal symptoms. These can be very severe and painful. In some cases, they can cause death.

People can be *mentally addicted* to a drug if they require its use to meet emotional needs. All drugs have the potential for mental

Ch. 5: Personal Decisions

*Habitually using drugs can lead to physical or mental addiction.*

dependence. In most cases of mental addiction, the body does not build a tolerance for the drug. Thus there is little or no need to keep increasing the doses. If you stop the use of a drug to which you are mentally addicted, you may have discomfort in many ways. These can include nervousness, crossness, and other mental distress. This is in contrast to the specific set of physical withdrawal symptoms that go with the physically addicting drugs.

When Karen stopped using the diet pills that her doctor prescribed, she found life unpleasant. She was cross and irritable with others. Relying on the pills for energy, she seemed unable to accomplish any work when she stopped taking them. She found herself sleepy and depressed.

Karen's experience in withdrawing from diet pills was unpleasant. However, it differed from Dave's physical symptoms when he began withdrawal from alcohol, the drug to which he was addicted. At first, he seemed to be sobering up normally. Then he began to have the shakes. An hour later, Dave started to vomit and run a high fever. He began to have hallucinations that someone was after him.

Most people who begin taking drugs feel confident that they will not become addicted to them. No one believes that he or she will be an addict. However, it is impossible to tell before drug use starts who will become addicted. Therefore, when you use any drug, you face the risk of either physical or mental addiction.

Unit 2: Relationships Begin with You

## experiences in human relations

### DRUGS IN THE NEWS

Drugs frequently are in the news. The headlines may report a major new drug for the treatment of cancer. A new drug law may be debated in the legislature. A teenager may have been arrested for illegal possession of drugs. This experience will help you explore just how often drug-related stories appear in the news.

Read your local paper carefully over the course of one week. Clip out all the stories that deal in any way with drugs. There will probably be a wide range of topics covered, including accidents related to drug use and legal violations. Other stories may discuss drug abuse or addiction or medical advancements or research about drugs.

After you have saved a week's clippings, sort the clippings according to subject. How many were about the legal status of drugs? How many about drugs used medically? Drug abuse could be another category. Make as many categories as you need.

How many stories were about alcohol use or abuse? Marijuana? Other drugs? Does your paper seem to put the most emphasis on one particular drug? Can you see a reason for this emphasis?

It may be interesting to watch the evening news on television for the same week. How many drug-related stories were carried on the television news? How does this compare with the number of newspaper stories?

What do these stories tell you about your community? Does there seem to be a drug problem which your paper or television station is uncovering? What kinds of stories do you think news media should be carrying about drugs?

### TO SUM UP...

1. What is a drug?
2. Explain the difference in the terms drug use, drug misuse, and drug abuse.
3. Define drug addiction.
4. Compare and contrast physical addiction and mental addiction.
5. What is tolerance?
6. Describe the withdrawal symptoms for physical and mental addiction.

### KINDS OF DRUGS

Although there are many kinds of drugs, this chapter will discuss drugs which are commonly used for non-medical purposes.

#### NICOTINE

One of the common and widely used drugs is *nicotine,* found in the leaves of the tobacco plant. You may not consider using tobacco as a method of taking drugs. However, the effect of nicotine on the body makes it a drug, just as alcohol or heroin are drugs.

People take the drug nicotine mainly through smoking cigarettes. Other forms of tobacco use, such as pipe or cigar smoking or chewing tobacco, are also sources of nicotine.

Nicotine is one of the legal drugs since there are no penalties for possessing or using it. All forms of tobacco are easily obtainable. However, cigarette packages and advertising must carry a warning that the Surgeon General has determined that cigarette smoking is dangerous to your health.

## The Effects of Nicotine

Nicotine has a definite mood-changing effect on its user, for it gives the smoker a "lift." Nicotine speeds the heart and breathing rates and at the same time cuts the appetite. It causes the blood vessels to narrow and disrupts the bodies' defenses against disease.

In women, nicotine influences reproduction. Women who smoke often find it more difficult to become pregnant and are more likely to have miscarriages than non-smoking women. Smoking mothers are prone to have smaller babies. One study showed that the babies of smoking mothers weighed 140 to 224 grams [5 to 8 ounces] less than those of non-smoking mothers.

## Dangers of Smoking

The main dangers of smoking come from the fact that nicotine is one of the most powerful poisons known. It causes cancer in many forms, although lung cancer is the most common cancer related to smoking. Bladder cancer is twice as likely to occur in smokers as in non-smokers. Smoking triples a person's risk of heart attack.

Mr. Carstairs had a heart attack a month after his fortieth birthday. His doctor had told him that he must stop smoking immediately. Mr. Carstairs' heart attack at such a young age was blamed on the fact that he had smoked up to two packs a day, sometimes more, for over twenty years.

Emphysema and other lung diseases are common in those who smoke. Smoking also increases the risk of gum disease which leads to losing the teeth at an early age. Smokers are also more likely to become ill from colds and flu.

People may not think about the danger of nicotine as an addicting drug. When people addicted to nicotine stop smoking, they have uncomfortable physical symptoms. They may feel dizzy and drowsy. Other problems may be chills, shakes, headaches, and diarrhea or constipation. Mental addiction causes withdrawal symptoms of nervousness, tenseness, and short temper.

Some people are able to quit smoking without any problems. Many ex-smokers, however, still crave nicotine. Martha hasn't had a cigarette in three years. She says, "It's really something I have to face every day. I still want a cigarette after I finish a meal. The fact that I've stopped smoking doesn't mean that I've stopped wanting to smoke."

## ALCOHOL

Alcoholic drinks are made from the fermented or distilled juices of various kinds of grapes or grains. Alcohol is a legal drug if you are of age in the state where you are drinking. Being legal, however, has not stopped the misuse and abuse of alcohol. In the United States, alcohol addicts are second in numbers only to nicotine addicts.

## The Effects of Alcohol

Alcohol acts as a depressant on the body in that it slows down body processes. To many, alcohol seems to be a stimulant because they feel excited or emotional when they begin to drink. What happens is that alcohol first slows down the thinking processes and the mental centers that control judgment and a sense of responsibility. At this stage, the drinking person doesn't know that reflexes and judgment are impaired. Because the emotional centers have still not been depressed, the drinker may feel happy and excited. After more drinks, the emotional centers are also slowed down. Later, the muscle-controlling sections of the brain are affected. Stumbling, slurring speech, and falls

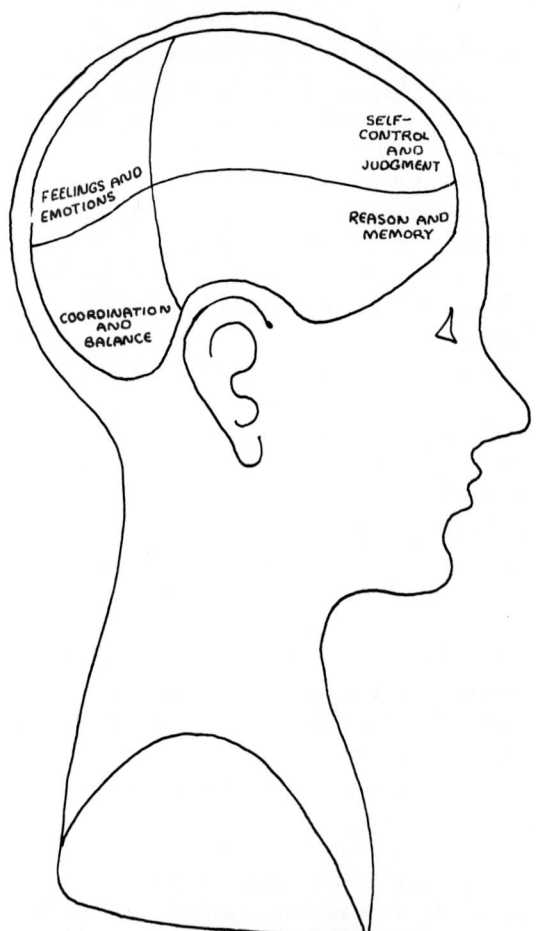

*Alcohol first depresses the brain areas involved in reason and judgment. Later the emotional centers are influenced. Coordination and balance are then affected. Finally, the drinker falls into a stupor as vital centers are involved.*

are common. Then the drinker falls into a sleep-like stupor.

Nancy sometimes drinks alcohol at parties. When she has her first two drinks, she is laughing and happy. However, drinking more than two affects her emotional center. She becomes depressed and sleepy.

**Dangers of Alcohol Use**

Because of the early loss of the drinker's judgment, even small amounts of alcohol can be dangerous. Perhaps the greatest danger is the possibility of accidents while driving a car or operating other machinery. The role of alcohol in causing fatal accidents has been established.

Norman and Marny had had some beer and pizza after the movie. Although Norman seemed to feel fine, his reflexes had been slowed and his judgment impaired by the beer. As a result, when he turned the corner, he hit a car stopped in the road. Neither he nor Marny was hurt although the car was heavily damaged. Many accidents involving a drinking driver have more serious results than this one did.

The dangers of mixing driving and drinking are well known. However, alcohol is also involved in deaths other than those caused by traffic accidents. Drinking increases a person's chances of killing another and the odds of being killed by someone else. Alcohol is also linked to suicides and suicide attempts.

Alcohol can be very harmful when used with other drugs. Alcohol and barbiturates or heroin used together can often cause death. Some people have died because they drank alcohol while taking a prescribed medicine such as an antibiotic.

Although alcohol is legal, people who drink raise their chances of arrest. Over half of all arrests are alcohol caused. Besides arrest for drunken driving, others cited are for public drunkenness and disorderly conduct.

Drinking causes damage to the body and mind. Alcoholism is the leading cause of entrance to mental hospitals. Physically, the liver is harmed by alcohol, leading to cirrhosis, which can be fatal.

Because alcohol is an addicting drug, withdrawal symptoms are very painful. These symptoms are called *delirium tremens*. They include shakes, fits, vomiting, delusions, and sometimes high fever.

## DEPRESSANTS

The *depressants* are drugs such as barbiturates and tranquilizers. These drugs, also called *sedatives,* have a calming effect by slowing down the body's systems. They are widely prescribed by doctors to bring relief from nervousness and insomnia. They are also used in the treatment of epilepsy and high blood pressure.

Barbiturates and tranquilizers are most often taken in pill form. Some drug abusers inject them into the muscle or vein.

### The Effects of Depressants

When sedatives are used in prescribed amounts, the body processes are slowed. The drug slows the action of the nerves and muscles. Depressants can lower blood pressure and slow down the rate of breathing and of the heart beat.

Mrs. Garcia was very worried and upset about the upcoming grand opening of the Craft Shop she and a partner were opening. Her concern and fears made it hard for her to sleep at night. The doctor prescribed a mild sedative, which helped her relax. It also allowed her to get enough sleep so that she could continue the hard work that was needed before the shop opened.

## experiences in human relations

### YOUR STATE'S DRUG LAWS

The legal status of most of the drugs discussed in this chapter is very complicated. While there are federal laws which cover the use of drugs, each state also has laws relating to drug use and control. These state laws vary a great deal, depending on the state. Some state laws authorize severe criminal sentences for drug users. Other states have decriminalized certain drugs. This means that their possession and use is not punished by jail sentences. In most of these states, violators are given tickets which might be compared to parking tickets.

This experience is to help you explore the drug laws in your state.

Choose a drug and prepare a report of the laws relating to that drug in your state. For example, you may wish to find out about the laws controlling stimulants or marijuana. Information on the laws may be obtained through books or talking with a lawyer. You might want to interview a police officer or discuss the matter with someone from your district attorney's office. People who work in drug control or abuse clinics are likely to be familiar with the local drug laws.

You may wish to discuss the current laws and the punishments that are associated with the laws. What is the status of possession of the drug? Use? Sale? What happens if you are arrested with someone who has the drug? Are you responsible if a guest in your home has the drug? What if you are found riding in a car where the drug is hidden? If you are exploring one of the legal drugs, you may wish to discover how the drug is distributed. Are there any restrictions on advertising and selling the drug? Are sellers required to be licensed? If so, who has control of that process? Are there any bills pending in the legislature which pertain to your drug?

When you have gathered your information, compile it into a report. Share your findings with your classmates.

**Unit 2: Relationships Begin with You**

### Dangers of Depressants

The dangers of abusing depressants are similar to those of abusing alcohol. Judgment is affected and reaction time slowed down. A person who is drunk on depressants also suffers from confusion, slurred speech, and staggering. Depressants cause many car accidents. Abusers are likely to become cross, quick-tempered, and angry.

Depressants are a leading cause of poison deaths, most often when they are used with alcohol.

The depressants are addicting. The body builds a tolerance for them so that ever-larger doses are needed to get the same results. Withdrawal causes the same physical symptoms as withdrawal from alcohol.

The depressant drugs are legal by prescription but other sales are considered criminal. Therefore, the depressant abuser who obtains pills through non-prescription sources is breaking the law.

## STIMULANTS

Stimulants speed up the central nervous system. Their action gives a sense of well-being known as *euphoria*. Cocaine is the main "natural" drug which is used as a stimulant. It is obtained from the leaves of the South American coca plant. The amphetamines are a large group of synthetic drugs that produce effects similar to those of cocaine.

The amphetamines are usually taken in pill form. Injected, they are known as "speed." Speed is one of the most dangerous drugs to abuse because it can lead to long-term mental illness. Large doses of speed can cause death. Cocaine is often taken through sniffing, although it too can be injected.

### The Effects of Stimulants

Stimulants are best known for their ability to curb tiredness and sleepiness. The user has a feeling of excitement and strength. A feeling of increased mental power often leads the user to overestimate ability.

James sometimes uses stimulants to help him stay awake when he is studying late for an exam. Carol Clark drives a truck. Some of her long-distance runs involve night driving. On these trips she takes an amphetamine to help her stay awake and alert.

*Because barbiturates slow down reaction time, their use has resulted in many automobile accidents.*

*Students sometimes take amphetamines to keep awake to study for important exams.*

Because the stimulant drugs depress appetite, they are sometimes prescribed by doctors as diet pills. Bert is trying to lose fifty pounds. His doctor prescribed diet pills containing amphetamines to help curb his hunger.

Stimulant drugs increase the heart rate and raise the blood pressure. Large doses can cause dry mouth, sweating, headache, diarrhea, and paleness. The abuser usually seems restless and overexcited.

**Dangers of Stimulants**

One of the dangers of stimulants is that their use often leads to exhaustion. The user stays awake and active long past the body's normal capacity. When the drug finally wears off, the body collapses.

Many people are like Janie, a college student who used amphetamines to stay awake to study for a final exam. She went to bed around 5:00 a.m. for several hours of sleep. By then, however, she was so exhausted that she slept through the morning, missing her exam, which was scheduled at 9:00 a.m.

The physical effects of withdrawal from stimulants are mostly confined to exhaustion. However, even moderate use of stimulants can lead to depression when the use is stopped.

Heavy users who stop often suffer from self-destructive depressions. The heavy use of cocaine and amphetamines (especially the use of speed) can cause hallucinations. One common feeling is that ants, insects, or

## Unit 2: Relationships Begin with You

snakes are crawling over or under the skin. Heavy use is also likely to cause mental problems which can lead to mental illness.

Those injecting either cocaine or speed risk hepatitis and abcesses from dirty needles.

Malnutrition may become a problem as users lose their appetites and eat little, if anything.

Amphetamines can be legally prescribed by doctors. However, their non-prescription use and the use of cocaine are illegal.

### NARCOTICS

The *narcotic drugs* include opium and the drugs made from opium, such as heroin, morphine, paregoric, and codeine. Synthetic narcotics have also been made in the laboratory, although these are used mostly for medical purposes.

Opium comes from the juice of the opium poppy pod. The dried juice is brown and gummy and can be used to prepare the other narcotic drugs. Since heroin is the narcotic most abused by people in the United States, this discussion will center on its use.

Although many of the drugs described in this chapter have a medical use, heroin does not. Heroin is a white powder with a bitter, sharp taste. It can be taken by inhaling or injecting it. Heroin can be injected into a muscle, shot directly into a vein, or injected just under the skin.

### The Effects of Heroin

In general, heroin slows down the functions of the body. It can reduce hunger, thirst, and the sex drive. Usually the first response to a dose of heroin is relief from all tensions. It produces a deep sense of well being. However, this feeling of euphoria or excitement may be followed by almost complete stupor.

The influence of the drug depends on the size and frequency of the dosage. The purity of the drug can also influence the effect of heroin on the user.

### Dangers of Heroin

Because heroin is an addicting drug, even infrequent users run the risk of addiction. The body builds up tolerance to narcotics easily, so larger and larger doses are needed. These larger doses do not give the euphoria that the

*Heroin users are especially apt to get in trouble with the law. Not only is heroin use illegal, but most addicts also commit crimes to get money to buy the drug.*

earlier ones did. Instead they are needed simply to avoid withdrawal pains.

Withdrawal pains begin about 18 hours after the last dose. The user may sweat, shake, and have a running nose and tearing eyes. Chills, diarrhea, nausea, and stomach and leg cramps are likely.

Users who have been able to stop taking heroin also suffer from *post addiction symptoms*. These are feelings of anxiety and depression and a craving for the drug. The craving may not be constant, but often comes and goes in waves. It may happen for months and years after an addict has stopped taking the drug.

Larry was once addicted to heroin. He says, "The withdrawal symptoms I went through when I quit taking heroin were terrible. They were so horrible that I couldn't imagine ever wanting to have to go through that again. I vowed I wouldn't take the drug again. But it isn't as simple as that. When I get upset and anxious, I still want and need my injection. My wanting nags at me until my whole being is focused on that one thing. It's really almost impossible to stay away from the drug. So far, I've been strong enough."

Because heroin is illegal, there is no control over the quality of the drug which users buy. This is true of other illegal drugs but it can be very important to heroin users. They have no way of knowing either the quality or the strength of heroin they purchase. Therefore it is impossible to control the doses that users take.

Because heroin is so costly, most addicts are forced to resort to theft or prostitution to support their habit. Thus their exposure to the law is doubled. Not only are they using illegal drugs, but they are breaking the law to get money to buy the drugs.

Heroin addicts are very apt to have health problems. Because heroin lessens the appetite, many users are malnourished. Some users get hepatitis from the use of dirty needles. The health problems and the physical effects of heroin cause addicts in their twenties to have a death rate as high as that of people in their seventies.

## experiences in human relations

### BUILDING A NEW DRUG LAW

The control and regulation of drugs have always been a controversial matter. Many people feel that the current drug laws are unrealistic. They feel that Americans should have learned a lesson from Prohibition: making a drug (alcohol) illegal didn't stop its production and use. These people feel that current drug laws should reflect the realities of drug use. They propose changing the laws so that all drugs would be distributed and controlled in much the same way as alcohol.

Other people feel that this would be a serious mistake. Instead of less strict laws, these people feel that the country needs harsher penalties for drug violations. They feel that the problem of drug abuse will cease only when drugs are strictly controlled and banned.

This experience is to help you think through your beliefs about controlling the use of drugs. With your classmates, pretend that you are a law-making body in a new country. Your job is to write a new set of laws regulating drug use and control.

There are a variety of issues for you and your classmates to decide. Which drugs should be legal and illegal? What will be the penalties for the use of illegal drugs? At what age should people be allowed to buy legal drugs?

How should legal drugs be distributed? What regulations should govern the new system? Will drug sellers need licenses? What taxes should be assessed on the drugs? Should only one grade and strength of a drug be marketed? Or would the sale of varying strengths be accepted? How could this be controlled?

Where should drug use be permitted? Should people use legal drugs in public or only in private? If they use them in public, where should this be allowed? Can drugs be used in all public places or will people have to go to special "drug houses" which would be like cocktail lounges or bars?

How will you handle the problem of operating an automobile or other machinery while a person is under the influence of drugs? Should there be drug advertising? Should there be warnings of the dangers of drug use on the packaging?

Committees can be formed to work on specific parts of your new set of laws, if that seems helpful.

It may be possible to get your proposed laws printed in the student newspaper for feedback and response from other students.

● ● ● ● ● ● ● ● ● ● ● ● ● ● ● ● ● ● ●

## HALLUCINOGENS

The *hallucinogens* are mind-affecting drugs. The most well known is LSD. It is made from the lysergic acid in wheat and rye fungus. Peyote and mescaline are other hallucinogens which are less well known.

LSD is a very powerful drug. Twenty eight grams [one ounce] of LSD can provide 300,000 average doses. LSD can be taken in pill or tablet form. It is also often taken on a sugar cube, a cracker, or a cookie.

### The Effects of Hallucinogens

The hallucinogens cause both physical and mental reactions in the user. Physically, there is a more rapid pulse and heart rate. Blood pressure and temperature rise. The pupils of the eyes may dilate, the hands and feet may shake, and chills and shivering may result.

The mental changes from taking LSD cannot be predicted. Reality and perception are distorted in unusual and unlikely ways. Some users can taste color, see music, and feel happy and sad at the same time. The sensation that they can fly occurs in some users, who lose the feeling of a barrier between land and space. Perceptions of time and space are changed. Other users have more frightening mental changes. These include feelings of helplessness or loss of control. Some become scared and panic at the changes that occur.

The hallucinogens are not physically addicting so users who stop do not suffer withdrawal symptoms. However, it appears that some users become mentally dependent on these drugs.

The hallucinogens, especially LSD, do have limited medical uses. However, their nonmedical use is illegal.

### Dangers of Hallucinogens

The main danger in the use of the hallucinogens seems to be the panicked reaction to the distortion of reality that the drug brings. The user may grow frightened because he or she can't stop the drug's actions. Other users feel they are losing their minds. Often users are suspicious that someone is trying to harm them or control their thinking. The occurrence of mental illness is more related to the use of these drugs than any other.

The first time Art took LSD was a very frightening experience for him. He felt as if the walls in the room came alive. They seemed to lean over and try to listen to his thoughts. Then they seemed to want to smother him. Even after the effects of the drug had worn off, Art occasionally relived the panicked feeling he had when the walls seemed to close in on him.

Physical harm can also occur to the LSD user. This most often happens because of the distortion of the senses. Drug users have fallen and hurt themselves by not knowing they were doing something dangerous.

## MARIJUANA

There is perhaps more debate about the use of marijuana than of any other drug. Marijuana is made from the top leaves or the dried flowers of the hemp plant. The dried plant is crushed or chopped into small pieces. The strength of the drug varies according to where and how it was grown, prepared, and stored.

Marijuana can be used in many ways. It can be smoked in pipes or in cigarettes. It can also be eaten or drunk. When smoked, marijuana gives a distinct burnt-rope smell.

The labels given to marijuana can be confusing. Chemically, it acts like a mild hallucinogen. It does not act chemically the way the narcotic drugs (opium, heroin) do. However, by law, marijuana has been labeled as a narcotic.

### The Effects of Marijuana

As marijuana enters the bloodstream, it affects the brain and nervous system. The user experiences rapid heartbeat and a lowering of body temperature. The eyes may redden and the user may be hungry.

The effect of marijuana on mood is unpredictable. Some users get depressed while others feel excited and euphoric. Others have no change in mood at all. Often, the user's sense of time and distance is distorted. To Susan, it seemed as though the chair in front of her rose and floated off into space. She also said that time seemed expanded—minutes seemed like hours.

### Dangers of Marijuana

Just how harmful marijuana is has long been a disputed issue. Because of time and space distortions, using machines or driving a car may be dangerous to users. The smoke from marijuana is harmful to the lungs, just as is the smoke from tobacco.

Other findings on marijuana's effects are less clear. Some studies have shown it is a dangerous, body-damaging drug. Others have indicated it causes little or no permanent harm. Scientists do not yet understand all the drug's long- and short-term effects.

While the body does not become physically addicted to marijuana, many users become mentally dependent on it.

Finally, as with many of the other drugs discussed here, marijuana use is against the law.

## TO SUM UP...

1. Why is nicotine considered a drug?
2. What common effects do nicotine, amphetamines, and cocaine have on the body?
3. Why is nicotine considered one of the most dangerous drugs from a physical standpoint?
4. Compare and contrast alcohol and barbiturate misuse, addiction, and withdrawal symptoms.
5. Describe the feeling of euphoria.
6. Explain what is meant by post-addiction symptoms in ex-heroin users.
7. What is meant by the statement that the hallucinogens are mind-affecting drugs?
8. How can marijuana be labeled both a narcotic and a hallucinogen?

Unit 2: Relationships Begin with You

## WHY PEOPLE USE DRUGS

With all the physical, mental, and legal dangers that go along with the use of drugs, why do people take them? People seek drugs or aids of some kind to produce feelings of well-being or euphoria, to relieve mental anxiety, and to ease physical pain. Drug taking has become a way of life in the United States. People live "take something" life styles. They take aspirin for headaches, antacid for stomach upset, and tranquilizers for tension.

*Advertising has influenced Americans to turn to pills and tonics to ease their physical and mental pains.*

## experiences in human relations

### DRUG ADVERTISING

Many of the advertisements that you hear on radio and television and see in newspapers or magazines are "cures" for minor ills. These ads promise that if there is anything not perfect in your life, there is a product to help you. This experience is to help you become more aware of drug advertisements.

- As you watch television, keep track of the drug advertisements you see. Keep a log of the name and type of product, the program that it is seen with, and the time of day. What was the length of the commercial? Toward what group of people was the advertisement directed?

When you have a number of entries in your log, look over the ads and think about their impact. How would each ad influence your attitudes about medicines, drugs, pain, anxiety, or solving problems? What are the psychological appeals used in the ads? How do you think these ads contribute to our drug-oriented society?

- Collect exaggerated slogans and claims from drug ads in magazines and newspapers. Use these slogans and claims to make a collage or a poster showing the exaggeration in advertising.

### NEGATIVE SELF-CONCEPT

Many people take drugs because of a negative self-concept. They feel hopeless, helpless, or inadequate. Using drugs *seems* to make them feel more mature and independent. Joanie started smoking marijuana because she thought it made her feel more

## Ch. 5: Personal Decisions

adult. Robert never felt comfortable around other students. He didn't believe he was as good as they were. After he had a couple of beers, however, he felt he was equal to everyone else.

Although Joanie, Robert, and many others think that the use of drugs makes them feel better about themselves, it is a false confidence. Actually, drug use reinforces poor self-concepts. Because people feel they can't rely on their selves without a crutch, their self-concepts become poorer. Instead of facing up to and solving their problems, they avoid the problems through drug use. They don't make the effort that could solve their problems and, as a result, improve their self-image.

Owen had a lot of trouble handling frustration. When he became upset because something didn't go his way, he was irrational. He almost always took a barbiturate or two when something went wrong. Because he didn't work to solve whatever had gone wrong, he didn't have a chance to feel better about it and himself. Owen's use of pills prevented him from growing as a person and building a better self-concept.

### PEER PRESSURE

Many people take drugs because of pressure from their peers. Most teenagers are introduced to drugs by their friends. Because they need to feel a part of the group, they join their friends in the drug use.

Laura started smoking cigarettes after her two best girl friends began smoking. At first, she didn't really like the taste of the cigarettes or the smell of the smoke. But she felt left out when her two friends smoked and she didn't, so she continued until she learned to like it.

Adult users also can feel pressure from their peers. Mr. Gordon usually didn't drink much alcohol. At parties, he often had one or two alcoholic drinks, then switched to soft drinks. When the other men urged him to have another drink, Mr. Gordon often found it hard to refuse.

### FAMILY EXAMPLE

Many teenagers use nicotine, alcohol, or other drugs because someone in their family does. Most young people who smoke have parents who smoke. Teenagers who drink heavily often have parents who are heavy users of alcohol. Some studies have shown that the children of drug abusers often abuse or misuse drugs, too.

Donald's parents both drank a great deal of alcohol. From the time he was a small boy, Donald saw his mother and father "have a drink" when anything went wrong. He followed their pattern. Now, at age sixteen, Donald is an alcohol addict, an alcoholic.

## experiences in human relations

### FAMILY INFLUENCES

It has been discovered that if parents use or abuse certain drugs, their children will also be likely to do so. However, many people feel that the family influences children's drug use in other ways, too.

Form a group with three other classmates. In your group, talk about the factors in a family that you think encourage drug use or abuse. Also discuss those factors in a family that you think might discourage the use and abuse of drugs. Make two lists, one of factors that encourage drug use and one of factors that discourage drug use. Read your lists to the other class members. Listen as they read their lists. How were the lists similar and different?

## CURIOSITY

Many drug users first try drugs out of curiosity, without giving any thought to the possible results. For some, one experience is enough. For others, curiosity leads to more drug use and possible abuse and addiction.

Sara tried LSD out of curiosity. Many of her friends had used it and she was interested in their stories. She never took it again since the drug caused her to feel as if she were losing her mind.

## ESCAPE

Some people find their lives so unhappy that they take drugs simply to escape. They seek pleasure through drugs, blocking out the worst aspects of their lives.

Keith used heroin to escape the miseries of his life. His father was in jail, and his mother paid little attention to any of the children. At first, Keith found that heroin made his life seem more pleasant. As he became addicted, his life became even more unhappy. All he could think of was getting money for his next dose to prevent withdrawal symptoms. Keith found out what many drug users have discovered. Taking drugs for escape can easily become a trap from which there is no escape.

## TO SUM UP...

1. Why does a negative self-concept often lead to the use of drugs?
2. How can drug use prevent a person from developing a more positive self-concept?
3. What is peer pressure?
4. What is the relationship between parents' use of drugs and their children's use?
5. Describe a situation in which a person might take a drug out of curiosity or a wish to escape.

## DECISION MAKING ABOUT DRUGS

Most people do not make conscious decisions about whether to take drugs. Somehow, they drift into drug use without thinking of the consequences. Yet an action with so many important physical, mental, and legal consequences deserves careful thought.

The process of decision making was described in Chapter 4. You will recall that the first step involves defining the decisions you must make. Are you faced with deciding whether to smoke tobacco or marijuana cigarettes? Whether to drink alcoholic beverages may be another choice you are facing. Has pressure been put on you to take stimulant or depressant drugs? Is your problem whether or not to begin taking drugs? Or to continue taking them?

What are the various options you have in regard to drug use? Is your choice between one drug and another or none?

Have you given serious thought to all your options? What would be the results of the various actions you have considered? What physical and mental effects would each choice have on your body? What legal results, if any, should you consider? How would your drug choices affect your relationships with others?

Making a choice about drug use should reflect the values that are important to you. Will your choice bring you satisfaction and growth? Will it help you become the best person you can be?

**Ch. 5: Personal Decisions**

Finally, you need to be ready to take the consequences of your decisions. Too often, drug decisions are made with little or no thought for the consequences. Many teenagers expect their parents to be able to prevent legal convictions. Others aren't prepared to live with the fact of physical or mental addiction. If the positive attractions of drug taking appeal to you, you must also be ready to live with the unpleasant results.

- You were riding in a car with a drunk driver?
- You took drugs when you were driving a carload of friends home?
- Your sister or brother was becoming an alcoholic?
- You were arrested for having amphetamines?
- Your parents forbid you to smoke, drink, or use drugs?

## experiences in human relations

### WHAT WOULD YOU DO?

Decisions about drugs are never easy. They involve thinking about the physical and mental effects of a particular drug. The legal status and consequences of drug use can be important. But not all the decisions relating to drugs are simply a matter of legality. The following questions are suggested for your private decision making. You may wish to discuss some of these questions with your family or friends.

### What Would You Do If . . .

- You were called a chicken because you refused to take LSD?
- You found out other guests at a party had marijuana?
- You discovered the thirteen-year-old next door was selling drugs?
- You were riding in a car which contained drugs?
- Someone offered to swap pills with you?
- You discovered a friend had used heroin?
- You found out your best friend was selling drugs?

### VALUES AND DRUGS

Through all the steps in the decision-making process runs the theme, "What is important to you?" The taking of drugs is a very controversial area because people hold such different values about drugs.

*Most teenagers find a sense of belonging without using drugs.*

97

**Unit 2: Relationships Begin with You**

George feels very strongly that taking any drugs non-medically is wrong. He wants complete mental and physical control over his body.

Martin thinks it's very important to be a part of a group. He is willing to try any drug that someone else suggests to him.

Carol has strong values concerning the legality of her actions. She is not willing to put herself in the position of being open to arrest. Therefore she avoids illegal drugs.

Alex values the carefree feeling that he gets from amphetamines. He puts his personal pleasure ahead of physical, mental, or legal consequences.

Other people have other values. The values that you hold influence your thinking about drugs. Your values are important in every step of the decision-making process. What you decide is a consequence of what you believe is important.

No one but you can make decisions about the drugs that you take. The consequences of drug use can be so serious that you need to make a conscious decision, rather than drifting into use at the urging of your friends. What is right for them may not be right for you. Responsible drug use involves considering just what is important to you. Then, using the facts about the effects of specific drugs, you will be able to make your own decision.

### experiences in human relations

#### FEELINGS ABOUT DRUGS

The whole area of drug use is surrounded by controversy. It touches the values that people have and what they feel is important. Many times, just knowing the facts about a drug is not enough. How you feel about drugs and their use and abuse may be more important in influencing your use of drugs than simply knowing the facts. The following experience will help you explore your feelings about drugs.

Number down the side of a separate sheet of paper from one to twelve. Beside each number, write "yes" or "no" as an answer for each of the questions below.

1. Do you ever take drugs because of your problems?
2. Do you get mad when someone says you're taking too much or too many drugs?
3. Have you ever forgotten something you did while taking drugs?
4. Do you ever do anything when you are on drugs that you are ashamed of?
5. Do you feel you can handle drugs better than your friends?
6. Do you look forward to the times when you can use drugs?
7. Do you stay away from non-drug users?
8. Do you avoid talking about the dangers of abuse of drugs?
9. Do you tell yourself that others use more drugs than you?
10. Has taking drugs ever caused you any trouble?
11. Do you ever take more drugs than you planned?
12. Have you ever taken drugs to "pay someone back"?

Think about your answers to these questions. What kind of a pattern do your feelings about drugs produce? Are you relying on drugs or on your own self and strengths for living? What kind of drug decisions are your feelings leading you to make? Is there some kind of balance between your feelings and the facts in your decisions about drugs?

Ch. 5: Personal Decisions

## TO SUM UP...

1. Describe the process of decision making.

2. Why is it important to think about the consequences of each option you have?

3. Explain why taking responsibility for your choices is especially important in decisions about drugs.

4. Why are values so important in making choices about drugs?

## PATTERNS OF PREMARITAL SEXUAL BEHAVIOR

Almost every society in history has had rules about sexual behavior. Some rules specified which parts of the body had to be covered. Other rules had to do with who could have intercourse with whom. The age at which people could marry and have children was also covered by rules.

It appears that today the rules in the United States are changing. Over the years, there has been a trend toward greater sexual permissiveness. People also feel more free to talk about sex and their sexual behavior. Thus there have been increases in sexual behavior outside of marriage. At the same time, people are talking more about what they do and believe.

This talk reveals many sexual values and behaviors. On one hand are those people who accept no limits on their behavior. Debi read an article about a man who said he had sex whenever, wherever, and with whomever he wished. On the other hand, there are those who choose not to have any sex, such as some religious leaders. Other people may choose to have intercourse only to bear children.

This wide variety in patterns of behavior can be confusing to teenagers. This is the time of your life when you are discovering your sexual feelings and urges. How do you know what pattern of behavior to assume? If and when you marry, you will assume the pattern of regular intercourse. Until then, it is often hard to know just what pattern is right for you.

Sociologist Ira Reiss has found four patterns of sexual behavior in unmarried people—abstinence, double standard, permissiveness without affection, and permissiveness with affection.

### ABSTINENCE

*Abstinence* means that the partners do not have intercourse before marriage. Abstinence is the standard which American society tries to uphold and which most religious groups support. Most parents and teachers encourage teenagers to abstain from intercourse.

Not having intercourse does not mean that there is no sexual behavior at all. Most teenagers who do not have intercourse still have some form of sex play. Jake and Wilma do not have intercourse with each other. However, they enjoy kissing and stroking each others' bodies.

### THE DOUBLE STANDARD

The *double standard* is a traditional pattern. In it, the female is expected to be a virgin at marriage. However, the male can have sexual experience wherever he can get it.

This pattern has become less common over the years. It is partly due to the progress being made toward equal standards for women and men. However, many people still believe in the double standard.

**Unit 2: Relationships Begin with You**

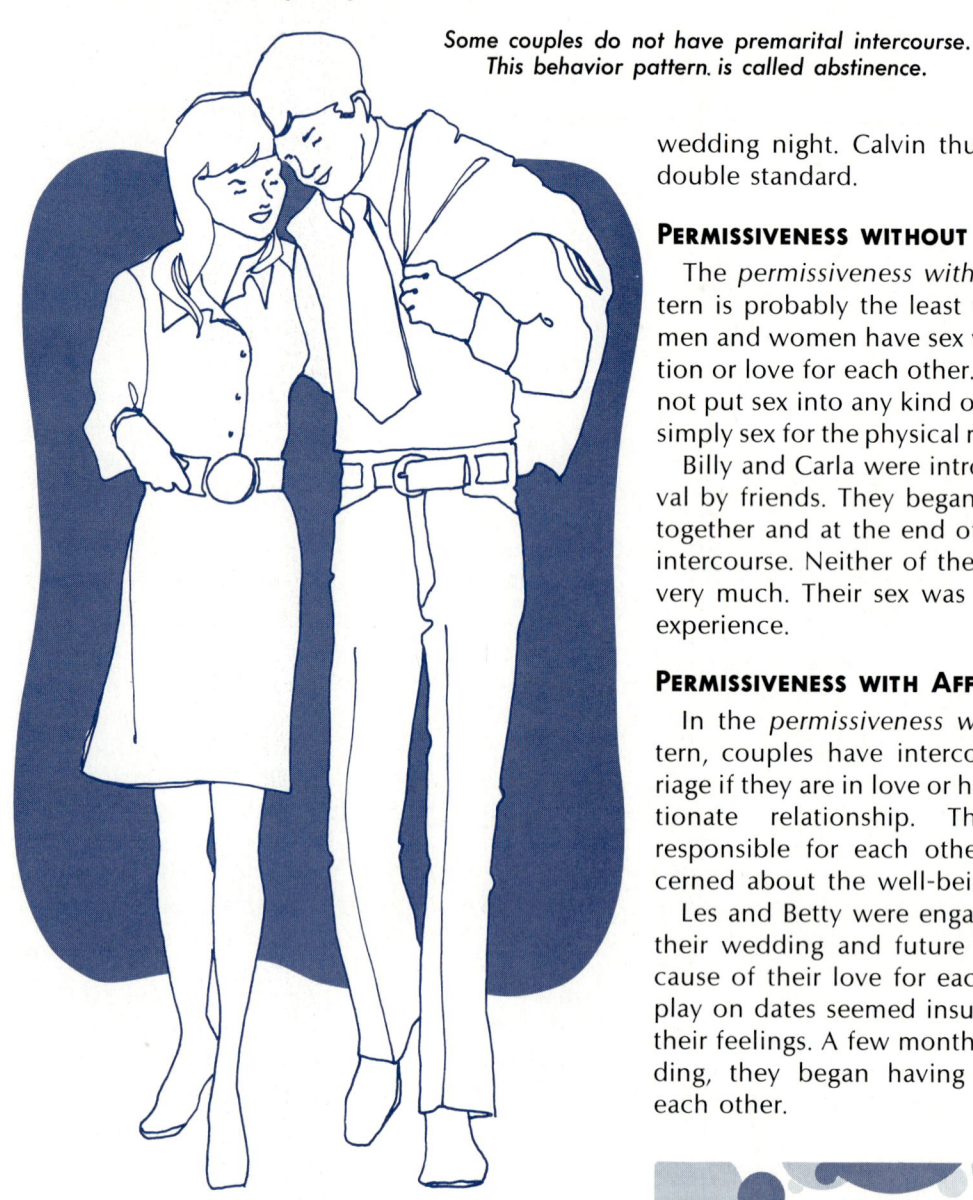

*Some couples do not have premarital intercourse. This behavior pattern is called abstinence.*

wedding night. Calvin thus believed in the double standard.

### Permissiveness without Affection

The *permissiveness without affection* pattern is probably the least widespread. Here, men and women have sex without any affection or love for each other. This pattern does not put sex into any kind of relationship. It is simply sex for the physical release of tensions.

Billy and Carla were introduced at a carnival by friends. They began to see the sights together and at the end of the evening had intercourse. Neither of them liked the other very much. Their sex was simply a physical experience.

### Permissiveness with Affection

In the *permissiveness with affection* pattern, couples have intercourse before marriage if they are in love or have a strong affectionate relationship. The partners are responsible for each other. They are concerned about the well-being of each other.

Les and Betty were engaged and planning their wedding and future life together. Because of their love for each other, their sex play on dates seemed insufficient to express their feelings. A few months before the wedding, they began having intercourse with each other.

Calvin had had sexual experiences with several different partners. However, he did not have intercourse with Marcia, his dating partner, whom he hoped to marry in about a year. He expected her to be a virgin on their

## experiences in human relations

### PATTERNS OF BEHAVIOR

The sexual activity of non-married persons tends to fall into four patterns. These are:

1) abstinence; 2) the double standard; 3) permissiveness without affection; 4) permissiveness with affection. The particular pattern a person lives depends on the values that person holds about sex. This experience will help you think about what you value in a sexual relationship.

Take a sheet of paper and fold it into eighths. In each eighth write one thing which you value or think should be important in a sexual relationship. When you have finished, tear your paper along the fold lines. This means that each value will be on a separate piece of paper.

Now, arrange the slips of paper according to their importance to you. In other words, place the most important value first and the second most important next. Continue arranging the slips until you have put the least important value last.

Now find a partner. Read your slips to your partner and describe how you decided upon their order. Explain your feelings about your sexual values. Listen when your partner explains his or her values.

Later, think privately about your values. Does your behavior reflect your values? Which pattern seems to fit your values best? Is it the pattern of your sexual behavior? Why or why not? What have you learned from this experience?

## TO SUM UP...

1. What is the main change involved in the sexual revolution?
2. Describe the pattern of abstinence.
3. What is the double standard?
4. Compare and contrast permissiveness with and without affection.

## SEXUAL RESPONSIBILITIES

Sex sometimes seems a carefree and pleasurable experience. However, it also involves responsibilities along with its pleasures.

### TO YOUR PARTNER

Most people know that the best sex happens in a loving relationship. This means that you have some responsibility to your partner. You care about what happens to her or him. Sexual behavior, including sex play and intercourse, becomes a process of mutual concern for both people. Being responsible means that your behavior rises from a strong emotional bond to each other.

Sexual behavior can bring great pleasure to a couple. It can also bring pain and heartache. It is almost impossible to know in advance what behavior will cause you or your partner to be hurt. Responsible sex occurs in a way that minimizes the possible hurt to either of you.

Couples who are responsible to each other feel free to talk about sex. Those who are too embarrassed to talk about sex are not ready for its responsibilities. Talk about sex should include pregnancy and venereal disease. The couple should also be at ease talking about their feelings and behavior.

Being responsible about sex means that you and your partner have plans for the future. If you have no mutual plans, sex is apt to be a matter of using each other. You need to decide how important sex is in your relationship with your partner.

You are not being responsible to your partner if you use sex to "hold" a dating partner or to be "popular." Jody could tell that Curt was losing interest in her as a dating partner. Her love for him was still strong, so she considered having intercourse with him to keep his interest. However, after more thought, she

Unit 2: Relationships Begin with You

decided that she wouldn't feel good about herself and her actions if she did.

## To Yourself

Although it may not seem apparent, you have a responsibility to yourself for your sexual behavior. Sex can easily be misused in ways that keep teenagers from growing as persons.

Some teens try sex play and intercourse because it makes them feel better about themselves. They have negative self-concepts, and they feel more manly or womanly after having sex. In other words, they use sex to prop up their poor feelings about themselves. This kind of sexual behavior usually doesn't help their self-concepts. Instead, they need to work on other ways to improve self-concept.

Zeke's family often teased him because he was so thin and short. He didn't feel very good about himself as a male. Therefore he always tried to persuade females to have sex play or intercourse with him. Through sex, he seemed to feel more manly.

Those people who have good self-concepts usually have fewer sexual experiences before marriage. They like themselves and what they do nonsexually. Therefore they do not try sex in order to feel better about themselves.

Another way in which people may not be responsible to themselves is using sex to prove that they are grown up. These teens use sex to get back at or rebel from their parents. Tammy felt this way about her parents. Her actions seemed to say, "You can't control me any more. I'm independent and to prove it, I'm having sex whenever I please."

This use of sex actually shows immature attitudes. Instead of showing how mature the teenagers are, it shows how much they still have to grow.

Responsibility to yourself also involves considering the way you were brought up. Some teens don't feel guilty about sexual experiences. However, it would be unrealistic to deny that many others do. They feel badly about doing something that their parents have taught them is wrong outside of marriage. Also, many students with strong religious beliefs feel guilty if they do something banned by their faith.

Barbara had been taught that intercourse was sinful outside of marriage. When her dating partner wanted her to have intercourse, she gave it much thought. However,

*People with poor self-concepts may try to use sex to feel better about themselves.*

she knew that she would feel very guilty afterward. Therefore she decided that, for her, intercourse would be a mistake.

Being true to what you have learned is right or wrong is being responsible to yourself.

## To Health

Another responsibility is to the health of you and your partner. It is not a responsible action to have intercourse with a partner when you know either of you has a venereal disease. To do this shows a great lack of concern for yourself and the other person. Venereal diseases are easily treated. Therefore it is important to show your respect for yourself and your partner by seeking medical help before having more sex.

## Toward Pregnancy

Sex was made to create new human beings. Therefore any time you have sex, you need to be ready to assume the responsibility of pregnancy. You need to be willing and able to support a child, both with money and with love.

Some people rely on birth control to prevent pregnancy. Others do not because of their values and religious beliefs. A physician or Planned Parenthood Clinic can give you guidance if you wish to choose a method of birth control. It is important to remember that birth control methods vary in effectiveness.

Studies have shown that most teenage intercourse occurs without the use of any birth control method. Over a million unmarried teenage females become pregnant each year. Most of these pregnancies occur because the partners took a chance.

Scientists say that half of all first-time premarital teenage pregnancies occur in the first six months of sexual activity. One-fifth of these pregnancies happen in the first month of sexual activity. The younger the woman is when she begins sexual activity, the more likely she is to become pregnant.

Having a child is an important part of the process of forming your own family. Having one accidentally as a result of premarital intercourse is not being responsible to yourself, to your partner, or to the child.

Meeting sexual responsibilities is not an easy task. As a result, most people feel that the marriage relationship best insures that the responsibilities will be met. It is true that some people can meet their responsibilities in a non-marriage setting. However, responsibilities to your partner and yourself are hard to meet unless you have a very strong, long-term, loving relationship.

### TO SUM UP...

1. Identify how you are responsible to and for your sexual partner.
2. What are your sexual responsibilities to yourself?
3. Describe your responsibilities toward health and pregnancy.

## DECISION MAKING ABOUT SEX

Making a decision about sexual behavior is very personal. No one but you can make choices about your behavior. Your parents, religious leaders, and teachers may try to influence your decision. However, you alone control your own behavior.

You cannot make a rational choice about sex if you are having sex play in the back seat of a car. Decision making about sex needs to

## Unit 2: Relationships Begin with You

be done at a time when your emotions and passions are cool.

### VALUES AND SEX

The whole area of sexual behavior is laden with values. People's sexual choices reflect their values about sex. For some people, sex is valued only as a release of tension. These people might decide to have intercourse with someone for whom they had no love or affection. They might also masturbate a great deal.

For others, the physical aspects of sex are less important. What they value is the sense of intimacy and mental oneness they experience during sex. These people may restrict sex to their marriage partners.

## experiences in human relations

### VALUES AND SEX

Because values are so closely related to sex, it is important that people think about their sexual values. This experience will help you think about your own values regarding some sexual matters. It will also help you learn about some of the values of your classmates.

On a separate sheet of paper, copy the following incomplete sentences. Finish each sentence so that it expresses your values. Do not write your name on your paper.

When it comes to the opposite sex . . .
Most people think premarital sex is . . .
I see marriage as . . .
I am most loving and affectionate when . . .
The double standard is . . .
The most frustrating thing in a relationship is . . .
Premarital sex causes guilt feelings when . . .
Virginity is . . .
If I became pregnant (or got a female pregnant) . . .
Permissiveness without affection is . . .
Ten years from now, premarital sex will be . . .

When you and your classmates have finished completing the sentences, place all the papers face down on the table. Mix the papers up, then draw a paper from the pile. Read a few statements from the paper you drew to the class. Listen while others read from the papers they drew.

● ● ● ● ● ● ● ● ● ● ● ● ● ● ● ● ●

### MAKING YOUR CHOICE

Making a decision about your sexual behavior before marriage is not easy. It involves your values—what you feel is important about sex. You need to think about how you can cope with your sexual feelings while still meeting your sexual responsibilities.

Jerry used the decision-making process in thinking about what pattern of sexual behavior he would live by. First, Jerry considered what his problem was. He was in love with Corrie and had strong sexual feelings when he was with her. Jerry had to decide what his behavior should be with Corrie.

Jerry thought about his alternatives. He could continue the kissing and hugging that he and Corrie did now. Another possibility would be further sex play. Finally, he and Corrie could have intercourse.

Jerry thought seriously about the results of each of these options. Most of his thinking was about intercourse. Since neither he nor Corrie had had intercourse before, there was

## Ch. 5: Personal Decisions

no chance of getting venereal disease. However, Jerry knew that neither he nor Corrie were ready to face a possible pregnancy. He also knew that they would both be embarrassed to arrange for birth control.

Jerry was also worried about his responsibilities toward Corrie. He knew that if they ever had intercourse, Corrie would feel very guilty. It would be very hard for her if their relationship broke up. He also considered his responsibility toward himself. He felt that he would not be using intercourse just to prop up his self-concept. He also did not think he was using it to rebel against his parents. His sexual feelings were a result of his love and caring for Corrie.

After much thinking, Jerry decided that abstinence would be the best pattern for both of them. Pregnancy was his main concern as well as the possible guilt feelings for Corrie. He felt that they might advance to more passionate sex play. However, he knew that he would have to be careful not to let his sexual feelings get too strong.

Jerry's values for himself and his relationship with Corrie influenced his decision. Other people might consider their sexual responsibilities differently. Their values might lead them to make different decisions about their behavior.

What should you consider in making a decision about your sexual behavior? You need to think about your responsibilities to yourself and others. What are your values about sexual behavior? Can you live your values through what you do sexually?

Learning to understand and cope with your sexual feelings is an important part of growing up. Because sex is a powerful force in everyone's lives, it needs to be used and controlled. Making thoughtful, responsible choices about your sexual behavior is a vital step in your growth as a mature adult.

*Making thoughtful decisions about your sexual behavior is an important part of becoming a mature adult.*

Unit 2: Relationships Begin with You

## experiences in human relations

### SEXUAL DECISION MAKING

What values do you hold about sex? How do these values influence your decisions about sexual behavior? Sexual behavior includes many actions. Masturbation, sex play, and intercourse are all sexual acts. The meaning of such sexual acts is important in making choices. This experience will help you think about the meaning you feel a sex act should have.

Write the following statements on small separate pieces of paper.

- A sexual act should help build trust between partners.
- A sexual act should bring fun and pleasure.
- A sexual act should increase honesty and openness between partners.
- A sexual act should give release from sexual tensions.
- A sexual act should give complete freedom to each person.
- A sexual act should help the partners talk easily with each other.
- A sexual act should free a person from the rules of family or society.
- A sexual act should improve the partners' self-concepts.
- A sexual act should let the partners be free to be themselves.
- A sexual act should be based on and express the partners' bond or commitment to each other.
- A sexual act should be consistent with the spiritual beliefs of the person involved.

Now sort the papers on which you have written the above statements into three piles. In the first pile, put the one slip which best describes for you what a sexual act should do or be.

In the third pile, put the one slip which least accurately describes for you what a sexual act should do or be.

Put the other slips in the center pile.

As you are sorting your slips, remember that the term "a sexual act" includes behavior in addition to intercourse.

You may find it very hard to make your choices. You may find that you wish to place several slips in the first pile and none in the third pile. However, in sexual decisions you have to decide what is most important to you. Therefore, choose the statements that seem best for you.

When you have sorted the statements, think about your choices. Why did you choose the one statement for pile 1? Pile 3? Does your sexual behavior reflect your choices? Why or why not? What have you learned from this experience?

### TO SUM UP...

1. When should you make decisions about sexual behavior?
2. How do values influence choices about sex?
3. What factors do you need to consider in deciding what your sexual behavior will be?
4. Describe how the decision-making process can be used in making choices about sex.

# UNIT THREE
## Relating to Others

Chapter 6. Building Relationships, 108
Chapter 7. Communicating with Others, 136
Chapter 8. Role Relationships, 165
Chapter 9. Conflict in Relationships, 189

# CHAPTER 6
## Building Relationships

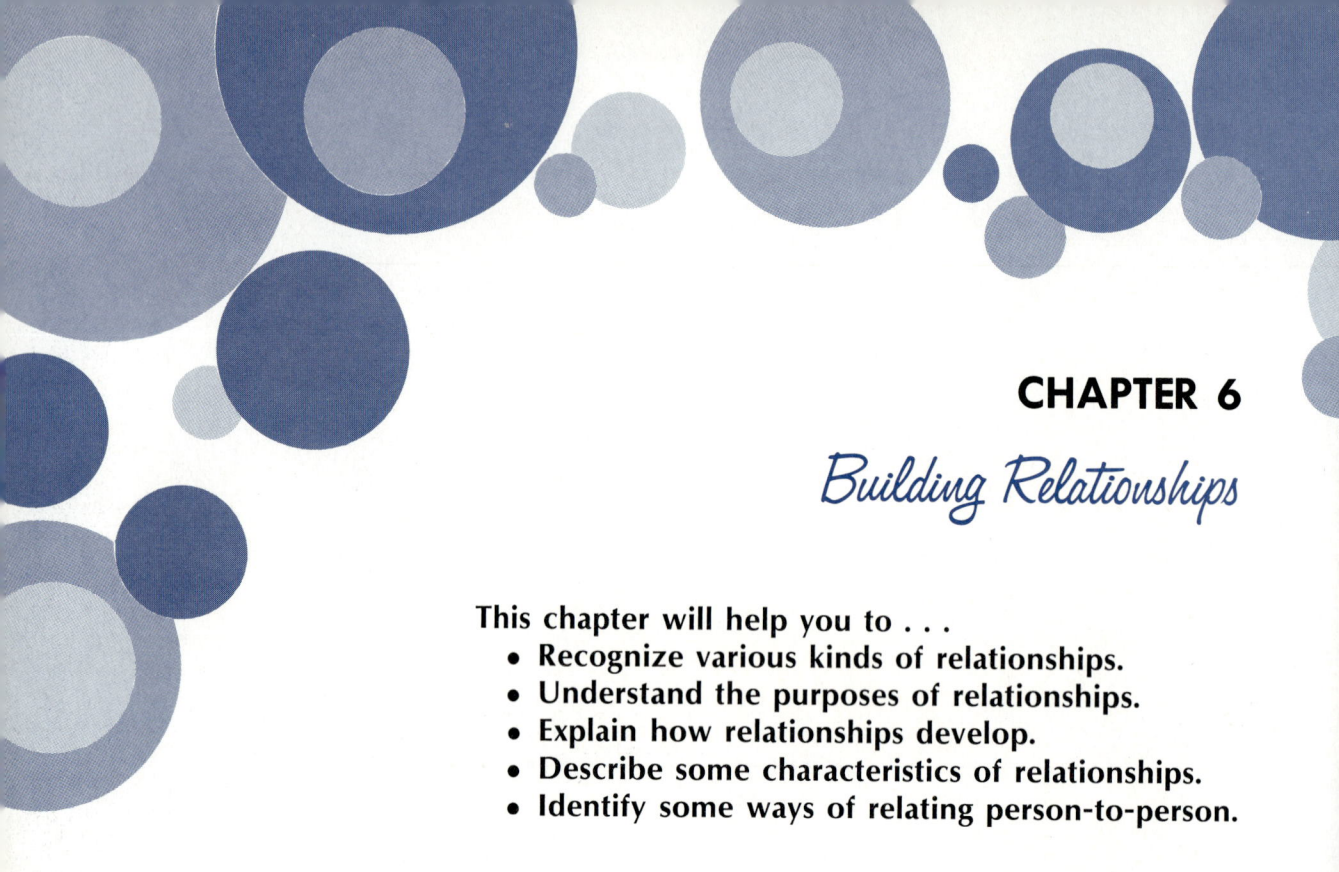

This chapter will help you to . . .
- Recognize various kinds of relationships.
- Understand the purposes of relationships.
- Explain how relationships develop.
- Describe some characteristics of relationships.
- Identify some ways of relating person-to-person.

People live in a world filled with other people. They live with others in families. They see people at school and at work. Shopping and most recreation involve being with others. These contacts are known as *relationships*.

### KINDS OF RELATIONSHIPS

Relationships between people are not all the same. You relate to your parents in a different way than to your teachers. The relationship between you and a special friend is different from your relationship to your doctor. Your relationships tend to fall into the categories of family, friends, acquaintances, and dating partners.

## experiences in human relations

### KINDS OF RELATIONSHIPS

You have a variety of relationships with other people. The following experience may help you begin to see the patterns in the relationships you have built.

On a large sheet of paper, draw five circles, one inside the other. Be sure that there is enough room to write people's names between the lines of the circles. In the smallest center circle, write "Me." The next circle you label "Close Friends," the next "Relatives," then

*In today's world, a person meets, interacts with, and forms many relationships with others.*

"Friends," and finally, the outside circle "Acquaintances."

Place the names of as many people as you have relationships with in the appropriate circles. The chart begins to make clear just where your place is in the center of a web of relationships.

Using different colored pencils, underline the names of people that you know through school, clubs, employment, church, or other sources. Is your relationship pattern balanced or are the majority of your relationships from one source?

Look at the names of the people on your chart. Which people have a positive effect on your growth? Which people stimulate you, are fun to be with, or bring out the best in you? You may wish to draw circles around their names.

On the other hand, are there people in your relationship pattern who have a negative impact on you? You may wish to plan a way to lessen their impact on your personal development.

Finally, are there people that you would prefer to relate to on another level? Are there acquaintances that you wish were friends? Are there friends that you would like to become closer to? What could you do to promote a closer relationship with these people?

## Unit 3: Relating to Others

### FAMILY

While families can differ a great deal, most people live in some kind of family. Wayne lives with his parents, brothers, and sister. Wayne has grandparents, aunts, uncles, and cousins whom he sees once in a while. He especially enjoys listening to his great grandfather tell about his boyhood.

Like others, Tina lives with her mother, several half sisters and brothers, her aunt, and cousins. Her grandmother lives down the street so the children see her often. Tina has no contact with her father's family and rarely sees other relations on her mother's side of the family.

Other people live in other types of families. Your family may have a different number of people than other families you know. The relationship of the people living together in your family may be different from other families. There are differences between families in the closeness with other relatives. Sometimes the relationships in families are rewarding while at other times they are not.

Membership in a family can change if new babies are born, parents are separated, divorced, or remarried, or grown-up children leave home. In spite of changes or sometimes unhappy relationships, your family is one very important part of your relationships with others.

### FRIENDS

The main purpose of *friendship* is to promote mutual growth and the development of each person's personality. A person's relationships with friends are usually rewarding. If they are not, it is possible to break off unsatisfactory friendships. Friends play an important part in the lives of most people.

A person can have many kinds of friendships. Friendships can be close and personal or more distant, which of course affects how rewarding the friendships are. Mattie and Joan are best friends. They walk to school together, have most of the same classes, talk frequently on the telephone, double date, and know each other's secrets. Their closeness is very different from the friendship that George has with Sam, a seven-year-old boy he sponsors through the YMCA's "Big Brother" program. Another type of friendship exists between Carol and Miss Broker, the drama teacher at school. Carol is the librarian for the drama department. In working with Miss Broker, Carol has come to consider her a friend in addition to an employer and teacher.

Thus friendships can vary in strength, with some friendships being closer and stronger than others. Friendship can join people of different ages as well as peers.

## experiences in human relations

### CHARACTERISTICS OF FRIENDSHIPS

Friendships play an important part in everyone's lives. However, it is often difficult to describe why a relationship with a certain friend is special. The following brief experiences and activities help you explore what qualities make a good friend.

1. Print the word "friendship" vertically on a piece of paper. Across from each letter, write a word beginning with that letter that describes a characteristic that you think a friend would have.

2. With your classmates, list as many descriptive words or phrases as possible to describe friendship. Is this easier than thinking of

words that began with the letters of the word "friendship?" Why or why not?

3. Conduct a survey among fellow students at your school about the qualities they look for in a friend. Compile the responses. Compare the all-school survey with your personal ideas and with the ideas that you and your classmates suggested.

4. Observe children at play with each other. What characteristics do their friendships have? Do children's friendships seem to have the same characteristics as those between teenagers? Compare the similarities and differences that you observe.

● ● ● ● ● ● ● ● ● ● ● ● ● ● ● ● ●

## Acquaintances

Those people whom you know, yet who are not your friends, are your *acquaintances*. Everyone has a variety of acquaintances. They can be someone you know at school, the person who pumps gas at your local station, or a family who lives in your neighborhood.

You may see acquaintances often. However, relationships with acquaintances are generally without much closeness or strength. Most people develop friendships from among their acquaintances. This happens if you behave in such a way that your relationship has a chance to grow.

## Dating Partners

One special kind of relationship is between dating partners. Dating relationships are like other relationships, but also include some amount of sexual attraction. As with friendships, your dating relationships may be weak and mild, close and strong, or anything in between.

Calvin and Mary's relationship is the most important thing in the world right now to them. They are together as often as possible

**Ch. 6: Building Relationships**

and hope to become engaged at Christmas. Robert and Connie consider each other special. However, they are not so wrapped up in each other that they have no other interests. Dating relationships often grow out of friendships and, for most people, end eventually in marriage.

### TO SUM UP...

1. What are the main kinds of relationships?

2. Describe ways that families can be different from each other.

3. Why are friendships generally satisfactory relationships?

4. Give some examples of people who are your acquaintances.

5. What makes dating relationships different from other kinds of relationships?

### PURPOSES OF RELATIONSHIPS

People use their relationships for many purposes or goals. Your special needs will determine which purposes are most important as you build relationships.

### experiences in human relations

#### RELATIONSHIP DIARY

It is very difficult to study your own relationships. It is hard to try to discover your purposes in any particular relationship with another.

111

## Unit 3: Relating to Others

Most of the time people's motives are hidden deep in their subconscious minds.

The first step in trying to understand your relationships with others is to collect information about them. One way to do this is to keep a relationship diary. A relationship diary is not a general diary about all of your daily activities. It is a specific kind of diary in which you record information about the relationships you have with others.

Over the course of the next two weeks, record an account of your relationships with others. You may wish to focus on one type of relationship, such as friendships. On the other hand, you may record information about a wide variety of relationships. Your records should be kept so that they are meaningful to you.

What you record about each relationship is a personal decision. Are you most interested in discovering what your purposes are in entering specific relationships? What you give to your relationships? Get from them? Many other questions will occur to you as you begin to think about the contacts you have with others.

After the two weeks of keeping your diary are over, spend some time looking back over your entries. Think about the information you gathered. What benefits did you get from your relationships in those two weeks? Were you mainly a "giver" or a "getter" in your relationships? Can you figure out which relationships gave you enrichment, which gave you acceptance, understanding, and support, and which helped meet your emotional needs?

Who began most of the relationship contacts you had with others over the two weeks? Were you able to go out and meet and interact with others? Did you wait until they came to you? Did a pattern emerge in your approaches to and separations from others? Was there a difference between family, friends, acquaintances, and dating partners? In other words, did you act differently with different types of relationships?

Which relationships seemed particularly satisfactory to you? Can you identify any relationships which were especially growth producing? Did any of your relationships seem to be growth inhibiting? Do you spend most of your time in growth producing or in growth inhibiting relationships?

Other questions, ideas, and patterns about your relationships will occur to you as you think about your interaction with others. Understanding how and why you act as you do can be a starting point to making your relationships more meaningful and satisfying.

## MEETING EMOTIONAL NEEDS

All human beings have basic emotional needs to love and be loved, to be needed and wanted. Your emotional needs are met through the kinds of relationships you build with others.

Tammy has strong emotional needs. The relationships she builds with her family and friends reflect these needs. She is very close to her parents and sister, has several best friends, plus an intense dating relationship with Keith. Outside of these strong, intense relationships, she has few other friends. These strong attachments seem to meet her emotional needs.

Reba has a very small need for intense kinds of relationships, which she says always make her feel trapped. She is quite close to one girl friend, but otherwise avoids intense relationships with her family, other females, and with men. Her emotional needs cause her to build calm, placid relationships with a variety of people.

**Ch. 6: Building Relationships**

meet these needs. Often the search for these new relationships centers on dating partners. Those who are unable to build relationships with dating partners often feel overwhelmed by their emotional needs. They usually try to meet their needs by building strong friendships instead.

### SEEKING ACCEPTANCE

The wish to be accepted by others is another need people have. To seek acceptance is to want people to understand and support you. Acceptance needs can be met in any relationship area—family, friends, acquaintances, or dating partners.

Having a job allows Shawn to live away from her family. At the same time, she still loves them and wants their understanding and acceptance.

Carleton seeks acceptance and understanding from his dating partners. He enjoys dating, but is not yet ready to settle into an intense dating relationship. He finds that a milder, accepting type of relationship suits his present needs.

Jenny gets understanding in her special group of female friends. Their acceptance and support allow her to feel good about herself and at ease with the others.

Sylvester's soccer teammates are acquaintances rather than friends. It is important to him, however, that they accept him as a player and a teammate.

### ENRICHMENT

Another purpose of relationships is the enrichment of people's lives. You share experiences, feelings, and ideas with others as you interact and relate to them. This adds variety, depth, and breadth to your life.

A world without other people would be very dull indeed. From others, you can learn

*Everyone has a need for love and acceptance, which is met through relationships with others.*

During the teenage years, the ties between parents and children are weakened. The emotional needs which used to be met by parents now must be met by others. Because these emotional needs are strong, it is important to build new relationships which can

## Unit 3: Relating to Others

about different life styles, tastes, values, and ways of doing things.

Andrew, who comes from a quiet family that does not participate in many activities, likes to be with Mark's family. They are always active and busy, and he is involved and active when he is with them.

Sonja and Kate love to argue over politics. Sonja's family is very conservative and her views often clash with liberal Kate's, yet both learn and benefit from their discussions.

Cherie is learning to cook new dishes from Orlando, who was taught by his grandmother. She has opportunities to prepare many foods that she has never tried before.

In these and other ways, people learn from each other. This allows them to grow and develop in new and different directions.

## experiences in human relations

### LIKENESSES AND DIFFERENCES

The likenesses and differences between people help to make relationships with others enriching. Searching for likenesses and finding differences is an important part of relating to friends and acquaintances. Likenesses help you to be comfortable and have rapport with others. Differences provide variety, which helps to keep relationships interesting. The following experience helps you identify likenesses and differences with another person.

Find a partner (someone you don't know well is best) and sit facing each other. To begin, in a brief sentence that makes only a single point, tell your partner one way in which you *believe* you are like each other. Your partner then replies by stating in a brief sentence one way in which he or she thinks you two are similar. You then state one way in which you think the two of you differ. Your partner responds the same way.

Don't try to discuss your statements as you make them. Keep on making alternate statements until you have mentioned all the major likenesses and differences that come to mind. Each of you should begin your statements with the word "I" to show that you are describing your own perceptions.

When you've finished your statements to each other, you may want to talk over the experience with your partner. What was said that you'd like to talk more about now? What was said that was unexpected? Were there times when you wanted to debate what your partner was saying? If so, discuss those times.

If you and your partner were to develop a closer relationship, would the differences between you be interesting to explore? Or did the differences between you make you uneasy? How could these differences help to enrich your relationship?

● ● ● ● ● ● ● ● ● ● ● ● ● ● ● ● ● ● ● ●

### BUSINESS

Many relationships are simply to carry on the business or work of the people involved. You may often have only a business aspect to your relationships with acquaintances.

Tom and Ted are acquaintances whose only contact is through their work on the Student Council. Maria knows many of the customers who shop at the store where she is a checker. She is cordial to them, yet the relationships are based on the service she provides as she does her job.

## Ch. 6: Building Relationships

~~~~~~~~

### TO SUM UP...

1. Explain how people meet their emotional needs.
2. Describe the main change which occurs during adolescence in terms of meeting emotional needs.
3. How does seeking acceptance differ from working to meet emotional needs?
4. Explain how relationships can enrich your life.
5. What are business relationships?

~~~~~~~~

### DEVELOPING RELATIONSHIPS

Building and developing a relationship does not happen automatically when two people meet. The relationship grows and flourishes as the people come together and relate to each other. Thus building a relationship with another person is basically the process of developing feelings and interactions between the two of you.

#### THE RELATIONSHIP WHEEL

Many experts have studied why certain individuals come together in love or friendship and are able to build strong relationships. One idea compares building relationships to a wheel. The *relationship wheel* contains four spokes which represent the four steps of relationship building. These four steps are rapport, self-revelation, mutual dependency, and need fulfillment.

*Rapport* is the feeling you get when you are at ease with another person. If you do not have rapport when you meet someone, you are likely to feel uneasy. Good rapport leads to more interaction between the two of you. Poor rapport makes it unlikely that you will want to further your relationship.

As you develop rapport with someone, you tend to "relax your guard." You become more open and tell more about yourself, which is called *self-revelation*. When two people feel at ease with each other, they are likely to talk about their feelings, experiences, and attitudes. They go beyond talking about the weather, what play the Thespians are presenting next, or the newest record of a popular rock group.

As you reveal more and more about yourself to another person, you begin to develop *mutual dependency* on each other. You learn each other's habits and develop habits of your own to respond to your partner. You learn to depend on the other person to talk and laugh with, to go places with, or to rely on.

Finally, this mutual dependency grows into *need fulfillment* as a fourth step. At this level, you begin to get respect, confidence, and love or affection from the relationship. If both you and your partner are able to fulfill each other's needs, your relationship grows.

### experiences in human relations

#### NEED FULFILLMENT

It is hard to discover what purposes people have or rewards they get in their relationships. It is also hard to determine the needs that people seek to fill in their interaction with others. The fourth spoke of the relationship wheel

### Unit 3: Relating to Others

is *need fulfillment*, which is a vague term and hard to define. This is especially true because people have their own special needs to be met.

With your classmates, brainstorm to make a list of all the possible personal needs that you think could be met through relationships with others. Some examples might be:

I need someone to...
- Love me.
- Appreciate what I want to do.
- Understand my moods.
- Look up to.

This short list is only a very small beginning. You will probably be able to come up with a long list. When your list is finished, think about the needs you have included. Do all the needs apply to all people? Do people feel their individual needs in the same intensity as others? Which of these needs are important to you? How could you build relationships that help you meet these needs? Could any of the needs you have listed be met in a relationship without the partners first going around the first three spokes on the relationship wheel?

● ● ● ● ● ● ● ● ● ● ● ● ● ● ● ● ● ● ●

These four steps are compared to spokes on a wheel, which can go forward or backward. Part of the initial rapport between people often comes from a feeling that the other can meet some need. The partners move around the wheel through need fulfillment, which leads to more rapport. This starts the whole cycle again at a higher level.

The wheel can also move in the opposite way, causing the destruction of the relationship. Sometimes the rapport you feel with someone leads to self-revelation that causes arguments or bad feelings. This is likely to cause less self-revelation. In turn, your rapport will decrease and fewer of your needs will be met.

Here are some examples of how the relationship wheel works in real life. Arnold and Harry met the first day of school when they were assigned to the same English class. As Arnold later said, "I don't know what there was about it, but I liked the way he looked right from the start."

There was good rapport between them as they chatted before the class began. During the first week of school, they began to discover things about each other as they revealed their ideas and feelings. They learned that they both liked stock car races so they formed the habit of going to the races together on Friday nights. Soon they relied on each other for a variety of things. Their relationship fills a need for companionship, affection, and respect for both of them.

Sandra was hired to be a stock girl after school in Mrs. Drake's dress shop. She had liked Mrs. Drake when she went in for her interview. She assumed that since she had been hired, Mrs. Drake had liked her too. Although the relationship of employer and employee is different from that of two same-age friends, Sandra and Mrs. Drake went through the same wheel cycle. The initial liking became a strong rapport as Sandra began to learn her duties at the shop. They soon learned much about each other and came to depend on each other as they worked together. In terms of need fulfillment, they were able to provide respect and affectionate regard for each other's work skills.

An example of how a relationship can begin to "unwind" happened with Rhonda and Joe. They had been dating for almost six months and had been happy together. Then, somehow, Joe discovered that Rhonda bothered him with what seemed to be a new possessiveness. While many of his affection and love needs had been met during his relationship with Rhonda, he didn't like this new

### Ch. 6: Building Relationships

possessiveness. He began to find excuses which kept him from picking Rhonda up in his car every morning for school, as had been his habit. This irritated Rhonda a great deal, since she felt that most of his excuses were phony. In turn, she stopped telling him as much about the things she was doing, which soon reduced the rapport between them. At that point, Rhonda's needs were not being met so she stopped typing Joe's English papers. The cycle continued to unwind and the relationship finally broke up.

Even in families, where individuals have no choice in the matter of partners, the relationship wheel applies. The wheel may have gone forward and backward many times over the years. However, it can still be seen in action between teenagers and their parents.

## experiences in human relations

### THE RELATIONSHIP WHEEL

Once you are familiar with the relationship wheel, it is interesting to see if you can actually observe it happening in real life. Think about some relationship with which you are familiar. You may want to choose a new relationship that is just beginning or a long-term relationship that you know. You might like to look at one of your own relationships, although it may be easier to observe a relationship between two other persons.

Now, think about the relationship in terms of the relationship wheel. Select examples in that

*The relationship wheel is one way to explain how relationships can grow or be destroyed. (Adapted from Ira Reiss, "Toward A Sociology of the Heterosexual Love Relationship," Marriage and Family Living 22(1960), p. 143, Copyright 1960 by National Council on Family Relations. Adapted and reprinted by permission of author and publisher.)*

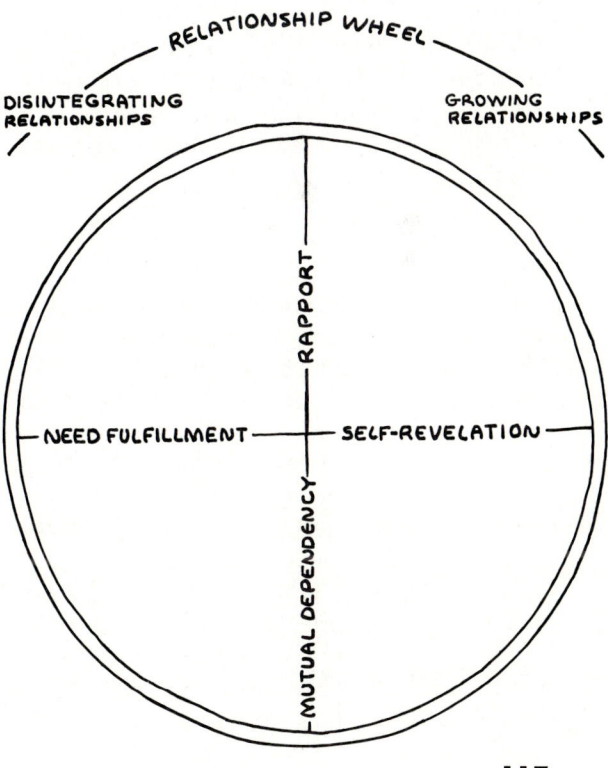

relationship which show the four parts of the wheel. Is the relationship growing stronger or weaker? Which way is the relationship wheel turning?

Using fictitious names, prepare a report of the relationship you have studied. If you wish, discuss the report with your classmates. You may find it interesting to prepare your report using a tape recorder, sketches, pictures, or records.

• • • • • • • • • • • • • • • • • • • •

Lorna was waiting eagerly for her mother when she returned from work at 5:30 one night. "Mom," she burst out, "the best things have happened. Paul asked me for a date for Friday and I got a B on that child development test I thought I had flunked!" Her mother was pleased that things were going well for her. As they worked together fixing supper, Lorna told her mother the details of her day. They sat down to supper with the rest of the family with some of their love needs met and with a better sense of rapport from which to proceed.

The progress of two people through a revolution of the wheel can be fast or slow. People who think that they have "fallen in love at first sight" may go through the entire cycle in one evening. Other people develop their relationships more slowly and may take weeks to proceed through the cycle. Some relationships may go many times around the wheel, both forward and backward. Other more short-lived relationships may not even complete one cycle.

Most people never consider how and why their relationships with others grow or die. The relationship wheel describes one way of looking at relationships. It explains some of the things that happen as two people interact and relate to each other.

## THE INTIMACY LADDER

Another way to look at building relationships is through the idea of an *intimacy ladder*. People climb the ladder as they build relationships with others. Each rung on the ladder describes one way of being close, or intimate, with another person.

The lowest rung on the ladder is *intellectual intimacy*. Two people who meet begin their relationship with words and ideas. They may discuss the new television series that just started, the last election, or the latest news about a famous movie star. On this rung of the ladder people usually hold their feelings in reserve. They keep their interaction on a nonpersonal basis.

The second step on the ladder is *physical intimacy*. People who have reached this stage are comfortable with closeness and may touch or caress each other. Curt gives Howard a hearty slap on the back when he sees him in the hall. Mr. Ossian puts his hand on Merrill's arm as he discusses an extra-credit project. Walking hand in hand has become enjoyable for Steve and Patty, now that they know each other.

### experiences in human relations

### PHYSICAL INTIMACY

Many people think that physical intimacy is sexual. However, physical intimacy includes many kinds of physical expression.

• Begin to notice how people relate to each other in a physical manner. Who touches whom? What is the relationship between those people who touch each other? Are they dating partners, family members, friends of the same or opposite sex? Do some people seem to need

Ch. 6: Building Relationships

a lot of touching in their relationships? Are there others who seem to have a "hands off" attitude?

- Make a list of at least ten examples of physical touching and intimacy that you have observed outside of marital or dating relationships. Share your list with others in your class. Did they find similar examples? Was it hard to find examples other than those between marital or dating partners? What conclusions can you draw about physical intimacy in relationships?
- To explore further how you react to physical closeness, form a circle with your classmates. How do you feel about being in the circle? Do you feel crowded by the nearness of others? Make the circle small enough so that you can place your arms about each others' shoulders. How do you feel? Are you comfortable or uncomfortable with the physical contact? Now step back until the circle is quite large and there are spaces between each of you. Are you more comfortable? What distance is the most comfortable for you? Would your feelings of what distance is most comfortable change if the circle were composed of members of your family or some of your special friends? What if all the other members of the circle were complete strangers?

• • • • • • • • • • • • • • • • • • • •

The last step on the ladder is *emotional intimacy*. This level is reached when two people are able to be completely natural with each other and show their feelings. Emotional intimacy allows people to lower their social masks and get rid of their defenses. They are able to receive understanding, affection, and support from each other. People who have reached emotional intimacy trust each other and share their most private feelings and ideas.

## experiences in human relations

### EMOTIONAL INTIMACY

Emotional intimacy is difficult to define and describe. The following experience will help you think about what emotional intimacy means to you.

Think of an experience you have had that was especially significant—in either a positive or a negative way. What would be hardest to tell about it? Would it be the shame and embarrassment of some part of a bad experience? If the experience you are remembering is a good one, is there some part of it which is so special to you that you would fear to tell others in case they might laugh or spoil it for you? These feelings, either good or bad, are the emotions which the experience arouses in you.

Now think about the people you would feel comfortable telling about this feeling. Those are the people with whom you have emotional intimacy. How many of them are there? Have you developed many or few relationships to the level of emotional intimacy? Are these the relationships in which you feel most rewarded? Are these relationships growth producing for you?

• • • • • • • • • • • • • • • • • • • •

The relationship wheel explains more fully than the intimacy ladder how relationships are built. However, the intimacy ladder gives insight into many relationships. For example, those who are acquaintances are likely to relate only through intellectual intimacy. Many friendships are also only on this level. Physical intimacy is obvious in the case of husbands and wives and between family

119

**Unit 3: Relating to Others**

*The intimacy ladder shows three kinds of intimacies which develop as a relationship is built.*

EMOTIONAL INTIMACY

PHYSICAL INTIMACY

INTELLECTUAL INTIMACY

members. It also can be found between friends and dating partners. Emotional intimacy is found mostly between close friends, family members, and some dating partners.

The three rungs on the intimacy ladder differ in importance to people because of their unique needs. In some people, physical needs are strong. In others, emotional or intellectual needs may be most important. Of course, all people have some amount of all three needs. You will find relationships with people that can fill your special needs most rewarding.

## TO SUM UP...

1. List the four steps of building relationships as described in the relationship wheel.
2. What is rapport?
3. What kinds of things do people tell each other in self-revelation?
4. What happens when the relationship wheel moves forward? Backward?
5. Describe the three rungs on the intimacy ladder.

## CHARACTERISTICS OF RELATIONSHIPS

As a relationship grows and develops, certain characteristics influence how it will proceed. Three of these characteristics of relationships are trust, affection or liking, and power.

### Trust

The ability to *trust* other people is to place your confidence in the fact that they will not reject, betray, or hurt you. Trusting means that you expect another to give you acceptance and support. Trust usually begins during the first two phases of the relationship wheel. As you build rapport and begin to share feelings with a partner, trust becomes involved.

If your revelations are met with acceptance, you are likely to begin to trust the other. However, if what you say is ridiculed or belittled, or if your partner betrays your revelations, no trust will be established. The first crisis of most new relationships involves your ability to trust yourself and the other. Whether or not trust is established determines how the relationship wheel will move.

Marcy moved to a new school district where she knew few students. She became friendly with Belle through a shared class and membership in the Future Teachers Club. Soon the girls were sharing ideas, feelings, and experiences. The rapport they had led Marcy to tell Belle about a horrible experience. The previous year she had been attacked and almost raped. To her dismay, the next day, most of her new friends and acquaintances had heard the story. By telling others Marcy's secret, Belle destroyed the trust that had been building between the two of them. Their friendship was at an end. Had Belle respected Marcy's confidence, it is likely that trust would have increased between them. The relationship probably would have continued to grow.

Trust can be a problem area between teenagers and their parents. Teenagers often complain that their parents don't trust them. On the other hand, some parents say their children are not trustworthy. Since the parent-teen relationship is a long-standing one, trust is built through the years as the parents and child move around the relationship wheel. If the child acts in a responsible manner, parents are more willing to be trusting.

*One aspect of trust between people is the ability to respect a confidence.*

Rex's parents had always imposed a curfew when he took the family car out alone. When he first started to drive, he was very careful to get home well before the deadline. Now that he has shown his parents that he can be trusted, they allow him later hours and more flexibility in setting his own time to come home.

Building trust involves both partners in the relationship. Not only do you expect certain behavior from your partner, but you must also act in a trustworthy manner. You can add to the trust between you and another by using what you know about the other to build your relationship. You avoid using your knowledge to hurt the other. Your ability to risk yourself through revelation and to express warmth toward others helps build a high level of trust. Because of these characteristics, others expect you to respond with warmth, acceptance, and support when they tell you about themselves.

A relationship can be established and continued without trust between the two partners. However, it is not likely to have much potential for future intimacy and closeness. In fact, little growth can occur in a relationship until the partners learn to trust each other.

## experiences in human relations

### DEVELOPING TRUST

Developing trust is important in building a relationship. The following experiences will help you think more about why trust is so important, how it feels to trust, and how trust is developed between people.

Ch. 6: Building Relationships

- People often think of trust as being important only in close relationships. However, all kinds of relationships require trust to proceed smoothly. With your classmates, try to think of all the types and kinds of relationships where at least a small amount of trust is necessary. Have you included relationships such as between dentist and patient, sports team members, orchestra members, employer and employee? What other kinds of relationships can you think of where trust is important? What would happen if many of these relationships became untrustworthy?
- This activity is to help you begin to experience how it feels to trust another person. Find a partner and have one of you put on a blindfold. The partner who can see then leads the other on a walk around the school and grounds. After about ten to fifteen minutes the positions are reversed. The previous leader is blindfolded, and the walk is repeated. Afterwards, describe how it felt to trust your partner when you were blindfolded. Did your partner deserve your trust? Did you find any relationship between trust and touching? What might this mean in terms of the development of trust and the intimacy ladder?
- What exactly can you do to build trust in a relationship? What do you expect of others when you trust them? With a partner, spend some time listing all the things that people can do to show trust or to be trustworthy in a relationship. From this list, choose the ten aspects of trust that you think most important. Talk about your list with your classmates. Do they agree with your list of the ten most important aspects of trust? What other suggestions do they have?

● ● ● ● ● ● ● ● ● ● ● ● ● ● ● ● ● ● ● ● ● ●

Carolyn and Walter have been dating for almost a year and seem to be devoted to each other. While their relationship appears loving and caring to their friends, Carolyn does not completely trust Walter. Early in their relationship, he lied to her about his interest in another girl. This did not cause Carolyn to break the relationship, but she has never fully trusted him since. Because of her mistrust, their relationship does not seem to go anywhere. In terms of the relationship wheel, they are in a rut. Unless Carolyn learns to trust Walter, they will eventually break up.

## AFFECTION OR LIKING

The need for affection can be one purpose of a relationship. However, the amount and strength of affection in a relationship is also a factor in how it develops. Not all relationships have affection. For instance, affection is not generally present in business-type relationships. It may also not be present in a family relationship, where it would be more expected. As shown in the example of Carolyn and Walter, affection can be present without trust.

The question of why people like each other is a complex one. Some ideas that help explain why affection grows or dies include reward and punishment, exploitation and benefit, and self-concept.

### Reward and Punishment

In general, people like others who reward them and dislike or like less those who punish them. People usually consider "reward" to mean something material and "punishment" to be physical. In the area of relationships, rewards and punishments are not so obvious. In fact, you are probably not aware of the things that reward and punish you in your relationships. Like most people, you probably have little idea why you have affection for certain persons.

Unit 3: Relating to Others

# experiences in human relations

## REWARDS THROUGH RELATIONSHIPS

Each person seeks rewards from relationships with others. However, the kinds of rewards sought vary because personal needs and desires differ. One reward that most people seek, at least to some degree, involves agreement with others. It is rewarding when others agree with you. You tend to like people who agree with you and agree with the people you like. Disagreement is a form of social punishment. Often people dislike those who disagree with them. The following experience was designed to help you explore the effect of agreement and disagreement on how you feel about others.

For this experience, prepare three value statements which do not need to reflect your own values. A sample set might include:
- To have understanding friends.
- To get a good job.
- To be an outstanding athlete.

Read your statements to the others. Listen as they read theirs. As you listen, decide which one of the three statements is most important to you. Find others who agree with you and form a group with them. Spend a few minutes in your group talking about why that particular statement is important to all of you.

Form a different group each time another set of value statements is read. Each time, join others who agree with you about which of the three statements is the most important.

When all the value statements have been read, talk about your feelings with the others. Did you feel close to the others in each of your groups as you talked about why you chose the same value statements as important? How did you feel about the other groups who chose other statements? Did you feel on a personal basis how like and dislike can vary as people agree or disagree with you? Although the time in each group was short, could you imagine how your feelings might be influenced if you spent more time with each other in the groups?

• • • • • • • • • • • • • • • • • • • • • • • •

For example, look at some of Roosevelt's relationships. In his family, Roosevelt is much closer to his mother than to his father. In part, this is because his mother is interested in Roosevelt's affairs and "rewards" him with her attention and interest. Roosevelt's father does not seem to care about what Roosevelt is doing. Although his disinterest is not what is commonly called "punishment," it is enough to cause the relationship to be distant.

Roosevelt's particular circle of friends "rewards" him with acceptance and friendship. However, Roosevelt's close friendship with John seems to be breaking up. This is because John has been criticizing and downplaying the things Roosevelt does. This criticism is a form of "punishment" and, in this case, has caused the relationship to break down. Roosevelt's favorite teacher is considered an easy grader while the teacher whom he dislikes the most is one that rarely gives outstanding grades. Thus Roosevelt is attracted to people who can give him rewards in the form of attention, non-critical acceptance, and good grades. Other people seek other kinds of rewards in their relationships.

**Exploitation and Benefit**

In much the same way, people come to dislike those whom they exploit or misuse and like those whom they benefit. In other

**Ch. 6: Building Relationships**

*Having others listen when you are talking is a rewarding experience.*

words, you will generally like those people you help and dislike those people you hurt. At first glance, this may appear an unlikely influence on relationships.

This factor is at work in some of Ken's relationships. Ken's relationship with his middle brother, Brian, has never been smooth. They have a long history of arguments, fights, and playing dirty tricks on each other. Somehow, after each dirty trick, Ken seems to hate his brother more. In contrast, Ken's relationship with his youngest brother Gene is affectionate. Ken helps Gene with his model building, and they frequently play football and catch together. Their good experiences almost seem to snowball and create more good experiences. The negative experiences of Ken and Brian create more bad feelings between them.

In another area, Ken recently convinced his dating partner, Barbara, to let him copy a math paper which he had not had time to do himself. After he had copied the paper, he felt embarrassed when he was with Barbara and started to avoid her. Within a week, they had stopped seeing each other and Ken began dating Julie.

Everyone on occasion exploits or uses other people. However, constant or major exploitation of someone else usually poisons your relationship. Helping and rewarding another person usually strengthens your relationship with them. It is almost as if, in your subconscious mind, you think, "I've spent my time on this person, so he or she must be pretty nice."

**Self-Concept**

Another factor which affects the amount of liking between people is related to the self-concepts of those who build a relationship. People who have a positive self-concept and

125

**Unit 3: Relating to Others**

*A person with a negative self-concept can be very hurt by rejection.*

who feel good about themselves are likely to believe that others like them. Marilyn is a friendly person who enjoys being with others. When she meets new people, her self-concept leads her to assume that they will like her. Her open and friendly manner is rewarding to others, so most people do like her.

Gary's low self-concept makes him afraid that new people he meets will reject him as unworthy. His fear tends to make him act unfriendly. As a result, many people he meets do *not* like him. In these examples, the amount of affection and liking Marilyn and Gary find in their relationships is directly influenced by how they feel about themselves.

There is another link between self-concept and affection. People with positive self-concepts view acceptance and rejection by others differently than do those with negative self-concepts. Olivia has a positive self-concept. However, she realizes that she is not going to like everyone, nor will everyone like her. When Toby did not ask her for a second date, she was not terribly upset. His rejection did not hurt much. Marsha's negative self-concept, however, caused her to feel greatly hurt when a similar thing happened to her. Rejection or lack of affection hurts a great deal more if you have a low self-concept.

In much the same way, acceptance and affection are usually more rewarding to those with negative self-concepts than to those who have positive self-concepts. A person with a low self-concept craves love and affection. Acceptance from another person fills a strong emotional need.

People with high self-concepts tend to have rewarding relationships with others. They approach people with a positive frame of mind, which others usually respond to easily.

If you have a positive self-concept, you

126

have accepted yourself. Therefore, you do not have to rely only on others for acceptance and affection. Lack of love is not so fearful if you have a positive self-concept. Thus, the amount of affection in your relationships with others may depend on whether you first feel affection for yourself.

## experiences in human relations

### SELF-CONCEPT

How you relate to others depends in large part on how you feel about yourself. The following experience dramatizes how people have their own style of interaction based in part on their self-concepts.

With your class members, imagine yourself at a large party. Your hostess has given you a cup of punch and left you to find your own way around. As you stand there drinking punch, role play how you would act in such a situation.

After a few minutes, think about the following questions. As you began role playing, what was your first desire?
- To look for a familiar face?
- To stand, hoping someone would come to you?
- To think, but not move, about how you should introduce yourself?
- To go immediately to someone you don't know and begin talking?
- To get your old friends together and stay together throughout?
- To check for people who do not have someone talking to them and go introduce them to someone?

Did you act out your first impulse? Were you meeting your needs as you interacted with the others or were you trying to meet the needs of others? What kinds of self-concepts do you think might cause each of the behaviors listed above? Did your first reaction reflect your self-concept?

● ● ● ● ● ● ● ● ● ● ● ● ● ● ● ● ● ●

## POWER

*Power* is the ability of one partner to influence the other's behavior. Power is obvious in some relationships. Parents have power to punish their children. Highway police have power to issue speeding tickets to drivers. An employer has the power to fire employees.

Power is not always as one-sided as these examples seem to show. A child can overcome parents' power in many ways. An example of this is the toddler who is being toilet trained but who keeps wetting the diapers in spite of the parents' instruction. Drivers and employees also have ways to use power in their relationships with police and employers. Motorists often speed when no police are around. Employees may use power against a boss by working slowly, wasting time, or deliberately making errors. Power is an important part of any relationship. Who holds power and how it is used are important in understanding how relationships work.

### Identifying Power

Power is usually associated with making decisions. If parents make most of the decisions concerning their children's bedtimes, clothes, and television watching, they are using power over their children. As the children grow up and begin to make some of these decisions themselves, they come to hold more power over their own lives.

The quarterback on a football team usually holds a great deal of power over his team-

*Some people use their ability to get along well with others to gain power.*

mates since he calls the plays. If the coach sends in the plays from the sidelines, the coach is using the power.

Ira and Sue usually go where Sue wants on dates. Thus she uses power in this aspect of their relationship. Ira uses some power in the matter of how late they stay out, how often they date, and who they go with when they are in a group.

In Sara's family, her father has the most power, including power over her mother. The family is expected to abide by his wishes and desires and make their plans around him. In Rodney's family, his mother has a great deal of power, while in Tony's family the children have a large say in planning family activities.

**Who Has Power**

It is often hard to discover how two partners will decide who is going to have the most power in a relationship. There are several factors which usually go along with power.

Age is usually associated with power. An older person is likely to have more power than a younger one. This works to strengthen the power which parents and teachers have. A problem often occurs when a supervisor is younger than those supervised. The older workers may not like taking orders from a younger person because of the feeling that age should be in power.

The person with more education usually holds the most power in a relationship. Again, this helps uphold the authority of teachers and parents over children. Problems can arise when a child has more education than the parents.

Money can be very important in the power balance of a relationship. Carla has a much larger allowance than Jill and she uses her money to gain control over Jill's behavior.

## Ch. 6: Building Relationships

When Jill does what Carla wants, Carla buys her presents or pays her admission to the movies.

In the past, the fact that men were the breadwinners and women stayed at home with the children influenced power in the home. Since the man earned the living, he made the decisions. Recently, women have taken a more equal part in the working world. Their income has often shifted power in the home to a more equal balance. If a male dating partner is paying, he is likely to feel he has more control over what the couple will do than if they are each paying their own way.

A person's skills or talents can influence power. Edna is learning to water ski. Since she knows nothing about it, she lets her teacher tell her exactly what to do. In other words, because her teacher is an expert water skier, Edna gives the teacher power over herself.

In addition, interpersonal factors influence who has power. A person with charm and personality will often be able to use power over another. Someone who knows how to communicate well may have more power than someone who never seems to be able to get ideas across to others. Thus the way in which people interact with others is important in holding and using power.

One person may often take power in a relationship because the other doesn't. Lucy and Ellen spent much of their free time together. Lucy always planned their activities and Ellen was happy to go along with the plans. One day Ellen protested. "Lucy," she said, "We have gone to so many movies lately that I'm really tired of them. Don't make plans to go to any more because I just won't go." Lucy had held power to decide what they would do together. Ellen took back some of that power when the plans Lucy made didn't meet her approval.

Another influence on how power is used is called the *principle of least interest*. The partner with the least interest in the relationship has more power. The person who cares less whether the relationship grows or dies does not have to work at maintaining the relationship. If you don't care what happens between you and your partner, you are able to do just about what you want.

For example, Nancy and Vern are dating partners. Vern is not strongly attracted to Nancy although he does care for her. Nancy, however, is very fond of Vern and will do almost anything to please him and hold him. Therefore, Vern has a great deal of power to influence Nancy's behavior.

In much the same way, this principle works between same sex friends, siblings, spouses, and others. Sherrie works at a fast food restaurant, but doesn't really care if she keeps her job or not. Therefore she uses power in often doing just as she pleases rather than as her employer wishes. On the other hand, if her employer didn't care whether she stayed or not, she would need to do exactly as she was supposed to if she wanted to keep her job.

## experiences in human relations

### POWER IN RELATIONSHIPS

Power is a subtle factor that is present in every relationship. It can be used either for the growth or the destruction of that relationship. The following experience will help you begin to see how power works in some of your relationships.

You and a partner are to plan an activity for the two of you to share together. Begin by

**Unit 3: Relating to Others**

suggesting a plan or proposing something you would like to do. Your partner responds by indicating willingness to participate in the activity. If your partner says "No," you must suggest another plan until your partner agrees to some idea. At that point, work out a plan in detail together. Include the time, place, and other arrangements which are necessary to make the plan a reality. Your partner then begins the process again by suggesting an activity. Go until agreement is reached and a second plan is made.

When you have finished, think about the interaction between the two of you. Who seemed to hold the most power? Did one of you reject several suggestions the other made? Was the rejector using power then? If you and your partner are well acquainted, did the power shown in this experiment reflect the usual situation between the two of you? If you are not well acquainted, how did you solve the question of who should hold the power? Did one of you attempt to hold the power or did you share power?

• • • • • • • • • • • • • • • • • •

**Power Conflict**

Power is a source of much conflict in many relationships. If one person holds power and both feel that this is all right, the relationship is likely to go smoothly. However, many partners try to gain control over each other. These relationships are not likely to be a source of growth and development.

One of the main causes of parent-child conflicts is that the child feels the parent is trying to use too much power. Friends and dating partners often struggle over who will hold power. Most teacher-student conflicts result from the teacher wishing to use more power than the student is willing to submit to. Rebellion and expressions of indepen-

*The need or wish for power in a relationship is a possible area of conflict.*

dence indicate an unwillingness for others to hold power. Taking orders, giving in, and usually agreeing with others indicate a willingness to let others hold power.

There is no easy way for power conflicts to be settled. Some people have a great need for power and are happiest when they can use it in their relationships. Others wish to have only a small amount of power. The best relationships occur when people are able to mesh their power needs to move around the relationship wheel. People who fight for power usually find their relationships unwinding and ending.

Power is a characteristic that is very important in every relationship. It is usually not thought about, talked about, or looked at directly. The ability to use power and let others do so when appropriate shows skill in getting along with others.

## TO SUM UP...

1. What does it mean to trust another person?
2. Explain where trust begins on the relationship wheel.
3. What kinds of rewards and punishments are the result of relationships?
4. Why do people often dislike those they use or exploit?
5. Describe how helping another person can strengthen the relationship between you.
6. Identify some reasons why people with positive self-concepts usually have good relationships with others.
7. What is power in a relationship?
8. Why is power related to decision making?
9. Explain how the following factors influence power: age, education, money, and communication skills.
10. Describe how the "principle of least interest" works.
11. Why is power often a source of conflict in a relationship?

## RELATING PERSON TO PERSON

There is one characteristic which can influence how rewarding a relationship really is. It is important whether you are looking at a relationship between acquaintances, friends, or dating partners. This is whether the partners are able to relate person-to-person.

### RELATING ONE TO ONE

One interesting aspect of relating to others is the fact that people primarily relate on a one-to-one basis. Miss Walker calls on one student at a time and that student responds before she goes on to another class member. Chuck, Tim, and Matt are standing in the hall talking. Yet, as they talk, the conversation shifts and floats so that Chuck and Tim talk while Matt listens. Then Matt and Chuck may exchange comments. Even in conversations between many people, at any one time, what is being said is generally between two individuals.

This same idea holds true for family relationships. Interaction flows mainly between two people regardless of how many family members are present. At the supper table, the Carroll family shares their experiences of the day. One night, Mr. Carroll teased Don about his favorite baseball team being beaten that afternoon. Then Anita and Jane talked about

## Unit 3: Relating to Others

*Talk is usually between two people even when several family members are present.*

the latest fall fashions while Mrs. Carroll discussed the next day's transportation needs with Mr. Carroll. Later Anita and Don began an argument over who was to have the last piece of dessert. While the Carrolls would have told others that they held "family" discussions during supper, most of their talk shifted around between two people.

### PERSONS VS. OBJECTS

In spite of the fact that most relating is done on a one-to-one basis, many people act as if they are relating to "objects." In some way, they have learned to think of people as "things" or objects rather than human beings. They are unable to see people as persons in their own right. By acting as if others were objects they fail to get much satisfaction in their relationships with them. Relationships are rewarding and growth producing only when people are able to relate as human beings.

Shelly always acted as if the people around her were there for her convenience. A regard for other people's feelings never bothered her at all. She borrowed her sisters clothes without asking. Any secrets that came her way she promptly told. She often played cruel practical jokes on her friends. She treated people as objects, but couldn't understand why she was unpopular with others.

Many people use roles to make people into objects. Instead of seeing others as people, they see them only as roles. Roles and how they affect relationships will be discussed in a later chapter. For now, two examples may make this idea clearer. Students often forget that teachers are human beings who love, hate, eat, and sleep just like they do. Instead they may consider them as robots who dispense knowledge and assignments.

Patrons of restaurants are sometimes rude to the service personnel. They excuse their behavior by saying, "Oh they're paid to take it—the customer is always right." By assigning the role of "paid object" to those who serve them, they avoid facing them as human beings.

The characteristics of trust, affection, and power influence how others are seen. People are more likely to trust, feel affection for, and avoid power conflicts with others whom they relate to as people. Those who see others as objects often mistrust them, feel no affection toward them, and try to use power over and against them.

Many individuals make people into objects even in their close relationships. They see their friends and family as objects to do things with, talk with, and be with. They don't see them as people, individuals in their own right, to relate to. Most relationships where partners are seen as objects are rather cold ones. It almost seems as if the partners are standing back and watching what is happening rather than being involved.

People who are able to accept themselves as they are—and like themselves—are more able to accept others as human beings. They are able to see each other as individuals and can relate on a person-to-person basis. In a person-to-person relationship, both open themselves to each other, without the need for masks to hide the self. They are able to experience each other as people, which helps them avoid loneliness.

# experiences in human relations

## PERSON-TO-PERSON RELATIONSHIPS

When you look—really look—at the person with whom you are interacting, it is hard to keep on treating that person as an object. Eye contact is important in building person-to-person relationships with others since you look more at those you like. In addition, more frequent eye contact indicates a willingness to begin or maintain a relationship with the other.

Choose a partner and begin a conversation. While you talk, keep constant eye contact. Since people normally only look at each other thirty to sixty percent of the time, this will seem very awkward. However, continue to talk with and look at your partner. After a while, you will begin to have the feeling that he or she is a "real" person. This feeling will grow as you learn to relate person-to-person instead of object-to-object.

• • • • • • • • • • • • • • • • • • • • • •

## ACCEPTING OTHERS' PERCEPTIONS

Because of their backgrounds and experiences, people tend to perceive or see the same events in different ways. You see and feel things differently than others do because you are different. The ideas that you have about what you have seen or done are called *perceptions*. In learning to relate person-to-person, it is important to accept other people's perceptions as real for them. This is very hard to understand because people tend to think they know what another person is thinking or feeling.

For example, during a session on life styles in a family living class, Les got into a long and

Unit 3: Relating to Others

*These two people have different perceptions of the concert. Learning to relate person-to-person involves accepting others' perceptions as real for them.*

somewhat heated discussion on communes with Mrs. Jason. As Cassie and Virgil left the class together, they were talking about the exchange. Virgil said, "Gosh, did I ever think Les had Mrs. Jason on the spot—he had a lot of good information and asked some good questions. I really think he got the better of her."

Cassie looked at Virgil as if she couldn't believe her ears. "Why, I can't believe that's what you think. I thought Les was really rude and awful. All he was doing was causing trouble and wasting time in class. I was sure you'd agree with me since I know you don't believe in communal living."

Cassie knew that she and Virgil agreed that communes were undesirable. She thought that he would also condemn Les's arguments. She was therefore unable to believe that Virgil admired Les's ability to present an argument based on facts that he had discovered. Cassie couldn't let Virgil have his own ideas about the class discussion, so she promptly started to argue with him about who was "right."

In starting an argument, Cassie and Virgil show one way in which different perceptions can harm a relationship. In most cases, partners tend to want to establish that their perceptions are right. It is very hard to realize that your perceptions are right for you, that another person's perceptions of the same event are right for them, and *the perceptions don't have to be the same.* A person-to-person relationship can stand disagreements in perception between partners.

Accepting the perceptions of others is not easy to learn. First, you have to be able to see others as persons in their own right, with their own personalities, needs, strengths, and weaknesses. Then you have to allow them to be themselves—to see things differently than you, to act differently than you, and to think differently than you. Only then will the relationship that you are building between you grow, develop, and flower into something meaningful.

## experiences in human relations

### PERCEPTIONS

Part of the uniqueness of people is the way they look at the world and their perceptions of what they see and experience. The following activity will point out how one concept or idea can cause several responses and perceptions.

Divide into groups of four people. Have one group member make up a list of words and read them one at a time to the others. The list could include words such as yellow, cat, blue jeans, bare, drink, game, backyard, boots, and recording. The person who reads the list also writes down what the others say.

The other three group members respond to each word from a different perspective. One gives a word association related to people. Another associates the given word with ideas. The last group member associates each word with material goods or items. For example, the word "football" could have the following associations: people—quarterback; ideas—violence; and item—goalposts. Thus, for each word in the list, your group will make three kinds of associations—people, ideas, and items.

When you have finished, talk over what happened with the others. Was it easy to make your assigned association for each word? Did the type of word association assigned someone else often occur to you before your own category? Did you tend to make the same kinds of associations with each word? Was there any way to judge whose ideas were best? Can you think of any situation where one person's perceptions were best for everyone? Why do people find it so difficult to realize that their perceptions are not right for everyone?

### TO SUM UP...

1. Explain how a conversation in a group of friends is on a one-to-one basis.
2. Describe the relationships that result when a person relates to others as objects.
3. What are perceptions?
4. Why is it so hard to accept other people's perceptions as right for them?

# CHAPTER 7

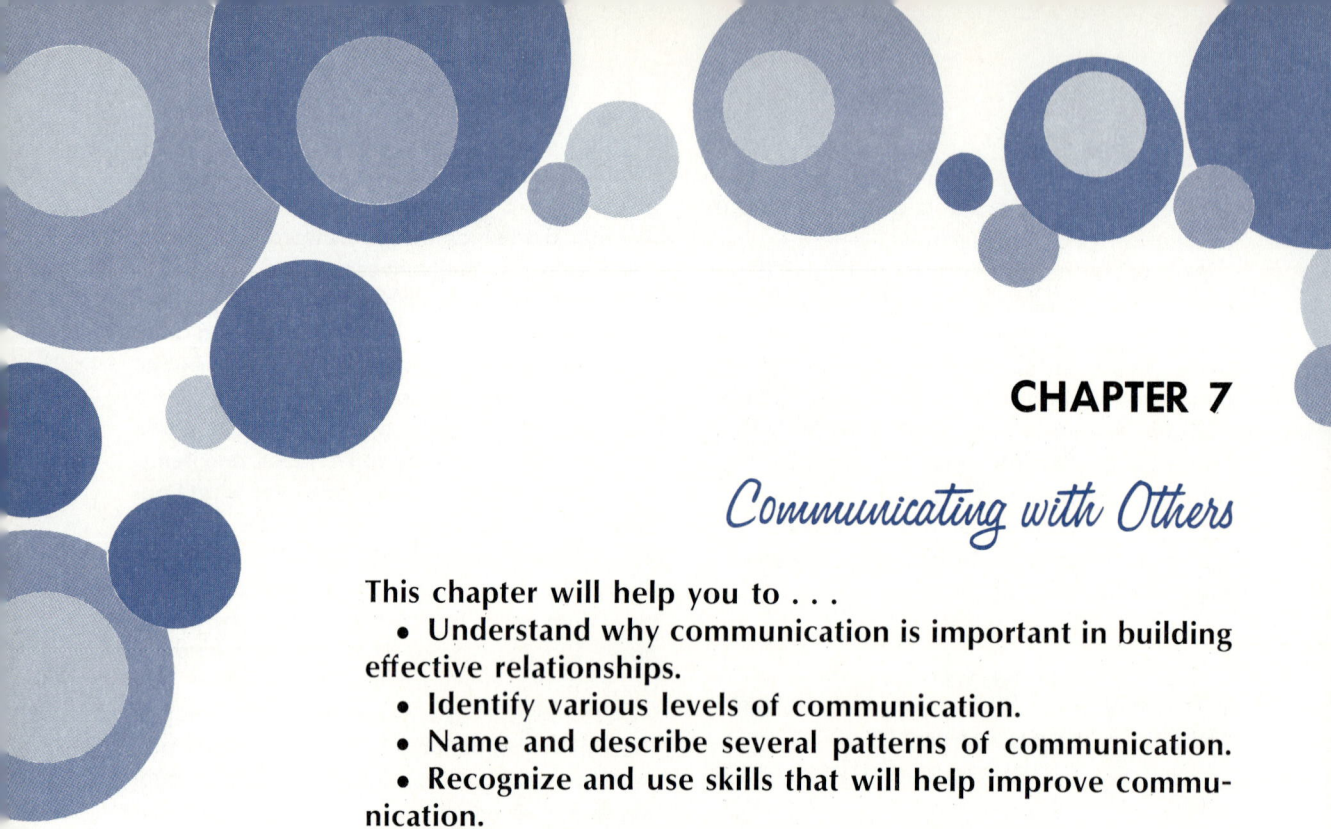

## Communicating with Others

This chapter will help you to . . .
- Understand why communication is important in building effective relationships.
- Identify various levels of communication.
- Name and describe several patterns of communication.
- Recognize and use skills that will help improve communication.
- Explain how people use nonverbal messages to communicate with others.

As people begin to relate to others, they need some way to express themselves. It is not possible to build strong relationships unless you are able to communicate. Most people think of communication as the spoken or written word. However, *communication* is any behavior that carries messages which can be figured out by other people.

Communication includes all the ways people give and receive information. Some of these ways are speech, action, letters, books, motion pictures, newspapers, radio, and television.

### COMMUNICATION IS IMPORTANT

Communication plays an important part in your life. The kinds of communication you have with others affect the kinds of relationships you have with them. If you have good communication, it is likely that your relationships will be good. Poor communication often leads to problems between people.

Communication has taught you what you know. Messages from your parents, peers, and teachers gave you information about the world. You learned how to behave from them. In fact, it is largely through communication that you became the unique person you are today.

Communication keeps you in touch with the world. Through radio, television, and newspapers you are able to find out about events that occur all over the globe.

### Link to Others

Communication is the behavior that links people to people. Communication influences the movement of the relationship wheel. The

**Ch. 7: Communicating with Others**

*Communication is the behavior which links people together.*

climb of two people up the intimacy ladder is helped by communication. Growth of affection, trust, and a good power balance depends on communication. Thus, a relationship will only be as good as its communication.

Through communication people begin and end relationships. They learn to like each other, to reach some understanding of others, and to influence one another. Communication helps you learn about yourself and how others see you. It is the way you learn to understand others as persons and help others understand you as a person.

## Never No Communication

Communication between people takes place constantly. In fact, there is never *no* communication. Even though they do not speak, people are communicating with others. Some type of message always gets through. When Drew passes Lisa in the hall without saying a word to her, he is communicating his lack of interest. If Craig fails to turn in a paper in class, he is indicating his feelings toward the assignment, the teacher, or the class itself.

Many times, when you think you have not communicated anything, you may have sent several messages. Peter was standing by his locker, not joining his friends in conversation. His shoulders were bent and his whole body drooped. It was obvious to his friends that he was quite upset even though he hadn't talked with them or even paid any attention to them.

You may feel that if you haven't told your friends what you are feeling, they don't know what is going on inside you. What is more likely is that your friends will have drawn their own conclusions, which may be wrong. Unless you tell others how you feel, the constant messages you send will lead them to guess your feelings. Therefore if you want accurate communication with others, you must be ready to tell them about yourself.

## Destructive and Constructive Communication

Communication can be either destructive or constructive. It can have an effect on how relationships proceed.

Destructive communication includes those messages that cause people to feel judged or

137

guilty. It makes people feel unworthy. They may even develop a negative self-concept. Growth is often blocked or stopped by destructive communication. Most people do not know how common it is. When a parent says to a child, "You are such a brat, I don't know how anyone could love you," the child's self-concept is going to be affected negatively.

When Mary says to Sally, "I don't know why I waste my time being friends with a dummy like you," a destructive message has been sent.

In contrast, constructive communication can be healthy. These messages make people feel better. They help people talk and express their feelings. Constructive communication can cause feelings of worth to become stronger. It can reduce threat or fear and promote growth and constructive change. A parent could say, "Well, I see you had a bad accident. Can you tell me about it?" What would have been the effect on the child in this case?

A constructive message that Mary could have sent to Sally might have been, "I sure am mad that you didn't wait to walk home from school with me like you said you would." This message gives Sally a chance to explain. It gives the relationship a chance to grow rather than being destroyed by a quarrel.

## experiences in human relations

### DESTRUCTIVE AND CONSTRUCTIVE COMMUNICATION

It has been said that good communication occurs when the other person does what you want. However, this does not consider that feelings may go with the other person's actions. People rarely think about the emotional effect they have on others. How people feel about the messages they receive is important in thinking about whether the results are destructive or constructive.

Choose a partner for the following experience. Begin by telling your partner about some idea you have that you think would improve your school. While you are talking, your partner is to make destructive comments to you. These comments should be negative, sarcastic, and belittle your ideas. Some examples might be:

"Oh, that's impossible, it would never work."

"You've got to be crazy to think of an idea like that."

"That sure is a stupid idea."

After two or three minutes, your partner is to tell you about an idea. You are to make the same kind of destructive comments about that idea.

Next, spend a couple of minutes telling your partner about something you would like to do that you have never had an opportunity to do. Your partner is to make constructive comments such as:

"Say, that sounds interesting."

"Where did you hear about that? I'd like to know more."

"How did you get interested in that?"

Switch again. Your partner is to describe an activity and you are to make constructive comments.

When you have finished, think about what happened. How did the destructive comments make you feel? The constructive ones? Which comments were easier for you to make? Do you tend to respond to others in a destructive or a constructive manner? In this experience, you knew that your partner was supposed to make certain comments. How would you feel if simi-

*This conversation may be on any one of the five levels of communication. It depends on how much of themselves these people are revealing to each other.*

lar comments were made to you in normal conversation?

### TO SUM UP. . .

1. Define communication.
2. Explain why communication is important in people's lives.
3. Why is communication called a link to others?
4. Explain why there is never *no* communication.
5. What is destructive communication and what is its result?
6. What are some possible outcomes from constructive communication?

## LEVELS OF VERBAL COMMUNICATION

Verbal or spoken communications can differ. The message, "It sure is windy today," is sent and received differently than a whisper of, "Darling, I love you." These are examples of different *levels of communication*. There are five levels of communication. Each level represents a degree of people's willingness to share themselves with others.

These five levels of communication go along with the way a relationship is built. As people become closer to each other, they are able to communicate with more depth and meaning. In turn, communicating at higher levels helps the relationship grow further. Communication and relationship building go together. Being able to communicate at all levels help build relationships that last.

Unit 3: Relating to Others

## CLICHÉ CONVERSATION

The first level of communication is the lowest level of telling about yourself. In fact, in most cases of cliché conversation, there is no sharing of the person's self. The conversation is based on clichés or what is often called "small talk." Ernie calls, "Good morning, how are you?" to Martin when he passes him in the hall.

Martin responds, "I'm just fine." Each has greeted the other but there has been no sharing of personal feelings.

When Dottie tells Karl that she had a very nice time that evening, it well may be true. However, that evening Dottie spilled a soft drink all over her clothes and Karl's car had a flat tire, which caused them to be late. Therefore you probably would assume that Dottie was using the cliché phrase to be polite.

Cliché conversation has a place in casual talk with acquaintances and friends. It is also useful in meeting new people. In fact, many people who are ill at ease with others often become more poised when they learn to chat with people they meet. On the other hand, a relationship cannot go very far with only this low level of communication.

## REPORTING THE FACTS ABOUT OTHERS

The second level of communication still does not involve telling much about the self. People mainly tell what so-and-so has said or done. Much of what is called gossip comes under this level. Those who communicate do not tell their ideas or feelings about the events, but simply report them.

Talking about their practice one night in the shower, Jefferson told Ted about the argument that another player had with the coach.

Karen announced to her family one evening that Mort and Allegra just got engaged. Lynise told her older sister that she overheard their parents talking last night. It sounded to her as if they were considering a divorce.

In each of these examples the people probably have ideas or feelings about what they are saying. However, if they only report the facts, communication stays at the second level.

## TELLING YOUR IDEAS

At the third level of communication, there is some sharing of the self. People take a small risk in telling others their ideas, judgments, and decisions. Each person has ideas about how things should be done and what should happen. To share these is the first step in really revealing to others who you are.

This level of communication corresponds to the second spoke on the relationship wheel. In telling your ideas you are beginning self-revelation. However, at this stage, trust usually hasn't been established. You are apt to be watching for acceptance or rejection. If it appears that rejection is likely, you will go back to earlier, safer levels of communication.

As Tom and Sandy walked down the hall after sociology class, Tom remarked, "I think Mr. Clapp should give the assignments at the beginning rather than the end of class. That way there will be enough time to ask questions about what he expects."

Sandy replied, "Well, I'm sure he thinks we're all smart enough to be able to figure it out." Tom took her comment as rejection and quickly changed the subject.

### experiences in human relations

COMMUNICATING YOUR IDEAS

There are many direct and indirect ways of communicating your ideas and judgments to others. One interesting way people do this is through the symbols they have printed on their checks when they have a personal checking account.

From a bank, obtain a brochure which shows all the possible symbols which can be ordered on checks. If you were opening up a checking account, which symbol would you choose for your checks? Why do you think this symbol represents you? Find out what symbols others in your class would choose. How do these choices communicate something about their ideas? It might be interesting to talk with someone who handles a great number of checks each day (such as a grocery store checker) and find out his or her reactions to the symbols which people have on their checks.

● ● ● ● ● ● ● ● ● ● ● ● ● ● ● ● ● ● ●

### SHARING YOUR FEELINGS

It might appear that by telling your ideas, your decisions, and your judgments you have communicated your self to others. However, there is much more of yourself that you can share. Sharing your feelings or emotions with another allows you to begin to know each other. It helps you reach emotional intimacy and begin to get your needs met.

Marion announced to her group of friends that she had decided to go to State College next fall. When she begins to share her feelings about her decision, she will communicate on the fourth level. She might tell her feelings of anticipation at the new experience ahead of her. She could confide her fear that she may not do well at such a big school or her excitement at living away from home for the first time.

One block which keeps people from telling their feelings is that they may have been taught that emotions are bad. Children are told that it is "silly" or "sissy" to cry. Teenagers are instructed to "stop moping around!" People learn to feel guilty or ashamed about certain feelings. Therefore they feel very naked or exposed if they tell those feelings to others.

In addition, some people think that certain emotions are better than others. Love is better than hate, happiness is better than sadness, and joy is better than anger. Therefore these people deny that they feel the "bad" emotions.

There is nothing basically good or bad about any emotion. It is the actions that people take as a result of their emotions that can be called good or bad. You do not have control over the emotions you feel. However, you do have control over what you *do* about your feelings.

Tanya was afraid whenever she thought about starting her new job as a nurses' aide. She was afraid she might not be able to do the work or that she might do the wrong thing for a patient. Her fear was a natural part of starting a new job. She could have let her fear control her and quit the job before she started. However, she used her fear to keep her extra alert the first month on the job. Her fear actually helped her do a good job learning her duties. Feelings of fear can have either good or bad results. Tanya was able to control her feelings and use them to work to a happy outcome.

## experiences in human relations

### SHARING YOUR FEELINGS

Individuals often find it hard to tell their feelings and emotions. The following experiences will give you practice in telling how you feel.

• Face your partner and rapidly exchange

Unit 3: Relating to Others

*Everyone experiences a wide range of emotions. People learn to control and express their emotions differently.*

brief sentences based on the sentence forms given below. When each of you has given several examples of one sentence form, go on to the next. Try to be as honest as you can in saying what you feel.

I need _____ and that (or it) makes me feel _____

I want _____ and that makes me feel _____

I expect _____ and that makes me feel _____

I lack _____ and that makes me feel _____

• Many things happen to people each day and they have an emotional, feeling response to each event. In some cases, the reaction is so slight that the person is not even aware of it. At other times the response can be very powerful and strong. This experience will help identify some of the emotional responses which people can have to specific events. It should help you become more aware of how the same event or judgment can cause a variety of emotional responses.

Prepare a statement or a judgment about some event or idea. Ask your classmates to do this too. In turn, read your statements and suggest some possible emotional reactions.

For example, you might say, "I think that Sue is intelligent." Some possible emotional reactions might include:

". . . and I am jealous."

". . . and I feel frustrated."

". . . and I am proud to be her friend."

". . . and it makes me ill at ease to be with her."

". . . and I feel inferior to her."

". . . and I feel like running away from her."

## PEAK COMMUNICATION

The fifth and highest level of communication is called peak communication. It is based on complete openness and honesty. At these times, which are usually quite rare, the partners are in perfect accord or harmony with each other. They know that each one's reaction is shared by the other, that both feel each other's happiness or sadness.

Peak communication is never a permanent condition. When it does occur between intimate friends, family members, or dating partners, it is usually a memorable experience.

Mario and Anna had spent their Saturday painting the living room in their apartment. That evening, tired from their work, they went for a leisurely walk through the wooded park in their neighborhood. As they paused to watch the sun go down, they felt in perfect communion with each other. They shared their satisfaction of a job done together, their pleasure at the beauty of the trees and sunset, and their joy at being together.

## experiences in human relations

### LEVELS OF COMMUNICATION

There are several levels of communication between people. It is easier to talk about what happens to others than it is to talk about what happens to you. It is easier to talk about distant events and feelings than those which are taking place right now. The following experience will show how some levels of communication are easy to use. However, as messages become more intimate and revealing, communication becomes more difficult.

Choose a partner with whom you are comfortable. As you go through the following steps, think about how difficult or easy it is for you to do each one. Insert the names of people you know in place of the letters, when appropriate. When you have finished all six steps, your partner should repeat the steps while you listen.

- Tell your partner how A felt about B, neither person being present.
- Tell your partner how A now feels about B, neither person being present.
- Tell your partner your past feelings about C, who is not present.
- Tell your partner your present feelings about C, who is not present.
- Tell your partner your past feelings about him or her.
- Tell your partner your present feelings about him or her.

Did you find it easier to talk about feelings concerning someone else than about feelings toward your partner? Why are people uncomfortable dealing with their present feelings toward others? Were you more uncomfortable listening to your partner's past and present feelings toward you than listening to feelings about someone who is not present?

### TO SUM UP...

1. What are the five levels of communication?
2. What does each level of communication represent?
3. Describe the purpose of "small talk."
4. How is gossip related to the five levels of communication?
5. Which levels of communication involve self-revelation?
6. At which level of communication do people really begin to know each other?
7. Why is the highest level of communication not permanent?

Unit 3: Relating to Others

*Specific body positions and mannerisms go along with the five communication patterns.*

## PATTERNS OF COMMUNICATION

A person can communicate in a number of different ways. Studies of how people communicate with each other show that certain patterns occur often. Most people become comfortable in one pattern or style of communication. As a result, they use that style in most of their interaction with others.

When people are anxious or under stress, they use one of the communication patterns called placating, blaming, computing, or distracting. These patterns are used to avoid a threat of rejection. In addition, people use these four patterns to help conceal weaknesses. These patterns, plus a fifth pattern called leveling, have body positions which go along with the pattern. These positions show through the body what the person is saying through words.

### Ch. 7: Communicating with Others

### BLAMING

Another pattern of communication is that of *blaming* others. The blamer is a fault finder, a boss, and a dictator. Blamers act superior to others and hope people will think they are strong. They give the impression that, "If it weren't for you, everything would be all right." A person who uses the blaming pattern is loud and tyrannical, putting everything and everyone down. The blaming pattern of communication often goes with an effort to control others.

Blaming is a communication pattern that often occurs among brothers and sisters. Laura and Carol share a bedroom and have many fights over the use of the space. A typical argument begins when Laura says, "You are the sloppiest person I ever saw. You ruin this room with your big messes. Why do I have to have such a mess for a sister?"

In reply, Carol says, "Well, I like that! You're the one that is always coming in here messing up my projects. You've ruined some of my best work by throwing it in the corner. I don't know why you can't appreciate the creative work I do. You are about as big a slob as I know."

Each sister resorts to blaming the other. Little true communication exists which could begin to solve their differences.

### COMPUTING

People who use the *computing* pattern of communication are very careful to hide all their feelings. They are sensible, correct, and "calm, cool, and collected." The computer uses big words and tries to stay away from all emotional upsets.

Many people would like to be a computer since they feel that it is good to hide all emotions. However, the computers are never able to get close to other people to develop intimacy. Unable to communicate with others

*The blaming pattern of communication is often used during arguments between family members.*

### PLACATING

People who are *placating* communicate so that other people don't get angry. In essence, they say, "Whatever you want is OK. I'm just here to make you happy." People who use this pattern of communication are sometimes known as "yes-men." No matter what, placaters never disagree with others. They communicate in a manner they think will please others.

Jenny and Joe had been dating for quite a while. Jenny wanted to break off the relationship, but Joe didn't. In an effort to please her and hold her affection, he became a placater. He agreed with everything she said, did everything she told him to do, and tried to win her approval in every way he could think of. Many people are like Joe in their relationships. They have so great a fear of being rejected or ignored that they turn all their efforts toward pleasing others rather than expressing themselves.

### Unit 3: Relating to Others

on the most meaningful levels, they rarely go above the level of telling their ideas.

Gina tries to be calm and cool in her relations with others. One night, Don came to pick her up for a football game, but she wasn't ready. Twenty minutes later, she came downstairs to find Don upset. He muttered, "Hurry up, I particularly didn't want to miss the kick-off."

She replied, "Why Don, don't be so upset. I came as fast as I could. Whether we are there for the kick-off or not won't affect the game."

At the game, Gina saw someone from the opposing school with whom she was acquainted. She spent almost an entire half sitting and chatting with her friend.

After the game in the car, Don blew up at her. "I could have strangled you tonight," he said. "First you were late. Then you spent half the game sitting with your friend and ignoring me entirely. I expect you to give me some consideration when you go out with me."

In a calm voice Gina replied, "I really don't understand why you are so upset. I only had a nice talk with an old friend. I expected you to be mature and adult about it. Instead you have been acting in a very childish way all evening." As you can imagine, Gina's calm, detached reply just made Don more angry.

### DISTRACTING

The fourth pattern is the *distracting* pattern. Whatever the distractor does or says is not related to what anyone else is saying or doing. Distracters rarely make a response to the topic under discussion, and may ignore everyone's questions or ask their own on a different subject. The distracting person often acts as if the surroundings are meaningless.

Joan often uses the distracting pattern and as a result is known as a scatterbrain. In the space of a few minutes one afternoon, she managed to confuse everyone. First, a group of friends were discussing their grades on a paper that had been returned that day. When someone asked Joan how she had done, she replied, "Sophie, did you buy that skirt at the boutique downtown?" The conversation then turned to places where the newest fall fashions could be found.

Suddenly Joan interrupted, "Lola, you have mud all over your shoes." Shortly after this, the group broke up and everyone went home.

### LEVELING

The leveling response is the only one which can help build better communication. Many people use the placating, blaming, computing, or distracting patterns to communicate. However, these patterns do not help them build good relationships which will meet their needs. The leveling response goes along with relating person-to-person.

In leveling you say what you think or feel instead of what the other person expects. You can agree if you really want to—not just because you think you should. Leveling lets you disagree if you really want to, not just because you want to impress someone by disagreeing. Finally, leveling lets you change your mind if you want to and if there is a need to do so.

The leveling response is a total response. If you are truly responding with what you feel, your words, voice tone, and body will all send the same message. Leveling helps you live as a whole person. It allows you to be in touch with your thoughts, values, feelings, and body. It is the best way you have of letting others know who and what you are.

In leveling, you take responsibility for yourself and for what you see and feel. Some people think this means that they are free to criticize others. They think leveling means telling what they see or feel is wrong about someone or something. However, leveling does not mean attacking others. It simply means describing how *you* feel. It means telling both the positive and negative things you feel in a way that does not hurt others.

One night when Mr. Juarez came home from work his wife met him at the door with her usual kiss. He said, "Honey, I've had a terrible day at work. My supervisor was really down on my back and I don't think anything went right. If you start telling me about your day at school, I probably won't listen. I'm sure that will make you upset, too. I'd like to just go lie down for about a half an hour and calm down and relax. I think then that I can be reasonably pleasant."

Since Mrs. Juarez was sympathetic, she left him alone as he requested. Later, Mr. Juarez was able to participate as usual in the family activities that evening. If Mr. Juarez had not been able to level about his feelings and need for quiet, the result could easily have been a quarrel with his wife and a ruined evening.

Being able to level with others in telling your true feelings and thoughts is important if you wish to build strong relationships with others. The leveling response helps to establish trust and understanding. These are essential in a good relationship. It may be a risky process to open up your inner self to others. However, that is the only way that people can truly come to know and care for each other.

## experiences in human relations

### PATTERNS OF COMMUNICATION

The patterns of communication known as placating, blaming, computing, distracting, and leveling have body positions which are often easy to identify. In this experience take the exaggerated position described for each pattern of communication. Hold each position for one minute.

*Placating:* Get down on one knee, wobbling a bit, and put out one hand in a begging fashion. Put your head up as if looking at someone towering over you. Talk to the person over you. How does your voice sound? Does it seem more natural to say "yes" in this position?

*Blaming:* Stand with one hand on your hip and the other arm stretched out with your index finger pointing straight out. Screw up your face, curl your lips, and hold your throat muscles tight. You are now ready to call names and criticize everything in sight.

*Computing:* Sit down in a chair and imagine that your spine is a long, heavy steel rod reaching from your buttocks to your neck. Pretend that you have an iron collar, ten inches wide, around your neck. Stay as motionless as possible and try to talk without moving your mouth any more than necessary. Do not gesture with your hands. When you speak, do you find yourself talking in a monotone?

*Distracting:* Stand with your knees together and your feet apart. Hunch your shoulders and have your arms and hands going in opposite directions. Imagine you are a lopsided top, that is constantly spinning.

*Leveling:* Stand with your feet firmly on the floor spread at a comfortable, stable, distance. Have upright, but not rigid, posture. Hold your arms loosely at your sides. Keep all your muscles relaxed, but ready to move. Look ahead rather than down or up.

When you have held all the positions for at least one minute, think about how you felt in each position. Which position seemed the most natural to you? Was that because it is a position which you use frequently? Which position was most unnatural or uncomfortable for you? Did this position go with a communication pattern that you rarely, or never, use? Were any

Unit 3: Relating to Others

of the positions that you assumed common ones for people that you know? How does this experience help you see that more is involved in communication than mere words?

● ● ● ● ● ● ● ● ● ● ● ● ● ● ● ● ● ●

## A Comparison of Patterns

A noted family therapist, Virginia Satir, suggests that she can predict when meeting a new group of people how patterns of communication will be used. Fifty percent of the people will say "yes" no matter what they feel or think (in other words, placate). Thirty percent will say "no," no matter what they feel or think (blame). Another fifteen percent will say neither "yes" nor "no" and will give no hint of their feelings (compute). One half percent will behave as if "yes," "no," or feelings did not exist (distract). Finally, four-and-a-half percent will be real and express their true feelings (level).

The case of Langston and Gwendolyn, who have been dating each other for quite a while, compares the five patterns of communication. One day Langston heard from a friend that Gwendolyn was seen the previous night with Leroy. Consider the different responses Gwendolyn might make when Langston asks her about it.

Placating: "Langston, I'm so sorry. Please forgive me for being so disloyal. I'll never do it again!"

Blaming: "Well, it's your own fault. If you'd take me to the places where I want to go, I wouldn't have to go with anybody else."

Computing: "I don't see that I have to answer to you about it. We never agreed to see each other exclusively so I can't see that who I go out with is any concern of yours. I have the situation under control."

Distracting: "Langston, I'm so excited that we're going to be able to get tickets for the next concert. I've been just dying to see that group perform!"

Leveling: "Golly, I'm sorry if my seeing Leroy hurt you. I guess I should have told you ahead of time about it. I like you a lot, Langston. But I'm just really not ready to settle down to seeing only you."

## TO SUM UP...

1. What are the five patterns of communication?
2. Why do people act in a placating manner?
3. How do people act when they are using the blaming pattern?
4. Describe a person who uses the computing pattern of communication.
5. What is the main characteristic of the distracting pattern of communication?
6. How can the leveling response help build better relationships?
7. Describe the characteristics of the leveling response.

## LEARNING COMMUNICATION SKILLS

Most communication with others is casual and "off the cuff." People rarely notice how they communicate with others or how others communicate in return. Often attention to how you communicate can lead to better communication skills. As a result, you can have better relationships with others.

**Ch. 7: Communicating with Others**

*Improving communication skills can lead to better relationships.*

## experiences in human relations

### A COMMUNICATION QUIZ

Most people think that they communicate fairly well with others. When it comes to learning new communication skills, they are likely to think that they "know enough to get by." The following communication quiz will help you judge how well you are able to communicate.

*Instructions:* Use a separate piece of paper to record your answers to this quiz. Read the entire quiz before answering any of the questions. You must work quickly, for only those people who do will be able to finish the quiz within the three-minute time limit.

1. Put your name in the upper right hand corner of your paper.
2. Put your address under your name.
3. Number from 1 to 10 down the left side of the paper.
4. Put three small boxes beside number 1.
5. Underline your name.
6. Write the word communication beside number 2.
7. Wet your finger and put a fingerprint on the other side of your paper.
8. Put a small X in each of the three boxes.
9. Punch three small holes beside number 3 with your pen or pencil.
10. Next to number 4, add the numbers 136 and 244.
11. Take the sum of question 10 and subtract 58 from it.
12. Divide the answer to question 11 by 2.
13. Tear off a small corner of your paper.
14. Place a circle around your fingerprint.
15. After reading all the questions, answer only 1 and 2.

## Understand the Context of the Message

Each communication message takes place in a specific situation called a *context*. The context can include the physical setting where the message is sent. It can also include the mood or feelings of the people who are communicating. The events or activities people have done or are doing are part of the context.

Vera received a low grade on a civics test which Mrs. Rossman handed back one Thursday. Because she wanted to talk about her grade with the teacher, Vera stopped by the classroom after school. The context of their discussion had several aspects. The classroom where Mrs. Rossman taught was the physical context. Vera's poor test score caused her to be worried and upset during their talk. Mrs. Rossman was tired after a long day teaching. In addition, she felt as if she were catching a cold. All of these factors made up the context of their talk about how Vera could improve her civics grade.

The context of a message may determine the meaning of what is said. Most people tend to ignore or not think about the context when talking to others. However, many problems can be avoided if you notice the context when you are communicating.

A certain context may have very different meanings for two people who experience it and try to communicate. Understanding the context means you are aware of what has happened to others to influence the messages they send. This part of communication is similar to the idea that people have different perceptions of the same event.

For example, Will and Marshall went biking one Sunday afternoon. Will was pleased to get out of town and do one of his favorite activities. The messages he sent were happy and full of excitement. Marshall, however, had had an unsuccessful job interview the day before. As they left, he was still upset and depressed over not being able to find a job. The messages he sent were negative ones, which reflected his gloom. Neither partner was aware of the context of the afternoon for the other one. Before too long, Will was mad at Marshall for being such a "wet blanket." Marshall thought Will was unsympathetic and a show-off. The afternoon that had been planned with such promise was a disappointment to both.

## Send "I-Messages"

One of the most destructive kinds of communication results in blaming and accusing other people. These kinds of messages are known as "You-messages." "You-messages" are common in all types of relationships but are perhaps most often used in families.

Mrs. Blake tells her fifteen-year-old son Tim, "*You* are the most impossible son! Don't *you* ever get in on time? *You* shouldn't stay out so late at night. If *you* don't stop that, then we're going to have to do something about it."

The foods and nutrition teacher, Miss Thompson, stopped to look at the lunch Clara was preparing. The lunch was for the children in the play school which the home economics department ran. "Clara," she said. "*You* should know better than that! *You*'ve got to be neater—your work area is a mess. I don't know how *you* can expect to get a job in food service working like that."

"You-messages" such as these are accusing and blaming. The person receiving "You-messages" feels unworthy and judged by the other. In contrast, people send "I-messages" when they simply tell how a situation makes them feel. When you send an "I-message,"

**Ch. 7: Communicating with Others**

you tell how the other person's actions seem to you. You make your messages statements of fact about you.

In the example above, Mrs. Blake could have sent "I-messages" by saying, "Tim, *I* am really upset about the times you have been getting in at night. When you are so late, *I* worry that something has happened to you and *I* can't sleep. *I* would feel much more comfortable if you could get in a bit earlier. How do you think we could come to some agreement about this?"

For Miss Thompson, an "I-message" might have been, "Clara, *I* am concerned that the food you are preparing might not be healthy for the children. This is because your hands are not clean and your hair isn't tied back. *I* can see that you have lots of equipment and supplies scattered over your work area. *I* would find it very hard to work in such cluttered conditions."

"I-messages" are more effective than "You-messages" for a number of reasons. An "I-message" is less likely to cause bad feelings and rebellion. It is not very threatening to communicate to others the effect of their behavior on you. It is much more harmful to suggest that there is something bad about others because they behaved that way.

"I-messages" place control for action right on the other person. This helps avoid power conflicts. People may choose to continue to

*This father is using an "I-message" to tell how a situation makes him feel.*

## Unit 3: Relating to Others

do something that you don't like, that hurts you, or that you disapprove of. However, they have done it knowing exactly what you think about that action. An "I-message" tells others that you are leaving the responsibility of changing to them. You trust them to handle the situation well and to respect your needs. You give them a chance to act constructively to build your relationship.

Sending "I-messages" is not easy. They don't come naturally to most people. Just as in making the leveling response, it takes courage and inner self-confidence to show your feelings in a relationship. When you send honest "I-messages," you risk becoming known to others as you really are. Sending "I-messages" also says that you are no longer trying to control the other person's behavior. Some people with a high need for power find this very frightening.

By sending messages that tell what you feel, you build intimacy with others. This leads to the kind of strong relationships which give the most satisfaction.

## experiences in human relations

### SENDING "I-MESSAGES"

Being able to say sentences which begin with "I," describe what you see, and tell how you feel, is essential in order to communicate with "I-messages."

Choose a partner and take turns making statements beginning with the word "I." Start with "easy" messages. As you become used to doing this, try to tell more and more of what you feel as you go along. Make each statement short and avoid sentences that say "I_____ because _____." This experience is to emphasize *what* you feel rather than *why*.

• • • • • • • • • • • • • • • • • • •

### LISTEN

When people think of improving their communication skills, they most often think about expressing themselves more clearly. However, the most perfectly worded message will not be communicated if the other person is not listening. Being able to receive a message is as important as being able to send one. Effective communication occurs only when the listener hears and receives the message in the same way the speaker meant it.

Most people do not really listen to each other. They may be concerned with what they have said and what they will say next. As a result, they basically ignore what the other person is saying. Another barrier to really listening is the tendency to judge what the other person is saying. People also become used to "listening with half an ear." Parents and children are often guilty of this as they halfheartedly listen to the words the others are saying.

Listening is perhaps the hardest communication skill to learn. Listening involves more than hearing the words of the speaker. It includes hearing the meaning and the feelings behind the words as well. To listen well, you must suspend your own value judgments. This way, you can understand the speaker's thoughts and feelings just as he or she is experiencing them. This means having *empathy* for others as you listen—feeling their feelings and seeing the world through their eyes.

Tammy and Robin were walking home from school one day. Tammy was telling Robin about the latest argument with her current dating partner. Suddenly Tammy stopped talking, then finally said, "You know, Robin, I have finally figured out why it seems like all your friends end up telling their troubles to you. It's because you listen! I never thought about it before. When I talk to you, you always pay close attention to what I'm saying. I feel that you almost experience what I do. It's sure nice to have someone you can talk to."

## experiences in human relations

### LISTENING SKILLS

Listening is perhaps one of the most neglected communication skills. Most people listen to others, but often they don't "hear" what the others are saying. The following experiences will help you become conscious of how you listen. They may help you improve your listening skills.

• This experience is to be done during a class or group discussion. Before telling your ideas, you are to restate the essence of the last speaker's statement. When the last speaker says that he or she has been understood, you can go on with your contribution to the discussion. One member of the group should act as a monitor to see that the process is carried out. This means that each person restates and understands the last speaker's meaning before making other comments.

This procedure will probably seem very awkward to you because it is slow and often frustrating. However, it gives you a chance to see how often people don't listen to the messages of others. Instead, they are thinking ahead to what they will say next.

• This next experience will help you realize how frustrating it can be to send messages to

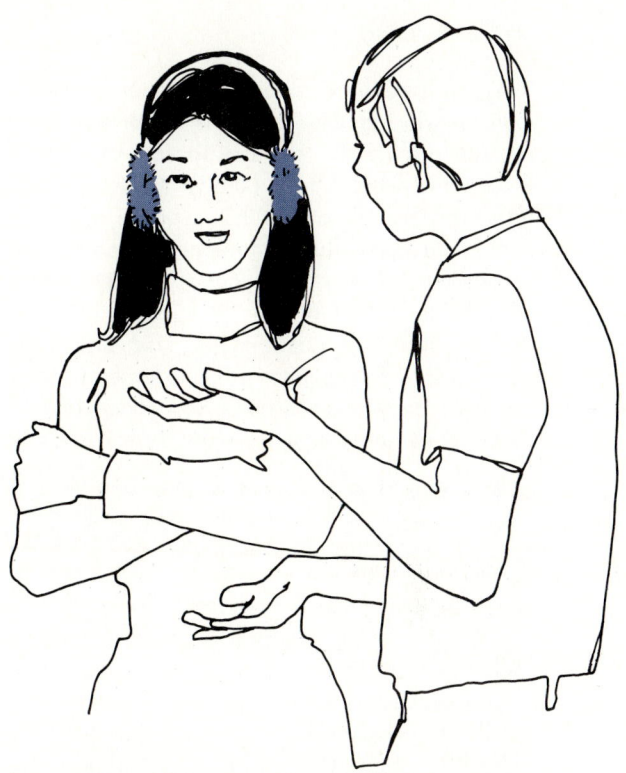

*No communication can occur unless the other person listens.*

someone who isn't listening. Talk to a partner about something that is important to you. As you speak, your partner should be silent, avert the eyes, and slowly move away—in other words, your partner is obviously not listening. What is your reaction to this? Do you feel like pushing or pulling your partner back?

Change roles and be aware of how it feels to not respond to someone. Do you want to walk away? Do you resent your partner? Do you have feelings of power over the other person since they need to keep talking to fill the gap you've created by your silence?

• One reason people don't listen carefully to others is that they are busy preparing their own contributions to the conversation. This experience helps show how this can happen.

## Unit 3: Relating to Others

With three other people, conduct a discussion on why communication is important. During the discussion, you are to talk about the topic. However, what you say must be unrelated to what the others in the group say. This should illustrate what can happen when people are so busy thinking of what to say next that they forget to listen.

After three or four minutes, stop and think about how it felt to ignore the statements made by the others in the group. How did it feel to make statements and have no one respond?

● ● ● ● ● ● ● ● ● ● ● ● ● ● ● ● ● ● ● ● ●

### Passive Listening

People who have learned how to listen well generally use two skills in listening. One is called passive listening. In passive listening, your responses do not tell any of your own ideas or judgments. Instead, you invite the others to share their feelings or ideas. The simplest responses in passive listening are: "Really," "I see," or "How about that!"

Other responses can be more direct such as "I'd like to hear more about it," "Tell me the whole story," or "This seems like something important to you."

Terry used passive listening skills when he met Al after a golf tournament. Al was jubilant and hailed Terry with, "Hey, did you hear that I made a hole in one today?"

Terry replied, "Why you lucky dog. Tell me how it happened."

As Al began to relate the story, Terry's comments included, "Wow," "No kidding?" and "You did, huh?" He was able to feel Al's excitement, and his interest allowed Al to relive that special moment.

### Active Listening

Active listening is the other listening skill. It usually is more effective than passive listening. In active listening, both the person who is sending the message and the one who is receiving it are involved in the process.

In active listening, you try to understand what the speaker is feeling or what the message really means. Putting the message in your own words, you send it back to see if you really heard what the speaker meant. You do not send back a message of judgment, advice, or logic. You send back only what you feel the sender's message meant—nothing more and nothing less. You can focus on sending back the content message or the feeling message you have received.

Melinda and Janet were talking one day about Melinda's parents. Melinda said, "The thing that really bothers me the most is that my folks can't stand George."

Janet answered, "You feel upset that your parents don't like your boyfriend."

Melinda said, "That's for sure. They have never tried to get to know him."

"You feel disappointed," commented Janet, "because they haven't made any effort for you."

In this example, Janet was sending back just what she thought Melinda's messages meant, without adding any of her own ideas. To be a good active listener, you must want to listen. It takes time and effort to pay attention to the feelings of the other person. Good listening is basic to understanding others. Skill in active listening is one way to learn to know and understand other people.

## experiences in human relations

### ACTIVE LISTENING

Active listening involves listening to the feelings behind the words of another speaker. This

**Ch. 7: Communicating with Others**

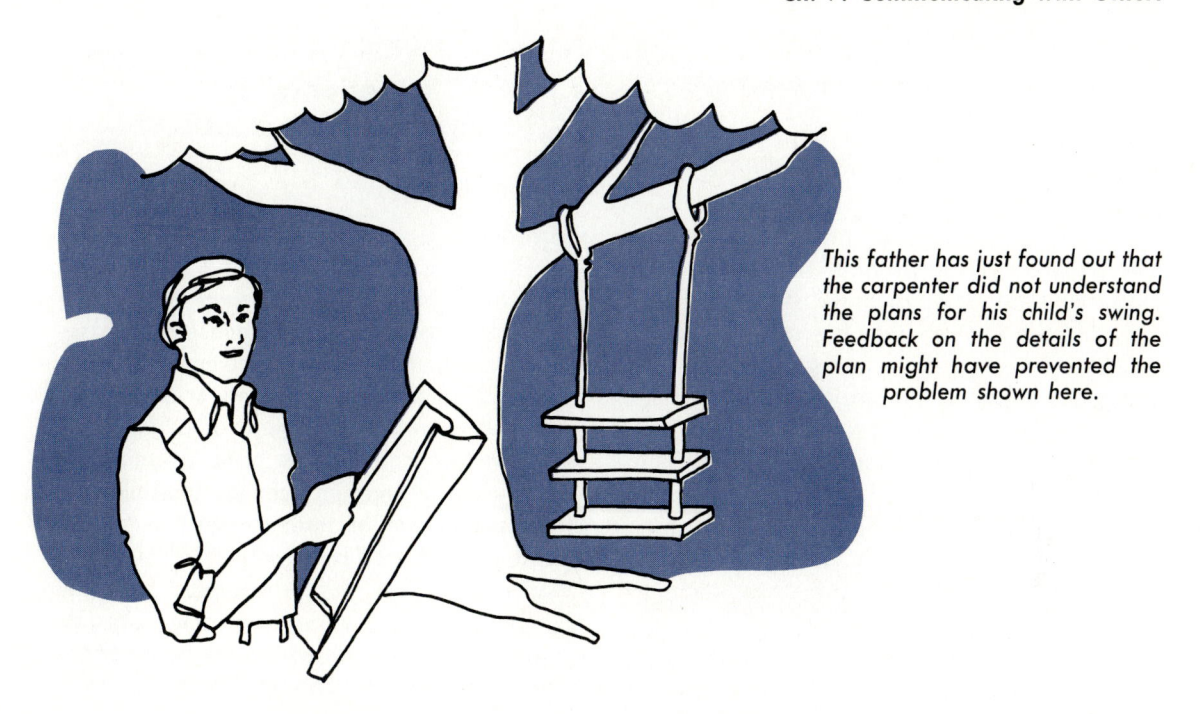

*This father has just found out that the carpenter did not understand the plans for his child's swing. Feedback on the details of the plan might have prevented the problem shown here.*

can be very hard because, when most people listen, they listen only to the words being spoken. The following experience will help you begin to learn the skills of active listening.

Sit facing a partner. Think about some of the disappointing moments of your life and some of the most meaningful experiences you have had. When you are ready, in a few sentences, tell your partner about one of the disappointing experiences. Your partner then reflects back the meaning of what you said, beginning with the words, "You must have felt. . . ."

Exchange roles and have your partner tell a disappointing experience while you respond with, "You must have felt. . . ."

When you have talked about several disappointing experiences, begin telling some of your most meaningful experiences. Again, respond using the sentence beginning, "You must have felt. . . ."

Active listening can be called "listening between the lines." Practice asking yourself, "What is my partner really trying to say? What is my partner feeling?" Being able to feel another person's disappointing and joyful experiences helps build strong relationships.

● ● ● ● ● ● ● ● ● ● ● ● ● ● ● ● ●

## Feedback

*Feedback* is a way of checking out the meaning of messages. Because words, ideas, and gestures are often vague, the people receiving messages are sometimes confused as to what the sender means. Feedback helps listeners be sure that they understand what the speaker actually means.

Active listening is one form of feedback. As listeners send back their version of the speaker's message, they have a chance to clear up

155

## Unit 3: Relating to Others

any misunderstanding. Beryl said, "I sure wish we weren't going to have that physics test on Friday."

June answered, "You feel worried because you won't have enough time to study before Friday."

However, Beryl then said, "Oh, that's not it. There's plenty of study time, but Friday's my birthday. I sure hate to think of my birthday being spoiled by an old physics test!"

Active listening or restating your partner's message is only one method to give and receive feedback. More direct feedback can be had by simply asking questions. When Sam came in after school one afternoon, he asked his mother, "Hey, when are we having supper tonight?"

His mother replied, "About six o'clock. Why? Are you hungry?"

"No," said Sam, "but Dick and I are going to work our consumer economics problems together tonight. I needed to know what time we would be eating."

You may also give and get feedback by making a statement that tells how you feel about the matter. Tony was treasurer of the Glee Club. He was worrying about a few members who still hadn't turned in their money from a recent club fund drive. Danny finally said, "You know, I think you're worrying too much about it. Most people will turn in their money sooner or later."

Tony answered, "Yes, but I've got to have $86 by Friday to pay for cleaning the blazers we wear for concerts. Unless the rest of the people turn in their money, I won't be able to pay the bill."

Feedback is important to listeners so that they are sure they understand what the speaker has said. Feedback is also important to the speaker. When you send a message to another person, you need feedback to know if you have been understood.

## experiences in human relations

### FEEDBACK

Feedback is essential to good communication. When both the listener and the speaker know that they understand and have been understood, more leveling responses are possible. In addition, the level of communication is likely to be higher. These experiences will help you become aware of some kinds of feedback and how they can improve communication.

• Have your partner complete the following statement in two or three sentences: "I can best describe myself by saying. . ." You are to listen and in your own words feed back the main points of your partner's statement. You do not approve or disapprove of what your partner says. Instead you respond by completing one of the following sentences:

"What I hear you saying is. . . ."
"By that you mean. . . ."
"It seems that. . . ."

Your partner must be satisfied that you have given back the essence of what was originally said. If your partner does not feel that you have understood, the message should be restated. More information should be given until you understand and can repeat the message to your partner's satisfaction.

Exchange roles, with your partner giving feedback to your statement describing yourself.

• Make what you believe to be a true statement to your partner. Your partner is then to repeat it to you mimicking your voice, tone, inflection, facial expression, body position, and movement. If your partner is not accurate in the feedback, say so and provide specific evidence of the differences. Then reverse roles, with you giving the feedback to your partner's statement.

Were you surprised at the amount of feedback there was from just one simple statement? Did any of your nonverbal messages conflict with the verbal one? Were you leveling as you sent your message?

• In this experience, sit facing your partner, while your partner makes a statement. You then respond with, "Do you mean. . ." to discover whether or not you have understood. Your aim is to ask "Do you mean. . ." questions until your partner has answered "yes" three times. For example:

"I think it's cold in here."
"Do you mean you are uncomfortable?"
"Yes."
"Do you mean that you think I should be cold, too?"
"No."
"Do you mean you want me to be aware of your coldness?"
"Yes."
"Do you want me to try to do something about it?"
"Yes."

Change roles so that you make the statement while your partner asks, "Do you mean. . . ."

## TO SUM UP. . .

1. What is the context of a communication message?
2. How can the same event have a different context for two people?
3. Give an example of a "You-message." Explain why "You-messages" are usually destructive.
4. What is an "I-message"?
5. Why are "I-messages" generally more effective than "You-messages"?
6. Why do people often not "hear" each other in conversation?
7. Explain why listening is considered a difficult communication skill.
8. Describe passive and active listening.
9. How is the listener involved in active listening?
10. What is feedback?
11. How can feedback promote more effective communication?

## NONVERBAL COMMUNICATION

Research has indicated that between sixty-five and seventy percent of people's communication with others is nonverbal. The way you walk, stand, dress, hold your head, drum your fingers, smile, or frown is important. These actions often tell others far more than your words. To communicate well with others, you must be aware of the nonverbal messages you send and receive.

### BODY LANGUAGE

Messages sent by the body often have specific meanings. A raised eyebrow shows disbelief, while a shrug of the shoulders can indicate indifference. When one person winks at another, that is often a sign of intimacy between them. Arms and legs which are crossed can indicate a tight, defensive posture. A person whose arms are loosely at the sides is more likely to be open and receptive to ideas and exchange. The pupils of the eyes tend to widen when the person has seen something pleasurable. A slap to the forehead shows forgetfulness.

Posture is very important in body language. A salesman trying to make a sale will sit erect on the edge of the chair while talking with the client. A student's slouching posture when listening to a lecture may show bore-

**Unit 3: Relating to Others**

*Becoming aware of the nonverbal messages people send can be important in learning to understand others.*

dom and lack of interest. Tenseness and nervousness can be indicated by a straight, rigid posture. Posture is quite closely related to fatigue, for a drooping posture often shows tiredness.

One problem in interpreting body language is that it is often vague and misleading. Even more than in verbal behavior, the message sent may not be the message that is received. In the area of nonverbal communication, feedback is used even less than in verbal exchanges.

For example, John was talking to Rosa one day in the hall. All of a sudden Rosa stopped answering John and became very withdrawn. John couldn't understand what had happened. From Rosa's body language, he thought that he must have angered her in some way. He was just about to walk away, but instead decided to find out what the problem was. He asked if he had done or said something to upset her. She replied, "Oh, no. It's just that I remembered that Mama said I should pick up some food after school at the grocery store. I was trying to think what I did with the list!"

Usually body language and spoken communication go hand in hand. When the body position reflects the words that are said, the message sent becomes stronger. This is what

## Ch. 7: Communicating with Others

happens in the leveling response. Leveling is a strong communication pattern because all the messages sent reinforce each other.

Problems sometimes occur in understanding body language. Sometimes the words a person says contradict the message of the body. This happens when people do not level with each other. The receiver is more apt to believe the body language because somehow it seems easier to fake a few words.

One night after school, Reba stopped in to talk with the home economics teacher, Mrs. Wong. When Reba asked if Mrs. Wong had time to talk about an assignment, Mrs. Wong said yes. However during the entire conversation, Mrs. Wong kept looking at her watch and moving nervously, as if she were worried about being late for another meeting. Her verbal and nonverbal messages did not match.

In another example, three-year-old Kim had broken a toy in the play school. She went up to Matt, the child development student who discovered the accident, and asked, "Do you like me?"

Matt replied, "Of course I do, now go back and play with the other children." However, Matt's tone of voice was cold, and he did not smile at Kim. The nonverbal message that he sent was that he was upset with her.

## experiences in human relations

### BODY LANGUAGE

Nonverbal messages are important in communicating with others. These experiences will help you become more aware of the many ways in which people communicate nonverbally.

- With a small group of your classmates, sit in a circle facing each other. Maintain complete silence for ten minutes and watch the nonverbal messages the others are sending. Watch their posture, their hands and feet, and how they place their arms and legs. Facial expressions may tell something of what the others are feeling. Can you recognize nervousness, edginess, confidence, or other feelings through the messages you are receiving?

- With other class members act out certain nonverbal messages. Some examples which you can easily communicate nonverbally are:

"I can't hear you."
"Come here."
"I'm cold."
"Quiet, Shh."
Hitchhiking.
"I'm tired."

What other examples can you act out? As the messages become more complex, are they harder to interpret correctly? Do others always receive your nonverbal messages in the way that you intended?

- Often people assume that the emotions they are feeling are obvious to others. However, emotions can be very easily misinterpreted.

Write a variety of emotions or feelings on small slips of paper. Examples might include energetic, bored, nervous, excited, loving, helpless, surprised, scared, happy, angry, stubborn, depressed, or disgusted. Put these slips of paper in a bowl, and you and your classmates each draw out one.

Along with your classmates, act out the emotions you drew, using gestures or nonword sounds. The others try to guess what emotion you are portraying. If you are self-conscious, it may be easier to close your eyes, concentrate on your assigned emotion, and let the expression come naturally to your face.

*Unit 3: Relating to Others*

This experience can be very interesting. People are often surprised that the messages they send, which seem very clear to them, are interpreted in many ways by others. This points out how hard it may be to figure out correctly others' nonverbal messages.

- Body language is important in carrying on a conversation. Often people give incomplete verbal messages, but "finish" their statements with gestures. This experience points out how hard it can be to communicate with others without body language.

You and a partner place your chairs back to back, about 46 centimeters [18 inches] apart. Sit down and talk to each other. After a few minutes of conversation, move your chairs about 5 meters [16.5 feet] apart, remaining back to back while you continue to talk.

When you are finished, talk about your experience with the others. How did you feel when you weren't able to look at your partner while you talked? Were you physically uncomfortable trying to carry on the conversation? Were there any changes when you moved your chairs farther apart? Does this experience tell you anything about why some people prefer not to talk on the telephone? Do you often communicate this way with others in your family? How important are eye-to-eye contact and gestures to your ability to feel comfortable in talking with another?

- Your choice of clothing can send strong nonverbal messages to others. With your classmates, collect a number of magazine pictures of people dressed in a variety of ways. What does their clothing tell you about each person? Now, imagine that all these people are attending the same event. What would their clothing tell about them then? Would all the garments be appropriate for school, a concert, work, a religious service, the beach, or other event? What message does inappropriate clothing give to others? How can people become more conscious of the messages their clothing gives to others?

● ● ● ● ● ● ● ● ● ● ● ● ● ● ● ● ● ● ● ●

## USE OF SPACE

Another way in which people communicate nonverbally is through the way they use the space around them. The distances people keep between themselves and others vary with the closeness of the relationships. There are four basic distances which most people use with others. They are:
- Intimate distance.
- Personal distance.
- Social distance.
- Public distance.

*Intimate distance* is the amount of space between people when they are very close to each other. It is usually less than 46 cm [18 in.]. Very close intimate distance is used in making love, in very close friendships, and when children cling to parents or to each other. The physical part of this distance is very important.

If two people do not have a close relationship with each other, intimate distance can be embarrassing. When a crowded subway or bus brings strangers into each other's intimate distance, people hold themselves tense and avoid touching, if possible.

*Personal distance* is from 0.5 to 1 m [1.7 to 3.2 ft.]. At this distance, you can still easily touch your partner. However, the physical aspect is not as important as in intimate distance. Conversation at a personal distance is private. When two people stop on the street to talk, they use this distance naturally.

*Social distance,* from 1 to 4 m [3.2 to 13 ft.], is the distance from which people transact business. Mr. Shallot uses this distance when he is talking to his employees. Teachers and students usually keep a social distance when they discuss class business.

*A crowded bus can make some people uneasy because they do not like strangers in their intimate or personal distances.*

**Ch. 7: Communicating with Others**

The last distance is *public distance,* which is over 4 m [13 ft.]. This distance is used with a group or in other impersonal situations. A speaker may use public distance to talk to a club meeting or to a classroom group.

## experiences in human relations

### INTIMATE DISTANCE

The intimate distance is generally reserved for those closest to people. When others with whom a person is not close enter the intimate distance, it is often uncomfortable.

Choose a partner with whom you are not well acquainted. Sit face to face with your knees touching. Put your right hand over your partner's left. Look directly into your partner's eyes and hold this position for two minutes while having a conversation.

Now do the same thing with a partner with whom you are well acquainted. Was there a difference in how you felt with the two partners? Were you more comfortable with your close friend? What was the most uncomfortable part of the experience for you? Do you think you are a person who enjoys having others enter your intimate distance? Or are you more comfortable if others stay at a personal or social distance?

• • • • • • • • • • • • • • • • • • • •

In addition, people have their own personal distances which are most comfortable. All people have *body bubbles*—invisible envelopes or bubbles of space around them which they consider their own.

Unit 3: Relating to Others

*Most people share their body bubbles as they develop close relationships with others.*

People usually become very uneasy when their body bubble is entered by strangers. This is why crowded elevators make most people uncomfortable. In contrast, when you are with people with whom you have close relationships, it is easy to share your body bubble.

Some people have larger body bubbles than others. When Ron goes to the library to do homework, he spreads his papers over half a table, as if to show that he needs that much space. In contrast, Arnold's body bubble is much smaller than Ron's. In the library, he always uses just the space in front of his chair. He isn't uncomfortable when someone he doesn't know works beside him.

One interesting aspect about the use of space is that different cultures and countries use space differently. Many people from the Middle East use what some Americans would consider an uncomfortably close distance for normal conversation. Instead of talking at a personal distance, the Arabs, for example, will go into their partner's intimate distance. Very often, some Americans find themselves slowly backing away when talking to someone who tries to decrease the distance.

Another way people use space is in the question of what belongs to whom. If Dad has a favorite chair, he will feel his space is invaded when he finds one of the children sitting in the chair to watch television. Often places aren't assigned in a classroom. However, many students sit in the same places day after day. They may resent someone else sitting in "their" chairs, even though they have no formal claim to the seats. How the space is used in a shared bedroom is often a source of conflict in families. In extreme cases, even putting something a few inches into the other person's "side" brings an instant fight!

## experiences in human relations

### USING SPACE

The way people use and react to the space around them is a very personal thing. People use space in ways that relate to their ability to communicate *with* others. Indeed their use of space communicates *to* others. Being able to relax often depends on whether people feel comfortable with the distances between them and others. This experience is to help you explore the distances at which you and others feel most comfortable.

Begin a conversation with a partner while the two of you stand about 5 meters [16.5 feet] apart, facing each other. As you talk, walk up to your partner (who remains still) until you touch each other. Then back slowly away until you reach the right distance to make conversation the most comfortable for you. At that point, stop the conversation. Measure the distance between you. Repeat the procedure with your partner walking toward you and then away from you while you remain still. Measure your partner's most comfortable distance.

Were there differences in the distance at which you each felt most comfortable? What might be the implication of this in your relationship with your partner? Repeat the experience with others whom you may not know as well or whom you know more intimately. Do you stop at a further distance with those people you don't know as well? Are you more comfortable at closer distances with those people you know intimately?

● ● ● ● ● ● ● ● ● ● ● ● ● ● ● ●

### Ch. 7: Communicating with Others

### TO SUM UP...

1. Approximately what percent of communication is nonverbal?
2. What are some examples of body language?
3. Why is it difficult to interpret body language correctly?
4. Why do people tend to believe nonverbal messages rather than verbal ones?
5. Describe the four distances which people use in communicating with each other.
6. What is the relationship between distance and the intimacy of the relationship?
7. What are body bubbles and how do people use them?

### COMMUNICATION RISKS AND BENEFITS

This chapter has covered many aspects of the communication process. In several places, it was pointed out that to communicate well is to risk attacks from others. You can be hurt by telling what you are feeling and by being honest in using the leveling response. It is easier to hurt and be hurt by another when open communication has occurred. This is because each knows where the worst hurt can be given to the other.

At the same time that effective communication has risks, it also brings benefits. As people learn to communicate verbally and nonverbally, they learn to know themselves and others better. Communication can help build relationships which satisfy and help

163

Unit 3: Relating to Others

"I KNOW YOU BELIEVE YOU UNDERSTAND WHAT YOU THINK I SAID, BUT I AM NOT SURE YOU REALIZE THAT WHAT YOU HEARD IS NOT WHAT I MEANT."

*Communication may be difficult at times, but learning to communicate well brings many rewards and satisfactions.*

both partners grow. It can bring profound moments in close relationships. Without these moments, human beings cannot grow and develop to their fullest potential.

### TO SUM UP...

1. Why is it easier to be hurt by others when you communicate honestly and openly?

2. Explain how effective communication can bring benefits to a relationship.

# CHAPTER 8

## *Role Relationships*

This chapter will help you to . . .
- Understand what roles are, how people assume them, and why they are important.
- Explain the advantages and disadvantages of relating to others through roles.
- Describe kinds of role conflict.
- Identify some of the changes which have occurred as traditional sex roles have broken down.
- Describe the kind of relationships people can develop when they go beyond the roles they play.

Josie shouted with glee when she saw the notice on the bulletin board. She had been chosen to play Mrs. Dolly Levi in the school performance of the play, *The Matchmaker*. Her excitement gave way to hard work as rehearsals began. She worked to learn her lines, to talk and gesture as Mrs. Levi would have done, to act like Mrs. Levi. She even tried to think as if she were Mrs. Levi. In every way possible, she tried to fit into the role of being Mrs. Levi.

Just as actors and actresses perform roles in the theatre or movies, people act out roles in real life.

## WHAT ARE ROLES?

A *role* is a position or part which you assume in your relationships with others. In *The Matchmaker*, Josie played the role of Mrs. Levi. In real life, Josie plays many roles as she relates to her family, friends, teachers, and drama coach. Some of her roles are daughter, sister, friend, and student.

Roles are an important part of living with and relating to others. In *role relationships*, people interact with each other in terms of the roles they are playing. People have always felt the need for roles and role relationships to define who they are to themselves and to

165

**Unit 3: Relating to Others**

*Roles people play in real life are very much like the role that this actor and actress are playing.*

others. In the middle ages, people were peasants or knights and ladies. Today, roles and the way people use them are more complicated than they were a thousand years ago.

**A Variety of Roles**

You fill many roles. Some are associated with your family life, your school life, and your social life. All people who live in a par-

166

ticular country are citizens, and anyone who spends money becomes a consumer. Many roles are related to leisure-time interests and hobbies.

Lonnie fills a variety of roles. Living with his father and stepmother, he is both son and stepson. He assumes the role of brother to his older sister. In his family, he is also nephew, uncle, grandson, brother-in-law, and cousin. He is a consumer, a citizen, a student at school, and a worker and employee at his job at the grocery store. In addition, he is a member of the YMCA's basketball team and a friend to his pals.

Belinda is a daughter to her parents but she doesn't have any other family roles. Her interest in music leads her to the role of church organist and director of a chorus she organized in an elementary school. She sings in the mixed choir and is an orchestra member. A friend, a student, a consumer, and a citizen, as Lonnie is, Belinda also is a dating partner and a member of student government.

The roles you hold are not permanent. As Belinda grows older, she may become a wife, homemaker, mother, and piano and organ teacher. At the same time, she will drop the roles of student, choir and orchestra member, and chorus director. She will still be a daughter, friend, consumer, citizen, and organist. Thus the many roles you fill vary over time as your life changes and you grow and develop new interests.

*Every person fills a variety of roles throughout life.*

## experiences in human relations

### THE ROLES YOU PLAY

You fill many roles in your daily life. You have roles you play in your family, in school, with your friends, and on a part-time job, if you have one. This experience is to help you become aware of the roles which you play. It also will help you become more aware of which roles are important in how you see yourself.

For this experience you will need at least ten index cards or small pieces of paper. On each

Unit 3: Relating to Others

card write one word or phrase which describes "who" you are. These phrases or words will actually be some of the roles which you fill.

When you have written your descriptions, arrange your cards in order of importance. Place first the card which gives what you think is your most important role. The cards at the bottom of your pile will contain the roles that you feel are less important to you as a person.

Think about how you have ordered your cards. Are there any cards that you wish you could eliminate? Are there ways you could exchange some of these cards for others? How could you do it?

If you feel comfortable doing so, compare your cards with those of others in the class. Do you have different cards? Have you arranged your cards differently? Discuss why and how the differences occurred.

● ● ● ● ● ● ● ● ● ● ● ● ● ● ● ●

### KINDS OF ROLES

The roles you fill include given, learned, and chosen roles.

### Given Roles

Some of your roles are given to you automatically. At birth, a male child becomes a son while a female child is a daughter. A baby is a sister or brother if there are other children in the family.

In the United States, children generally have the role of student between the ages of six and sixteen. When children begin handling money, they automatically become consumers.

Roles are given to children by their sex, the kind of family into which they are born, and the laws and customs of the country in which they live.

### Learned Roles

Other roles are learned by children as they grow up. Franklin learned to play the role of an athlete. He excelled in sports of all kinds and was rewarded by his parents for his skill in athletics. Sancha learned an entirely different kind of role in her deeply religious family. Her religious beliefs became very important to her as she assumed the role of worshipper. She learned to be devout because of her training and background.

Every family teaches its members to fill certain roles by the values and beliefs of that family. Just as families can help teach the roles of athlete and worshipper to their children, they can also teach the roles of gambler, thief, or alcoholic. Many roles which adults fill were originally learned when they were children living with their families.

As children grow older, they begin relating to their peers. New roles are learned from friends and acquaintances. In fact, children and adults are constantly learning new roles as they have new experiences and meet new people.

As Mr. Hall reached his early sixties, he became friends with Mr. Andress, who was retired. Mr. Hall had not known many retired people before, so he learned about the role of a retired man through his friendship with Mr. Andress. Several years later, when he retired, he knew what to expect in his new life.

An important point about roles is that the same role can be learned differently. Janis learned early that her role as a daughter was to be her mother's helper. She babysat for her younger brothers, often cooked and cleaned, and did other household tasks to help her mother.

In contrast to Janis, Avadner learned to play the role of daughter much differently. She wasn't taught any homemaking skills, but

*This couple has chosen to assume the roles of husband and wife.*

instead was encouraged to spend time playing outside, participating in sports, and working with her rock and mineral collection. Her parents expected her to tell them about her many experiences. Thus Avadner learned that a daughter could do many interesting activities away from home as long as she shared her experiences with her parents.

In much the same way, children going to school learn the role of student in various ways. Juan really enjoys school and spends much of his time reading and studying. He learned from his parents and teachers that to be a student means that he is expected to earn high grades. He is also expected to take advantage of opportunities to learn in out-of-school settings. For Sam, being a student involves showing up at school each morning, attending classes, and doing enough work to keep from failing.

How you fill certain roles and how you think certain roles should be filled depend on what you have learned. If Juan and Sam have different ideas about what it means to be a student, it is because of what they have learned from their parents, their peers, or their experiences.

## Chosen Roles

A final kind of role that people play involves those roles that are deliberately chosen. Generally, people begin choosing roles as they grow up, become more independent, and start making choices of their own. Orlando chose to continue in the role of student by going to college after high school

169

## Unit 3: Relating to Others

graduation. The opposite decision was made by Gina, who took a job, thus taking the role of worker. People chose to get married and become husbands and wives and later, perhaps, parents.

Sometimes it is hard to tell the difference between learned and chosen roles. If Tansy decides to be a student by attending college, that role may be chosen. However, if she has been taught that it is only by going to college that she will amount to something in life, her decision to continue being a student may be a learned role.

In much the same way, Karin decided to drop out of school during her junior year to get married. Her decision to give up the role of student and take on the role of wife would appear to have been deliberately chosen. However, her years of schooling taught her that there wasn't much reward for her in being a student. In addition, her mother, who had been married and divorced several times, taught her that life isn't worth living without a husband. So, in many ways, Karin's decision actually involves what she has learned about roles.

## experiences in human relations

### SOURCES OF ROLES

The roles that people play come from various sources. Some are given, others are learned, and some are chosen. This experience will give you some practice in thinking about these three kinds of roles.

Choose a person as a subject for a case study about roles. You may wish to choose someone you know very well or someone you'd like to know better. Talk with your subject about the various roles that he or she plays. Make a list of all the roles that your subject fills. Then try to figure out which of these roles were given to your subject, which were learned, and which were chosen. You may wish to check with your subject to see whether your ideas agree with his or hers.

Report your case study to your classmates. Compare the similarities and differences of your cases. Did some subjects fill many more roles than others? Were there any subjects who had most of their roles in one category? Did most of the subjects have their roles balanced between the three kinds? Can you see any differences between the roles of older and younger subjects? Male and female ones? What kinds of conclusions can you draw about the kinds of roles people fill?

### TO SUM UP...

1. What is a role?
2. Why are roles important?
3. What are some common roles that most people fill?
4. Explain why roles change over time.
5. Describe the three kinds of roles.
6. Why do different people learn the same role in different ways?

### HOW ROLES WORK

It is no surprise that people learn to think of themselves and others in terms of the roles they play. Roles are such a central part of people's lives that they become very important. However, there are advantages and disadvantages in relating to others only through roles.

**Ch. 8: Role Relationships**

*The roles of employer and employee help these two people know how to relate to each other.*

## ADVANTAGES OF ROLES

Roles make living with others much easier and comfortable. Just about any role that you play carries with it certain ideas about behavior, called *role expectations*. A person is expected to behave in a specific way for a certain role. This makes it easy for you to know how to act when you assume the role. Instead of having to find out by trial and error what you should or shouldn't do, the role itself sets your behavior.

When two people who are each filling a specific role meet, they have a ready-made basis for knowing how they are supposed to act with each other. Employer and employee, parent and child, teacher and student all have role expectations which they act out as they relate to each other.

When Bill joined the other fellows on the corner by the bowling alley, his role was as a member of his group of friends. They whistled at the passing girls and called to the people driving by in cars. Bill whistled and called as loudly as anyone, for that was the way members of his group expected each other to act.

In the same way, when Joan was hired to work part time at the florist's shop, she knew what to expect. As an employee she was to be prompt, work hard, and follow her boss's instructions.

When Carla and Fred became engaged, their roles as an engaged couple meant that they were to date only each other. Making plans for their future marriage and life together is an important part of their new roles.

## Unit 3: Relating to Others

Another way roles make relationships easier is by providing labels or ways of identifying others. Very often people are known by the roles they fill. Tom is pointed out as the captain of the swimming team. Janie is known as Tom's dating partner. President of the student body is Juanita's identifying role. Mrs. Vasquez is known to Juanita's friends in her role as Juanita's mother. In contrast, if someone is being pointed out who has no special role, a common comment is, "Oh, that's just somebody I know."

Many adults are known to others by their occupational roles. Mrs. Gary's role is daily maid at a local motel. Being a teacher is Mr. Terriscovich's occupational role. Teresa Barren is proud to be a bus driver. Everyone in the neighborhood knows Theodore Washington as the priest at the church on the corner.

## experiences in human relations

### ROLE BEHAVIOR

Roles help people know how to act in certain situations. In particular, when two people who are interacting with each other are both filling roles, certain behavior is expected. The following experience will help you see how people know how to act when given roles to play.

With a partner, act out the following situations:

- A *teacher* reminding a *student* that an assignment is overdue.
- A *parent* telling a *son* to run the cleaner in the living room.
- A *parent* giving the keys to the family car to the *daughter* for the evening.
- A *policeman* telling two *dating partners* parked in a car to move along.
- The dining room *supervisor* telling a new *employee* how the dishes are to be stacked.
- A *female* asking a *male* to go to a movie with her.

How did you feel as you played each role? Were the roles easy or hard to play? Did there seem to be a number of ways the situation could be handled? Or did there seem to be one main way that was most appropriate? How would the situation have been different if the roles to be played had not been given? For example, how would you have acted out the following: One person reminding another that an assignment is overdue, one person telling another to run the cleaner in the living room, one person explaining to another how the dishes are to be stacked?

● ● ● ● ● ● ● ● ● ● ● ● ● ● ● ● ●

### DISADVANTAGES OF ROLES

Filling certain roles can also be a disadvantage in getting to know others and relating to them on a person-to-person basis. When people fill certain roles and role expectations, they limit themselves. The role of employer may suggest that a person act in a certain way toward an employee. That cuts out many ways of relating to each other that both might have found satisfying.

Parents and children and brothers and sisters quite often find their family roles keep them from seeing each other as people. When Mr. Rabin says to Josh, "No son of mine is going to act like that," he is denying Josh has feelings and ideas of his own. It is as if he feels that Josh is his *son* and not a *person*. In turn, Josh calls his father "The Jailer" behind his back. He feels that his father is just being mean and stubborn when he forbids

## Ch. 8: Role Relationships

Josh to do something. Josh doesn't see his father as a person whose feelings of love and concern make him attempt to control his son.

Venetia and Pat are sisters who bickered and fought when they lived at home. Now that they each have their own job and own apartment, they have discovered that they like each other as people. After all those years together, they are now friends. Their roles as sisters prevented them from relating to each other as people.

Roles can lead people to *stereotype* others. A stereotype is usually based on a role or some other personal characteristic. It is a standardized idea of what people are or how they should behave. When you stereotype others, you expect everyone in a certain role to be the same, to "fit the same mold," to have no individuality. It is easy to stereotype all people who play the same role. When you use role expectations to stereotype others, you are kept from seeing them as people.

What are some common stereotypes? A football team captain may be stereotyped as an unfeeling "animal." A beauty queen may be considered a "dumb blonde." "Cold-hearted egghead" may be the label attached to the class valedictorian, while the student who smokes marijuana may be considered a "juvenile delinquent."

### experiences in human relations

**IS IT APPROPRIATE?**

When you fill a certain role, your behavior is often limited. You are expected to act in ways that are suitable for the role. Other behaviors are considered inappropriate.

The following checklist will help you begin to see how some behaviors may not be considered appropriate for certain people. Listed below are statements which ask if a certain behavior is appropriate for a specific person. List the numbers 1–15 on a separate piece of paper. Write "yes" beside the number for each item if you feel the behavior is appropriate. If you feel the behavior is not appropriate, place "no" beside the number.

Is It Appropriate . . .*

1. for a man to stay at home as a househusband and for the wife to be the main wage earner?
2. for a female to open doors for her male companion?
3. for males to knit or crochet for gift giving?
4. for a female student to work toward becoming a heart specialist or a United States Senator?
5. for a male to marry but not want children?
6. for male children to play with dolls?
7. for females to be on the school golf or tennis team?
8. for females to play basketball with males?
9. for teenage males to babysit?
10. to ask a male why a good looking man like himself isn't married?
11. for males to cry?
12. for males to arrange flowers?
13. for males to enjoy sewing?
14. for females to like woodworking?
15. to ask a male what he plans to do until he gets married?

Compile the answers of all the members of your class. How much agreement was there? Give reasons why you answered as you did.

*Checklist is from "Expanding Role Options for Males and Females," *Tips and Topics*, Vol. XV, No. 3, February 1975, p. 2.

Unit 3: Relating to Others

*Stereotyping people can be compared to trying to fit people who play certain roles into the same box or mold.*

Does being male or female limit how you can behave? How does it limit how others behave toward you?

• • • • • • • • • • • • • • • • • • • • • •

When you stereotype people, you do not allow them to be themselves. You keep them from having a personality beyond the role that they are playing. As a result, you lose the opportunity to relate to people as individuals.

In summary, roles can help make it easier to relate to others and to know the proper way to act in certain situations. At the same time, roles can interfere with knowing yourself and others. Roles can turn you into the kind of person the roles you play demand, instead of being the kind of person you are or would like to be. Roles and stereotypes can limit your ability to see others as they are and learn to relate to them as people.

## experiences in human relations

### SEX STEREOTYPING

Is your life limited by stereotyped roles? Are you missing many rewarding activities because they are stereotyped for the opposite sex? This experience will help you become more aware of how stereotyping may occur in your life.

On a piece of paper list twenty things that you love to do. When your list is finished, code what you have written in the following manner.

• Write SSM (sex-stereotyped male) beside the name of each activity that is considered more appropriate for males than for females.
• Write SSF (sex-stereotyped female) beside each activity that is considered more suitable for females.
• Write an N (neutral) beside those activities that are appropriate for either sex.

Now choose the activity on your list that is most important to you. Place a 1 in front of that activity. Identify four other activities that are especially important to you and label them in order, 2 through 5. Finally, write the approximate day when you last did each of the activities.

Think about the things you have written. Do you avoid certain activities because they are stereotyped "male" or "female"? How many sex-stereotyped activities for the opposite sex are included on your list? Are your five most important activities stereotyped for your sex? How long has it been since you did something that is an activity considered more appropriate for the opposite sex? What activities that you have previously avoided would you be willing

**Ch. 8: Role Relationships**

to try? If you like, discuss your list and conclusions with your classmates.

## TO SUM UP...

1. Define role expectation.
2. Give an example of a role expectation.
3. How do role expectations make relationships easier?
4. Describe how roles can limit people's behavior.
5. What is stereotyping and what is its result?

## ROLE CONFLICT

The roles that people play are a potential source of conflict with others. Many times the various roles that a person fills interfere with each other. Mattie is finishing her last year of high school. She is married and has a three-month-old baby. Her role as a mother is difficult for her, and recently she has been very tired. Her tiredness has interfered with her role as a student. She is too tired to do her homework in the evenings. Her roles as mother and student have also interfered with her role as a wife. She is so busy she has little time to spend with her husband.

Phil is always short of money and finds that the many roles he fills help keep him that way. He gives part of his salary from his after-school job to his mother to help pay for groceries for the family. However, this keeps him short of money when he wants to date, to be with his friends, or to participate in school activities. His family responsibilities as a son interfere with his roles as student, dating partner, and friend.

Another way that roles can cause conflict is when two people have different ideas about how a certain role should be performed. Maynette has recently been elected president of her homeroom. She feels that in this role, she should get ideas from the others, appoint committees to develop the ideas, and conduct the meetings. However, Mr. Tanner, the homeroom teacher, feels that she should be more active in thinking of ideas herself. They have had several disagreements over how she should perform her role.

Roosevelt and Thelma went to a party together one evening. When they got there,

*Role conflict can result when the roles a person plays interfere with each other.*

175

## Unit 3: Relating to Others

Roosevelt went into another room and didn't come back to Thelma until the party was almost over. Thelma was furious with him. She said, "When I go to a party with someone, I expect to see him at least a few times during the evening. I came to be with you, not to have you leave the minute we walked in the door. If you want me to ever go anywhere with you again, you'd better stick around a little more!"

Roosevelt couldn't understand why she was angry. He said, "I don't understand—we came together and we're going to leave together. We'll have some more time together before I have to take you home. I was interested in seeing the guys in that room and I figured you were enjoying the people in here. Why should I have to stay by you when we're at a party?"

In this example, what Thelma expected from her dating partner was very different from the behavior that Roosevelt felt was appropriate. They were arguing over Roosevelt's behavior in his role as dating partner.

A final way that roles can cause conflict occurs when people fill roles that relate to each other. Some roles are naturally tied together, such as parent-child, husband-wife, and employer-employee. When two people who fill these roles have the same ideas about what their relationships should be, the interaction between them is smooth. However, when they have different ideas about the relationship, conflict is involved.

Anthony lived at home the summer after he graduated from high school even though he had a good job as a plumber's apprentice. He planned to live at home for about a year to save money for a new car. Then he expected to move into an apartment. He felt that since he paid his parents a small amount for room and board he should be treated as an adult and should have adult privileges. However, his father tended to treat him the same as ever, asking where he was going and scolding him about some of his actions. An argument soon resulted because Anthony and his father had different ideas about their father-son relationship, now that Anthony was earning money of his own.

Mildred had problems in her family living class in her role relationship with the teacher, Ms. Carrodine. Mildred had never been in a class before where the teacher didn't make assignments. When Ms. Carrodine passed out sheets with suggestions for individual activities, Mildred didn't know what to do, so she did nothing. At the end of the grading period, Mildred was failing the course. When she went in to talk to the teacher, she said, "The trouble for me is that you don't act like a teacher. Teachers are supposed to tell students what to do, not to give them a choice."

Ms. Carrodine replied, "Well, I'm sorry that we have different ideas about how teachers and students should act. I think teachers should use any ways they can to get students to learn. I happen to think that students learn more when they choose for themselves what they are going to study." The role conflict in this example was what teachers and students expect from each other. Mildred and Ms. Carrodine had different ideas about what their role relationship should be.

## experiences in human relations

### ROLE CONFLICT

Very often, the activities that go along with one role a person fills conflict with the activities of another role. Role conflicts such as these can make life complicated and can cause strain and friction between people.

**Ch. 8: Role Relationships**

With a partner, read and discuss the following situations. Answer the questions which follow the descriptions of the situations. When you have finished, present your answers to the rest of your classmates.

*Situations*

- Marty has basketball practice at the same time that one of his teachers requested an after-school conference.
- Darren's sister is getting married the same afternoon that his drum and bugle corp is to march in a parade.
- Carla has a Future Homemakers of America committee meeting after school when she had promised to babysit with her brother.
- Pete recently took an after-school job at the car wash, so he is not able to walk his dating partner home after school.
- Shirley has a dentist appointment at the same time she needs to pick up her daughter after kindergarten.
- Ruth's boss asked her to work late one evening on a special project. She called and asked her husband to cook supper for the family.

*Questions*

- What two roles are in conflict in each situation?
- What is likely to be the result of the role conflict?
- How could these situations be resolved so that the requirements of both roles are met?
- Think of examples in your life where role conflict occurs.

### TO SUM UP. . .

1. Explain how several roles a person fills could interfere with each other.
2. Describe the role conflict which can result when two people have different ideas about how one of them should act.
3. Give an example of what can happen when people don't agree on how their role relationship should be.

### SEX ROLES

One of the most important roles in your life is the *sex role,* which is what it means to be a boy or girl or a man or woman. Sex roles are learned in the family. Children learn what is appropriate for their sex in many ways. They learn about sex roles from the clothing they wear, the toys they play with, and how they are taught to act.

How you interpret what you learned about sex roles influences your self-concept as well as how you relate to other people. Therefore, of all the roles that you fill, the sex role is probably the most important.

*Television programs are one way that children learn about sex roles.*

Unit 3: Relating to Others

## experiences in human relations

### LEARNING SEX ROLES

Children learn what sex role they are supposed to fill from their parents, their peers, and their experiences in the world. Books, television shows, and toys are all important influences as children learn what roles are appropriate for their sex. The following experiences will help you become more aware of the ways children are taught sex roles.

- Find a book of nursery rhymes or fairy tales. Read at least five selections from the book. Compare the roles played by the boys and girls (or men and women) in the stories. What do these roles teach children? Can you think of ways which these stories might affect children's self-concepts?
- Play children's records and be alert to sex stereotyping. Do songs about dolls always have a feminine character while songs about trucks are masculine? Which songs do women sing and which songs do men sing? What roles are described in "story songs"? What are children learning from the records they hear?
- Look carefully at a toy catalog or the toy section of a general catalog. With what kinds of toys are boys pictured? Girls? Do the labels suggest that a particular toy is appropriate for only one sex? What toys would you buy for your brothers and sisters or your own children?
- Watch television after school or on Saturday mornings. Notice the roles that males and females fill on children's programs. Are males strong, brave, and clever? Are females quiet, gentle, kind, sweet, and passive? Do any males show more tender feelings? Are any of the girls active and aggressive? What do these programs teach children about sex roles?

### BREAKDOWN OF TRADITIONAL ROLES

In the past, people were taught that some behaviors were best for men and others for women. For instance, men were expected to hold a job and earn a paycheck. It was felt that since men were tough and strong their place was out in the world. Woman's place was in the home, caring for children and doing what she could to make home a pleasant place for her family. Women were considered soft, fragile, and not fit to participate in the real world. Their qualities were best fitted to staying in the home. When Tony and Alice got married, they lived in the traditional way. Tony worked at his job at the airport and Alice was a homemaker and mother.

In addition to traditional roles in the family, men's and women's interests were expected to be different. Women were supposed to be interested in fashion, babies, cooking, sewing, and housework. Sports, automobiles, and electronics were men's areas. In the occupational world, men were builders, plumbers, electricians, scientists, and executives. If women did hold jobs, they were expected to be teachers, librarians, nurses, beauticians, or secretaries.

But the traditional roles and interests have often been only a dream for many people. When Danny and Kathy married, they expected Danny to earn their living while Kathy stayed home with the children they hoped to have. However, Danny's job in the electronics factory didn't bring in as much money as they had counted on. Therefore Kathy worked as a waitress in a local restaurant. After their first baby arrived, they found they couldn't make ends meet. Kathy went back to her job in the evenings while Danny took care of the baby. Even after their second baby was born, Kathy continued to work and Danny watched the children and did some of the housework. Kathy and Danny still say that someday Kathy

**Ch. 8: Role Relationships**

hopes to stay home with the children. For now, however, they simply can't afford it.

People like Danny and Kathy continue to believe in the traditional roles even when they know these roles don't work for them. The breakdown of traditional roles has been speeded because many families now need two incomes to live.

On the other hand, traditional roles have also broken down because many people take little interest in them. Some people have always had interests that did not hold to what was expected of their sex. Marion has never been interested in homemaking, but is wrapped up in her work as an engineer. She hires a housekeeper to cook and clean for her family. Her husband and children help with other household chores.

Many men are like Drew, who has always enjoyed cooking. He does most of the food preparation for his family. His wife prefers to do other tasks. As people have found that they enjoy activities that were not thought suitable for their sex in the past, sex roles have become more flexible. With this flexibility has come more freedom and opportunity for growth as a person.

*There have always been people who did not fit the traditional sex roles.*

## experiences in human relations

### BREAKING DOWN TRADITIONAL ROLES

The breakdown of traditional sex roles has been a gradual process. Many people still believe the traditional roles to be most appropriate. Others find the traditional roles too limiting and restricting. Therefore people choose what seems to fit best with their ideas and needs. To explore further what your ideas about sex roles are, try the following experiences.

• From magazines, cut out pictures of people of various facial types. Show your pictures to your classmates and tell what you think those people may be like. Try to imagine what their lives are like.

When you have finished, think about your descriptions. Did you generally react more favorably to women who fit the usual idea of "feminine" and to men who represented the

179

## Unit 3: Relating to Others

traditional ideas of "masculine"? What types of life styles were described for each sex? Did you guess about marriage and the number of children more frequently with females than with males? What types of jobs did you suggest for males and females? What sex roles did you assign to the people in the pictures? Did you tend to give them traditional roles?

• During the next week as you watch television, become aware of the sex roles that people play. How often are men strong and tough, while women are soft and delicate? Are men shown as workers while women are homemakers? How traditional are the roles you observe? Are there examples of how roles are changing?

• Take a piece of paper and fold it in half lengthwise. On one side, list the characteristics you look for in male friends. On the other side, list the qualities you desire in female friends. Now open up the paper and compare your lists. How similar are they? Do you seek friends on the basis of traditional roles?

• Think of a newborn baby boy. Try to imagine what he will be doing when he is thirty years old. Now think about a newborn baby girl. What will she be doing when she is thirty years old?

How easy was it for you to predict what the babies would be doing in thirty years? Did you find it easier to make the prediction for the girl? Did you suggest that she is likely to be a homemaker and mother? Often people automatically assume females will be homemakers without considering whether they have any interest in that role or not.

Was it harder to predict for the boy? Is there any way that you can know what kind of role he will fill? Did you suggest that he would also

*There are often more differences between one female and another and one male and another than there are between males and females.*

be a homemaker and parent? Did you tend to think of the babies only in terms of the traditional roles? Are roles likely to be as traditional in thirty years?

• • • • • • • • • • • • • • • • • • • •

## Changing Role Expectations

In the past few years, many people have come to believe that the traditional roles just don't work for everyone. Too many people act in ways that, in the past, would not have been thought appropriate for their sex. Studies show that more differences exist between one man and another and one woman and another than between men and women. As a result, sex role expectations are losing their importance.

People are now free to choose whatever life style they desire. They may want to live according to traditional sex roles. On the other hand, they are able to make less traditional choices, if they wish.

Changing sex role expectations have increased people's ability to express themselves. Unlimited by their sex, people can choose careers, hobbies, and activities which express their own personalities.

Chuck's sister taught him to sew. He enjoys making tee shirts and trousers. Although his friends sometimes tease him, they envy his large wardrobe. Recently, Douglas has been talking about the advantages in knowing how to sew. He plans to sign up for a sewing course in school next semester.

Adelle is a long-distance runner on the track squad. Not many girls share her interest in running. However, Adelle's hard work at practice is admired and she has earned the respect of others through several high finishes at track meets.

Chuck and Adelle are like others who have found that they can be themselves in expressing their interests. They are respected as human beings for their special abilities and skills.

## experiences in human relations

### CHANGING ROLES

People learn their sex roles early in life and then often don't consciously consider them much afterwards. These experiences will help you begin to think about the sex role that you fill and the roles that you expect others to fill. They may also help you think about how sex roles are changing.

• Given below are a number of characteristics for females and males. Copy the lists below on a separate sheet of paper. Then, as you read the first list, place a 1 in front of the quality you believe most important in females. Place a 2 by the quality you believe is second most important, a 3 by the third most important, until you have assigned a number to all the characteristics. Repeat the procedure again for males.

*Female*

    Considerate and cooperative
    Relates well to others
    Respectful toward adults
    Creative and imaginative
    Clean and neat
    Trustworthy and responsible
    Carefree and fun loving
    Makes friends easily
    Curious
    Independent and assertive

*Male*

    Considerate and cooperative

**Unit 3: Relating to Others**

  Relates well to others
  Respectful toward adults
  Creative and imaginative
  Clean and neat
  Trustworthy and responsible
  Carefree and fun loving
  Makes friends easily
  Curious
  Independent and assertive

Look at your two lists. Were they different? Did you think different qualities were most important for females than for males? Do you think you would have answered the same way two years ago?

Compare your lists with those of your classmates. How alike or different were they? Did males and females tend to have different orders on their lists? Did the females see themselves differently than the males saw them and visa versa? What conclusions can you make about how you view sex roles?

• If you are a female, complete the following statements: "I would like to be a male because . . ." and "I would not like to be a male because. . . ." If you are male, complete the sentences with the word "female" substituted for "male." Discuss with your classmates how each sex sees the duties and privileges of the opposite sex. Do you see your sex role the same way as others do?

In the same way, complete the following sentence: "If I were a male (female), I would. . . ." Again, discuss this idea with your classmates. What activities would you enjoy if your sex was different? Why can't you do them anyway?

● ● ● ● ● ● ● ● ● ● ● ● ● ● ● ● ● ● ●

**Social Changes**

One important social change is that people now look at their worth as people rather than as members of a sex. People appreciate that both men and women can make contributions as individuals.

Men and women are taking equal roles in marriages, at work, and in their relationships with others. Being a specific sex does not make a person better or worse than another, but simply different.

Social roles are changing in many settings. Mr. and Mrs. Trent wanted each of their children to use their abilities as individuals. However, there wasn't very much money to help the children. After many discussions, the family decided that Cassie should be helped to go to college. The Trents would be able to meet expenses if she got a part-time job.

Calvin had not done very well in school, but was a good musician. Mr. and Mrs. Trent continued to pay for his organ and voice lessons. Calvin's training helped him get a well-paying position in a five-piece band when he graduated from high school.

In the Trent family, the decisions made about the kind of training each child received were based on abilities, not sex.

When Mr. Carter posted the list of members of Highland High's golf squad, the list included three females and seven males. Mr. Carter explained that he had chosen the best ten players available to represent the school. He noted that the players had been selected on the basis of their scores during tryout rounds. Thus, the players were chosen for their golfing abilities.

Rogine and Will started work as bus personnel at the Steak House Restaurant at the same time. As they learned their duties, their boss, Mr. Cary, observed their abilities carefully. He used his judgment of their special talents when it came time for a raise and more responsibilities. Will got a chance to work more with the customers because of his outgoing personality and friendliness. Mr. Cary took advantage of Rogine's skill at organization. He assigned her to help with inventory and ordering food and supplies.

Another social change is that people are more comfortable with their own differences and uniqueness. It can be very hard to be different than others. At the same time, your differences are what make you special.

Darrell's friends were all musicians. Sometimes this was hard for Darrell because he had no musical ability. Darrell didn't let his "difference" bother him. He knew his worth as a friend didn't depend on his ability to play a guitar. During their senior year, four of Darrell's friends formed a country and western group. He was able to contribute his share to the group by acting as a manager for his friends.

Many of Sharon's good friends are very interested in makeup and hair styling. She enjoys seeing the results of their latest experiments. However, she isn't concerned about her skin and hair beyond keeping them clean. She is much more interested in working with her father in the family garage. Her interest in auto mechanics is so important to her that she doesn't want to spend much time on grooming.

Changes have also taken place in the expression of emotions. All people experience tender feelings as well as feelings of anger and aggression. The changing sex roles make the expression of any emotion by any person more acceptable.

**Changes on the Job**

The world of work used to be a man's world. Now, more than half the women between 18 and 64 years of age are in the labor force. Labor experts predict that nine out of ten females will work outside the home at some time in their lives. Thus role changes in the world of work affect both sexes.

In the past, most women held low-paying jobs with little chance for promotion and higher salaries. The higher-paying jobs in the construction or skilled trades or in business management were not open to women. Three-fourths of the women who work are clerical, service, or factory workers, or sales clerks.

*Men and women now share the role of worker and wage earner.*

## Unit 3: Relating to Others

Women now have more choices open to them when selecting a job or career. They are beginning to hold higher-paid positions requiring more skills. These positions also have more potential for advancement. Nora is the first woman member of the local Tool and Die Makers union. She has almost completed her apprenticeship and already makes a higher salary than her mother, who has worked in one office for 17 years.

At the same time, more men are moving into areas where women were traditionally strong. People expect both men and women to be school teachers, nurses, librarians, and social workers. Alan works in a day care center with three-year-olds. He really enjoys being with the children. Since many of them come from homes without a father, he feels he is an important man in their lives.

Today young men and women are more involved in career planning. Even those women who leave their jobs while their children are small still spend over 25 years in paid employment. This means it is important that both sexes develop work skills. They need to plan how they can best use their working years in a productive way.

### experiences in human relations

#### SEX ROLES ON THE JOB

The working world has had a long history of separating men's and women's jobs. Certain jobs were considered more suitable for women while others were more appropriate for men. These experiences will help you explore some of your ideas about what is appropriate work for males and females.

- Review the want ads in a local paper. Make a list of the jobs which traditionally call for a woman and those which want a man. What jobs do not ask for a specific sex? What reasons do employers have for seeking one sex or the other for a certain job? Call three employers who requested a specific sex and ask why the other sex could not do the job.

- Look at the want ads in another day's paper and choose a job you would like to have. Don't worry if you aren't qualified for the position, but simply choose something that sounds interesting to you. Discuss your choice with others in your class. Did you choose a job that was traditionally considered all right for your sex? What kinds of choices did others in your class make? Does your paper still list jobs under "Men Wanted" or "Women Wanted"? If so, did you even look for a job in the column labeled for the opposite sex? Which jobs, "Male" or "Female," offer the highest salaries?

- Look through a variety of magazines and clip out pictures which show men and women at work. What kinds of jobs do most of the men have? The women? Do the pictures you have show men and women working at jobs traditional for their sex? Why are there not more pictures of nontraditional jobs?

- A list of different occupations is given below. On a separate piece of paper write whether you think each job is more appropriate for a man, a woman, or either sex.

  Garbage collector
  Nurse
  Welder
  Bank teller
  Nursery school teacher
  Astronaut
  President of the United States
  House painter
  Computer programmer
  Typewriter repairperson

*One role change in the home involves more sharing of household tasks.*

Telephone operator
Assembly line worker in an electronics plant
Accountant
Automobile salesperson
Cosmetics salesperson
Farmer
Animal trainer
Mayor
Janitor
Professional athlete

How many jobs did you assign to men? Women? Either? What were your reasons for choosing as you did? Did your choices reflect traditional job assignments? Why would it not be appropriate for either sex to do any of the jobs?

●●●●●●●●●●●●●●●●●●●●

**Changes at Home**

As more women have begun working, role changes have occurred at home. Both men and women now help earn the family's income and both help run the family's home. Couples share housework and other chores such as cooking or laundry. When there are children, both partners share the child care. Men and women function as a team, sharing the responsibilities and the pleasures of working together.

Reba and Ted Stone are teachers at Central High School. Since they are both busy with school activities, they have worked out a routine to share the work at home. One week Reba does the cooking while Ted takes care of the laundry and house cleaning. The next

185

## Unit 3: Relating to Others

week, they exchange jobs. Both spend time with their son, Andy. Reba does the shopping while Ted takes care of their car. They live in a condominium so they don't have yard work to do. Their arrangement allows them both to have free time for personal enjoyment and family fun.

Occasionally, men and women completely change sex roles. Carmen and Troy have been married five years. About two years ago, Troy became a "househusband" who does the housework, cooks, and cares for their children. He is able to spend time on his woodworking hobby. Sometimes he sells his carvings and furniture. Carmen loves her job as a computer programmer and has no desire to stay home. For Troy and Carmen, exchanging sex roles has been rewarding for both of them.

## experiences in human relations

### SEX ROLES IN THE HOME

Many changes in sex roles are taking place in the home. These experiences are to help you think about what sex roles may be appropriate in families.

- Think about "who does what" at your house. Who does the laundry, washes the car, makes the beds, washes the dishes, mows the lawn, or pays the bills? Are certain jobs done by the family members of a certain sex? Do the females (mother or daughters) always do the laundry and the dishes? Do the males (father or sons) take care of the car and yard? List as many household jobs as you can and decide whether they are done by the traditional sex in your family.

If you live in a family with only one parent, think about all the roles that your parent fills. If you were to get a step-parent, which roles would that person assume? Which roles do you think your mother or father would be willing to give up? Are these according to traditional ideas?

Now imagine what your own family will be like. Which jobs will you be willing to be responsible for? Which jobs will you expect your spouse to do? What are your reasons for this division? Have you based your choices on sex roles? What jobs or chores will you expect your children to do? Would these be different if your children were boys or girls?

- While you are watching television, notice what household chores men and women do. Are men ever shown performing household tasks? What jobs do the women do? Do any of the shows you watch reflect changing sex roles in the home?

- Below are two lists of items which are often used by families. If you are a female, on a separate piece of paper, try to estimate the cost of each item in the list "For Females." If you are a male, do the same with the "For Males" list.

*For Females*
  Car battery
  Can of motor oil
  Package of nails
  New 360 cc motorcycle
  Muffler installation
  Lawn fertilizer
  Phillips-head screwdriver
  Furnace filters

*For Males*
  Jar of mayonnaise
  Ironing board
  Box of detergent

Non-stick loaf pan
Package of weiners
Can of household cleanser
Single-bed fitted sheet
Coffee maker

Now, if you are a female, complete for "For Males" list. If you are a male, try the "For Females" list. Compare your answers. Which list was easier for you to complete? Are these items purchased by different sexes in your home? Do they need to be? What might be some results of spending money in terms of sex roles?

## TO SUM UP...

1. What is a sex role?
2. Explain the old saying, "People are born male and female but must learn to be men and women."
3. Why is the sex role probably more important than any other role a person fills?
4. Describe the traditional sex roles for men and women.
5. Give some examples of why traditional sex roles and interests have not always worked for everyone.
6. Explain some of the social changes that have occurred in sex roles.
7. What percentage of women between the ages of 18 and 64 now work?
8. Why is it important that both males and females think about planning their careers?
9. Describe some of the role changes that have occurred in the home.

### Ch. 8: Role Relationships

## BEYOND ROLES

Roles are important in relating to other people. No one can be completely free of role relationships. To attempt to eliminate roles would be to lose useful ways of organizing your life and your relationships. Yet, roles can be restricting because too frequently, roles limit behavior and the choices that you have. Make it your goal to avoid being controlled by the roles you play. You can fulfill your many roles, yet go beyond roles to still be yourself. What you do can be determined by what you feel as a human being.

People can go beyond the roles that they play. Mr. Farley was the night manager at the drug store in the shopping mall. He noticed that the employees seemed to talk and laugh together except when he was around. Then they were quiet and talked only when he spoke to them. Mr. Farley felt as if he were missing out on the friendship and affection that existed among the other employees.

When he thought about the situation, he realized that he was acting like "The Boss" when he related to the others. He began to try to step out of his role as manager to be friends with the others. Within a few days he was pleased to notice that the talk didn't stop when he was near. Mr. Farley was able to overcome his ideas of how a boss should act in order to relate to the others as a person.

Learned roles can be very hard to overcome. Sophia George had learned about being a mother from her mother. When her son Gary was bad, she beat him with a belt just like her mother had done. But Sophia could see that Gary wasn't learning the right behavior by being beaten. And she could remember that being beaten never made her want to act better. Sophia was sure that there were better ways to teach children than by

### Unit 3: Relating to Others

beating. Her problem was that she didn't know what they were.

Then she saw a poster about a night course in parenting offered by the high school home economics department. Sophia signed up for the course and learned many new ways to fill the role of mother. Another idea that she learned was that she could relate to Gary as a person by not playing the mother role all the time. When Sophia get very angry, she still find herself reaching for the belt. But most of the time, she is happy in her new re-learned role of mother.

Many people find it hard to go beyond the role expectations which others hold for them. Toby's parents expected him to go to college. They had a savings account to help pay for his expenses. Catalogs from many good schools arrived at his house so he could, as his parents said, choose the school best suited for him. His parents wanted him to study business since all the men in his family had been accountants or businessmen.

But Toby felt smothered by his parents plans and expectations. He didn't want to major in business in college—he didn't even want to go away to college! Finally he worked up the courage to tell his plans to his parents. He loved tinkering with radios, televisions, and stereos. A year of electronics technology at the City Technical College would give him the skills to open a repair shop.

His parents were shocked and disappointed. But gradually they came to see that they had made plans for their son without considering the *person* that he was. They realized how much courage it took for Toby to tell them about his own desires and ideas. When the time came, they used the college savings for his schooling and to help him open his own shop.

Sometimes people find it hard to overcome role stereotyping to be themselves. Miranda's brother Gene had done the basketball team statistics for two years. When he graduated, Miranda went to Mr. Grabill, the coach, to ask if she could have the job now.

"Absolutely not," said Mr. Grabill. "No girl has ever done the statistics for my team and no girl is going to do it. Girls don't know enough about basketball. I'd have to spend too much time teaching you how to chart the shots and all the other things."

"Oh no, you wouldn't," answered Miranda. "Gene taught me everything he knew about the job. Please at least give me a chance to show you I can do it. Could I come and figure the statistics at a practice just to show you I can handle the job?"

Mr. Grabill reluctantly agreed to let Miranda show what she could do. When he saw her work, he realized that she could handle the job better than any of the males who had applied for the job. In telling her the job was hers, he commented, "I guess I have to eat my words. I really never thought a girl could handle this job. But you showed me that being a male isn't a qualification for the job. It's having the skills that is important."

The ability to see beyond the roles people play is important in building relationships. It is only as roles become less important that the person appears. At this point, genuine person-to-person relationships are possible. Going beyond roles allows people to experience themselves *as* persons and to relate to other *as* persons.

### TO SUM UP...

1. How can people avoid being controlled by the roles they play?
2. When people go beyond roles, what kinds of relationships develop?

# CHAPTER 9
## Conflict in Relationships

This chapter will help you to . . .
- Identify common relationship problems that lead to conflict.
- Recognize that conflict can have destructive or constructive results.
- Identify various conflict styles.
- Describe some characteristics of constructive arguments.
- List and apply the steps in the no-lose method of solving conflict situations.

When you relate to other people, conflict is certain to occur sooner or later. This is because you think differently and have different needs and wants than others do. These differences are the basis from which disagreements, arguments, and physical violence often spring.

Every day you can see many examples of people who do not get along with each other. Disagreements can be as small and trivial as when two three-year-olds fight over who will have a certain toy. In contrast, war or murder are examples of how serious the results of disagreement can be.

### WHAT IS CONFLICT?

*Conflict* is an open struggle between two or more people. A conflict results whenever one person tries to prevent or interfere in some way with the actions of others. Conflicts can be about anything. Many of the topics covered earlier in this book are sources of conflict. Conflicts can be about different values or ways of relating to each other. Power is very often a source of conflict when two people try to gain control over each other. Role conflicts are common, as are conflicts about people's needs, their goals, and their behavior.

Eric and Sophia have a conflict over interests and needs when they argue whether to attend a movie or go roller skating on their Saturday night date.

Mr. Singleton and Victor have had disagreements all year about Victor's behavior in physical education class. Their conflict is

Unit 3: Relating to Others

*You can't go out until your room is cleaned!*

*But I'll be late to meet Claude for the movies.*

**This conflict is developing because a mother and son are interfering with each other's actions.**

about power and whether Mr. Singleton has the power to make Victor behave in a certain way.

Mr. and Mrs. Tillis frequently disagree over how to spend their money. She feels she needs all the money they have for groceries and household needs. He wants to spend more on entertainment and having a good time. Mr. and Mrs. Tillis are in conflict over values relating to money.

Another husband and wife, Mr. and Mrs. Washington, disagree on who should do household chores. Since Mrs. Washington works, she feels that Mr. Washington should

## Ch. 9: Conflict in Relationships

help her with the housework. He thinks housework is for women. Their conflict is over the role each should take at home.

### experiences in human relations

### CONFLICT AROUND YOU

Conflict is a common part of your everyday life. You are involved in conflicts with others. In addition, various kinds of conflicts go on around you. People are perhaps more aware of conflict today since television, newspapers, and radio give many examples of conflict.

Take a newspaper and clip out all the stories that tell about some kind of conflict. Be sure to check the political news, the sports news, the advice-to-readers columnists, and the international news.

As you read and clip the stories, think about who is involved. Do most of the examples tell about conflict between individual persons? Are many stories about conflict between countries, conflict between companies, or conflict between companies and the government? Is the disagreement personal or do the people involved represent others, as when a person speaks for a political party?

How was the disagreement expressed? In a fist fight? A legal case? A war? Did the article tell how the conflict was solved? Did it seem to you that the solution was a good one?

When you have finished, think about what you discovered in this experience. Were there many more examples of conflict than you expected? Did the people involved seem able to solve their differences peacefully? Do you think most people handle conflict well?

### DESTRUCTIVE RESULTS OF CONFLICT

It often seems as if conflict is bad, that it should be avoided. Families with a great deal of conflict are often unhappy. Les's parents have terrible fights. They scream and yell, calling each other names. Les often feels he can't stand listening to the two people he loves fight that way. He tries to go to a friend's house when the arguments get too bad.

Conflict between friends can seem harmful because it can lead to the breakup of the friendship. Ozzie and Jeff's friendship was weakened when Ozzie asked to copy a paper of Jeff's. Jeff would not allow Ozzie to copy it and this made Ozzie very angry. He said, "What are friends for if not to help out? I don't have time to do this paper and now I'll get an F if you won't let me copy yours."

Jeff answered, "I'm sorry you feel that way. I don't believe friends are to help each other be dishonest. It doesn't help either of us if I do your work. It just doesn't pay to cheat—for friendship or anything else." The conflict over values and role expectations for a friend led to the breakup of this friendship.

Most dating partners break up their relationship because of conflicts. When Carol got to school one morning, she found her friend Anna waiting for her. Carol said, "You won't believe the awful thing that happened last night. Don and I have broken up. We had the worst fight I've ever had with anyone and all over a really stupid thing. He saw me in the drug store with Gus and thought I was interested in Gus. Oh, it was terrible!"

Anna replied, "But I don't understand. He should know you weren't with Gus on purpose. I mean, Gus is his best friend." The two continued to talk about the argument until the bell for class rang.

Another place where conflict can have unhappy results is at work. Conflict with your

**Unit 3: Relating to Others**

boss or with another worker can make going to work very unpleasant and can even cause you to lose your job. Robert was fired from his job at the restaurant because of an argument with his boss over how long his hair should be. When Robert refused to have his hair cut, his boss told him not to come back to work again.

Because of these negative situations which seem to result from conflict, many people try to avoid it. They feel that good relationships are those with no conflict.

## Constructive Results of Conflict

Conflict and disagreement themselves are not necessarily harmful. It is the failure to handle conflict in constructive ways that causes problems. Most people deal with conflict in destructive ways. Conflict can be a force for good in your relationships if you learn to handle it.

Conflict can be positive because, through conflict, issues can be brought out into the open. By using listening skills and trying to hear and feel others' viewpoints, you can understand people better. Conflict can lead to new respect for others' ideas.

By learning to know people better through conflict, you will have a base for your relationship to grow. Overcoming conflict together can draw you closer to each other in a feeling of accomplishment. Thus conflict can

*Conflict or disagreements at work can lead to losing your job.*

actually help a relationship if you know how to handle your misunderstandings.

One Friday night, Carolyn and Richard had been with their group of friends. On the way home, Richard was very quiet but when Carolyn asked him what was wrong, he exploded. "It's you," he said. "Every time we're out, you do nothing but flirt with all the other guys! It's always bothered me, but before I didn't know if you were just trying to get in good with everybody else in case you dropped me. But now you say you love me, so I don't think you have any right to be so friendly with anybody else."

By the time Richard finished speaking, Carolyn was upset, too, and was about ready to return Richard's attack. But, instead, she took a breath and tried to speak calmly. "Richard, I had no idea that my behavior bothered you. I think our problem is that what you call flirting, I think of as being friendly. After all, the others in our group are my friends, but I don't want to date any of them."

Carolyn's quiet answer seemed to calm Richard down, and they talked about the problem. The result of their talk was that Carolyn agreed not to be quite so friendly with the other males. In turn, Richard promised to have a little more faith in her affection for him. One result of this particular disagreement was that they came much closer together. The argument helped them talk about how they felt about each other. This conflict actually strengthened their affection for each other.

Teresa and her mother were always arguing over the clothes which Teresa did or did not wear. Her mother didn't think the clothes Teresa wore were suitable and often suggested that Teresa wear some of those "pretty dresses" she had. Frequently their arguments were over a particular expensive shirt which

*Handling conflict constructively helps people understand each other better.*

Teresa refused to wear. One night, when it looked as if another fight over clothes was about to start, Teresa said to her mother, "Look Mom, do you think maybe we could sit down and talk this over? We fight and fight over my clothes, but we never settle anything. We're going to be fighting over the same issue for the next five years unless we can figure out something!"

"All right, let's try," answered her mother. "There are two problems that worry me. I just don't think you look attractive, for one. The other is that we don't have that much money that we can afford to let all those pretty clothes just sit in your closet unworn."

"Now let me try to give my side of the story," said Teresa. "Remember that sweater of yours that you let me have because you never wore it? When I asked if I could have it, you told me that you'd be the laughing stock of your friends if you showed up in it. Well, you may not think my clothes are very pretty, but if I wore some of the things you liked, my

## Unit 3: Relating to Others

friends would laugh pretty hard at me. I understand about the money, too, Mom, but you bought some of those clothes without ever showing them to me or asking me if I'd like them. I've been thinking about some of those dresses. There's a couple of them that would make pretty nice looking tops. If you would help me fix them up, I'd be glad to wear them."

The result of this discussion was the two of them made plans to alter some of the clothes Teresa didn't wear. Teresa's mom also agreed not to buy her any more clothes without her approval. In addition, both Teresa and her mother gained appreciation of each other as *people*. Their ability to talk about their problem without shouting and calling each other names helped their relationship in other areas, too.

## experiences in human relations

### THE RESULTS OF CONFLICT

Most quarrels can have either destructive or constructive results. The following experience will help you begin to think about what makes the results of a quarrel destructive or constructive.

Working with three or four other students, make a tape recording of an argument. Few people will quarrel normally if they know they are being taped. Therefore it may be easiest to record a conflict from a television program.

Later, listen to the recording of the conflict. What were the people fighting about? Did one of them win? What would be the worst possible result of this argument? What would be the best thing that could happen because of this disagreement? Which of these seems most likely to happen (or did happen) as a result of what was said?

In your group's opinion, were the results of this conflict destructive or constructive? Why do you feel this way? How do you think this conflict could have been handled more constructively?

### TO SUM UP...

1. Why is conflict a normal part of relating to others?
2. Define conflict.
3. What are some causes of conflict in relationships?
4. Describe some destructive results of conflict.
5. Discuss some of the constructive outcomes of conflict.

### HANDLING CONFLICT

People handle conflict in many ways. Small children seem to handle any conflict by automatically hitting the other person. As children grow older, they learn new ways of handling arguments from their family members. When they begin to attend school, they also learn from their peers. People rarely have a style of meeting conflict that they have not seen other people use.

#### CONFLICT STYLES

A *conflict style* is simply the way people behave when faced with disagreement. Most people have certain ways of behaving which seem to fit their personalities. They use these ways of behaving, or conflict styles, whenever they have conflict with another person.

## Physical Violence

One of the most destructive conflict styles is physical violence. This occurs when a person's feelings of anger or resentment grow so strong that the only way to relieve them seems to be to strike out at another person.

Physical violence often occurs in families. Some men beat their wives. Whenever Mr. Gordon has had too much to drink, he gets violent. He usually takes his feelings out on Mrs. Gordon, saying that she spends all his money on unnecessary things. Mrs. Gordon is afraid of her husband because of the beatings he has given her when he was drunk.

Other examples of violence in families occur between brothers and sisters. This is particularly common when children are young. Mark got into Bob's collection of aluminum cans and bent the sides of several. Bob was so angry that he hit and punched his younger brother.

Most parents use some mild forms of physical force to discipline their children. Most children are spanked at least a few times as they are growing up. Babies and toddlers often get their hands slapped when they reach for the television knobs or a glass ashtray.

Possibly the most destructive form of violence in the family is called *child abuse*. This is much more than spanking or slapping and occurs when parents physically harm their children. Child abusers have psychological problems which lead them to harm their chil-

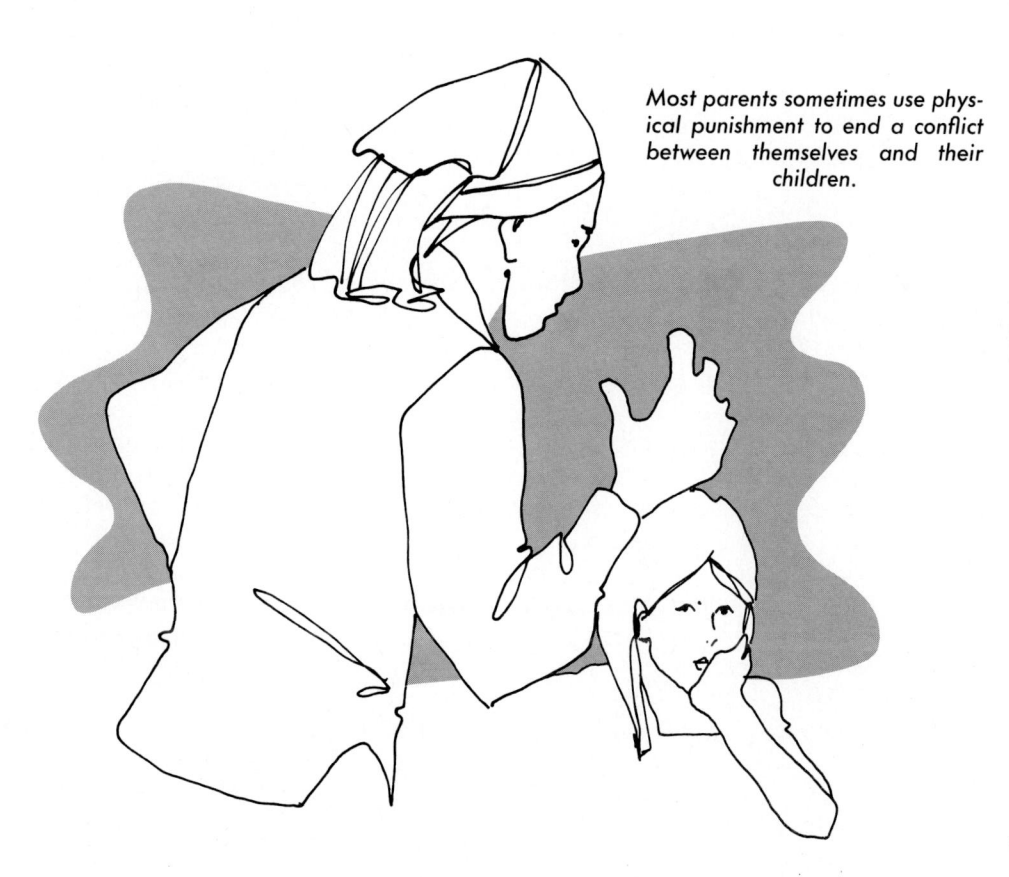

*Most parents sometimes use physical punishment to end a conflict between themselves and their children.*

dren. Thus child abuse is more than simply using physical violence to resolve conflict. On the other hand, child abuse is related to using violence as a conflict style. If a parent strikes out at other adults during conflict, that parent is also apt to harm children physically when stress and strain arise.

Two-year-old Tracy cried all the time because of colic. Her crying was very irritating to her parents. One night, her mother just seemed to be unable to listen any more. She ended up beating Tracy to make her stop crying. The next day, Tracy's small body was covered with bruises.

Parents who abuse their children were usually beaten themselves as children. If you were beaten as a child, you are likely to beat your children. They, in turn, will be likely to beat their children. Children are often seriously hurt by child abuse and sometimes even die. As a result, government and private agencies are making an effort to teach parents to discipline their children without using physical violence.

## Withdrawal

Some people use a conflict style just the opposite of physical violence. These people simply leave, or *withdraw,* when conflict begins or when their feelings get too strong to control. They withdraw because they are very uneasy when arguing with another person. They also may be afraid that they will lose control over their feelings and either say or do things for which they will be sorry.

When Jason went in after school to see Mr. Braun about his grade in building trades, he was upset. He just kept getting more and more angry as Mr. Braun explained why his grade was so low. Jason didn't ask any questions or try to explain why he had been having problems. All of a sudden, right in the middle of one of Mr. Braun's sentences, Jason got up and ran out the shop door. Mr. Braun was disturbed at Jason's leaving, but he had come to understand Jason during the school year. He realized that Jason's feelings of anger, shame, and embarrassment had become so strong that he had to get away.

Benjamin didn't like arguments, even though it seemed that he and his mother were always fighting. Whenever a new argument would begin, Benjamin would just walk out of the house and stay away until he thought his mother would be calmed down. He usually went down to the playground and shot baskets.

Marcia had the same kind of reaction to arguments with her parents although she would lock herself into her room whenever a fight started. When her parents knocked on the door and demanded that she open it, she just ignored them.

When Bart and his dating partner, Karen, had an argument, he would usually take off in his car for a long drive. Bart used his car as a way of escaping from conflict.

Sometimes, people who simply leave when a conflict begins also hope to punish the other partner. By leaving and not saying where they are going and when they plan to return, they hope to worry the other. Mr. Myers was likely to leave the house when he fought with his wife. Sometimes he would walk around the block and return home within fifteen minutes. When he was really angry, he would stay away a long time.

He would be gone so long that Mrs. Myers would imagine him killed in an auto crash or other accident. By the time he came home, she would be so relieved to see him that she would give in to him about their argument.

Mr. Myers used staying away as punishment for his wife and also as one way to "win" arguments.

**The Silent Treatment**

People who use silence as a conflict style refuse to talk to the other person about the conflict. Two people who are using this conflict style may talk enough to carry on their "business." They just don't talk about anything that would lead to or increase confidences or emotional intimacy. In some cases, they may even use others to carry messages.

Mr. and Mrs. Barnes don't speak to each other when they are having a fight. They often use their children to carry messages. For example, Mrs. Barnes may ask Timmy to tell his father that he is wanted on the telephone. Mr. Barnes might tell Sam to ask his mother to pass the carrots.

Friends or dating partners who quarrel may act as if the other were invisible. When Larry joined the group standing beside Ruth's locker, she acted as if he weren't there. She talked to the others, refused to look at him, and didn't answer when he asked her a question. Her silence toward Larry was the result of a quarrel they had over how Ruth's mother was interfering with their relationship.

**Blow Up**

Some people blow up or seem to explode when they get angry. Their fights are fast, furious, and over quickly. After the anger has left their systems, they are ready to "forgive and forget." People who use this style of conflict rarely hold grudges.

Andy was known to his friends for his hot temper. One night, he was talking with Ricky about his desire to make the first team of the basketball squad. Ricky commented that he didn't think Andy was tall enough. At that, Andy blew up and started making all sorts of negative comments about Ricky. He called him various names as well as saying that Ricky wasn't good enough to be able to judge whether Andy could make the team or not. After about five minutes, however, Andy had his anger out of his system. He started talking calmly with Ricky about a girl they both knew.

Mrs. Smith also blew up when faced with conflict. If her 16-year-old son tracked mud on the floor, she was likely to scream at him. She would accuse him of trying to make extra work for her. When her 14-year-old daughter brought home a failing grade in math, she carried on and on about how her daughter had let her down. Both the Smith children knew, however, that their mother's "bark" was worse than her "bite."

**Bagging**

One method of dealing with conflict, which many people use, is called *bagging*. This conflict style is a combination of the silent treatment and the blowup. The name comes from the idea that people put their hurts and anger in an imaginary bag or sack and carry them around instead of talking them out. Then one day, all the hurts and feelings that have been in the bag come tumbling out. The person who has been carrying the sack around really "lets loose" in a rage. When a big fight occurs over a little incident, it is likely that at least one partner has unloaded a bag of resentments.

Mr. Thomas put all of his complaints about his son, Joe, in his bag. He tried not to nag Joe, but every time Joe was late for curfew, ate sloppily at supper, or left his room a mess, Mr. Thomas stored his feelings in his sack.

### Unit 3: Relating to Others

One Saturday Mr. Thomas wanted Joe to mow the lawn. Joe said he didn't have time since his group of friends was going on a picnic. At that point, Mr. Thomas's bag exploded. He shouted, "What kind of a son are you anyway? You sure are good for nothing as far as I'm concerned. You are the sloppiest person I ever saw. Your table manners are so bad they almost make me sick eating at the same table with you. Your room looks like a pig pen and so do you lots of times. You can't seem to get in on time. You don't get good grades like I want you to. And now you say you can't do a simple little job like mowing the lawn to earn your keep around here!"

The conflict in this particular instance was whether Joe would mow the lawn. However, Mr. Barnes brought up all the complaints he had in his bag. He included in the conflict all the issues over the past weeks that had irritated him.

Tina also was the kind of person who used the bagging style of fighting. She had been dating Roger for several months and liked him very much. She had been worried about how much he liked her in return. Therefore she never said anything when Roger did something to irritate her. She saved her complaints and kept them in her bag. One afternoon Roger called to say he wasn't going to keep their date that evening because he was going night hunting with his brother. A disappointed Tina suddenly felt she couldn't be silent any longer. After she had shouted out her dissatisfaction with Roger and his attentions, she slammed down the telephone with her bag empty.

The danger of bagging complaints and conflict is that when the blowup finally comes, it usually is much more damaging to the relationship than a few fights all along might have been. In the case of Roger and Tina, Roger felt that Tina's attack was completely uncalled for. His interest in her dropped and he soon found a new girl.

*The conflict style called bagging can be compared to carrying around a bag of anger, hurts, and resentments.*

## experiences in human relations

### YOUR CONFLICT STYLE

Many people don't realize that they have a certain style to the way they handle conflict. The first step in learning to handle your conflicts more constructively is to become aware of your conflict style.

Think about the conflicts, disagreements, or fights you have had with others during the past month. Who were these conflicts with? Did you fight with friends, dating partners, parents, brothers and sisters, or teachers? On a separate piece of paper, list five conflicts that you have been involved in recently. Beside each conflict, write a brief statement telling how the conflict was solved.

Now, think about these five conflicts. Did you act in the same general way in each situation? Do you seem to have one particular style of conflict? Did your conflict style vary with the situation?

Does your way of handling conflict seem destructive or constructive? What was the end result of the five conflicts you have listed? Did your conflicts improve or worsen relationships between you and others? Think of some ways you could improve your handling of conflict.

### TO SUM UP...

1. What is a conflict style?
2. Describe the feelings which lead people to physical violence as a conflict style.
3. What is the most destructive form of physical violence?

Ch. 9: Conflict in Relationships

4. Why do some people just leave when an argument begins?
5. Explain why the silent treatment can be harmful to a relationship.
6. Describe the actions of a person who blows up during conflict.
7. Explain what bagging is.

### LEARNING TO FIGHT

Most people laugh when it is suggested that they need to learn to fight. "Why, I've been fighting from the day I was brought home from the hospital," Dell might say, "and I do all right for myself." But the kind of fighting that people do naturally is very different from the kind of fighting that can strengthen a relationship.

Quarrels begin when you and another person disagree over some issue. However, most quarrels don't center around the issue in question. Instead, the quarrelers attack each other and try to find hurtful comments to make. If you are quarreling with someone with whom you are emotionally intimate, you know just what to say to hurt the other the most. The more serious the fight, the more likely it is that you will say something to damage your relationship.

**Focus on One Issue**

In contrast, quarrels which have constructive results focus only on the issue involved. The argument is directed at the problem or condition rather than the other person. The first step is for both people to agree on the issue over which they are fighting.

Vera and Lorne had a running argument all day Friday at school. Vera wanted Lorne to take her to a concert on Saturday night. Lorne

**Unit 3: Relating to Others**

*Establishing one problem or issue for an argument is the first step in learning to fight constructively.*

was tired of Vera always selecting the places where they would go. He always went where she wanted but she never would go to the events he suggested. While Vera was arguing about *where* to go, Lorne thought the battle was over *who* was to decide where to go. When they couldn't agree on what they were arguing over, it was no wonder they couldn't reach a solution!

Second, when two fighting partners agree on the problem, they need to stick to the issue. This helps avoid the situation where one partner unloads a bag during a quarrel. By only working on one area of disagreement at a time, the partners are much more apt to solve their problem. The more issues that are brought up in a quarrel, the less likely it is that anything will be solved. However, sticking to the issue can be very difficult.

Toby and Sally have been dating for quite a while. Toby wants Sally to participate in more sexual intimacies than she is comfortable with. One night they decided to try to talk about the conflict between them. Toby tried to explain how he felt about the situation.

Then he said, "And another thing, it really makes me mad that your parents won't let me come over to your house on school nights. Isn't there something that you can do to convince them?"

Sally replied, "Well, maybe that is a problem, but that's not what we agreed to talk about tonight. Do you have anything more to say before I try to explain my side of the argument?"

By agreeing to stick to the issue, neither person "hits below the belt" by attacking the other person. Carla and her sister Gwen were trying to learn to quarrel more constructively. One morning, Gwen wanted to wear a top that Carla had borrowed the week before and hadn't returned. When she asked Carla about it, Carla finally found it on the floor under the bed, still dirty. Gwen was furious. She almost blurted out. "You are sure a slob. It's no wonder that Dan found a new girlfriend!"

She stopped herself just in time because she knew how much Carla had been hurt when she and Dan broke up. Instead, she was able to say, "It sure does make me furious when I can't even wear my own clothes because you wear them and get them dirty. If you are going to wear my clothes, you'd better start returning them clean—and a whole lot faster!"

In the course of a fight, one or both people may begin to get very angry and upset. If this happens, it may be time for an "intermission." The quarrelers can sit quietly until their intense feelings begin to calm down enough so they can stick to the one issue under disagreement. When feelings get out of hand in a fight, the most likely result is an attack on the other person. This usually leads to a destructive end to the quarrel. By stopping and waiting for a few minutes, the partners increase their chances for a positive solution to their problem.

## experiences in human relations

### HURTING OTHERS

Most people know what hurts others. In any close relationship, people know what they can say or do to hurt or anger the other. When these "weapons" are used in conflict or disagreement, the result is likely to be destructive.

Think about the people you are close to. What do you know that you can do or say that will make them angry? It may help you to make a list of people and the comments that you know will hurt them. Do you use these "weapons" in fights with the others? What happens when you do? Do you feel that saying or doing things to make others angry generally works to help you "win" the argument? Do you feel that these "weapons" help make a constructive fight? How could you fight without making comments which cause the other person to be hurt or angry?

● ● ● ● ● ● ● ● ● ● ● ● ● ● ● ●

*Finding a time when both people are ready to fight can be important in solving the conflict.*

### The Time and Place Are Right

If a disagreement is to be settled so that both people are satisfied, it means both must agree to fight. If one person does not want to argue, probably nothing will be solved.

One night Elaine came home from work excited because she had received a raise in salary. When she stopped inside the door, her husband, George, was waiting for her. "Elaine," he said, "I don't like having to start supper after work very much. I agreed to do it because I get home earlier than you do. However, if you expect me to be the kitchen help around here, you'd better have the food ready for me to fix. How can I make spaghetti and meatballs when the meat is frozen and there isn't enough tomato sauce?"

"Oh, George," replied Elaine. "I know you've been unhappy about our cooking arrangement. We do need to talk about it, but please not tonight! Let's go out and celebrate. I got a $10 a week raise today."

George was able to back down from the fight he had wanted. The next evening George and Elaine had a good discussion and fight which led to a new system of preparing meals that was agreeable with both of them. If George had forced an argument with Elaine the first night, probably neither would have been happy with the results of the fight.

In addition to choosing a time agreeable to both partners, the place should be selected carefully. A quarrel is a private matter between two people, which should be settled between them only. Quarreling in front of another person serves no useful purpose in

### Unit 3: Relating to Others

finding a solution to the problem. Sometimes one partner will find an advantage to picking a fight in public if the partner won't fight back. However, by making sure quarrels are private matters, the partners are able to approach each other as equals.

**Ending the Quarrel**

The quarrel should not be stopped until both persons agree that the issue is really settled. If one person does not want to stop the argument, that person is likely to put the "unfinished business" in a bag. Then, during some future quarrel, the same issue will come out again. It may be that the couple can *agree* to stop the quarrel, knowing that the issue isn't settled. But if one of the partners thinks the matter is settled and the other does not, the quarrel has not been constructive.

Tom and his father were arguing over what time Tom should be home after a big party on graduation night. Finally, his father said, "Well, there's nothing more to be said. You've got to be in by 2 a.m."

Unfortunately, Tom did not agree that there was nothing more to be said! He had much more to say, but he did not say it. Instead, he put his bad feelings about his father in his bag. The next time he and his father disagreed, he brought his resentments out of the bag, which just made that quarrel worse.

Learning to *compromise,* to "give a little to get a little," is another aspect of ending a quarrel. No one is always right, although many people act as if they think they are. Quarrels that end with one person always giving in are not constructive. If both people feel that they are able to get something from the other person, they are likely to feel better about their relationship.

Consider how Tom would have felt about his father and their disagreement if his father had said, "Well, I sure would feel better if I knew you were going to be home by 2 o'clock. But I know it's hard to leave a party when it's still going strong. Since you seem to think the party won't really get started until about midnight, how about if you aim to be home about 3 o'clock?"

Since Tom had been hoping to get a 4 o'clock curfew, he didn't feel he had won the argument. However, the fact that his Dad understood how important the party was to Tom made Tom feel good. The extra hour his father gave him made him feel as if he had won part of the fight.

The end result of a constructive quarrel is that both people reach a better understanding of each other. By arguing about and solving problems in your relationships, you can strengthen them. Instead of causing hurt feelings and harm, quarrels which stick to and solve one issue can help you build more satisfying relationships.

## experiences in human relations

### CONSTRUCTIVE AND DESTRUCTIVE QUARRELS

Constructive quarrels focus on the issue or problem involved. Destructive quarrels tend to involve attacks on the other person. The following experience will help you begin thinking about the differences in these two ways of fighting.

Clip pictures from magazines that show people in possible conflict settings. Prepare two captions for each picture. One caption should attack the person pictured (destructive quarreling). The other caption attacks the problem (constructive quarreling).

## Ch. 9: Conflict in Relationships

For example, if you have a picture with two women frowning at a little boy, a destructive caption could be, "If you weren't such a bad mother, you wouldn't have let him break that glass."

A constructive caption might be, "Yes, it does bother me to have that glass broken because it is one I really like. It shouldn't be too hard to replace, though."

When you have prepared several pictures, show them to other class members. Imagine the results of the quarrels when one person attacked the other. What differences would you expect when both people attack the problem instead of each other?

### TO SUM UP...

1. Why do people need to learn to fight?
2. What is the main difference between constructive and destructive fights?
3. Why is it important to stick to one main issue in an argument?
4. Explain why both partners should be ready for a fight.
5. When should an argument end?
6. What does it mean to compromise?
7. What should be the end result of a constructive quarrel?

### THE NO-LOSE METHOD

Most people think of conflict with others in terms of winning or losing. If one person "wins" the fight, then the other must "lose." When John and Pete argue over which television program to watch at 8 o'clock, John "wins" if they watch his choice. Pete therefore "loses."

There are ways of solving problems which do not require any winners or losers. In business, partners work out agreements over their differences. Labor unions and managers negotiate contracts which both agree to obey. Many legal conflicts are settled out of court through a process that lets both sides agree on a solution.

The no-lose procedures that businessmen, legal cases, and management and unions use can be applied to everyday conflicts in relationships. Solutions can be found to conflicts so that no one wins or loses. Both partners win when a solution is acceptable to both.

The no-lose method actually involves six separate steps:
- Identify the conflict or problem.
- Suggest possible solutions.
- Judge the solutions.
- Pick the best solution.
- Work out ways of handling the solution.
- Discover how well the solution works.

The first step is actually the same as the first step in learning to fight constructively. Until you and your fight partner agree on the problem, no solution can be found.

In the second step, try to list as many possible solutions as you can. Both you and the other person should give ideas about solutions. You should not laugh at any solution given, no matter how silly it may seem. If you have a complicated problem or many possible solutions, it may help to write down the suggestions.

Next, judge the solutions. This is the time to comment if you don't find a particular solution satisfactory. Since you must be satisfied with the solution, you will need to let your opinions be known. In most cases, in

#### Unit 3: Relating to Others

this step, many of the suggestions will be discarded as being not acceptable to you or your partner. Probably only two or three suggestions will be left.

From these remaining ideas, the best solution is picked. In this step, ask yourself, "Would this solution be OK with me? Will my partner be satisfied with this solution? Will this work?" When a suggestion has been chosen, you both agree to cooperate in carrying out the solution.

In order to carry out the solution, you will have to make some choices about who does what and when. The details of the plan must be agreeable to both of you, too, just as the solution was.

Finally, the no-lose plan is put into action. Usually, these plans do work to solve a conflict or problem so that no one loses. Occasionally, however, a plan does not work. In that case, you will need to go back to the second step and suggest more possible solutions to the problem.

## experiences in human relations

### THE NO-LOSE METHOD

The no-lose method of solving differences is not difficult to learn, but it doesn't come natu-

*Most people believe fights or arguments should end with a winner and a loser.*

## Ch. 9: Conflict in Relationships

rally to most people. It must be practiced to be effective. Just as a beginning pianist needs practice to play a song, or a beginning tennis player practices to improve, the no-lose method must be practiced to be done well. This experience will help you gain some practice in the no-lose method.

Choose a partner for this experience. The experience will be more meaningful if you choose someone with whom you have a real conflict. However, you may choose to act out a conflict with someone just to have the practice.

Decide with your partner what conflict you are going to work on. When you have decided on a problem, try to think of many possible solutions. At this stage, the more suggestions you can think of, the easier other steps will be later. Some suggestions may be impractical or silly, but don't judge them now. Simply list all suggestions or combinations of suggestions.

Now begin judging the suggestions. Which ones would be impossible? Which ones would not be satisfactory to you? Which ones does your partner object to? If you eliminate all the suggestions, you need to go back to the last step and suggest some more possibilities.

Now, of the suggestions that are left, which one would be the best for both of you? The best solution *must* be agreeable to both you and your partner so that no one loses the fight. You both win by picking an answer that suits both of you.

Now figure out how you would work this solution. What arrangements would you have to make? What changes would have to be made? Think of all the items that would be necessary to make the solution work.

Finally, if you have been using a real situation, put your solution into action and see how it works.

Think about how this process worked in the experiment. Did it seem unnatural and strange? Did it seem to work better than your usual conflict style? How long do you think you would need to practice the no-lose method before it became easier for you? Are you willing to try to use the method in resolving some of your conflicts with others?

• • • • • • • • • • • • • • • • • • • • • •

Communication skills are important in using the no-lose method for solving problems. Active listening helps you understand the needs and desires of the other person. This will aid in thinking of solutions that will be satisfactory to both you and your partner. Also, sending "I-messages" is crucial throughout the whole no-lose process. "I-messages" let your partner know just what you are feeling, what you want, or how a particular suggestion strikes you. Sending "you-messages" often breaks off the no-lose process because the other person sends "you-messages" in return. "You-messages" tend to attack the other person, to blame the other, or to cause embarrassment and resentment. This usually turns the argument or conflict into a verbal battle, with each of you trying to hurt the other.

One morning, Gary hollered into the kitchen to his mother, "'Bye Mom, I'm off to school."

His mother said, "Gary, it's raining outside and you don't have your raincoat on."

Gary answered, "Oh Mom, I don't need it.!"

"I think it's raining quite hard," said his mother, "and I'm afraid that you'll ruin your clothes or get a cold."

"Well, I won't wear my raincoat," said Gary. "*Nobody* wears raincoats to school."

His mother replied, "Well, what other way can we think of to keep you dry this morning?

Unit 3: Relating to Others

*When many possible solutions are suggested, it is likely that a problem can be solved so that no one loses.*

Would you like to use my umbrella? Dad has a clear plastic raincoat that folds up into a pouch. Would that be any better?"

"No, I don't want any of them. How about my windbreaker? Or maybe I could take one of those big plastic dry cleaner bags you have in the closet. That would keep me dry."

"Your windbreaker isn't enough protection. That would soak in a couple of minutes," answered his mother. "I guess the plastic bag would be all right. In fact, if you want to, just put it in the garbage when you get to school. How about if you do that and I'll come pick you up tonight if it's still raining when school is out."

Gary agreed and went off to school, dry in his plastic bag. In this example, Gary and his mother both could appreciate each other's position. Gary understood why his mother wanted him to be dry, and his mother realized that Gary would have felt embarrassed in a raincoat. Through a combination of steps two and three, Gary and his mother thought of a number of possible solutions. It was only when Gary thought of the plastic dry cleaner bags that a solution was found that suited both of them. In another family, the umbrella might have been a good answer to the problem.

Here's another example of the no-lose method. Emily and her sister, June, were delighted when their parents agreed that they could give a Valentine's Day party for 32 guests. However, when they sat down to decide whom to invite, the disagreements began. Emily wanted to invite only couples while June didn't like that idea. June had 26 people on her first list, which Emily said was more than her share. When it was obvious that they couldn't agree, they decided to try the no-lose method for solving disagreements. Their problem was to agree on whom to invite to their party. They made the following list of possible solutions:

Invite all couples.

Invite all people by themselves.

Each invite everyone she wants.
Each invite half the total number.
Each hold a party for her friends on different nights.
Each invite her friends for half the evening.
Don't have the party.

In judging the list, June and Emily knew their parents would not allow more than 32 guests, so they would not each be able to ask all the people they wanted. Their parents also refused to have two parties. Finally, each agreed to ask 16 people. Emily planned to invite her friends as couples. June decided to ask her friends individually, without pairing them. They agreed that each would invite her own guests.

When the issue of whom to invite was settled, Emily and June went on to plan the refreshments for the party.

In the following example, several steps have been left out with a streamlining of the no-lose method. Sherrie and her mother argue constantly over the cleanliness of Sherrie's room. One day her mother said, "Sherrie, I'm really tired of nagging you about how messy your room is. I'm sure that you are tired of it, too! You do clean it up once in a while, but not often enough to suit me. It just makes me mad to look in there. Let's see if we can't find some solution that will make us both happy. I don't want to make you clean your room if that makes you unhappy, but I don't want to be embarrassed about how dirty your room is. Let's see if we can come up with something."

Sherrie listened while her mother was talking. "All right Mom," she answered, "but I know I'll just end up having to clean it oftener."

Her mother said, "No, if that is not a good solution for you, we don't want it. I want something that is good for both of us."

"Well, I have an idea," said Sherrie slowly. "You know you hate to cook and I hate to clean. You don't mind cleaning and I don't mind cooking. How about if I cook dinner and do dishes one night a week for the family and you keep my room clean?"

Her mother answered, "Well, that doesn't sound too bad to me. I surely couldn't complain about how messy your room was if it was my job to keep it clean. Do you think you'd be happy with the deal?"

"Oh, yes," Sherrie answered. "I'd really like to try. If it doesn't work, we can try something else. It sure sounds better to me than having to clean my own room!"

Sherrie and her mother found that their decision worked well for them. They both agreed that it was much better than their previous constant fights over the messy room.

The no-lose method may seem strange to you in the beginning because it is so different from the usual methods most people use to solve problems. With a little practice, you can learn this method. Solving problems with the no-lose method can pull people together in the intimacy of a joint search for a solution.

## experiences in human relations

### ROLE REVERSAL

One crucial factor in how well the no-lose method works is whether each person makes an effort to see the other person's side. Using listening skills and feedback and sending "I-messages" are important. This experience explores one way of discovering what the other person in a conflict feels. This is called "role

### Unit 3: Relating to Others

reversal" or taking the other person's part or role.

For this experience you will need a partner. With your partner, act out the conflict situations described below. Then change roles with your partner. Act out the situations again, with each of you in the opposite role. When you have finished, think about how it felt to play each role. Did you feel differently about the situation depending on which role you were playing? If you could "play the other person" in conflicts you have, do you think it would be easier to come to some constructive solutions?

*Situations:*

A teacher catches a student cheating, but the student denies it.

Two sisters argue over who is going to wear a particular pair of slacks. The slacks belong to one sister but both want to wear them on the same day.

Dating partners argue over where to go for a snack after a date. The male says he can't afford to go where the female wants.

A father and underage son argue over whether the son can go to a party where they know beer is going to be served.

### TO SUM UP...

1. List the steps of the no-lose method of solving problems.
2. Why is it important to list a number of possible solutions?
3. Describe how a solution is chosen in the no-lose method.
4. Why are communication skills so important to the success of the no-lose method?

# UNIT FOUR

## *Family Relationships*

Chapter 10. Living in Families, 210
Chapter 11. Forming Your Own Family, 236
Chapter 12. Changing Life Styles, 258
Chapter 13. Family Breakdown—Death and Divorce, 286

# CHAPTER 10
## *Living in Families*

This chapter will help you to . . .
- Define and describe characteristics of a family.
- Identify the functions which families fulfill.
- Give examples of family themes, tempos, rhythms, and boundaries.
- Understand why parents and teenagers often have conflicts.
- Consider ways to strengthen family relationships.
- Describe what causes a family crisis and how families can successfully resolve such crisis.

A *family* is a group of people, related by blood or other means, living in a common residence, and sharing common interests and goals. This definition means that families can be formed through childbirth, marriage, or adoption. Once a family has been formed, members can be added by the same three processes.

Rosa and Anthony have just formed their own family group through their marriage relationship. Janice and Eric became a family when Eric was born, even though Janice was not married to Eric's father. Alex Barnes, a single police officer, was thrilled when he was able to bring his adopted baby son home with him.

When you think of a family group, you may commonly think of a mother, a father, and their children. However, the definition given above says nothing about specific family members. Millions of people live in families that fit their individual circumstances.

The Jarrett family consists of Mrs. Jarrett, her three children, and her mother. Lorna and Saul live with their aunt and uncle. Bobby was adopted by Paula Krause, who has never been married, but Paula and Bobby have become a family. Marilyn Adams, age 19, is the head of a family which includes her 12-year-old brother and her 9-year-old sister. You probably know of families who have still other patterns of relationships.

Part of the definition of a family is "living in a common residence." This means that family members live in the same home. The Downs family lives in a high-rise housing project. Corky and Bill Ruiz live in an apartment. A mobile home is the Anderson's residence. Wayne Millott and his daughter live in a townhouse. Laura Vasquez and her mother live together in a house. Thus families may live in many kinds of residences. But the fact that they live together is one part of being a family.

Members of a family may stop living together. When this happens, the relationship ties stay the same. A daughter is still a daughter even when she lives in a college dormitory. A married son who lives in his own apartment is still a son. However, these children are no longer a part of their family on a day-to-day basis. Persons living separately still have ties to others, but are no longer part of their original family.

Another part of the definition of a family states that families share common interests and goals. This means that family members care about each other and about the family itself. It does not mean that family members must all like doing the same things.

At a very basic level, family members share the goal of having food and shelter. Mrs. Grace may or may not care whether the children in the next apartment have enough to eat. But she worries about her own children's diets when the money runs short.

Mr. Howard and his son Frank don't agree on many issues. In fact, their arguments go on almost daily. But when Frank began having trouble with his history course, Mr. Howard was very concerned. He talked to the teacher about Frank's problems with the course. The everyday interaction between Mr. Howard and Frank was often full of conflict. However, when a problem arose, their basic concern for each other as family members overcame their frequent arguments.

In these and other ways, family members show their interest in each other. Their concern for the well-being of all family members comes from the goals they share with each other.

*Many families consist of a single parent and his or her children.*

## experiences in human relations

### WHAT IS A FAMILY?

In this chapter, a family is defined as a group of people, related by blood or other means,

## Unit 4: Family Relationships

living in a common residence, and sharing common interests and goals. But just what does this definition mean? Who makes up a family? This experience will help you begin thinking about just what a family is or can be.

Form a partnership with two or three other class members. Together, read the descriptions of various groups given below. With your partners, decide which of the following groups is a family.

- Two close female friends who have known each other since childhood share an apartment. Neither has married and both feel that the other is very much a "sister."
- A young married couple are both attending school. They do not intend to have children until after graduation.
- A husband, wife, and their four children live with the husband's parents on a farm.
- A middle-aged married couple have chosen to remain childless.
- A woman who lives with and cares for her three grandchildren.
- A young man and woman live together while they attend college. They consider themselves married but did not have a legal ceremony.
- A husband, wife, and two school-age children live in the suburb of a large city.
- An eighty-year-old man and his fifty-five-year-old daughter live together in a mobile home.
- Two brothers share a bachelor apartment although each has his own job and social life.
- Four young men and four young women call their communal group "The Family." No one in the group is married.
- An unmarried woman lives with her two adopted children.

When you have finished, look over those groups that you have labeled as families. Can you identify the ways that people are linked together in family groups?

Were there groups about which you and your partners could not agree? What made these choices so difficult?

Is there any way the definition of a family could be changed to make it more specific? With your partners, write a new definition of the family. Include all the factors you think are important in a family group.

Finally, compare your list with the lists of other class members. Did you all identify the same groups as families? Report to the others your new definition of a family.

● ● ● ● ● ● ● ● ● ● ● ● ● ● ● ● ●

## FUNCTIONS OF FAMILIES

Families are found in every country of the world. They have existed since the beginning of history. What is it about families that have made them so important to people?

The reason families are so widespread is that they have filled *functions* that have served people in many ways. These functions help people live their lives as they wish. The importance of each function has changed over time. Thus family functions have varied in importance, depending on the place and time in history. Today, families serve their members through the following functions: economic, protection, education, recreation, religious, procreation, affection, and adaptation.

### ECONOMIC

The family is the center of economic activity for its members. Money is earned and spent to meet families' economic needs.

In most cases, one or more family members earn money to buy the goods and services they need and want. In the Marks family, Mr. and Mrs. Marks both work. In addition, the two Marks' sons have part-time jobs after

## Ch. 10: Living in Families

years, the production of goods moved outside the home into factories. Today, families consume goods rather than produce them in carrying out the economic function.

### PROTECTION

The family serves as one means to protect its members. It works to keep them from bodily harm. It provides care and security for members in times of illness, injury, unemployment, and old age.

Protection is especially important in the care of the family's children. When Pete reached the toddler age, Mrs. Hill spent a lot of time keeping him away from the range, electrical outlets, and the street. When children get into trouble, parents back them up to help solve the problem. Curt's mother talked to the police and the insurance agent to help Curt after he had been in an auto accident.

Families who live in high-crime areas often take special measures to protect themselves. The Grier's large watchdog growls whenever a non-family member is in their home. They rely on the dog to alert them to prowlers. In these and other ways, families work to protect themselves and their members.

The protection function of the family is less important in today's society than in the past. Families now share this function with other organizations. Police departments work to protect citizens from harm. Protection from fire is provided by public fire departments. Hospitals and doctors care for family members who are seriously ill. Insurance coverage has taken some of the financial burden of illness from the family.

Programs such as Social Security, Medicare, and Aid to Dependent Children and Families help people unable to provide for themselves. These programs remove the protection function from the direct control of the family.

*Family members earn money to buy the goods and services they need and want.*

school. Mrs. Grenfell works as a waitress to support her two children. Because Mr. Jordan is disabled, the Jordan family receives Social Security payments and a veterans' pension.

No matter what the source of money is, families use their income to purchase what they need to live. They buy food, clothing, and medicine. Homes are rented or bought by family groups. The values a family holds influence when and how money will be spent.

Today's families fulfill their economic function differently than in the past. Two hundred years ago, the home was almost like a "factory," producing everything the family needed or used. Parents and children worked together to produce food, clothing, housing, furniture, soaps, and medicines. Over the

Unit 4: Family Relationships

*One function of families is to provide recreational opportunities for members.*

However, individuals and families are still responsible for public protection programs through their payment of taxes.

## EDUCATION

The family is an important learning center for children. Newborn babies learn eating habits, how to attract attention, and whether other people bring pleasure or pain. As children grow older, they learn to talk, to control their bodies, and how to behave. Most people learn to relate to others in the family group.

Values, attitudes, and beliefs are some of the important items children learn in families. They quickly discover what is important to other family members. Children learn how the family looks at itself and at the outside world. Although people grow and change, most are influenced all their lives by what they learned as children from their families.

When the United States was being settled, families educated their own children. Only a small number could go to school. Most had to learn their lessons at the family fireplace. Today, few families teach their children academic skills. However, children learn their attitudes about education and school in the family.

Janet began to go to nursery school soon after her third birthday. She learned to value education and school from her parents. Will's father felt that school was a waste of time and encouraged him to drop out and get a job when he turned 16.

Whether students attend college or vocational classes after graduation from high school often depends on parents and family values. Miri is majoring in mathematics at the college in her city. She could not have continued to attend school without the support and help of her parents.

## RECREATION

Playing together has always been a part of family life. The family is where children first learn about recreation and fun. Many families take their children on outings or play games together.

Mrs. Murphy enjoys taking her children swimming, to the zoo, and to baseball games. The Andrews family likes playing board and word games together at home.

Families also teach members attitudes and values toward recreation. Mr. and Mrs. Rahming enjoy all kinds of fun. They have taught their children to play many card games and participate in a variety of sports. The Rahming family values the benefits of relaxing through recreation.

In contrast, recreation is not stressed by the Samuels family. Playing together is considered unnecessary because work is an important value. The Samuels and the Rahming children have learned different values about recreation in the family.

While recreation is a very important part of modern life, it is not as family centered as it was in the past. The growth of spectator sports, amusement parks, swimming pools, and tennis courts has been tremendous. These facilities offer opportunities for family recreation. They also promote recreation among peers.

Most people enjoy fun with others of the same age group. Family members often play with their friends instead of each other. Ten-year-old Billy bowls with his friends Sam and Arnie. Carol and Viola are teenagers who play tennis together. Mr. and Mrs. Trapp enjoy playing cards with other couples.

## experiences in human relations

### RECREATION IN THE FAMILY

Recreation is what people do when they are free to choose their activities. The family used to be the group with whom most people spent their free time. Today, families tend to do fewer activities together. Most recreation is done with the peer group. Still, family recreation can help build close family relationships. Playing together can help family members grow as a family. The following experiences will help you think about family recreation.

• Become aware of the recreational activities available in your area. Would your family enjoy any of these? Are there games or activities described in magazines, books, or newspapers which your family could do? What activities would your present family enjoy? What activities do you hope your future family will enjoy?

• Plan something to do together with at least one other member of your family. Choose an activity that you both (or all) enjoy. Do the activity as you have planned. Was it a success? Did you have fun? Can you plan something else which all your family members will enjoy? What part can you play in helping your family enjoy recreation together?

Unit 4: Family Relationships

- Think about television programs that involve family life. What do these television families do together for fun? Do their activities involve spending money? How many members of the family usually participate? Try to see if you can discover any patterns in your favorite television family's recreational activities. Write a brief report summarizing your findings.

### RELIGIOUS

Religion plays an important role in the lives of many families. The Singleton's attend church each week and encourage their children to participate in church youth activities. The Joseph family is very involved in the programs of their temple. Ruth and Malcolm Ali are active in the Black Muslim faith. As a result of his religious beliefs, Jack Walker served his church for two years as an overseas missionary. In these and other ways, families fulfill their religious function.

Families teach children attitudes and values about the worth of religious behavior. The Sorenson children were taught that religious beliefs were an important part of daily life. Their "born-again" Christian values and life style led them to participate in a variety of church activities.

*Providing affection and love for family members is probably the most important function of today's families.*

Mr. Thornton did not believe in any organized religion and taught his children what he believed. At the same time, he pointed out the good done by various religious groups. His children learned to accept the religious beliefs of others. Thus the Thornton children did not learn any particular "religion." What they did learn were attitudes of tolerance toward religion.

Moral training was once bound up with religious teachings. Today, some parents may not give a religious meaning to moral training. However, they still teach their children what they consider appropriate behavior.

When Gary Simon was growing up, his father used to tell him that it was a sin against God to tell a lie. Today, Gary works to teach his own son Mark honesty. However, he does not tell his son that God will punish him for lying. Instead, he explains to Mark that people will not believe in him or trust him unless he tells the truth.

## Procreation

The family has always been the accepted group for *procreation*—to bear and rear children. Most couples look forward to becoming parents. They plan for their children's births and do their best to raise their sons and daughters to be healthy, happy people.

The procreation function has changed over the years. When the United States was a growing, underpopulated land, families were encouraged to have many children. In fact, children were needed to help produce the goods the family used. Today, with overpopulation a concern, many families are having fewer children and some choose to have none.

Children in the past were often seen as economic assets or workers for the family. Today, children may be loved and appreciated more for themselves. Mr. and Mrs. Grey have three children who were conceived and born because the Grey's enjoy and love children. Each child is special in his or her own way to the Greys.

## Affection

One very important family function in today's world is that of affection. The love, acceptance, and support that family members give each other is very important. People meet many of their needs for love and affection through family life.

A family is formed on the basis of love between a man and woman. Children receive love as they are born into the family. Love and affection help family members build strong relationships with each other.

Love in the family can also help people meet other needs. When Marty and Jeff come home at night after work, they are often very tired. They find pleasure in spending quiet evenings at home together. Their love helps them meet each other's needs for quiet and relaxation.

Affection and love at home give family members a base to use in relating to the outside world. Jon was assigned a speech teacher with whom he always seemed to be in conflict. Their disagreements made Jon's school life unhappy. However, he could count on his mother's willingness to listen with love when he talked about his problems at school.

Caroline was very unhappy when she broke up with her dating partner. She never discussed her feelings with her father, but she knew he was aware of her misery. She could feel the extra love and care he gave her when she was feeling badly. His encouragement meant a great deal as she began dating others again.

In much the same way, Nita and Joel Perchek depend on each other's love and support when they have problems or disap-

## Unit 4: Family Relationships

pointments at work. They help each other cope with life both within and outside of their home.

## experiences in human relations

### SHARING AFFECTION

Providing each family member with affection is one important function of today's families. However, the meaning of affection can differ from one family to another. How do you show affection in your family? What might be other ways of giving love and support to family members? This experience will help you think about the various ways people show their affection for each other.

The following list contains a number of items which can be expressions of love. On a separate piece of paper, write down those items which *you* would interpret as love or affection when offered or given by someone in your family.

A lecture
Your own bank account
A slap on the back
A joke shared with you
A searching look
The set of a jaw
A bawling out
A gift of money
Your own house key
Fancy-worded statements
Long, serious discussion
Teasing
A kind word
Sending you to boarding school
A hand holding yours
A paycheck
Playful kidding
A special dessert
Ridicule
Being left alone when you want it
A nuzzle on the neck
A wink
A note left for you
A smile
Flowers in a room
A special dinner
Taking a walk together
Expecting you to help around home
An unexpected gift
A kiss
An arm around your shoulder
A soft voice
A gift on your birthday
Crying over you
Being held in someone's arms
Doing things together
Silence
A pinch
A pat on the back
Criticism
Someone helping you out
Ruffling up your hair
A cleaned-up house or room
Dinner ready on time
Someone listening to you
Expecting extra from you

When you have finished, form a group with several other classmates. Discuss the items which you have identified as being expressions of love. Do your lists differ? Explain why certain items seem to you to show affection. What did you discover in this group about the differences people have in how they express or interpret expressions of love?

Show the above list to other members of your family. What items do they identify as showing affection? Did their lists agree with yours? Does any of the conflict in your family arise over the different ways you show or share affection?

● ● ● ● ● ● ● ● ● ● ● ● ● ● ● ● ● ●

### Ch. 10: Living in Families

Jerry Neville, a worker at a truck factory, was laid off. He was told he would be called back as soon as possible. However, he was home for over four months before he started work again. During that time, his wife and children helped him become used to being at home. They assisted him in setting up a routine to replace going to work. They all worked together to adjust to their lowered income. With everyone's cooperation, Jerry's layoff was a time with little family conflict and disagreement. Everyone helped the others adapt to the changes in the family's schedule and financial standing.

*The family whose belongings are in this moving van will have to adapt to many changes as they move to their new home.*

#### ADAPTATION

One important family function in a world that changes rapidly is adaptation. New patterns of behavior are built in the family so that members can adjust to a changing world.

The building the Jason family lived in was destroyed in an urban renewal project. Their family was relocated in a housing project, where they were strangers. During the time it took to move in and get acquainted with others, family members helped each other. They worked together to get settled in their new home. Doug discovered which bus routes to take to get around the city. Together, Betty and Mark explored the shops near their new home and found where the best buys were. Each family member introduced the others to new acquaintances. The family group was crucial in helping the Jason's adapt to their new home.

### TO SUM UP. . .

1. What is a family?
2. What characteristics do members of a family share?
3. Why are families found all over the world and throughout history?
4. Describe the change in the economic function over the last 200 years.
5. What are some agencies that help families with the protective function?
6. Identify some learnings that children are taught in their families.
7. Why has recreation become less important as a family function?
8. Why is affection probably the most important function of the family today?
9. What is meant by the adaptation function?

### THE FAMILY STYLE

All families provide the functions described above. However, families differ in the way they handle these functions. Some families stress one function more than another.

## Unit 4: Family Relationships

*This family has a theme of enjoying the beauties of nature and outdoor living.*

Working toward economic security is very important to the Meadows family. On the other hand, the Jackson's don't worry much about money but place a great deal of emphasis on religious matters. Other families focus on other functions, although most families are involved in the affection and adaptation functions.

Whatever functions a family stresses, that family does them in its own way. Just as people are different from each other, so are families. Each family has its own style or personality in fulfilling its functions. Each family operates by a series of different patterns.

### FAMILY THEMES

A *family theme* is based on what the family wants out of life. It represents ideas about how things should be. The family theme is usually set when a man and a woman marry. They mesh their individual ideas into a pattern for the family. A family theme reflects the attitudes, values, and beliefs that members have. Many areas of family life are influenced by the family theme.

For example, the Willis family theme centers on fun and enjoyment of life with others. Very seldom are the Willis's home alone. Mr. and Mrs. Willis have their friends over often for parties or dinners. The Willis children bring their friends home. There are usually at least one or two extra people for meals, and overnight guests are common. When the Willis's are not at home, they are visiting or have gone out with other people. They rarely go anywhere alone or as a family.

Members of another family may spend much time with others, but for different purposes. The family theme for the Myers family is service to others. All of the family members work to help others, although each has a special interest. Mr. Myers uses his free time to help coach a swimming team at the Y Teen Center. Mrs. Myers does volunteer work at a local hospital. Sancha visits residents of a senior citizens nursing home three times a week and Mary is involved in the Young Democrats organization. All of these activities reflect the family theme of working for others.

The Abbotts stress thrift and getting the most for their money. Many of their activities center around comparison shopping, do-it-yourself projects, and free or inexpensive recreation.

Family togetherness is the main theme of the McNeal family life. Since her separation from Mr. McNeal, Mrs. McNeal works to plan family activities. She feels that it is important for her and the children to work and play together. In this way, she tries to promote family affection and support for each other.

Other families have different family themes. Some families may value getting ahead in the world. Adventuresome living is a theme of many families. Others may stress calmness and sobriety, or the freedom of outdoor living.

Your family probably has another theme. There are as many themes as there are families. Becoming aware of the theme of your family group may help you understand other family members better.

## Tempos and Rhythms

Just as families have themes, they also have a *pace* at which they live. This pace is how fast or slowly life is lived.

One way to describe the pace of life is by the *tempo*. This is the speed with which events happen. In some families, life moves very rapidly. In other families, events occur more slowly.

For example, the tempo of life is very rapid at the Mays. All of the members of the Mays family are busy people. Someone is always coming or going and there is much hustle and bustle. Sometimes it seems that family members arrive home from one activity only to leave for another.

In contrast, life at the Richmonds' home is much more slowly paced. No one ever seems in a hurry. There is always time to sit and talk for a while. Mr. Richmond is a calm, placid sort of person. He influences the others to take life easy, to spend time with each other.

Another way to describe the pace of family life is through *rhythms*. This is how steady the activity is—how regular the pace is. Some families always seem to move at the same pace. In the examples given above, the rhythm at the Mays' home is steady at a rapid pace. At the Richmond's, the rhythm is steady at a much slower pace. But in other families, the pace is not steady. Instead, it may go in spurts of activity.

The family life of Mr. Robbins and his three children tends to go in spurts. They may have a quiet life for several months just going to school and to work and relaxing at home. Then they will have a period of a more rapid pace, each busy attending events at school or in the community. A month or two of activity usually lapses again into a more slowly paced existence.

Obviously, the tempo and rhythm of a family's life will depend on the family theme. A family that enjoys being with others and going places is more likely to have a rapidly paced life. Families that stress relaxation and togetherness are likely to have a more slowly paced life style.

## Family Boundaries

Another trait which makes up the life style of a family is the *family boundaries*. The boundary is the line that divides the family from others outside the family.

In some families this boundary is very tight. These families are like the Davis family. Being together as a family is important to the Davis'. They do not have company very often. If

221

Unit 4: Family Relationships

*A family with loose boundaries welcomes its children's friends into the home.*

Tansy wants a friend to come over to play, she is expected to get permission first. If Tom wants to bring a date over to their apartment, he has to ask in advance. Neighbors do not "drop in" at the Davis'. For the most part, outsiders are not important in the family life at the Davis home. The boundaries between the family and others are strong.

In contrast, the Owens family has very loose boundaries. The Owens' children bring their friends home any time without asking permission. Whoever happens to be at the Owens' home at mealtime is free to eat with the family. Friends and neighbors visit the Owens' any time. They know they will always be welcome. Relationships with non-family members are important to this family. The boundaries between their family members and others are loose and weak.

Again, how tight or loose the family's boundaries are depends on the family theme. The theme determines how many extra people members can comfortably include in their family. How much members value togetherness as a family or the company of outsiders is influenced by the theme.

## Ch. 10: Living in Families

Thus the family theme, the tempos and rhythms of family life, and the family boundaries are important in understanding how families live. The family style influences which of the functions will be emphasized. It also determines how these functions will be carried out.

## experiences in human relations

### FAMILY STYLE

Every family has a personality, just as every person does. This personality is called a family style. The family theme, tempo, rhythm, and boundaries influence the style of a family. This experience will help you learn to recognize what makes a family style. Think of some family with whom you are familiar. This may be a family you know or a family from a television program, a movie, or a book.

The following list of words can be used to describe families. Some of the words will apply to the family you have chosen to study. Others will not apply to the family. First, read over the list. Then choose one word which you think best describes the family. This might be hard to do. When you have chosen one word, go through the list again. On a separate piece of paper, write down all the words which you think in some way describe the family. The words may pertain to the family theme, the pace, or the boundaries. Your list should give a good impression of the style of the family.

Bossy
Gentle
Stingy
Playful
Democratic
Generous
Fast-paced
Loving
Lonely
Modest
Witty
Outgoing
Silly
Apathetic
Bitter
Dependable
Relaxed
Sense of Humor
Shy
Creative
Proud
Efficient
Giving
Likable
Rigid
Warm
Nervous
Wasteful
Lively
Cheerful
Hard Working
Selfish
Calm
Intelligent
Honest
Anxious
Strong
Serious
Rejecting
Slow
Carefree
Friendly
Accepting
Controlled
Ambitious
Dignified
Responsible
Fearful
Independent
Authoritarian
Fun
Religious
Sociable
Organized
Energetic
Merry
Passive
Understanding
Worried

Now look over your list. Do you think members of the family would agree with your list? Could you explain to them why you chose the words you did? What did you learn about family styles from this experience?

### TO SUM UP...

1. What is a family style?
2. List examples of various family themes.
3. What is the difference between tempos and rhythms?
4. What are family boundaries?

Unit 4: Family Relationships

# RELATIONSHIPS IN THE FAMILY

When the family carries out its functions well, it promotes the growth and well-being of all family members. Family functions and relationships are closely connected. How well the family carries out its functions depends on the relationships within the family. On the other hand, family relationships depend to some extent on how well the family can fulfill its functions. Therefore building strong relationships in the family is important in helping the family fulfill its functions. Effective family relationships are also needed to help family members grow and develop as people.

Relating to another on a person-to-person basis is difficult in any setting. It becomes an even harder task within the family. The constant day-to-day living together can make good relationships difficult.

## experiences in human relations

### MEMBERS OF YOUR FAMILY

The previous experience involved identifying words which described a family style. This experience will help you think about the various members of your family and what they are like as people.

Imagine that a stranger is coming to visit your family. You are to meet her at the bus station. Since she has never met any of your family, write a description of each member of your family for her. Do not describe clothing that each person might be wearing. Instead try to describe what each family member is like, both in looks and in actions. Make your descriptions an introduction to the members of your family. Be sure to include a description of yourself.

To summarize your family descriptions, choose one word which would describe each person. For each person in your family, complete the following sentence: "He (or she) is the _____ one." What word would you use to describe yourself?

Think about what you have written about each family member. Did these individual descriptions help you realize how each person helps form your family's style? How did this experience help you begin to see the others in your family as people?

● ● ● ● ● ● ● ● ● ● ● ● ● ● ● ● ● ● ● ● ●

## PARENT-CHILD RELATIONSHIPS

As parents interact with their children, conflict occurs. Early in the child's life, the conflict may be as simple as the parent keeping a child from throwing food on the floor. However, as the child grows older, the natural conflict between parents and children becomes more complex.

### Different Outlook on Life

Some conflict will occur between parents and teenagers simply because of the age difference between them. The twenty to thirty years of age that separates you and your parents is important in understanding your relationships. The events that your parents lived through as they grew up were different from those you are living through. These various events cause parents and their children to look at the world from distinct viewpoints.

Mr. and Mrs. Lang grew up during the early 1950's. They are both quiet people who like to conform to the behavior of others. Their children, however, think that individuality is important. Both sets of ideas are a natural result of the world in which each generation grew up. However, they are also the basis of some conflict in the Lang home.

Not only do parents and teenagers look at the world in a distinct manner, but they also apply what they know about the world differently. Parents may sometimes try to apply what they learned as young adults to today's world. Because of the changes in the world, their learnings are out-of-date. Teenagers often try to apply their learnings without any notion of how events came to be the way they are. Thus, parents don't take into account the changes in the world, while teenagers are unable to see events in any kind of long-term perspective.

Jake's parents want him to go to college. Although neither of them was able to attend, they feel that it is important to Jake's future security that he go. They feel that college will give him a chance to get ahead in the world in a job with a good salary. Jake, however, realizes that a college degree doesn't guarantee a good job. He knows several college graduates who have been unable to find jobs in their areas of study. Therefore he has concluded that college would be a waste of time if he is going to end up driving a taxi anyhow.

Jake's parents may be overestimating the future security that college would bring Jake. He, on the other hand, is not able to appreciate the opportunities that college could bring him. The conflict between Jake and his parents centers around the way they have applied their understanding of the world to their own situation.

## Different Needs

The age difference between parent and child creates a different outlook on life. It also leads to a situation in which family members have different needs.

Teenagers are reaching the point of their lives when they will soon become independent. Adult life requires that they be self-supporting and self-sufficient. They will no longer be dependent and reliant on their parents. Much of the interaction between parents and teenagers is concerned with deciding how much independence the teenager is going to have while still at home.

*The teenage years help prepare children for independence from their parents.*

Martha's parents have established a weekend midnight curfew for her. She feels that now that she is 17, she should be able to decide for herself how late she will come home. She is trying to become more independent, getting herself ready for her future total independence.

On the other hand, parents have needs also. As their teenage children approach maturity, one of parents' needs is to be needed. They see their parent role coming to an end. Although they may be proud of their teenagers' new independence, they still want to

## Unit 4: Family Relationships

be a part of the teens' lives. Therefore, parents often try to exert more authority than teenagers wish.

Virgil has an after-school job. When he began work, it was understood that he would save part of his money for vocational school after graduation. Lately, however, he has been spending all of his earnings on dating and other recreation. His mother warns that if he can't spend his money wisely, he will be required to give half of his paycheck to her. That way, she can see that he saves it for his education. Virgil feels that his mother shouldn't interfere, since he earned the money. He feels the need to be independent and spend his paycheck as he wishes. His mother feels the need to continue to order and organize his life. Because of these conflicting needs, arguments occur.

Another difference in needs may relate to family style. Parents establish a family theme, tempo, rhythm, and boundaries to fit their own needs and personality. Some children find the family style right for them. Other children don't fit in with their family's style. This can cause problems in family relationships. Kurt's family lives a quiet life. Kurt finds them very dull and unexciting. He craves noise, companionship, and dangerous activities. His motorcycle racing appalls his parents. They cannot understand his love of risk and adventure.

## experiences in human relations

### FROM THE PARENT'S SIDE

You may have thought many times that your relationship with your parent or parents could be better. However, it is likely that you were looking at improvements from only one point of view—your own. Being willing to try to see the relationship from the parent's point of view is one of the first steps in working out differences.

Many of the things parents say and do may upset you. But have you stopped to consider that what you say and do may also upset them? This experience will help you think about the situation from the parent's side.

Choose three people from the class to assume the role of parents. You and your other classmates should take the role of teenage children. The "children" should choose one of the following statements. Using strong emotions, express the statement you have chosen to the "parents." The "parents" are to remain silent. They can use nonverbal methods to communicate their reactions to the others.

"I'm really sick and tired of the way I get nagged around this place. Nag, nag, nag, that's all you ever do."

"I don't ever get anything I want!"

"I've seen you drunk before. What's wrong with my taking a drink now and then?"

"Everybody has one but me."

"What did you do when you were my age that makes you so suspicious of me now?"

"You've ordered me around all my life, but this time it's going to be a different story."

"It must be awful to be getting so old, isn't it?"

"If I hear 'when I was your age' one more time, I'm leaving home for good."

"You don't understand anything but money. We're not money grubbers. We love each other and want to get married. We'll get by without help from you."

"You're just stingy; you're selfish."

"I don't care! I'm not going to college."

"Nobody has any privacy around here. I just burn up when you read my mail and my diary and listen in on my phone calls."

"Why are you so hard on me?"

You may wish to make up other statements to express to the "parents."

When you are finished, think about how you felt in this experience. Have those students who were parents tell how they felt. How did they react to the statements? Did they get angry? Did they feel that the accusations were fair?

How did the students who were children feel? Were the statements ones that they have used to their parents? Did you feel as if the statements were constructive or destructive kinds of communication? How could you use what you learned in this experience in your family life?

● ● ● ● ● ● ● ● ● ● ● ● ● ● ● ● ●

## Sibling Relationships

In addition to parent-child relationships, most families include relationships between children. Brothers and sisters are sometimes called *siblings*. Their relationships to each other are called *sibling relationships*.

Of all relationships, those between siblings are most likely to create conflict. This is because a child's first experience with competition usually occurs with a sibling. The affection function of the family is very important to children. Thus children compete with each other for parents' love and attention. The more children there are in a family, the more likely there is to be competition for love.

Tony and Jim compete for their parents' attention and praise. When they were small, their competition often led to fist fights and trying to outdo each other. Now that they are both in high school, each has an area where he shines. Tony is a good student and can hold his parents' attention with discussions about his work and grades. Jim excells in athletics. His parents attend his ball games and praise his skill. Jim is able to gain his parents' attention through his football and baseball talents.

*Jealousy occurs when a child feels he or she is not getting a fair share of parents' love and attention.*

Some children choose other ways to get their parents' attention. Karen learned early in life that the fastest way to attract her mother's attention was to be naughty. Coloring on the walls got much more action than coloring on a paper. Karen still draws attention to herself by getting into trouble. Recently, she was suspended from school for three weeks for having alcohol in her locker. Karen's need for affection and attention leads her to actions that are self-defeating. She gets her family's attention, but in such a way that they find it hard to show love or affection.

Jealousy is another reason for conflict among siblings. This, too, is related to the

## Unit 4: Family Relationships

affection function of the family. Because one child is different from another, parents treat the children differently. Although the parents may try very hard to be fair, sometimes one child becomes jealous of another.

Janine is very talented in relating to other people. She knows how to make people feel at ease with her. As a result, she has many friends. Her parents take her skill in getting along with others for granted. Her sister, Bobbi, is a talented singer. Because Bobbi's voice is often praised by her parents, Janine is very jealous. Her talent for getting along with others seems worthless beside Bobbi's voice. Janine's jealousy leads to frequent conflicts between the sisters.

### Relating as People

Most parents and children want to have good relationships with each other. But somehow, especially during the children's teenage years, they often seem unable to accomplish this easily. Instead, family members find themselves in conflict-riddled relationships. No one finds these kinds of relationships satisfactory. In addition, poor relationships decrease the family's ability to meet its functions well.

As a group, the family gives people a chance to seek the best expression of themselves in life. You can be accepted by and for yourself in your family. Thus people look to their family for help in growing. Parents and children can contribute to each other's understanding and growth. How can this occur in the family setting? How can family members learn to work together to meet their needs and keep the family fulfilling its functions?

One way that families can help each other grow is through improved communication. Chapter 7 describes in detail the communication skills which you can use with your family. Leveling with each other and working to send "I-messages" which describe how you feel can help your family members meet each other's needs. Listening and feedback are two other skills which are important in relating to family members. Good communication skills are crucial if family members are to relate to each other in healthy ways.

## experiences in human relations

### COMMUNICATION IN FAMILIES

Family members often take each other so much for granted that they communicate poorly with each other. You may assume that others in your family know you so well that you don't need to express your feelings and ideas. However, most family members are unable to read minds. It often turns out that communication problems interfere with good family relationships.

Choose one member of your family with whom you seem to have frequent conflict. Keep a journal for a week, recording your conversations and actions with that person. It may be hard to write down exactly what went on each time you were together. However, try to keep a record of your contacts and the kind of interaction you had.

After the week of record keeping is up, read over your entries. Did the two of you have pleasant conversations or were you often in conflict? Did there seem to be a pattern in your relationship? If so, describe the pattern.

Look back over the chapter on communicating with others. Pick two or three communication skills. Make a plan to use them in your relationship. Work to figure out exactly how you can use the skills to improve your commu-

Ch. 10: *Living in Families*

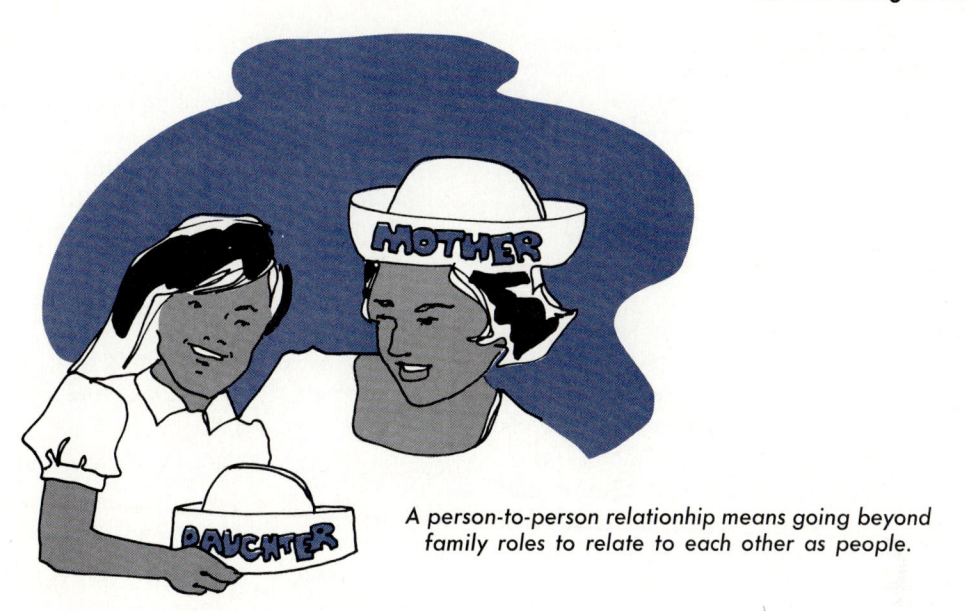

*A person-to-person relationhip means going beyond family roles to relate to each other as people.*

nication patterns. For example, you may wish to work on listening skills and feedback. Your efforts to improve communication could easily lead to a better relationship between the two of you.

● ● ● ● ● ● ● ● ● ● ● ● ● ● ● ● ● ● ● ●

People can help their families become more healthy by accepting conflict. When people live together and attempt to get all of their needs met, conflict is bound to occur. Accepting conflict as a normal part of family life helps you to be able to manage it. But besides accepting conflict, you must be willing to work to resolve it. The methods of solving conflict discussed in Chapter 9 can be used to make family relationships more harmonious.

Finally, family members can become closer to each other if they work to see each other as people. It is very easy to become used to relating to family members in terms of their family roles. When people are "Father," "Mother," "Sister," or "Brother" to you, it may be hard to see them as *people*. Your family roles interfere with relating as people.

Person-to-person relationships in families have the same traits as other person-to-person relationships. You need to trust and be trustworthy. You need to be able to use power and accept its use by others. Giving and receiving affection is important in person-to-person relationships. As you learn to accept each other as people, you will build satisfying family relationships.

Families serve many important functions for their members. These functions may only be partly fulfilled unless family members learn to relate to each other as people. Building relationships through good communication skills and effective conflict resolution results in strong families. Families that fulfill their functions through good relationships provide the setting for the growth and self-actualization of family members.

Unit 4: Family Relationships

## experiences in human relations

### YOUR IDEAL FAMILY

What is your ideal family like? Thinking about this question may help you understand what you value in family life.

Make up imaginary want ads headed "Father Wanted," "Mother Wanted," "Brother Wanted," and "Sister Wanted." In each ad, describe in a few words the characteristics you think are important for each person.

Next, compose an ad headed "Son Available" or "Daughter Available," depending on your sex. Tell the kind of son or daughter you are and how you might improve.

For example, Ozzie wrote:

> FATHER WANTED. To take his children seriously, but willing to let them be themselves. Needs to be warm and outgoing. Should be able to listen without shouting.
>
> SON AVAILABLE. Considerate and responsible when not hassled. Willing to learn if not forced. Is sometimes moody, but will work to improve.

When you have completed your ads, think about what you have written. What values were shown in your descriptions?

### TO SUM UP...

1. What is the connection between the family functions and the relationships between family members?
2. Explain how a different outlook on life can cause conflict between teenagers and their parents.
3. Which needs of parents and teenagers conflict most sharply?
4. What are siblings? Sibling relationships?
5. Why might sibling relationships be prone to conflict?
6. What are some communication skills which can be used to improve family relationships (see Chapter 7)?
7. Describe how conflict can be handled in family relationships (see Chapter 9).
8. How can good family relationships contribute to the self-actualization of family members?

### FAMILY CRISIS

Families face problems from the day they are formed. Most of these problems are easily solved. However, some problems create a situation which the family can't resolve by any of their normal problem-solving methods. A *crisis* occurs when normal routines and behaviors for handling situations are not effective. Changed behavior by family members is needed in order to meet the new situation successfully.

Crises differ in their sources. Some crises arise outside of the family while others arise from within. The Kent family was plunged into crisis when their 16-year-old daughter Anna ran away from home. The mental illness of Mr. Graves was the source of the crisis in his family. Alice's premarital pregnancy caused crisis in the Blankenship family. Other kinds of crises which can arise from within the family include infidelity, alcoholism, and delinquency. The breakdown of the family through death or divorce are two major causes of family crises. They will be discussed later in Chapter 13.

Many crises are imposed on the family from the outside. When Mr. Griffin announced that his company was transferring him to another city, a crisis arose in his family. Ruth Jasmine lost her job when three assembly lines in the plant were shut down, causing a financial crisis in her family. War and natural disasters are other kinds of outside crises.

## What Makes a Crisis?

A crisis arises when a family cannot cope with or handle a new or unusual situation. Therefore what makes a crisis differs from family to family. No single event will be a crisis for all families.

For example, a tornado struck the town of River Junction. It caused a severe crisis in the Scott family for Mr. Scott was killed and their home destroyed. The Garcia family, however, suffered a mild crisis. Mr. Garcia was out of work for two months before the feed plant where he worked could open again. Meanwhile, he was able to work part-time at community cleanup and salvage. In addition, the Garcia family had enough savings to help them live comfortably until their regular income started again. Finally, the tornado turned out to be an opportunity for John Malone. His old grocery store was demolished by the storm. With insurance money and a government disaster grant, he was able to build the new store that had been his dream for over 15 years.

In general, three factors determine whether a particular event becomes a crisis for a family. First are the hardships of the situation or event itself. The second is whether the family has the resources to cope with these hardships. Finally, the attitude of the family toward the event influences whether or not it will be a crisis.

Mr. Larkin and Mr. Rickey both lost their jobs when a munitions plant in their city closed down. The immediate hardship in both families was the loss of salaries. In the Larkin family, the job loss was a crisis. No one else in the family worked and they had no savings. Thus they had no resources to see them through until Mr. Larkin got another job. The family members felt panic and fear about how they would pay their bills until they had income again.

In contrast, the Rickey family was able to keep the job loss from becoming a crisis. Mrs. Rickey's salary was enough to pay the family's bills although they had to be frugal. Mike and Tina were both able to find after-school jobs to earn their own spending money. A savings account gave the family a financial cushion until Mr. Rickey found a new job. While the Rickey family considered the situation serious, they did not find it frightening or tragic. They worked together to keep the loss of Mr. Rickey's job from becoming a crisis.

Although money or the lack of it can be important in how families meet crisis situations, other factors are also involved. Personal strengths and relationship skills are resources that can be used to meet crises. The Curry family found it hard to build relationships with others. Although they had lived in their town for about five years, they had only recently begun to build strong friendships. When Mr. Curry was offered a large promotion if he would move to the company's main office in another city, the family caused a fuss. Because family members lacked the personal skills to build new relationships, they saw the proposed move as threatening and frightening.

The Streetman family was transferred about every two years by Mr. Streetman's firm. This family, in contrast to the Currys, looked forward to their moves. They made friends easily in each new town. They enjoyed the chance to meet new people and have new experiences wherever they went. Their relationship

### Unit 4: Family Relationships

skills helped them to look upon their frequent moves as opportunities rather than crises.

Some families, called *crisis prone,* seem to have more crises than others. In some instances, these families do suffer many hardships. But in most cases, a crisis-prone family is one that has not learned to meet crisis. Therefore family members are unable to cope with the hardships that come with crisis events. Because they are unable to cope, each crisis in turn looms larger than the one before. Crisis-prone families are apt to be in a constant state of stress and disunity. They have lost their ability to fulfill the family functions outlined earlier.

*Financial resources can sometimes help prevent crisis or make it less severe.*

### FACING AND MEETING CRISIS

Usually, a family facing a crisis goes through a typical pattern. Family members may at first act as if nothing had happened. Then as they begin to face the fact of crisis, they become disorganized. Family members fill their roles without enthusiasm. Resentments against each other come to the surface. Conflicts appear, often leading to strained relationships. Then just when matters often seem hopeless, family life begins to improve. New routines are found that help meet the problems brought by the crisis. Sacrifices may be made. Thoughtful planning begins to help the family reach some agreements about the future.

When Thad Grabill was expelled from school for fighting with a knife, his family was shocked. At first, neither Mrs. Grabill nor her mother, with whom Thad lived, could believe it. Then the resentments poured out. Thad's grandmother blamed his mother for never being home to care for Thad. Thad accused his mother and grandmother of not providing well enough for him. His mother shouted her bitterness at both of the others. For a few days, they all avoided each other and spoke little when they were together.

Finally, they began to regroup and talk about what could be done. Thad enrolled in a new school and was placed in a counseling group where students could talk about their problems. Mrs. Grabill took a part-time job in addition to her full-time one to help provide a little more money for the family. Thad's grandmother took over more responsibility for running their home. As the family learned to live with its new routines, the crisis began to be resolved.

The ability of families to meet and face crisis is directly related to how well they fulfill their functions. In particular, the affection

Ch. 10: Living in Families

*Love and affection between family members help them be better prepared to face crisis.*

and adaptation functions are important in meeting crisis.

When crisis strikes, a basic level of affection and support are needed for a family to work together to meet the crisis. When family ties and bonds are important, they are worth working to keep. When there is little love or affection, people often feel that it is not worth making an effort to face the crisis together. Family members who see themselves as a united group are apt to work together to maintain that group. Without love and affection, the conflict that goes with crisis can tear the family apart.

The Norton family had always had a close relationship with Mrs. Norton's mother, Mrs. Wilber. Mrs. Norton describes what happened to her family when Mrs. Wilbur suffered a severe stroke. "I have always had a real dislike of nursing homes for old people," says Mrs. Norton. "When my mother had her stroke, I was determined that she wouldn't be put in such a home. So we sold her small house and brought her home with us. Her stroke was a bad one and I had to spend most of my time nursing her. I guess I did realize that I was neglecting my husband and children, but all I could think of was keeping mother out of a nursing home.

"Then we were called to school for a conference about Tim. I just couldn't believe it when they said that he had become such a problem child that perhaps we should send him to a psychiatrist. When we got home, my husband and I started fighting about whether I was neglecting our children. Then my husband dropped his bomb—unless things changed, he was going to file for divorce.

"Now, looking back, I think what helped us live through the whole ordeal was how much we all loved each other. I loved my family too much to risk having it break up. So we compromised. We found a good home for mother where I can go care for her each morning. Then a nurse takes over and I have the rest of the day to devote to my family. Tim's problems have disappeared, which has been a big relief. Of course, it took a long time to work it all out, but we had too much together to let our love and family life just go down the drain."

While love is the factor which helps families make the effort to meet crisis, adaptation is the key to solving crisis. Families facing crisis must adapt and develop new ways of behaving. For instance, a shift in power may be needed in the family. Some family members may assume new roles. Improved communication patterns may help the family to new levels of functioning. The ability of the family to change their behavior patterns, to adapt, is the crucial factor in resolving crisis.

Mrs. Parrish became more concerned every time she took eight-month-old Tammy to the park to play with the other babies. The others about Tammy's age babbled happily as they played while Tammy was strangely silent. Mrs. Parrish noticed that the other babies had learned to recognize their mother's voices. Tammy had never responded to either Mr. or Mrs. Parrish's talking. Finally, they took Tammy for testing and found that she was profoundly deaf and, thus, also mute. The Parrish's were crushed at the news. They had no idea how to cope with a deaf child or how Tammy could be educated.

Slowly, they began to learn what they could do to help Tammy lead a normal life. They both learned sign language so that they could teach it to Tammy as she approached the age when most children learn to talk. Mrs. Parrish took a weekend job to earn money to pay for a speech therapist to work with Tammy. They joined an organization of parents who also had deaf children, where they learned more about deafness. In these and many more ways, they adjusted and adapted to their daughter's deafness. Because they were able to change and learn new ways of behaving, Tammy has grown to be a happy child who has accepted her deafness. She has many friends and can communicate through sign language, lip reading, and simple speech.

Most people consider the term "family crisis" as something negative or bad. Yet crises are not always bad for the family or its members. In many cases, a crisis leads to new ways of behaving that turn out to be better than the old ones. The Burks family moved to a new city reluctantly when Mr. Burks took a new job. The decision to move caused a severe family crisis. A year after the move, however, all the Burks family members say that the move was a good one. All agree that they are happier in their new home and city than they were before. Facing the crisis of moving led them to a more rewarding life.

In some instances, a crisis can bring a family closer together. When Althea Clark was stricken with meningitis, she hovered between life and death for several days. The Clark family was drawn together by their grief and concern during the days of her illness.

When she recovered, their joy at having her a part of the family again led to closer and more loving family relationships. The crisis of Althea's illness led to stronger family ties.

Finally, families who are able to meet one crisis well are better equipped to face the crisis that the future will bring. Crises can bring about family growth. Families can become strong and stable through successfully facing and overcoming crises.

## experiences in human relations

### FAMILY CRISIS

A crisis is an event which causes changes in a person's or family's normal behavior. What is a crisis for one family may not be seen as a crisis by another. This experience will help you explore what family crisis means to you and your classmates.

Given below is a list of events which could cause family crises. Read through this list and, on a separate piece of paper, write down all the events which you think would cause a family crisis.

Loss of an arm or a leg by a family member.
Pregnancy of an unmarried family member.
Death of a family member.
Loss of a job by a family member.
Failure of a family member to graduate from high school.
Pregnancy of a married family member.
Family income cut in half.
Relative coming to live with family.
Divorce.
Birth of a mentally retarded child.
A three-month hospital stay by an ill family member.
Alcoholism by a family member.
Destruction of the home by flood, earthquake, tornado, or hurricane.
Commitment of a family member to a mental hospital.
Arrest of a family member for theft or another crime.

Form a group with three other class members. Compare your lists of family crisis. Did your lists differ? Discuss with the others your reasons for including certain events on your list. Make a master list which contains those events all group members mentioned on their individual lists.

Compare your master list with those from other class groups. What events did all groups list as crisis? What differences did you find in the lists? How can you account for these differences?

### TO SUM UP...

1. What is a crisis?
2. List the three factors that determine if an event will lead to family crisis.
3. Identify characteristics of a crisis-prone family.
4. Describe a family's normal reactions to crises.
5. Why is the affection function important in meeting crises?
6. How does the adaptation function relate to resolving crises?
7. How can crises help a family to grow?

# CHAPTER 11

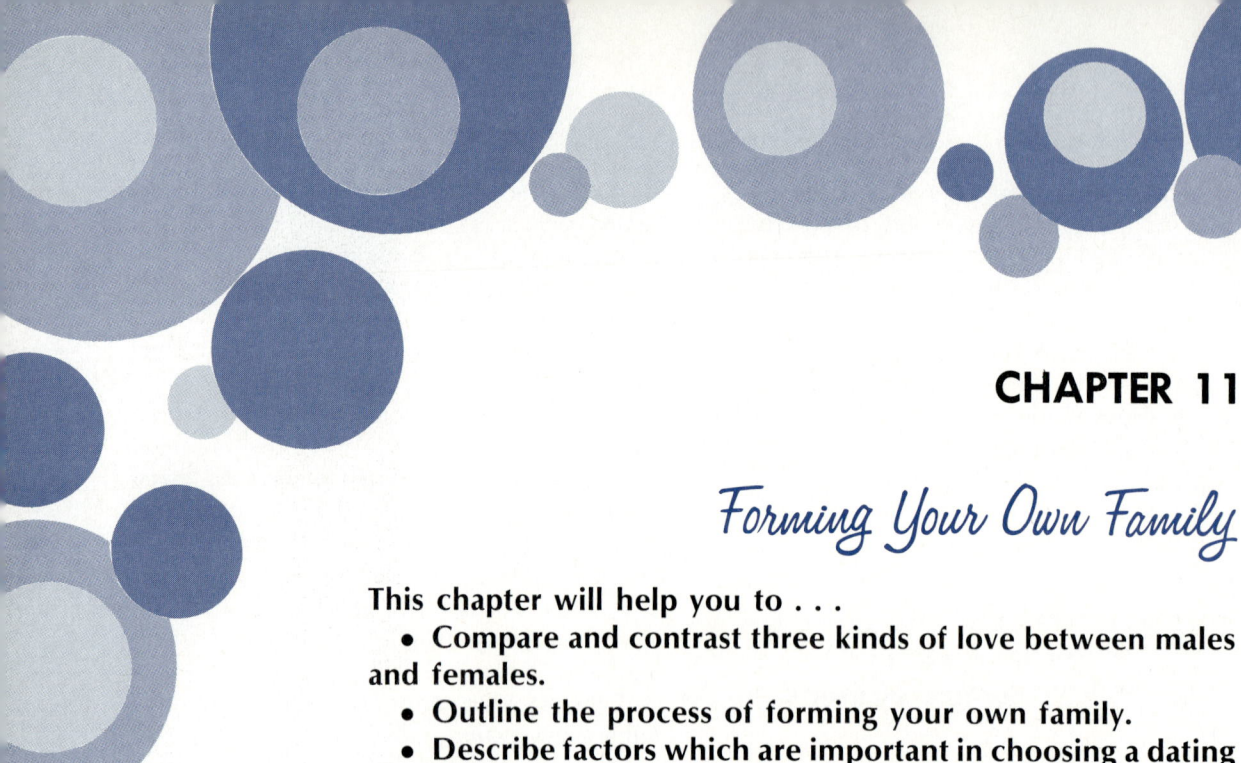

## Forming Your Own Family

This chapter will help you to . . .
- Compare and contrast three kinds of love between males and females.
- Outline the process of forming your own family.
- Describe factors which are important in choosing a dating partner.
- Discuss the value of dating as a preparation for marriage.
- Identify ways the engagement, wedding ceremony, and honeymoon help prepare a couple for married life.

As teenagers grow and mature, they become more independent of their parents and the family in which they grew up. At the same time, they still want love and the emotional support of someone they care for. This leads them to begin the process of forming their own family.

It is true that today a small number of people choose to live together without marriage. An even smaller number may have children without being married. However, most people form their own families through the marriage relationship. Therefore the marriage ceremony will be thought of as the beginning of a new family.

Why do people feel the need to marry? Because people are so different, their reasons for wanting marriage are different.

Some people just don't enjoy life by themselves. Marshall lived alone in an apartment. At first, he enjoyed the quiet and the freedom to do as he pleased. It was a welcome change after the noise and confusion of living with his siblings and his father. After about a year, however, Marshall almost hated to go home after work at night. He was lonely and bored with no one to talk to. Although he dated a lot, he missed having someone to share his life on a daily basis. His feelings of being alone helped him decide that maybe he was ready to think about marriage.

Joanie was unhappy living at home. Even though she had a good job, her parents didn't want her to move to an apartment. They treated her as if she were still their child instead of an adult. Joanie realized that the only

### Ch. 11: Forming Your Own Family

*Love is the reason most people marry and form their own families.*

way she would ever be able to move away from home without conflict would be to get married.

There are many reasons why people get married. Some people want to show the world that they are mature, married adults. Marriage may be an escape from an unhappy home, loneliness, or singlehood. In some cases, marriage may bring a more financially secure future. However, when people talk about why they want to marry, these reasons are rarely mentioned. People say the main reason they married or want to marry is for love.

## LOVE

Love is the subject of songs, books, articles, and poems. People sing about love, write about it, and talk about it. In fact, through overuse, the word love has almost become meaningless. It is used to describe everything from love of country to love of a special shirt or slacks. It is no wonder that you may find it hard to define love, even though you feel it is very important to you.

Just what is love? *Love* between a man and a woman is a strong emotional attachment. It is made up in part of sexual desire and tenderness for the other. It is a relationship in which the other person's satisfaction, fulfillment, and security mean as much as your own.

Lois says, "Well, when I love a man, I want what is best for him. I'm important too, but I don't think my wishes automatically come first. I try to put myself in his shoes and feel what he is feeling."

Another aspect of love is that a loving relationship gives people a chance to grow. Love offers warmth, understanding, intimacy, and loyalty. These are traits not always found at work, school, or in other situations. Thus love gives a security that lets people use their skills in relating to others. It lets them feel safe enough to try new activities.

Bill has felt this kind of security in his relationship with Althea. He explains it this way. "There's something about loving Althea that makes me feel safe. I feel good about myself because of our love. In a way, that helps me get along with other people better. It's really funny—I've become a much better listener. I guess it's just that I'm more interested in other people, so I take time to listen. Would you believe that she has even taught me roller skating? I've never done that because I always thought I'd look like a fool when I fell down. Well, I fell down all right, but it was really fun!"

Unit 4: Family Relationships

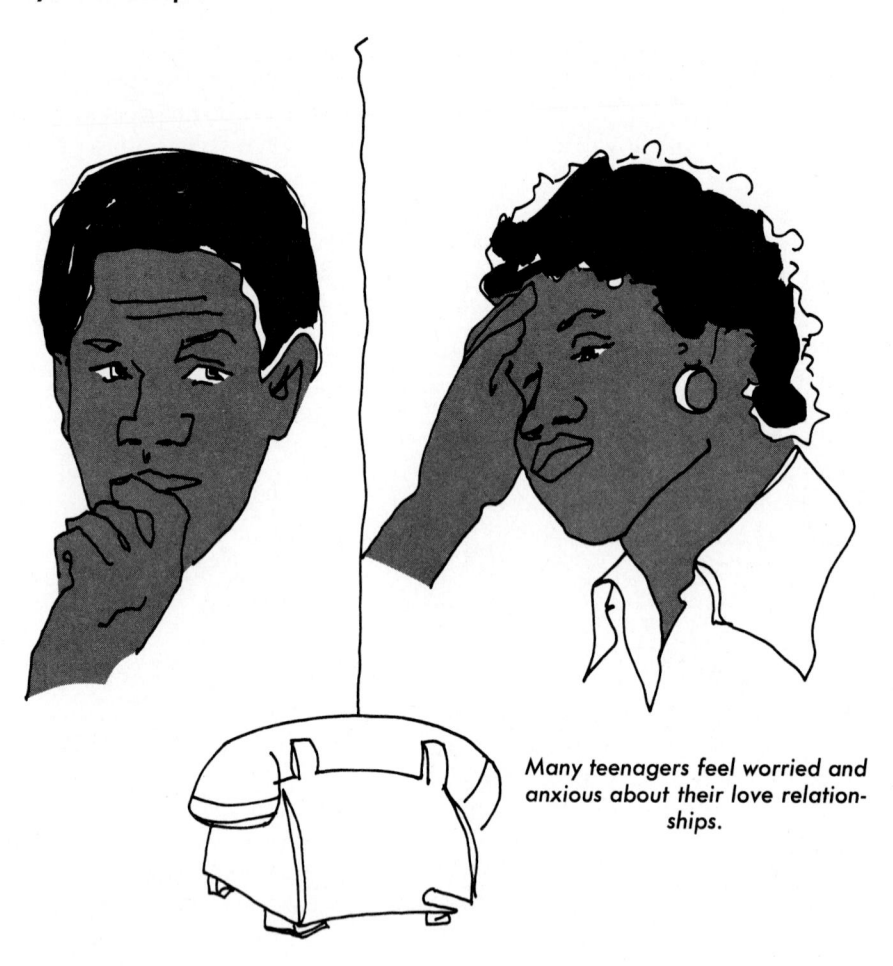

*Many teenagers feel worried and anxious about their love relationships.*

People often feel anxious about their love feelings toward members of the opposite sex. They are comfortable with their love for their parents, their siblings, and friends of the same sex. But when they begin a love relationship with someone of the opposite sex, the anxiety begins.

Jim began dating Marcia the weekend after he met her. He liked everything about her. He found her attractive and loads of fun. But along with his feelings of love came all sorts of questions. Would the relationship last? What would he do if it didn't? Jim wondered if he were really in love with Marcia. If so, what should he do about it?

Jim's questions and anxieties are to be expected at the beginning of a new relationship which matters to him. Because love is the emotion which leads to marriage, people often think all love should lead to marriage. Therefore instead of enjoying a love relationship and the pleasures it brings, they worry about it. A couple may know that they are not ready for marriage and a family. But because they are "in love," they feel pushed toward marriage. This pressure is bound to create anxiety.

Carol regularly falls in love every few months. Each new relationship seems the answer to all her longings. Each time, she dreams of a wedding and future married bliss with her dating partner. However, in a few months, love has gone. Carol then looks for a new relationship. Carol is obviously not ready for marriage. She justifies her love feelings toward her dating partners by assuming that if she feels love it will lead to marriage.

Another cause of anxiety is often the fear of being rejected. Dating partners are afraid that the other will no longer want to be with them. They may dread being without a dating partner.

When Marlon and Pasty started dating, Marlon was filled with anxiety. Each time he called Patsy he worried that she would refuse his invitation. After they had dated several times, people began to expect to see them together. Then Marlon began to fret that Patsy would tire of his company. He didn't want to lose her and be alone again.

Many teenagers are like Jim, Carol, and Marlon. They worry about their relationships, whether they will last, how they will turn out. In the process, they often don't enjoy the warmth and closeness of the relationship.

Love relationships can be divided into three groups—infatuation, romantic love, and conjugal love.

## experiences in human relations

### FALLING IN LOVE

People often say, "I don't know why I fell in love with him or her, I just did." Statements like this imply that love is mysterious and unexplainable. To some extent, it is. However, certain traits attract people to each other. The presence of a valued trait may help the relationship grow as the couple begin to know each other. This experience will help you think about the traits that you consider important in someone you love.

Copy the following list of characteristics on cards:

Is honest and truthful
Gets along with my family
Supports my ideas
Is cheerful and optimistic
Enjoys being with people
Cares about me
Has the same values and goals as I do
Is affectionate
Seeks adventure
Has the same religious background as I do
Is physically attractive
Is calm and even tempered
Is dependable
Makes me feel important

Place these cards around the classroom so that a silent auction can be held. There should be a space for bids next to each card.

Each of you in the class has $1,000 to spend to buy traits you consider important in someone you love. Look over the choices. Which quality seems most important to you? Decide how much money you would be willing to spend on that trait. On a small slip of paper, write that amount along with your name. Place your slip of paper face down near the card which lists the trait you value.

Using more small slips of paper, bid on other traits you want. Continue your silent bidding until you have "spent" your $1,000. While you are bidding, you will not be aware of which traits others are interested in. You will also not know how much others are bidding.

Unit 4: Family Relationships

When everyone in the class has bid to the $1,000 limit, check the bids. The person who bid the highest amount for each trait is given the card which lists the trait.

Did you get any of the traits you wanted? How did your bids compare with those of other class members? Were certain traits bid on by many class members? Why do you suppose these traits were so popular? Which traits received few bids? Why do you think these were not popular?

What traits do you think important that were not on the cards? How much would you have been willing to pay for those traits? What do you think you learned from this experience?

If you wish, this auction could be held with an auctioneer and open bidding instead of using the silent auction procedure.

## TO SUM UP...

1. What is the beginning of a new family?
2. List some of the reasons why people marry.
3. What is love?
4. How does love help people grow and develop?
5. Why do people often worry about their love relationships?

### INFATUATION

Many of the early love experiences teen-agers have are very intense and very short lived. These short love relationships are called *infatuation*. They often begin swiftly—"falling in love at first sight." While they are in progress, the couple is very involved with each other. Their feelings are very strong, but not too stable. In fact, there is no way to know that a relationship is or was infatuation until it is over!

Sara and Don had a very strong love relationship for a while. They spent as much time together as possible. They felt that they were very much in love. Then, as suddenly as it began, their relationship was over.

One characteristic of infatuation is that the partners are very involved with themselves. They have not yet reached the ability to be concerned and involved with their partner. During their time together, they are wrapped up in their own feelings, not those of the partner. Lester fell in love almost overnight with Sandy. He said, "I was so much in love I couldn't eat or sleep. My mom kept saying 'What is that girl doing to you?' My baseball batting average slumped—I just couldn't concentrate on hitting. I wasn't able to study too well either."

Lester's love affair was a very thrilling experience for him. However, his comments reveal that he was thinking about the effects of his love on himself. He was not thinking about Sandy or his relationship with her. This is a characteristic of infatuation. It also means that Lester will likely fall out of love with Sandy as rapidly as he fell in love.

Love relationships that turn out to be infatuation are often based on physical attraction. One partner may be very attracted by the way the other looks. In fact, people can be infatuated with others they have never met. June is in love with the star of her favorite television series. She imagines what their dates would be like and dreams of meeting him. While enjoyable, this kind of love is not based on a relationship, but on physical attraction.

Some people feel that infatuations are bad and that someone who is infatuated with

*Being in love is exciting as you learn to know each other as persons.*

Ch. 11: Forming Your Own Family

another is immature. It is true that infatuations are not the kind of relationships which lead to marriage. In that sense they are not mature love. However, infatuations are important in helping teenagers learn about love. Through these short love experiences, you learn more about the traits you desire in a longer-term relationship. You gain skill in relating to someone of the opposite sex in a loving manner. You have a chance to practice your skills in relating to others in an intimate relationship. These are valuable learning experiences in understanding your self and your needs and values.

Bob has had intense love relationships with several females. He says, "I've been in love lots of times. It's never lasted very long any time, but I learned something from each of my loves. For example, I thought I was really in love with Clara. She was something to look at! She dressed well and I just loved her long red hair. But we didn't have anything in common. She would be ready to go to the stock car races when I wanted to hear a choral concert. My family really likes to play games, and I do too. But Clara thought that was stupid. You learn a lot about yourself and what you value in a love relationship. I wouldn't trade one of mine, but I'm not sorry they're over."

## Romantic Love

The *romantic love* relationship is the basis for marriage. It is the kind of love people mean when they say they married for love. Romantic love can develop as a relationship between two people. It can also grow from the beginnings of an infatuation.

Christy and Art's relationship built slowly. They dated once in a while for several months. Christy said, "At first, I just thought he was a nice guy. We got along all right and always had fun on dates, but it was nothing special. Then somehow, the feeling between us just seemed to grow. I began to think that maybe there was more to our relationship than just friendship. During those first few months, I would never have believed that Art and I would end up engaged."

Tanya and Sam's relationship started rapidly. They went everywhere together. Sam felt like he was "head over heels" in love. After about a month, the excitement of their relationship settled down. They began to learn more about each other. As Sam explained, "The more I learned about Tanya, the more I loved her. I just couldn't believe that anyone who looked so good to me could have so many ideas like mine. In the beginning it was almost like we'd put a spell on each other. But now we know and love each other for what we are."

## Unit 4: Family Relationships

One of the main differences between infatuation and romantic love is in how the partners see each other. In infatuation, people are absorbed in their own reactions to the love relationship. In romantic love, they begin to consider their partner's reactions. Tony tries to look beyond his own feelings to consider the needs and feelings that Renee has. He is sometimes jealous of the time Renee spends with her female friends. Because her friends are important to her, Tony works to overcome his feelings of neglect.

Romantic love is exciting. It is thrilling to learn to know another person in a close relationship. In addition, physical affection goes along with the growth of love. Some amount of sexual exploration and play begins. The physical and mental thrill of building a love relationship makes it a rewarding experience.

Romantic love affairs are longer lasting than infatuations. Still, not all romantic love leads to marriage. Most people have more than one romantic love before they marry. Many of these are long-term relationships. Some people become engaged only to find that they have made a mistake. Dana dated Andy for two years before they became engaged. After being engaged for three months, Dana broke the engagement. She felt that somehow, their relationship was just not going to be strong enough for marriage.

Again, while romantic love may not turn out to be lasting, it is helpful in learning how to relate to others. It provides many of the same kinds of experiences that infatuation does. Romantic love helps people explore their feelings and needs about love relationships.

### Conjugal Love

Romantic love starts a couple thinking of marriage. However, the beginning of conjugal love is the final step that leads a couple to marriage. *Conjugal love,* or married love, differs from romantic love in quality. Because people in a loving relationship change and grow, their love does also. The change from romantic to conjugal love is a change in depth and committment of the relationship.

Joel and Corky have been married for almost four years. Joel says, "I was really in love with Corky when we got married. I thought I loved her as much as it was possible to love anyone. But you can't live together for four years and not change and grow. My love for her now is deeper and stronger. The excitement of being together is different, but in our case, different means better!"

There are four aspects of conjugal love. These are attraction, empathy, companionship, and concern. Some of these elements are also present in romantic love that is building toward marriage. The presence of all four aspects marks a growth toward conjugal love.

## experiences in human relations

### LOVE IN MUSIC

Love is the subject of many songs. Those which are popular with teenagers often center around love and the feelings love brings. This experience will help you think about how love is portrayed in songs. It will also help you think about how these songs influence your feelings about love.

Write down the names of five popular songs about love which you like. If possible, obtain a copy of the words of each song or write down the words as you listen to the song. Think about the words of these songs. Do the songs seem to describe infatuation, romantic love, or conjugal love? What kind of feelings do the songs bring? Do the songs describe love as happiness, excitement, tenderness, or misery? Do you think the words of the songs capture the complexity that is love? Do the songs tend to simplify love?

Now think about what these songs mean to you. Do you sing them often? Think about them? Daydream about them? Why do you think these songs are important to you? Are your ideas and feelings about love similar to those in the songs? Do you think your ideas and actions have ever been influenced by a popular song? Why or why not?

## Attraction

*Attraction* is a physical and mental bond between two people. It is often used to describe sexual desire. While sexual feelings are an important part of love, attraction also includes the rapport and closeness of emotional intimacy. The lift and stimulation of being with your loved one is part of the attraction aspect of love.

"There's something really good about going home to Lanie every night," says John. "There's nobody else I've ever met who makes me feel so mentally and physically alive. I was attracted to her from the beginning. That feeling hasn't changed one bit."

The attraction between a couple is important in marriage. This part of love is often stressed more in romantic love. In the process leading up to marriage, attraction is vital in bringing and keeping the couple together. It is the thrill of being with each other. During married life, attraction may decrease, but it is never unimportant. When married couples do not feel attraction, their relationship is apt to be empty and unrewarding.

## Empathy

*Empathy* is being able to sense what another person is feeling. It goes beyond under-

*Empathy is the ability to put yourself "in the other person's shoes."*

standing the other's feelings. Empathy is being able to put yourself "in the other person's shoes."

Empathy is related to the rapport which begins the action of the relationship wheel. However, in conjugal love, empathy is much more than rapport. It is the feeling of being "with" the other person in mind and spirit.

David and Joleen have always been empathetic. Since their marriage, their empathy has grown. Joleen says that she can tell how David feels as soon as he walks in the door after work. She notices the nonverbal messages that he sends. Her empathy lets her share his happy moods and help cheer up his sad ones.

**Companionship**

The third aspect of conjugal love is companionship. The partners enjoy being together and are glad to be with each other. Part of companionship is an awareness that you are good for each other.

Trust is important in the companionship aspect of love. Each trusts the other to be him or her self. Each expects the same privilege in return.

Companionship is shown by the ability of couples to be comfortable with each other. They enjoy playing, working, or loafing together.

Martha says, "Les and I really look forward to our weekends together. If there's work to be done in the apartment or on the car, we do it as a team. We spend some time playing with the baby together. We also plan at least one thing for us to do for fun without the baby. The rest of the time we just relax. We never see enough of each other during the week. Weekends are our special time to be with each other."

Companionship is another aspect of love that is very important in romantic love. Sometimes after couples marry, they cease spending much time together. This often weakens the bond between the pair. Sharing time together as friends and companions is important in keeping a strong conjugal love relationship.

**Concern**

The final aspect of conjugal love is concern for the welfare of the other. The partners can identify the needs of the other and give support and help as it is needed. Concern is shown by the genuine caring of one person for another.

When Loran lost his job at the service station, Anna knew how badly he felt. She was worried about what they would do until he got another job. However, she did her best to be loving and tender toward Loran. She helped him watch the want ads for new job openings. Her concern and support helped Loran keep his spirits up as he went through the process of looking for work.

Concern for the partner is one aspect of conjugal love that deepens in marriage. As partners move toward marriage, they become more sensitive to the other's needs. However, it is the living together day after day which gives each partner the insight into the other to show deep and loving concern.

When all four elements of conjugal love are present in a marriage, the relationship is able to grow. A growing relationship allows the partners to grow as people. Through their love for each other, they are free to grow toward self-actualization. Relating to someone through love is one way to have rewarding peak experiences as described in Chapter 3.

## experiences in human relations

### CONJUGAL LOVE

Teenagers often think conjugal love rather dull and boring. To them, it implies that the excitement and spark of romantic love is gone, with nothing to replace it. This experience will help you learn how several married couples view conjugal love. It will give you a chance to compare your ideas of conjugal love with theirs.

Find three married couples (or partners from three couples) who would be willing to talk to you about married love. You might try to find one couple who has been married less than a year. An interview with a couple married between five and ten years would given a different perspective. Finally, a couple married over 15 years would have other ideas about their love.

Talk informally with your interviewees about how they think their love has changed over the years. Which of the four aspects of conjugal love do your couples label as most important now in their relationship? Was this always true for them? Were there other times in their dating, engagement, or marriage when other traits were most important? Try to listen for their feelings about their love relationships.

When you have finished, write a report comparing the answers your three couples gave. Could you find any patterns in their answers? Explain why or why not. Did you change any of your ideas about conjugal love after taking this survey? What conclusions can you draw about conjugal love?

● ● ● ● ● ● ● ● ● ● ● ● ● ● ● ● ● ●

Ch. 11: Forming Your Own Family

### TO SUM UP...

1. Describe infatuation and how it usually develops.
2. What can be learned from infatuation and romantic love?
3. What is the main difference between infatuation and romantic love?
4. Define conjugal love.
5. What are the four aspects of conjugal love?
6. Why is attraction more than sexual desire?
7. Define empathy.
8. Why is companionship important in conjugal love?
9. Describe differences between conjugal and romantic love.

### FORMING YOUR FAMILY

Love is considered the reason for forming your own family. However, certain activities go along with the growth of love. These activities are generally done in a certain order. They are called *the process of forming your own family*. These activities are dating, dating exclusively, engagement, and marriage.

#### DATING

*Dating* is a shared activity between partners of opposite sexes. The term "dating" covers and defines a wide range of activities. Some dates are formal while others are informal. Most dates are for recreational purposes. However, some couples have study dates or dates to perform some job together.

Unit 4: Family Relationships

*On most dates, couples enjoy recreational activities together.*

Jake took Linda to the spring dance at their school. He asked her several weeks in advance and they made many plans for their evening together. He bought her a corsage of flowers to go with her long dress. After the dance, they went out to eat with several other couples.

In contrast to this date, one Saturday evening about six p.m. Linda called Jake on the telephone. She said, "Hey, guess what? I can have the car after all tonight. Why don't we do something?" They talked a few minutes about their choices. Finally, they decided to go bowling. The informality of this date was quite different from the formality of their date for the dance.

Wilma and Stewart enjoy movies, ball games, and dancing on their dates. They also like playing tennis together. However, many of their dates involve other kinds of activities. They often spend part of their evenings together doing homework. They enjoy playing cards at one or the other's home. They spent one Saturday "date" painting the kitchen at Stewart's house. Sometimes they shop together. Because they enjoy being with each

246

## Ch. 11: Forming Your Own Family

other, their dates involve many everyday activities.

### Choosing A Dating Partner

You will recall from Chapter 6 that relationships are built in four steps. These steps, or spokes on the relationship wheel, are rapport, self-revelation, mutual dependence, and need fulfillment. What attracts two people to each other to begin the movement of the wheel? Why do some couples build a relationship into love while others end their contact swiftly?

No one can predict for sure who will be attracted to each other. However, some factors increase the chances of two people developing a dating relationship that is satisfactory to both. These factors also increase the couple's chances of falling in love. This in turn furthers the process of forming their own family.

### Common Expectations

Certain expectations for dating partners are common in the United States. Most people expect the male partner to be older, taller, better educated, and to make more money than the female. There is no logical reason that says that dating partners who do not fit these expectations can't be happy together. However, people generally do not expect them to build strong relationships. It takes strong people to build a relationship in the face of public curiosity.

When Vernon and Della first began dating, they found people looked at them strangely. In fact, Della was very self-conscious about being three inches taller than Vernon. Gradually they became used to the stares. Because of their many common interests, they soon were very much in love with each other. Others, however, always seemed to expect their relationship to be on the verge of break-

*This couple attracts attention because people expect the male to be taller than the female.*

ing up. This was because their appearance as a couple was so unusual.

In other instances, the common expectations may indeed break up a promising dating relationship. Kate was an elementary school teacher. When she first began dating Ned, an electrician, many of her friends were sur-

## Unit 4: Family Relationships

prised. Ned had never been to college. Kate's friends asked many embarrassing questions about that fact. They made Kate feel that there was something wrong with the relationship because she had been to college and Ned hadn't. The difference in education led to a decrease in their rapport. This caused the relationship wheel to unwind. The common expectation that the male should have more education than the female helped break up this relationship.

### Nearness

Another factor which is involved in choosing a dating partner is simply nearness. Nearness is sometimes called *propinquity*. You can't date someone whom you don't know—unless you have a mutual friend who arranges a blind date. As a rule, your possible dating partners are limited to those people whom you know. You are most likely to know those near you.

When Jesse transferred high schools, he knew no one in his new school. As he became acquainted, he met a number of females. He felt he would like to know several of them better through dating. He also found the two-hour trip back to his old high school very inconvenient when he wanted a date. Therefore the nearness of his new acquaintances led him to begin dating females from his new high school.

### Homogamy

*Homogamy* means sameness. Scientists who have studied dating and marriage partners have found over and over that such couples are homogamous. That is, they are more like each other than they are different.

The fact that people tend to choose someone like themselves as partners can be partly explained through the relationship wheel. If you find you are similar to someone else, you are more likely to feel comfortable with that person. This causes you to have rapport with him or her. Since rapport is the first step around the relationship wheel, likenesses make it easy to begin a relationship.

Some of the traits which most couples share are race, religion, age, education, and family background. Of course, you may know couples who have striking differences. Still, the majority of couples are similar in these traits.

For example, Craig's father and mother both work in a truck manufacturing factory. Craig hopes to become a mechanic. He usually dates females from his neighborhood whose families are like his. One night, however, he had a date with a female whose father was a lawyer. Craig found himself uncomfortable all evening. Laurie talked about places Craig had never been. She described the tennis matches she'd been in at the country club. Although Craig thought Laurie was attractive, he never asked her out again. He felt as if the two of them lived in different worlds. These differences made it hard for him to feel at ease with her.

While Alma was in medical school, she found that she dated other medical students. Many of the males she had dated in college had stopped calling her. She decided that some of them felt uncomfortable with her since she had gone on to medical school. Thus her only source of dating partners was the males very like herself—other medical students.

In these and other ways, people tend to be friends with, date, and marry others who share similar traits.

### Ideal Mate

Another factor that influences the choice of dating partners is called the ideal mate. Most people have an image in their minds of

### Ch. 11: Forming Your Own Family

an ideal mate. For some people, this image is very clear. They can see how the ideal mate would look and act. Others have a more vague idea of some ideal traits a partner would have.

People who have an ideal mate in mind measure their dating partners against this ideal. They are more attracted to those who seem like their ideal mate.

When Toni met Matthew, he seemed like the perfect date. He was tall and dark as was her ideal. The clothes he wore were the latest fashion. They shared interests in music and sports. His appearance, manners, and interests attracted Toni to him because he seemed to match her ideal.

In summary, attraction is based on common expectations, nearness, homogamy, and notions of an ideal mate. These factors combine to encourage partners to date each other. Just which trait or factor is the "spark" that causes a relationship to grow into love, no one really knows. But the process of forming your own family begins when some combination of factors draws you to someone else. This attraction may be the beginning of a love relationship.

*Most people have an image or an idea of what kind of person would make an ideal mate.*

## experiences in human relations

### DATING PARTNERS

Think about a past or present dating partner or someone whom you would like to date in the future. This experience will help you analyze why you are attracted to him or her.

First, consider the common expectations about dating partners. Which of you is older, taller, or in a higher grade? Do you fit the

**249**

common idea of the male being older, taller, and more advanced in school?

Second, think of your convenience and nearness to each other. If your partner is someone you wish to date in the future, do you actually know each other? Do you attend the same school? How easy or hard is, was, or would it be to have dates? How does propinquity influence who you date?

Now, how are you alike? Are you the same race? About the same age? How alike are your family backgrounds? Do you agree on religious matters? In what other ways are you similar?

Finally, think about your ideal mate. In what way is your dating partner like your ideal mate? Different?

Which factor do you think is or was most important in your relationship with past or present dates? Which one would you think would be most important in setting up a future dating relationship? What characteristics seem to be most important to you? What do you think is most important in attracting you to dating partners?

● ● ● ● ● ● ● ● ● ● ● ● ● ● ● ● ●

### Dating As Preparation for Marriage

Dating is the first step in the process of forming your own family. However, it is a rare person who ends up marrying his or her first and only dating partner. Most people date a number of others before they move further toward marriage. All dating partners in some way help each other learn more about themselves and others. What each person learns is a help in being ready for marriage in the future.

Dating can be important in learning how to relate to persons of the other sex. Males and females may have been friends for years while growing up. However, when sexual interest arises in the teen years, they find themselves uncertain and awkward. Dating gives individuals a chance to learn to relate in the male-female relationship. The most satisfying relationships are those in which the partners relate person to person. However, they still must learn to be at ease in a situation where sexual attraction is a factor.

Ruthann and Tom had known each other for years. During her junior year in school, Ruthann found herself more and more attracted to Tom. At first, this made her very uncomfortable with him. They dated once in a while and were often in each other's company with a group of friends. Gradually, Ruthann became more at ease with her new feelings toward Tom. In turn, this helped her in other dating relationships.

Dating can teach you how to get along with a variety of people. Through knowing and interacting with dating partners, you can learn about the differences in people. These experiences can help you learn what traits in others you value. It can also help give you tolerance for those who believe differently than you.

Wayne says, "I never knew what a difference religious beliefs could make. My religion is important to me. I really didn't know how important until I dated Carla. She used to tease me and make fun of my church work. I can understand her feeling I was too enthused about it when she didn't have any religious beliefs herself. Some people believe and others don't. But I found out that I need a dating partner who respects my beliefs and maybe even shares them."

Dating is also a good setting for learning to resolve conflicts with others. All dating partners have disagreements. Learning to cope with differences in a dating relationship is good preparation for marriage. When Abbie and Sid first started dating, Abbie cried whenever they had a fight. She expected her crying to make Sid give in to her. As their relationship grew, Abbie learned better ways of resolving conflict with Sid.

On the other hand, some of the aspects of dating are not good preparation for marriage. They do not help build strong relationships between partners. However, by being aware of the nature of some of these aspects, you can work to build person-to-person relationships. Such relationships will help you be ready to move forward in the process toward marriage.

At times, especially in casual dating, dating is for self-promotion. Instead of being a chance to build a relationship, a date is a chance to be seen. It may be important to be seen with a particular person, or it may be important to be at a special event. Kathy accepted a date with Robbie for the talent review at her school. She didn't really care about dating Robbie, but all her friends had dates for the show. Therefore she accepted Robbie's invitation so that she would be able to go with a date.

Carl always enjoyed his dates with Eileen. She was so good looking and dressed so well that they always got lots of attention. It was a thrill for Carl to know that other males envied his being with such an attractive date.

The problem with dates based on such reasons is that they neglect the fact that the partner is a person. Dates such as these use the other persons for what they can give you, not for what you can enjoy together. Since the relationship itself is not important, this kind of date is not good preparation for marriage.

Another problem with dating is that often people don't reveal their selves. It is only as people learn to relate to each other as people that relationships grow strong. However, many dates only show masks to each other. Valerie tries to be cheerful and lighthearted because she knows that's what Chuck likes in a dating partner. She hides her cross and depressed moods. At those times she wears a mask to conceal what she is really feeling. Because she doesn't feel free to be her real self, Valerie and Chuck's relationship will never be a strong, rewarding one. Learning to know each other's unmasked self helps dating become preparation for marriage.

Likewise, there may be little honest communication between some dating partners. They communicate on the surface and fail to meet each other at the deeper levels of communication. Many dating partners may say what they think the other partner expects. Again, little true person-to-person communication can occur in this setting.

Finally, dating is often a leisure-time activity. Some couples may share work or study time on dates. However, most dates are for fun. Thus couples see each other when they are relaxed and ready for a good time. They are less likely to see each other when they are under stress or in conflict with their family members. Stress and conflict are a normal part of life. However, the emphasis on leisure in dating can give the partners one-sided views of each other.

Nora and Calvin always enjoyed their dates together. Because they didn't go to the same school, their only contacts were on dates when they did activities that both enjoyed. Because their evenings together were relaxed, Nora didn't know that Calvin had a bad temper. She knew him as a casual, calm person. She wasn't aware that he blew up when he was crossed or wasn't allowed his own way. Their dating relationship didn't show this side of his personality.

Unit 4: Family Relationships

*Often the dating situation does not reveal how partners react under stress or tension.*

## experiences in human relations

### DATING AS PREPARATION FOR MARRIAGE

Dating is the first step in the process of building a marriage relationship. In some ways, dating is good preparation for marriage. In other ways, it is not.

Form a group with three of your classmates. In your group, discuss the following statements about dating behavior. Try to decide what effect the behavior would have as preparation for marriage. As you discuss each statement, copy it on a separate sheet of paper. If you decide the behavior would be a good preparation for marriage, mark the statement with a + and list your reasons. If you think the behavior would be poor preparation for marriage, place a — by the statement. Again, give your reasons for your choice. If the behavior does not relate to marriage preparation, place a 0 by the statement.

- Jerry went steady with seven females during his senior year.
- Marge is engaged to the first and only male she ever dated.
- Cloris and Ted frequently babysit with Ted's younger brothers.
- Quinn and Mariana both work after school at the same restaurant.
- Janice has always dated several males, refusing to limit herself by going steady.
- Darryl and Sonja live over 150 miles apart so are only able to see each other on dates about once every two months.
- Donna has gone steady with three males during her high school years.
- Reggie has fallen in love with a cheerleader from a rival school whom he has never met.
- Frank and Reba attend religious services together each week.
- Barbara and Ray have never had an argument.

Ch. 11: Forming Your Own Family

- Tammy and Scott have lived next door to each other for five years.
- Lisa and Warren always double date with others. They have never gone on a date by themselves.

When all the groups have finished discussing each situation, report your decisions to your classmates. On a chart or a chalkboard, record the decisions of each group. Did all the groups give the same markings? What reasons were given when different marks were given? What conclusions can you draw from this experience?

### TO SUM UP...

1. What is dating?
2. Describe some common expectations in dating.
3. Why is propinquity important in the choice of a dating partner?
4. Define homogamy.
5. Give an example of a trait that homogamous couples might share.
6. Explain what is meant by an "ideal mate."
7. Describe some of the ways in which dating is good preparation for marriage.
8. When is dating not good marriage preparation?

### DATING EXCLUSIVELY

When two people begin to date only each other, this is often called *steady dating* or *going steady*. The agreement between the partners is that they will not date others. Instead, they agree to date each other exclusively.

Couples come to exclusive dating in different ways. Some couples drift into it. Raul and May began dating each other when each was also dating others. They never discussed only dating each other. But May gradually stopped accepting other invitations. Raul found that he always wanted to call May first when he decided to ask someone out. Thus, without any planning or decision making, they soon began dating only each other.

In contrast, some couples reach a deliberate conclusion to date only each other. Larry and Belinda were very attracted to each other when they started dating. After about a month, Larry asked Belinda to go steady. They agreed that they would date each other exclusively.

Some couples trade tokens of their affection when they decide to go steady. What these tokens are depends a great deal on the age of the couple and the custom in the part of the country in which they live. Wilbur and Beth exchanged class rings when they began dating steadily. Steve gave Gloria his fraternity pin. Others may exchange identification bracelets or friendship rings.

Other couples do not exchange any outward symbol of their relationship. Pete said, "What's important is how we feel about each other. I don't have to wear something of hers and she doesn't have to have something of mine. If she needs my class ring to keep the other guys away, then there's something wrong between us. Rings don't make the relationship strong."

Couples who date exclusively tend to date more often than others. Perhaps this is because they have "working" or "study" dates. It also may be that steady dates are more likely to plan activities on the spur of the moment. They are more comfortable with each other, so don't always feel the need for advance plans.

Unit 4: Family Relationships

*An engagement ring is the traditional symbol of a promise to marry.*

## ENGAGEMENT

Not all people who date exclusively become engaged. However, most engagements are between couples who have been dating steadily. An *engagement* is a promise to marry. An engagement is a period of planning and transition. The partners can test out their relationship as an established couple. At the same time, they have not made the final marriage promise. Therefore they are still able to break the relationship before it becomes legally binding.

The engagement is a time for partners to see each other in a variety of settings. They are able to discover their differences. During the engagement, they can learn which differences they can tolerate. If they find ones that they can't tolerate, the engagement may be broken.

Rosa and Al were very much in love. They became engaged soon after they started dating steadily. However, during their engagement, conflicts began to occur. Al assumed that they would have several children. Rosa admitted she didn't like children very much and didn't know if she wanted to have any. She did know that if she had children, she would continue her career. Al felt that a mother should stay home until the children were grown. In the conflict over their future roles as parents, the relationship disintegrated. Finally, the engagement was broken.

As the example of Al and Rosa shows, the engagement is a time to explore values. As the partners prepare for the marriage relationship, they find out what is important to each other. A couple does not need identical values to have a strong marriage relationship. However, they need to understand and respect each other's values.

Rich explains how he and Harriet have settled their differences. "Harriet is one of those people who is always involved in some project," says Rich. "She worked on a voter registration drive last winter. Right now she's helping organize a thrift shop where secondhand clothing will be sold. In one way, her involvement in these projects is part of what I love about Harriet. Life's never dull when she's got a project cooking. On the other hand, I don't get as involved. I'm a bit more cynical—I figure one person's efforts just can't make that much difference. That's an area where we sort of agree to disagree. What's right for me is not right for her. But we respect and understand the other's view."

The engagement period is a preparation for marriage. However, the emphasis on getting ready for the wedding sometimes seems to take first place. Even simple weddings take planning and organization. Couples need to work to keep their relationship growing even during wedding preparations. It is the relationship that is built during the engagement that determines how successful the marriage will be.

## Marriage

A marriage marks the beginning of a new family. The wedding ceremony is a public announcement of a change in the couple's relationship. Legally, they have become a family. The state considers that the couple have signed a civil contract which cannot be altered or broken except by action of a court of law.

### The Ceremony

Traditionally, the bride and her parents planned the wedding ceremony. However, recently, more couples are planning their own wedding. They work to add personal touches to the ceremony. These touches reflect their own personalities and make the wedding more meaningful to the couple. Sharon and Andrew rephrased the customary wedding vows to make them more personal. They also added poems and flute and oboe music to the ceremony.

Cheryl and Jeff kept the traditional ceremony of their church, but were married by their minister outdoors on the beach. Other couples adapt the ceremony in other ways.

There are two basic kinds of ceremonies—religious and civil. Religious ceremonies are regarded by most people as a commitment to each other made in the presence of their God. Civil ceremonies are performed by a justice of the peace or other government official. Civil ceremonies tend to be less expensive and less elaborate than religious ones.

## experiences in human relations

### THE CEREMONY

The ceremony of marriage establishes the legal tie between a man and woman. What is said and done at that ceremony expresses how and what the couple feels for each other. Many couples use the traditional religious or civil ceremony. Other couples personalize the ceremony in ways that mean something to them. This experience will help you think about the vows that you would wish to make to a marriage partner.

Think about how you expect to feel about your future partner. Plan a ceremony which shows how you feel. You may wish to include music, poetry, some thoughts on what marriage means, and the vows that express your feelings. Your ceremony should symbolize what you feel is most important in a relationship between people being married.

When you have written your ceremony, you may wish to compare it with actual ceremonies from various sources. Your teacher will give you help in locating copies of such ceremonies.

● ● ● ● ● ● ● ● ● ● ● ● ● ● ● ●

### The Honeymoon

The ceremony is the public beginning of married life, while the honeymoon is the private beginning. The honeymoon is the time

Unit 4: Family Relationships

*Leaving on a honeymoon is the beginning of a couple's married life together.*

when the couple begins to learn the new roles they have taken on as a result of the marriage. They start to learn their roles as husband and wife.

The honeymoon can be a time of joy and excitement for a couple. They begin their married sexual life together. They often are free to concentrate solely on each other and on their joy in being together for several uninterrupted days. Orlando and Lucy took a week's vacation from their jobs. They spent their honeymoon in a cottage on a lake. They swam, fished, and sailed as they enjoyed each other's company. The beginning of their life together was a memorable peak experience for them both.

On the other hand, the honeymoon can also be a disappointing time. Many couples find that their first sexual experiences are unsatisfactory. For other couples, the honeymoon is the first time they have had to cope with each other on a twenty-four-hour-a-day basis. They find the prolonged intimacy may cause problems.

Saul and Maria took a sightseeing trip for their honeymoon. Each evening when they stopped for the night, they were tired and cross. Saul didn't like the way Maria's cosmetics cluttered up the bathroom. Maria complained about being cold when Saul kicked off the blankets during the night. They couldn't agree on where and when to eat meals. They were both glad when the honeymoon ended.

Any change in your life can cause problems. The honeymoon is often an important beginning of a couple's life together. Therefore problems on the honeymoon are often seen as more serious than they actually are. It takes time and effort to work out a new sexual relationship. It also takes time to adjust to each other's personal habits. The loving atmosphere of the honeymoon is a place to begin working on these issues. Couples who expect the honeymoon to solve these problems completely are being unrealistic.

**Living Together**

The start of true family life begins when a couple returns from their honeymoon to live together. During the first year of marriage, the couple works out ways of relating to each other. They also learn how to relate as a couple to the outside world.

Becoming a family involves seeing themselves as "we" instead of as "I." They see themselves as a unit which interacts with others. How the couple interacts within this unit depends on their backgrounds, their val-

**Ch. 11: Forming Your Own Family**

*During the first year of marriage, a couple learns to face the world as a unit.*

ues, and the way they think husbands and wives should behave.

For Gary and Frances, one big step was in relating to their parents. At first, each tended to side with the parents against the spouse. However, after they had been married longer, they began to support each other. They began to act as a unit in their relationships with their parents.

Living together is the beginning of the fulfillment that comes from being a part of your own family. Couples who build a strong relationship in their life together find they can grow as individuals and as a family.

## TO SUM UP...

1. What is the agreement between partners who go steady?
2. Why are engagements a time for planning?
3. Why do couples often make changes in the traditional wedding ceremony?
4. Explain how the honeymoon can be a disappointment to a couple.
5. Describe ways that married couples learn to face the world as a unit.

257

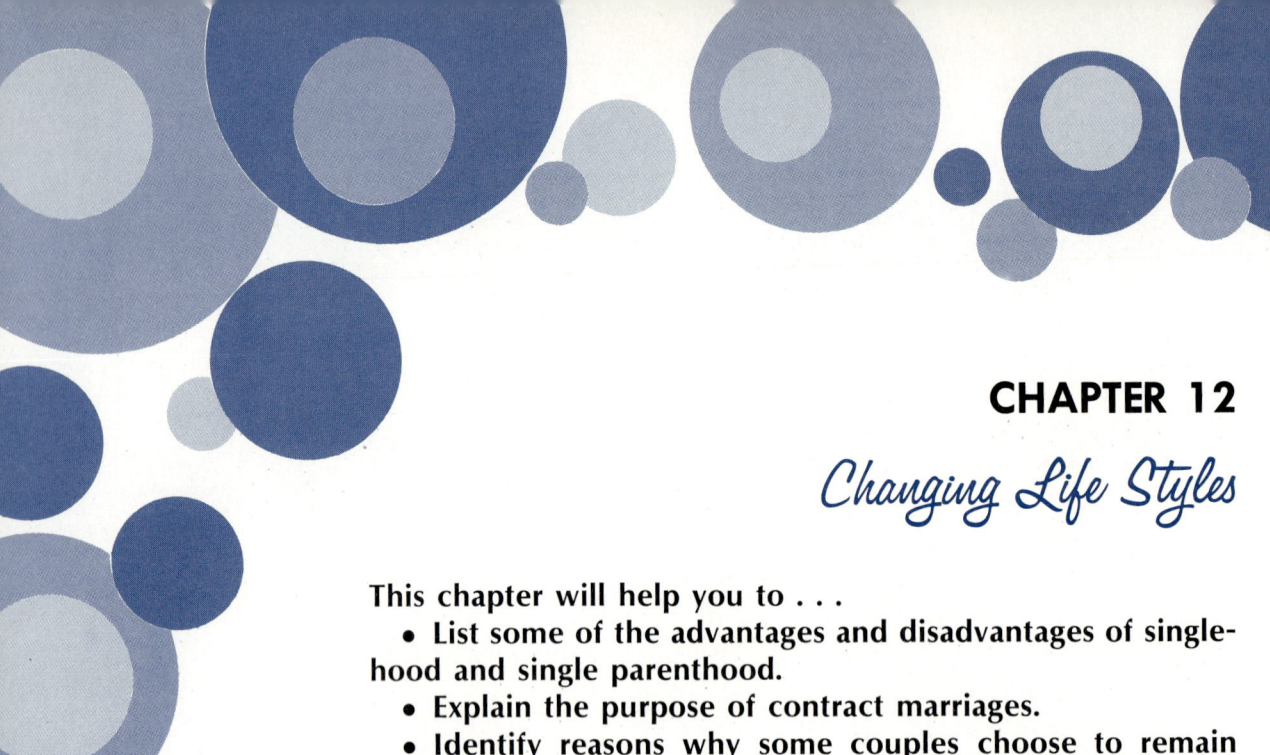

# CHAPTER 12
## Changing Life Styles

This chapter will help you to . . .
- List some of the advantages and disadvantages of singlehood and single parenthood.
- Explain the purpose of contract marriages.
- Identify reasons why some couples choose to remain childless.
- Know some characteristics of blended families and open and group marriages.
- Describe the differences in communal organization.

Most people in the United States follow the same pattern in forming their own families. They begin dating during their teenage years, then move on to marriage and parenthood. The ideal most people hold states that two people marry, have children, and "live happily ever after."

Some people do not agree with this ideal pattern. Lorena has no desire to marry, although she enjoys the company of men. Others marry and find that it doesn't suit their needs. Marilyn and Neill are staying together because of their children even though their marriage is unhappy. When Nancy and Bill's relationship broke down, they agreed to divorce. Some people have or desire sexual relationships outside of marriage.

Throughout history, there have always been those who were out of step with the common marriage patterns. It is only today that such people have received much notice or publicity. Newspapers and magazines often carry articles which describe unusual life styles. People have become more open in telling about behavior that might be different from others.

People who feel that the common pattern does not meet their needs are searching for other life styles that will help them grow as persons. They are looking for ways to build their potential and their enjoyment of life.

Annabelle and Mike feel that their marriage meets only some of their needs for closeness and intimacy. They are trying to find ways to

**Ch. 12: Changing Life Styles**

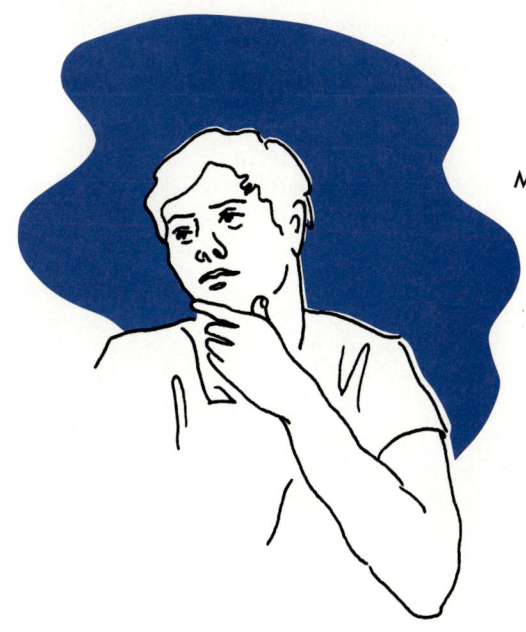

*Many people question whether the traditional life styles can meet their relationship needs.*

build new relationships with other couples and individuals while still keeping their marriage strong. People like Annabelle and Mike are developing new forms of marriage and family life. The new life styles often are quite different from the usual patterns.

It may be that new life styles add more warmth and satisfaction to people's lives than the traditional life style. On the other hand, alternate life styles may bring more problems than the more common way of life. Only a very small percentage of people in the United States live in changing life styles. It is too soon to know whether any of the other styles will meet family functions better than does the traditional family. At any rate, none of the alternate styles is likely to replace the family as you know it today.

The issue of alternate life styles is closely related to the values you hold. You may feel that the different life styles are immoral, sinful, or against your religious teachings. You may believe that a trustworthy and faithful spouse can and will provide for all your needs. However, because people are so different, it seems unlikely that the same family pattern could meet everyone's needs.

You may believe that a certain life style is right for you. Others may try to convince you differently. No life style is going to be right for everyone. In any way of life, problems will arise and adjustments will need to be made. In the end, you must choose a life style on the basis of what you know about your self and the people who are important to you. In turn, it is important for you to be tolerant of those who choose a life style different from your own.

## experiences in human relations

### ALTERNATE LIFE STYLES

Most people learn about changing life styles from the media. You may have read newspaper clippings about communes or unmarried couples living together. Your favorite magazine may have had an article about the people who live in single's apartments. Radio or television programs may have discussed childless or open marriage. This experience will help you think about the ideas that you have read or heard about.

Find an article or an interview about an alternate life style. You may find the article in newspapers or in magazines. After you have read the article, prepare a report. Your report should focus on what the author of the article wanted you to believe about the life style.

First, decide whether the author was for or against the life style described in the article. In what ways did the author try to get readers to hold the same opinion? Did the author include both the good points and the bad points about the life style? Or did the author emphasize one over the other?

What kind of examples did the author use? Were they included to attract you to the life style? Or did the examples disgust and repel you? What other ways can you find that the author tried to change or influence the ideas of the readers?

Share the findings of your report with other class members. Listen to and think about their reports. Were the articles for or against certain life styles? Did anyone report on an article that held the exact opposite opinions of your article? Can any life style be all bad or all good? Why or why not? What conclusions can you draw from this experience?

● ● ● ● ● ● ● ● ● ● ● ● ● ● ● ● ● ● ● ● ●

## SINGLEHOOD

Although remaining unmarried may be considered an alternate life style, it is certainly not a new one. There have always been people who did not marry. Some of these remained single through choice, some unwillingly. Between 5 and 10 percent of the United States population remain unmarried throughout their lives.

Today, singlehood is becoming a more important life style. To be unmarried used to be thought a sign of failure. Today it is seen as having positive value for those who choose it. Although most people marry sooner or later, the age at marriage is rising. This allows more time before marriage to be single. Many divorced, widowed, or separated people choose not to remarry. Others wait longer before marrying again. Thus, the total number of single people is increasing.

Within the last few years, singlehood has gained a new respectability. People are coming to realize that not everyone can fulfill their needs through marriage. Jonathan feels that marriage is restrictive. He believes he can be free to be himself only in the unmarried state.

While singlehood was always considered acceptable for men, it has only recently become more attractive to women. As they gain work experience and well-paid jobs in the labor market, women are able to be financially independent. Some women are interested in equality in their work and personal lives. They may postpone marriage and finally decide they do not wish to marry at all.

Tammy earns a good salary as a drill press operator. Because she works with men as an equal, she feels no urge to marry. She says, "I might marry if I met someone who could accept me as I am. I don't need a man to take care of me because with the money I earn, I can take care of myself. I have a lot of interests and I'm just not all caught up in thinking that I have to have a husband to be a whole person."

### Ch. 12: Changing Life Styles

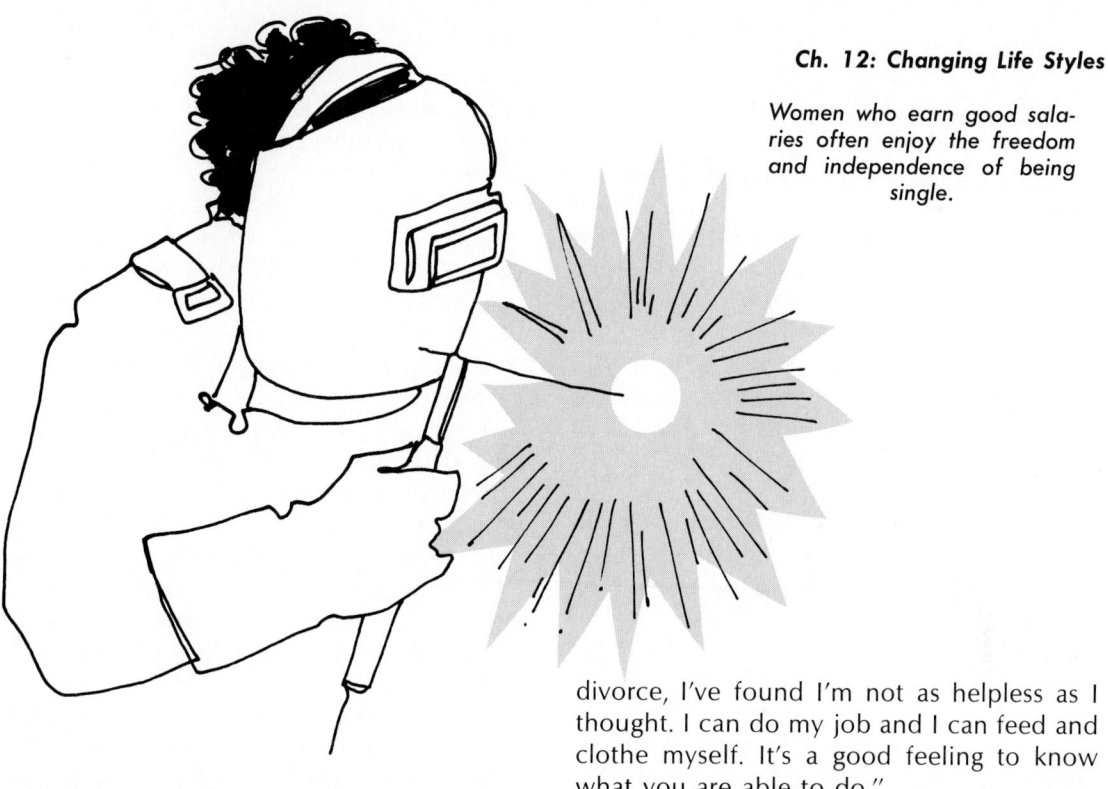

*Women who earn good salaries often enjoy the freedom and independence of being single.*

Those who are single claim freedom and independence are what they value most about their life styles. Jeanine says, "I like being able to come and go as I please. I don't have to be home to fix supper for a husband because my time (and my money) are mine. I'm not very tidy either. By being single, I can live in a big mess and not feel that I'm bothering someone else."

Other singles find that they have a strong sense of their own abilities. "I went from living with my parents to marriage with Judy," says Tony. "I never had to take care of myself. I found I relied on Judy's advice and help to solve problems with my sales job. She'd write speeches and promotional materials for me. I know she was only trying to be helpful and I wanted her help. At the same time, it got so that I didn't really know what I could do by myself. Since I've been living alone after the divorce, I've found I'm not as helpless as I thought. I can do my job and I can feed and clothe myself. It's a good feeling to know what you are able to do."

Most single people build up a group of family members and friends that they rely on. These people provide the intimacy and sharing that married couples receive from each other. Singlehood can be very lonely without some close relationships to give support and understanding.

Jeff was very lonesome when he started living alone. In fact, he commented, "I was close to deciding maybe it was time to get married. Then I became good friends with a married couple next door and started dating more often. I also met several other men through basketball at the park district. Now I don't feel the need for a wife so much. I have lots of people with whom I can share activities and ideas."

Scientists have found that single women, in general, adjust to their lives better than single men. Females have fewer physical and mental health problems than the males. They report greater happiness. This may be because they are more apt to build strong ties to family and friends than the men.

Compared to single men, single women are more likely to have a higher education. They earn more money than the men do and are more apt to be managers or professionals.

The health of single and married men and women has been compared. Never-married women and married women are similar in overall health. Married men are more healthy than never-married men.

The health risks for singles who are divorced, separated, or widowed are much higher. Divorced and separated people are the least healthy of all groups. They are especially likely to have "life style" health problems. These include diseases, injuries, or death related to smoking, alcohol use, and automobile driving. The stress of the marriage breakdown may cause some of these problems.

Gerald was very upset after his divorce. He began smoking heavily, which led to a chronic cough. He often stayed out late at night drinking, sometimes missing work because of hangovers. He was severely hurt when he was in an accident which was caused by his reckless driving after drinking.

To sum up, people choose a life style to meet their needs for personal growth and development. Singles feel they can do this best by remaining unmarried.

## experiences in human relations

### REMAINING SINGLE

This experience will help you explore how you feel about singlehood. On a sheet of paper, draw a circle about three inches in diameter. From the circle, extend six or eight lines outward, like the rays of a sun.

In the center of the circle, write the word "single." What is the first word that pops into your mind about being single? Write that word on one of the lines radiating out from the circle. On the other lines, jot down other words and phrases you associate with singlehood. Write down your responses quickly, without judging or evaluating your ideas. Make more lines if you need them.

When you have finished, circle the word or phrase you think best represents your feelings and values about singlehood. In turn, explain to other class members why this word symbolizes being single for you. Make a list on the chalk board of the word each person reports.

When everyone has contributed a word which represents singlehood to him or her, look at the list you have made. How many people listed the same word? Were the words positive, negative, or neutral about the value of singlehood? What was the most positive word? Negative? How did your words compare with the others?

### TO SUM UP...

1. Why do some people seek alternate life styles?
2. How common are alternate life styles in the United States?
3. Why is the issue of alternate life styles related to values?
4. What percentage of Americans never marry?
5. If most Americans marry, why is the single life style becoming more important?

**Ch. 12: Changing Life Styles**

*Women are head of the household in 15 percent of American families.*

6. Why is singlehood more acceptable for today's women than it was for women in the past?

7. What are some advantages of remaining single?

8. Why do divorced, separated, and widowed people have poorer health than those who are married or who have never married?

## SINGLE PARENTS

Another life style involving unmarried persons is that of single parents. Both mothers and fathers may live alone with their children. However, a single-parent family is likely to be headed by a woman. In fact, about 15 percent of all families in the United States are made up of a woman and her children.

Because of increases in divorce, single-parent adoption, and unwed motherhood, families headed by a single parent are on the increase. Forty percent of the American children born during the 1970's can expect to live part of their childhood with a single parent.

Most adults living in a single-parent family do not choose that life style on purpose. Instead, it is most often the outcome of either the death or divorce of the partner. Mary became a single parent to her son Carl when her husband was killed in a car accident. Pete

263

## Unit 4: Family Relationships

got custody of Kim and Kyle after his divorce from his wife Sancha. Others who become single parents are females who bear children while not married.

Single-parent adoptions are fairly new. Men or women who are unmarried but who wish to be parents can now adopt children. Tina was thrilled the day she found out her application to adopt was approved. Five weeks later she was the proud mother of a three-year-old son named Renaldo.

Single parents enjoy many of the advantages that other singles do. However, they also have a great deal of responsibility in caring for their child or children.

One of the biggest problems single parents face is financial. Mothers especially find themselves lacking enough money to care for their children. Many women do not have any special employment skills. After divorce they must take jobs whose low pay does not cover family expenses. Women who have chosen a career and have had training or education usually have fewer money worries after divorce.

Lucy is an experienced key punch operator whose salary is larger than most of the other women with whom she works. In spite of her higher salary, Lucy feels as if her income never stretches to all the needs of herself and her children. One or the other of her daughters always seems to need new shoes, jeans, or visits to the doctor or dentist. Lucy budgets her money carefully and lives frugally. She still finds money worries to be her main problem.

After a divorce, many fathers are required to pay child support if the children live with their mother. However, less than one-half of all fathers make full child support payments for even the first year after divorce. Thus single divorced mothers need to be prepared to financially support their children.

*A parent who works and manages a household alone may not have much time to play with a child.*

Fathers living with their children may face financial problems as well. Some mothers may pay child support after a divorce, but this practice is not yet common. As a rule men tend to have fewer money problems than women because their jobs generally pay more than do women's.

Another problem that single parents face is being both a mother and a father to their children. At times the children's needs conflict with the parent's job demands. Tim found that he had many problems working out a schedule for himself and his two children. He had to be at work a half an hour before the bus came to pick them up for school. There was a difference of three hours between the time the children came home

## Ch. 12: Changing Life Styles

from school and he came home from work. In addition, on school holidays, he had to arrange child care. The biggest problems were when the children became ill. Tim's former wife had worked in the kitchen of the children's school. Therefore they had been able to work out child care before and after school. It was only after the divorce that Tim realized the problems in scheduling a single-parent family.

It takes a great deal of time and energy for a single parent to make a warm and loving home for all family members. Money problems and the lack of a spouse to help during busy times are drawbacks. On the other hand, some people enjoy the advantages of living alone with the children.

Marion likes being a single parent. She says, "I really enjoy my life with the boys. Oh, I know we don't spend as much time together as I'd like—and there's no doubt that I'm cross and tired some of the time. But Joe and I had millions of fights over how to raise the boys. They learned to take advantage of our conflicts. Since the divorce, I haven't had to worry about what anyone else thinks about how I handle the boys."

Kenneth waited a long time before he was able to adopt his son. He took physical and psychological tests. A series of interviews took his free time for several months. The pleasure he finds in finally being a father more than makes up for any problems he faces as a single parent.

Finally, some single mothers simply choose not to marry. Clarice found herself pregnant while she was in her senior year. Her parents wanted her to marry the father of the child. Even though he was willing to marry her, she refused. She says, "It would have been a disaster for us to marry. We were both too young to be tied to each other. I don't know whether I'll ever get married. I sure haven't met anyone yet with whom I could build that kind of relationship. I get a lot of joy out of being Teddy's mother. He's really the most important person in my life. I don't need a husband."

Many single parents are simply doing the best job they can until they remarry. If the divorce rate continues to climb, many more people will live alone with their children. The satisfactions they find in this life style will determine whether it will be temporary or permanent.

## experiences in human relations

### SINGLE PARENTS

Although there are some rewards for single parents, most feel that raising children alone is a hard job. This experience will help you become more aware of the joys and problems in single parenthood.

You probably know a parent who is raising one or more children without a spouse. Arrange an interview with your subject.

When you are talking with your subject, try to find out what kind of experiences the person has had being a single parent. Does he or she like living alone with the children? What are some of the disadvantages in having only one parent in the home? Find out how the parent arranges any necessary babysitting or child care. If the parent works, what happens when a child is ill? Does the parent stay home from work to care for the child? Is discipline a problem for the parent? How does the parent find time for work, housework, and the children? What does your subject see as the biggest advantage of single parenthood? Ask any other

## Unit 4: Family Relationships

questions that interest you about single parenthood.

When you have finished your interview, try to summarize what your subject told you in a report. What seemed to be your subject's overall view of single parenthood? Was it positive or negative? How do you feel about the possibility of being a single parent?

### TO SUM UP...

1. What percentage of families are headed by women?
2. Why have single parent families increased over the years?
3. What are the differences in singlehood with and without children?
4. Describe some of the problems single parents face.
5. What are some advantages of being a single parent?

### CHANGING MARRIAGE STYLES

Changing life styles involve more people than those who choose singlehood. Many people who choose to marry are developing new marriage styles. They feel that it is too much to expect two people to share all of the same interests and needs for an entire lifetime.

Since couples can expect to live over 50 years together in marriage before death, some new patterns are emerging. These new patterns may help give more flexibility so that fewer marriages end in divorce. In addition, some of the alternate marriages allow the partners to build strong, creative relationships with a number of people. While most people can build these relationships within the usual marriage pattern, others seem unable to do so. Changing marriage styles may allow marriage to meet the needs of a greater number of people.

### Contract Marriages

A *contract* is an agreement between people or organizations. It outlines the agreement, noting how it is to be carried out, and states the responsibilities of all parties. Contracts have long been used in the business world. They have also found a place in family life.

Every marriage is a contract. The major terms of the contract are set in the marriage ceremony. The partners are expected to be loyal and faithful to each other in all kinds of circumstances. Their union is expected to last until one partner dies.

In addition, each partner brings an unwritten contract to marriage. This "contract," often ignored and unknown, consists of the expectations of each partner. Maria is entering into marriage expecting Bart to provide her with economic and emotional support. Bart, in turn, expects Maria to bear him children, keep his house clean, and provide regular meals. He also expects sex whenever he desires it because "we're married now."

The problem is not with the ideas which Maria and Bart hold. It is that they have not made their expectations clear to each other. The first time Maria refuses sex, Bart will feel that she has cheated on her marriage vows. In turn, if Bart expects Maria to hold at least a part-time job, she may feel that he is demanding more than she wants to give.

Couples can write a contract for themselves which spells out just what they want the marriage ceremony to mean. A written contract can deal with the length of the marriage or with the marital expectations of each partner.

**Ch. 12: Changing Life Styles**

*The contract this couple is writing will help them understand what each expects from their marriage.*

### Renewable Marriages

One of the suggestions for contract marriages deals with the length of the marriage relationship. To marry is a contract for life unless the couple divorces. Some people think the marriage license could be issued for a period of several years, then renewed if the partners wished.

Laws allowing renewable marriages of three or five years have been proposed in several states. However, they have never been passed, so renewable marriages are not now legal in any state.

Some couples who believe in the idea have drawn up private contracts. Todd and Wilma decided to set up a renewable marriage. They felt they would be cheating themselves if they assumed their love would last a lifetime. Their private contract was prepared by a lawyer. It said that if they did not wish to renew the contract after five years, Wilma would file for divorce. The contract could also be renewed for another five years. Thus they lived within their state's laws for licensing marriages and granting divorces. At the same time, they were able to work out their own contract for marriage renewal.

People who favor renewable marriage feel it helps build good relationships. Partners cannot take each other for granted. If they want to be sure the contract is renewed, they must work to keep their love strong and alive.

Some critics of renewable marriage say it really differs little from regular marriage. This is because divorce is so widespread and easy to obtain. They also feel that a contract which can be dissolved discourages people from working at marriages that are not going well.

As with traditional marriages, any disagreements over property and child custody would be settled by a court when the contract was not renewed.

267

Unit 4: Family Relationships

**Marital Expectations**

Another type of marriage contract does not involve the length of the marriage. Instead, it specifies the freedoms and the responsibilities for both partners. The couple includes in their contract those items of behavior or property which are important to them.

For example, Doris and Leroy were married after high school graduation. Both partners wanted to attend college. Therefore their contract was an agreement that they would both attend school part-time, hold part-time jobs, and share the household chores. They agreed in their contract to postpone having children at least until after both had graduated from college.

The contract set up by Chad and Salina concerned their money and property. They each agreed to keep their separate savings accounts. All money they saved during their marriage would be divided—half into Chad's account, half into Salina's. They agreed that as long as both were working, they would put half of their salary money into the household fund. The other half they could spend as they wished. If half the money turned out to be not enough, they would each put in more. When they were ready to have children, they would rework the contract.

A third kind of contract was set up by Lisa and Sam. They established which person would do which household chores. They agreed that Sam would cook the meals and do the shopping. The dishes and housecleaning were Lisa's jobs. Lisa was to care for their car and arrange for its servicing and cleaning. Doing the laundry was Sam's other main chore. Their contract stated that if either of them became a housewife or a househusband, they would rework the contract.

One type of marriage may especially benefit from a marriage contract. This is the family in which both the husband and wife have careers. In this type of family, both partners usually have college degrees. Both careers are equally important. It is often hard to work out the practical details of two careers. Making a contract helps partners decide how they will handle decisions. For example, what will happen if one of the partners is transferred? Will that partner turn down the job? Will the other partner move too, even if the only possible new job is inferior to the old? If the couple wants to have children, what kind of arrangements will be made? Many other decisions have to be made if both couples have professional careers.

Marty and Della were both lawyers when they married. Marty belonged to a law firm while Della was a government lawyer working with civil rights cases. Their marriage contract agreed that if Della should ever be transferred, Marty would sell his interest in the law firm and relocate in the new city. Thus when Della was promoted and transferred about three years after their marriage, there was no conflict about whether she should accept the transfer. She accepted her new job and in about six months, Marty was able to join her in their new home.

Many of the contracts that people make concern uncommon ways of doing things. However, a contract can simply put in writing any agreement that husbands and wives make about their marriage. Ruth and Gary were interested in a traditional marriage. They felt, however, that they would both know better what to expect if they put their ideas in a contract. Therefore their contract agreed that Ruth would continue to work for about 18 months after their marriage or until she became pregnant. She would quit her job before the baby's birth to become a full-time homemaker and mother. Gary would continue to support her and their baby. Ruth would stay at home until their youngest child

## Ch. 12: Changing Life Styles

reached school age. At that time, they would discuss whether she felt ready to reenter the labor market.

This type of marriage contract makes more concrete those expectations of marriage that are often not discussed. Couples may assume that they know what each other expects. Because of their love for each other, they think they have the same needs and wants and hold the same values. Writing a marriage contract may help couples have a clearer idea of their goals and expectations for themselves and their partners.

*This couple wrote a marriage contract that assigned chores by interest and ability.*

### experiences in human relations

#### MARRIAGE CONTRACTS

Marriage contracts are sometimes used to formalize an alternate marriage style. However, such contracts can also be useful in a traditional marriage. A contract is one way to make clear each partner's ideas and expectations for the marriage. This experience will help you begin to think through your ideas and expectations about what you want in a marriage relationship.

Imagine that you are engaged and planning your wedding and marriage. You and your future spouse have decided that a contract would help you discuss and formalize your ideas about your marriage. (If you are engaged or planning marriage at this time, you may wish to actually develop a contract with your partner.)

Write a contract stating your ideas. Begin with the statement, "We, _____ and _____, agree to the following items as a basis for our upcoming marriage. We agree to live and love following these guidelines."

Beneath this statement, list the items you feel would be important in your marriage contract. You will want to consider the following questions in developing your contract. You may choose to answer some or all of these questions in your contract. What you include depends on what is important to you and/or your future spouse.

Unit 4: Family Relationships

- Who will earn the money to support the family? If both work, will you pool income or will each keep his or her own salary?
- Where will you live? What would you do if one partner wanted to move because of a job or other reason and the other one didn't?
- What kind of birth control, if any, will you use? Whose responsibility is birth control?
- How many children do you plan to have? When? Would you consider adoption? Who will take the most responsibility for raising the children? Will one partner be expected to quit a job to care for the children?
- Who is going to do what around home?
- How will your leisure time be organized? Will you spend evenings and weekends together? Who will decide what activities you will do together? Will you take vacations together? With your future children?
- How important is privacy to you? Under what circumstances would you wish to live with others?
- Will you and your partner be free to make relationships with other people? Those of the same sex? Those of the opposite sex? Will you include each other in these relationships?
- Should the wife assume her husband's name or will she keep her own? If she keeps her own, whose name will the children bear?

As you are writing your contract, you will probably think of other questions you will want to include. The above questions are simply a guideline to help you begin thinking of issues to include in your contract.

When your contract is written, think about it. Does your contract make a statement about what you think is important in marriage? Do you think you would actually like to make a contract before you marry? What would you see as the advantages and disadvantages of doing so?

## TO SUM UP...

1. What is a contract?
2. How can a contract be used in marriage?
3. What is the unwritten contract between marriage partners?
4. Describe a renewable marriage contract.
5. What is the main advantage of such a contract?
6. Describe some marital expectations which could be included in a marriage contract.
7. Why are contracts especially helpful in two-career families?

### CHILDLESS MARRIAGES

Many couples are now choosing another growing life style, childless marriage. In the past, knowledge of birth control was limited, so methods of family planning were usually unreliable. Thus married couples produced children, whether or not they wanted them. Couples without children usually had problems in fertility.

Today, birth control technology has advanced a great deal. Couples who wish to remain childless are able to do so. There are many reasons why couples may choose not to have children.

Vivian says, "I was the oldest of eight children in my family. I had to spend a lot of my free time when I was growing up taking care of the others. I changed enough diapers, wiped enough noses, and scolded enough naughty kids to last me for a lifetime! I de-

### Ch. 12: Changing Life Styles

cided a long time ago that I wasn't going to have any children of my own."

Participating in sports takes up a large share of Paul and Barbara's time. "I really enjoy the way we live," comments Paul. "We both work and we just count on spending our time off together. There are so many things that we enjoy doing. We play tennis and bowl. Our own boat lets us enjoy water skiing and swimming. If we had a child, we couldn't afford to do all of those activities. In addition, we wouldn't be free to go out when we wanted. We'd have to worry about babysitting and child care. I suppose you could say we're selfish. But I know too many people with children who are unhappy with the way they live. We think our life is ideal—why should we change it?"

Margie is a sales manager for her firm. She has been promoted several times since she began working there. She feels that her career is very important. She says, "I know there are lots of women who can combine a career and a family. I don't think I would be very good at it and my career is too important for me to give up. I travel a lot in this job and that certainly would be hard with a baby. Even if I would get another promotion, I would still travel. So right now, I'm just not interested in becoming a mother. Jack is very involved in his work, too, so he understands and agrees that our marriage is just for the two of us."

People may choose to remain childless for a variety of reasons. Whatever the reason, research studies have found that couples in childless marriages rate themselves as happier than do couples with children. The studies report that children decrease marital satisfaction. Many more mothers than childless wives find marriage restrictive. Mothers also report more problems in their marriages and more dissatisfaction with themselves.

*Some couples choose not to have any children.*

In comparing husbands without children and fathers, husbands considered themselves much happier than did fathers. As with mothers, fathers felt marriage was restrictive with many problems.

The more children a couple has, the more unhappy their marriage tends to be. The poorest marriages are those with unwanted children.

On the other hand, many couples place a higher value on having children than on marital satisfaction. They find that the joy and pleasure they gain from their children more than makes up for their loss of satisfaction from their marriage.

Thus to choose to remain childless is a matter of what is important to a couple. Modern birth control methods give couples the chance to make their choice according to the values they hold.

Unit 4: Family Relationships

### TO SUM UP...

1. Explain why some couples decide not to have children.
2. Compare the happiness of childless marriages to those with children.
3. Why is the decision to have children a matter of values?

**BLENDED FAMILIES**

Many people who marry find themselves in an increasingly common family style called a blended family. They become "instant" parents to the children of their new spouse. These families are called "blended" because they are a blend of parts of other families. About one child in ten lives with a stepparent.

Members of new blended families must make many changes and adjustments. The adults are learning new marriage and parental roles. Children must adjust to the new parent and may have to learn to live with stepbrothers and stepsisters.

Ten-year-old Carole found her new family totally confusing. She had lived alone with her father for four years. Although happy when he married Pat, she hadn't realized how her life would change. Pat's two sons had loud voices, played rough games, and teased Carole all the time. The relaxed life she was used to changed as Pat started serving meals at regular hours and wanted Carole to help with household chores. It took a few months before Carole was comfortable with the new family routine. However, she soon learned not to cry when the boys teased her and the three became close friends.

It takes time to build strong relationships in a blended family. Trust and affection grow slowly and can't be forced. Closeness develops as new family members live together and share their lives with each other.

The new family is a blend of two sets of rules, values, and family styles. Some of these may be similar while others can be very different. Juan's mother had always welcomed his friends' visits. However, she wanted to know in advance who he planned to ask and how long the guests would stay. Juan found his stepmother enjoyed having his friends drop in unexpectedly.

Simply scheduling a blended family's activities can be a challenge. Habits set in the past can be hard to change. Mealtimes, bedtimes, curfew hours, and times for the family to be together have to be worked out.

Stepparents have to learn to adjust to the habits and personalities of the children. They work to be accepted as parents. Discipline is often a problem. Martin admits that he is harder on his own children than he is on his new wife, Kay's. He says, "Kay's daughter Laura likes to listen to records and tapes with the stereo on full blast. If my son Doug did that I would yell at him in a minute. But I find myself ignoring Laura when she does it because I hate to be too strict with her. Doug is beginning to resent it. I find it very hard to be evenhanded and fair to everyone."

The role of stepfather seems to be an easier one than that of stepmother. This may be because stepmothers tend to have a bad name in this country. They also spend more time with children than do stepfathers. This may mean more chance for conflict. Children are usually very close to their natural mother and may find it hard to accept someone else in the mother role.

Children in a blended family face their own adjustments. Those whose parents were di-

**Ch. 12: Changing Life Styles**

vorced often hoped they would get back together. Remarriage makes that dream impossible. Most children have had strong bonds with their single parent. They find it hard to include others in that close family circle. They may resent the attention the parent gives a new spouse or stepchildren.

Belle felt that way at first. "I was so jealous of Manny," she says. "I just couldn't understand why my mother loved him and wanted to marry him. To make it worse, Mom fussed over Manny's daughter Lil. I felt that she didn't love me anymore, that they were more important to her than I was. It took me a while to realize that she had more than enough love for us all and that I didn't get less because there were three of us. Now I can't imagine life without either Manny or Lil."

There are lots of changes and adjustments needed to build a happy blended family. Relationships are complex and take time to develop. Blended families are most successful when members go slowly and don't try to force instant love and intimacy. Studies have shown that stepchildren tend to be as happy as children who live with their natural parents. As a rule, younger children and adult children adjust to life in a blended family more easily than do teenage children.

Perhaps the happiest blended families are those where the stepparent is less a substitute parent than an added one. Patty Breen explains it this way. "Both my Mom and Dad have remarried. I live with my Dad and his wife, but I visit Mom often. It's really great to have two families. When I have a fight with Dad, I can go to Mom's house and get away for awhile—sometimes I even get some sympathy! Both my stepparents are great. It was one of the best things that ever happened when my folks got divorced."

*Shared experience help members of blended families develop love and trust.*

Unit 4: Family Relationships

## TO SUM UP...

1. What is a blended family and how is one formed?
2. Describe some of the adjustments made by members of a blended family.
3. Why does the role of stepmother seem to be more difficult than that of stepfather?
4. List some factors that help promote successful blended families.

### OPEN MARRIAGE

Most people enter into marriage without expecting much change. Rob said, "Well, I love Carol today, so why shouldn't I love her tomorrow? I expect we'll both always be the same people we are now. After all, people don't change that much, do they?"

People do change, and unless partners are prepared to cope with changes in themselves and the other, problems arise. Open marriage is one approach that tries to give couples a chance to change and grow as people.

Open marriage results from an agreement between the partners. Some partners may use a contract to formalize their agreement. Others may simply talk over the situation and agree to try an open marriage. Some couples begin open marriage after being spouses many years. Others agree to an open marriage before the wedding.

The key to an open marriage is that partners are bound together by love rather than by behavior or roles. Spouses each have their own interests and their own relationships with others. They are not bound by the usual marriage roles. Instead they live their lives as people who are free to act in ways that will bring personal growth.

In a traditional marriage, partners are expected to meet each other's needs. Couples are expected to share the same friends, interests, and activities. However, it is unrealistic to expect that any two people will be able to be all things to each other. Instead of providing an atmosphere of growth for both partners, marriage may come to seem like a cage.

A recent study of marriage found that people with few close friends and acquaintances are more apt to be unhappy with their marriages. Those people who had many friends did not have to rely on their spouses to meet all their social needs. Without this heavy pressure, the marriage relationship ended up being happy and satisfying.

*Open marriage allows spouses to develop their own interests.*

## Ch. 12: Changing Life Styles

### Outside Relationships

Perhaps the most unusual aspect of open marriage relates to the relationships which spouses build. Each partner is free to form relationships with others outside of marriage. Many people assume that the outside relationships in an open marriage are sexual relationships. This is often not the case.

All people have needs for relationships and companionship that marriage cannot meet. However, in traditional marriages, these outside needs are met with friends of the same sex or with couples who are friends of both partners. This eliminates many possible friendships.

In contrast, partners in an open marriage make friends where their interests are. They are honest with each other. They do not attempt to hide their friendships with others of the opposite sex. Bob comments, "Some people might feel that I shouldn't tell Kathy about my chess games with Patty. I suppose I could tell her I worked late or something. But it would hurt our relationship if I lied to her. We want open, honest relationships with all our friends. It would be silly to begin the lies at home."

### Individual Interests

Couples who feel free to have their own friends and to pursue their own interests feel their marriages grow stronger. They have more to talk over as they discuss their own activities. When each partner is enthusiastic and excited about what he or she is doing, that enthusiasm can give the relationship a lift. It is the sharing of separate activities that ties the couple together. This emphasizes the importance of good communication. If the couple can't share their excitements, the relationship will soon wither.

Arnie says, "Bess is all involved in electing her candidate to the state government. I think the woman will make a good legislator. But I don't get all worked up about it. So I babysit with the kids while Bess campaigns. I think it's worth it to me when she gets home. She tells me all about what she's done, the people she talks to, how the election is going. I really don't care that much, but I love to listen to her when she's excited about something. She's so snappy and sparkly when she's enthusiastic, I can't help but love her more."

Open marriage is a growing relationship. Each partner is free to grow as a person. Partners then use that individual growth to promote growth in their relationship together. To do so takes honesty, trust, and a strong sense of the value of it all.

## experiences in human relations

### OPEN MARRIAGE

The idea of an open marriage is very threatening to many people. They find it hard to accept the idea that their spouse could form non-sexual relationships with someone of the opposite sex. This experience will help you explore the feelings you and your classmates have about open marriage.

Each of you should have several small index cards. On each card, write the following sentence, "Open marriage is like _____." Fill in the blank with a comparison. Let your mind run free. Think of as wild a comparison as you can to express your ideas. For example, someone might write, "Open marriage is like opening the prison door to the convicts." Another response might be, "Open marriage is like playing with fire."

Try to think of several comparisons in two or three minutes. All class members then place

## Unit 4: Family Relationships

their cards face down on a table. Shuffle the cards and then each of you draw out one or more cards, depending on how many cards there are.

Read aloud the comparison(s) that you drew. If it is the one you wrote, do not let the others know. Read one card at a time and try to explain what the comparison means to you. Ask the others if they have other ideas about what the card means.

When you are finished reading the cards, think about the comparisons. Were there any cards that were similar? Were most of the cards favorable or unfavorable to the idea of open marriage? Why do you suppose class members felt as they did?

### TO SUM UP...

1. What is the possible outcome if people enter marriage expecting no changes in either partner?
2. Why do people with more friends tend to have happier marriages?
3. What is the most unusual trait in an open marriage?
4. Why is communication so important in an open marriage?

### GROUP MARRIAGE

A group marriage consists of three or more people who live together and feel bound or committed to each other as marriage partners. Such groups involve emotional closeness, economic sharing, and sexual access to all members.

Group marriage is one of the most radical of the alternate life styles. It also probably is one of the least acceptable life styles for most people. It is estimated that there are only a few hundred group marriages in the entire United States.

People who form group marriages have a great interest in relating to other people. They also firmly believe that people can grow through their relationships with others.

John says, "I have a need to relate to many people. Sara, my wife, is a fantastic person. I wouldn't want to break up with her for anything. Yet, I want more close relationships, too. I can form these relationships in our group marriage with Donna and Quinn. Another advantage that I see is the fact that our children have four parents instead of two. If I have a fight with one of them, they have another father who may be able to provide the love and support that I can't give right then. I also enjoy the sense of 'community' I get in our group marriage. We love and support each other as we try to grow as people."

However much the idea of group marriage appeals to some people, it does not seem to be a very workable idea. Group marriages are unstable and tend to break up rapidly. Finding three or more people who can live together in harmony is a problem. It is hard enough to live together in peace with one husband or wife. As each additional person is added to the marriage, the possibilities for conflict increase.

Working out the schedule for so many people can be another problem. Norma reports that scheduling was the main factor that broke up her group marriage. She said, "Each person had his or her own work schedule, activities, and commitments. It became almost impossible to set something so simple as what time to have supper. We usually ended up eating in two or three shifts. Wanting to spend time building our group relationship was the reason we formed a group marriage. However, we found that we couldn't even find the time to take care of business matters."

One proposal that is sometimes made is that group marriages should be promoted for elderly people. The number of men over sixty is considerably lower than the number of women. Thus most older women have no chance to remarry.

Group marriage with one man and two or more women would offer these women a chance to remarry and form a meaningful family group. Elderly people are often very lonely. A group marriage would allow them to again feel that they are needed. They would know that there are others who care for them.

In addition to the relationship needs which group marriages would meet, there are other practical advantages. Studies have shown that elderly married couples eat better diets than those living alone. Because most of the elderly have limited incomes, a group marriage would provide more money to obtain good living conditions. A group marriage would provide nursing care when one member of the marriage was ill. It also would allow several people to share the physical chores of keeping house and preparing food.

Group marriage is a life style that is probably more attractive in theory than in practice. However, it does appeal to a small number of people who try it. They see it as one way to have a full, rich family life built on strong relationships with several other people.

## experiences in human relations

### ATTITUDES TOWARD MARRIAGE

People hold different attitudes toward marriage. Some people see it as their life's goal. Others do not want to get married. Some people consider marriage a safe and secure base from which to enter the world. Others see marriage as their world. This experience will help you think about your attitudes toward marriage.

The following list of words describes a variety of attitudes toward marriage. Read over the list and on a separate sheet of paper write the three words which best express what you feel marriage is or should be.

| | |
|---|---|
| Equality | Taking |
| Exploitation | Commitment |
| Fun | Responsibility |
| Intimacy | A Cage |
| Sex | Freedom |
| Love | Growth |
| Dependence | Understanding |
| Trusting | Permanence |
| Liking | Harmony |
| Affection | Authority |
| Hate | Acceptance |
| Submitting | Strength |
| Independence | Security |
| Giving | Risky |
| Sharing | Children |
| Selfish | Cooperation |
| Happy | Agreement |
| Open | Disagreement |
| Stifling | Criticism |
| A Trap | Calm |
| An Ideal | Unexciting |
| Conflict | Exciting |

All class members should place their papers face down on a table. Shuffle the papers. Each member then draws a paper and reads aloud to the class the words written on the paper.

When you have finished, think about the words that were read. Were most of them similar? Did many people choose the same word or words? Were some negative ideas about marriage expressed? Given the words that were read, would you guess that marriage

## Unit 4: Family Relationships

will be able to meet the needs of all your class members? How might people come to desire an alternate marriage style? What conclusions can you draw from this experience? What did you learn about yourself and marriage?

### TO SUM UP...

1. What is a group marriage?
2. Why do some people seek to form a group marriage?
3. Describe some of the reasons most group marriages don't last very long.
4. Why are group marriages often suggested for elderly people?

### LIVING TOGETHER

Another life style which has received a great deal of publicity is that of two people living together without being married. Actually, only three to four percent of the American people choose this life style.

Delbert and Sally are living together while they are in college. They do not expect to marry because they feel their separate careers will take them to different parts of the country. In the meantime, they feel that living together provides each with love, affection, and support.

Norton and Eileen consider themselves in a trial marriage. They are engaged, but plan to live together for a year before the wedding. They consider marriage a permanent commitment and want a year together to show whether they are really right for each other.

George and Annie are in their mid-thirties. Both have been divorced after unhappy marriages. Neither is ready to marry again, but their feelings for each other are strong. Therefore they decided that George would live with Annie and her children.

Finally, sixty-eight-year-old Yolanda Smith and seventy-year-old Vince Garrett live together. They find the companionship of each other a great pleasure after several years of living alone. At first they planned to marry. However, they found that as a married couple, they would receive much less in Social Security benefits than they do now. Therefore, to avoid a drop in benefits, they decided not to marry.

One important aspect of most living-together arrangements is that they contain no built-in vow of permanence. The couple does not have any legal basis for staying together. They believe that their feelings for each other, not a marriage license, are the basis of the relationship. They accept the fact that if the relationship fails, nothing will keep them together. Thus most couples who live together work to keep their relationship close and meaningful.

Some couples feel that, by living together, they are avoiding the roles that are restrictive in marriage. They feel that if they legally became husband and wife, they would cease to relate to each other as persons. Betty says, "I have seen too many of my friends get married and then begin to take their spouses for granted. If that's what getting married does, I don't want any part of it. I want a relationship that changes and grows as I do, not one that stays in the same old rut."

Couples may live together for any length of time. College students often find that their living-together experiences end in a month or two. Some people look on living together as a short-term preparation for marriage. Others may consider it a substitute for marriage. These arrangements may be long term and fairly permanent.

Ch. 12: Changing Life Styles

mitment to each other led to the breakup of their relationship.

Living together can mean that a couple simply finds it convenient to stay in the same place. It can also be an expression of true affection and responsible caring for each other. Perhaps the main value of living together is that it helps people learn to relate intimately. As such, it may help build stronger marriages as partners grow toward permanent emotional bonds with each other.

*The most frequent cause of conflict between couples who are living together is differing expectations.*

One common idea is that people live together to fulfill their sexual needs. However, most people living together downplay the importance of sex in their lives. Instead, they stress the joys of living with someone you care for and who cares for you. In other words, they stress the rewards of closeness and intimacy with another person rather than sexual satisfaction.

Most conflict between couples who live together is over their expectations for their relationship. Partners may differ in the degree of commitment they feel toward each other. One of the partners may look at the relationship as building toward marriage. The other may simply be enjoying it for its present value.

Mark was very angry and upset when he found that Debbie, with whom he had been living for two months, was dating other men. He expected her to be totally committed to their relationship. Debbie, however, felt that living together did not commit her only to Mark. This difference in their degree of com-

## TO SUM UP...

1. What are some of the reasons people choose to live together without marriage?
2. Why do couples who live together work hard at their relationship with each other?
3. What is the main cause of conflict between couples living together?

## COMMUNAL LIVING

Communal living has been a minor part of human life throughout history. In hard times, people banded together to survive. Monks shared communal lives in monasteries. In the last century, communal groups formed such settlements as the Shaker communities and Amana Colonies.

A commune is a group of people who live together and who have a commitment to the group based on common needs and interests. Early communes were generally based on economic needs, or like religious groups, on shared ideas and philosophy. Today, communes usually center on ways to create new family ties.

279

## Unit 4: Family Relationships

In the 1970's what was a small, mostly unknown life style received a great deal of publicity. A way of life that involved less than one-half of one percent of the population was made to seem much more widespread. In addition, the publicity tended to focus on communal groups where there was drug use and promiscuous sex. Communes based on religious beliefs or on family life were not given such extensive reporting. Although their numbers have decreased in the last few years, there are still many functioning communal groups.

Most people who choose communal living do so because they feel the need for close, emotionally satisfying relationships with others. They feel that living alone or with their family keeps them from forming many strong relationships. Janie lived in a commune when she first moved away from her parents' home. It gave her a sense of family life. At the same time, it allowed her to be independent of her parents.

### VARIATION IN COMMUNAL LIFE

Communal life varies in a number of ways. Many different kinds of people choose to live together in groups. A common stereotype is that only young, unmarried people live in communes. Many of them seek an alternate family. They hope to find one in communal life. On the other hand, some successful and permanent communes are formed by people in their thirties or older. These groups are usually begun by several married couples and their children. They may also include some singles who seek a family life without being married.

The kind of behavior acceptable in communal groups differs a great deal. Some are loosely based on common drug use. Others forbid the use of drugs.

Tania belongs to a commune that is based on interest in health, diet, and vegetarianism. The group runs a health food store. Members believe that people ruin their bodies by improper eating and drug use. Therefore they do not eat meat or use any drugs. This includes caffeine, which is an ingredient in coffee and many soft drinks.

One area of public interest has been the sexual life styles of people living in communes. Some groups do allow members sexual experiences with each other. But many recognize that jealousy and conflict over sex create stresses in the group. Others see sex outside of marriage as morally wrong. Thus most require that sexual activity, if allowed, be with one's spouse or primary partner.

Communes differ in their support of some kind of belief. Some groups are organized around a creed that may be religious or spiritual. Meditation or yoga may be the focus in some groups. Others are affiliated with organized religion. Other groups have a political focus. Still more are interested in health foods or growing organic foods. Those groups which have some kind of creed or belief toward which the group works are the strongest.

In contrast, some groups have few common beliefs or goals. They are held together by an interest in forming some kind of substitute family group or by the desire to build relationships. However, without some strong central interest, membership changes often. The life of the communes without a creed is generally short, often lasting only a few weeks.

The geographical setting of a commune may influence the way the commune is organized. Some groups stress a "back to nature" theme and are located in rural areas. People living in these communes may try to

**Ch. 12: Changing Life Styles**

*Growing some of their own food is a common interest in many communes.*

farm or grow produce. The Freedom Commune was located on a forested acreage in the South. Members of the commune used trees from their land to handcraft wooden furniture, toys, and sculpture. They also sold wood for lumber when money ran short. Group members were very interested in conservation and reforested areas where they removed trees.

Other communes are located in urban areas. Some of these urban communes are loosely knit—teenagers arrive, stay for a while, then leave. Other urban groups are formed by older couples who work at their jobs daily, then quietly go home to their communal family. These communes often seek to avoid publicity. The members live quietly without attracting attention.

Roles vary in communes. Some groups hold that all members should share the work equally. In others, males and females perform the traditional roles. In a rural commune called Apple Farm, the traditional sex roles are lived. The women keep the house and take care of the children. The men do the farm work and have contact with the outside world.

In contrast, one urban commune consisting of two married couples, their five children, and two single people, divide the work without consideration for sex. Each person is assigned a household role for a week. The jobs are rotated each week. Thus one week Orlando is the cook, the next, housekeeper, and the next, shopper. All of the other commune members fulfill these household roles in their turn.

### DISADVANTAGES OF COMMUNAL LIVING

The life span of most communes is relatively short. There seem to be several major drawbacks which cause problems in communal living.

Disagreement often occurs over household chores or work. In communes where the work roles are highly structured, people may resent

281

## Unit 4: Family Relationships

being "assigned" work. In others, work is not structured or assigned. This may mean that it never gets done.

Art always seemed to end up being the cook in his commune. No one else ever wanted to fix any meals. When Art prepared food for himself, the others would expect him to make something for them, too. Art resented the fact that he was always expected to prepare the meals. Finally, he left the commune with many bitter feelings about the laziness of the others. He felt that they wanted the benefits of communal living but without having to help with the unpleasant chores.

Another area that often causes communal groups to break up is that of personal conflicts. It is hard enough to live with members of your family whom you love. It is even harder to relate to all commune members with equal affection and support. In some groups, differences in values cause the split. In others, jealousy over sex, work, or possessions may bring conflict. Most people do not have the maturity to maintain strong, close relationships with a large number of people. This causes most communes to be short lived.

Economic survival can be a problem for many communes. If most or all of the members work in outside jobs, the groups are least likely to break up for economic reasons. However, communes which try to be self-sufficient through farming or through a small business often have some problems. Even more severe financial problems are found where commune members rely on public welfare or on support from parents.

Jonah receives a small amount of money each month from his parents. Because none of the commune members have regular jobs, Jonah's money is the only regular income the group can count on. However, it is just not enough to care for the needs of nine people.

Some communes break up because of harrassment or hostility from the outside community. This is especially true when the life style and moral code of the group are very different from that of the surrounding community. Some people feel that communal living is in itself disgraceful or sinful. Others may feel that a particular communal group is a bad influence in the community. Residents of the community may ignore the commune members. Some communal groups have been the targets of vandals. Urban communes seem to be able to escape attention from their neighbors more easily. This may be because urban communities are accustomed to more diversity.

## experiences in human relations

### COMMUNAL LIVING

Those communes with a strong organization and structure tend to last much longer than others. The stable communes usually have a leader, a strong financial base, and a creed or belief that governs all members.

Starting a commune that will be stable is similar to building a new little nation. Many rules of government or organization must be established. This experience will help you begin to recognize the many issues which need to be settled before a strong, long-lasting group can be formed.

Form a group with five other class members. Pretend that you are a group of friends who have decided to form a commune after high school graduation. Your group consists of three males and three females. You have decided that your communal living arrangements don't include the right to sex with each other.

Your job, as this make-believe communal group, is to solve the issues facing the commune members.

First, who will be the leader of the group. How will you decide if two or more people want to be the leader? If no one wants the job?

Will your commune have a creed? Will it be a religious creed, a political creed, an interest in health, or something else? How will you decide what is to be your main focus and interest?

How will your communal group support itself? Do you all plan to hold jobs? What if one or more people cannot find or do not desire to have a job? Will the rest of you support them?

How will the housework be divided? Will everyone be assigned chores? Who will do what? What will you do if someone decides he or she doesn't want to share the work?

What kind of rules will your commune make? Will there be any kitchen rules? Rules about drug use? Rules about bringing outsiders into the communal group? What other rules can you think of that might help the commune function smoothly?

How will property be divided? Will individuals continue to own their own property? Or will all possessions belong to all commune members?

What happens when two or more members have conflict? When someone new wants to join the commune? When a commune member wants to leave?

Setting up a stable commune is a complex process. No doubt other questions will occur to you as your group talks about the features of your commune. When you have discussed the issues, report your ideas to your classmates. Listen to their reports of their communal groups. Was there much similarity in the organization of others' communes and yours? Did each commune's rules reflect the personalities of those people who were pretending to be

*The most stable and long-lasting communes are those based on religious beliefs.*

future commune members? Do you think most communes go through a process of organization such as you just did? Based on this experience, explain why many communes last only a short time.

• • • • • • • • • • • • • • • • • • • • • •

## STABLE COMMUNES

The most stable communes share several traits. They are founded on pre-existing conventional families. These families then become the basis of the commune as others join them.

Stable groups have a definite leader who has authority and uses it. Such communes also have some clear economic function. The members hold jobs or the group as a whole may operate a business or a resort.

Religious groups have the highest survival rates of any type of commune. This is proba-

## Unit 4: Family Relationships

bly partly due to the fact that they have a religious leader who has authority over commune members. In addition, such groups are highly structured. Members have their religious goals to tie them to each other and to the group.

Communes are most apt to be successful when their members are over 30. By that age, people usually have learned to know themselves. They have also made career and marriage decisions before joining the commune. Therefore they are free to focus their energies on the relationships between members.

Stable communes offer the advantage of a sense of closeness with a variety of people. Those who live in such communes feel that the advantages of the life style outweigh the disadvantages. However, communal life is attractive to only a small number of people.

## experiences in human relations

### CHOOSING A LIFE STYLE

Alternate life styles offer options. People can thus choose a life style that fits their values and needs. Most people will still choose traditional marriage, even though one-fourth of those people will eventually divorce. Some people will alter their life styles slightly. Others will make drastic changes as they try to make a life that is right for them. The following experience will help you think about the values involved in several types of life styles. It will ask you to think about what you want from your life style.

Listed below are various life styles that are mentioned in this chapter. Below the first list is a second list which gives a code for identifying the life styles. Copy the list of life styles on a separate sheet of paper. In front of each item, write the code number which describes your feelings about that life style.

Life Styles
- Singlehood
- Single Parenthood
- Communal Living
- Living Together
- Renewable Marriage
- Contract for Marital Expectations
- Childless Marriage
- Two Career Marriage
- Open Marriage
- Group Marriage
- Traditional Marriage (includes children)
- Divorce and Remarriage

Code
1. I like it very much
2. I like it quite a lot
3. I like it slightly
4. I am indifferent to it
5. I dislike it slightly
6. I dislike it quite a lot
7. I dislike it very much

Look over your codings. Do you find yourself liking the more traditional patterns? Or are you drawn to the alternate life styles?

Now, rank order the list of life styles. To do this, place a number 1 beside the life style that would be your first choice. Place a number 2 beside the one you would prefer second. Continue doing this until all the life styles have numbers beside them. This may be very difficult to do. You may have several choices that you are equally drawn to. There also may be several choices that you wish to place at the bottom of the list. However, make an attempt to rank your choices.

When you have finished both parts of this experience, think about your choices. What did your choices tell you about yourself? Do you think you will be happy in a traditional life style? Will the life style that appeals to you most place you in conflict with society? What did you learn from this experience?

## TO SUM UP...

1. What is a commune?
2. Why do people choose communal living?
3. Describe some of the ways communes differ from each other.
4. Explain why most communal groups are short lived.
5. Describe traits of the most stable communes.
6. Why do people over 30 tend to form successful communes?

## CHAPTER 13

*Family Breakdown—Death and Divorce*

**This chapter will help you to . . .**
- Describe various physical and emotional reactions to death.
- Identify steps in the mourning process.
- Become aware of the many arrangements which need to be made at the time of death.
- Understand characteristics of couples who are likely to become divorced.
- Discuss the advantages and disadvantages of the adversary and no-fault systems of divorce.
- Describe six different aspects of divorce.

Families are formed with a great deal of hope for the future. The couple envisions a long, happy life ahead, but every day, families break down. Some families are broken by desertion. Others falter when a family member is jailed or must be hospitalized for a long period of time. However, the most common causes of family breakdown are the death of a family member or the divorce of the married couple.

Both of these types of family breakdown are painful for everyone. Both require adjustment and changes in people's way of living. Confronting the fact that you may face either or both death and divorce in the future is difficult. Recognizing the possibility may help you to cope better when either crisis does arise.

### DEATH

In the past, people were born and died at home with their families. Most people died in their own beds. Death was considered a natural part of the life cycle. People understood the fact that just as life was to be lived, death would come and must be faced. Grief and mourning were accepted as necessary emotions in learning to live without the dead family member. Because death occurred in the family, children and teenagers were exposed to it as a part of life.

Today, however, most deaths occur in hospitals. In many cases, the dying person is surrounded by medical personnel instead of family members. Because of the hospital setting, death has become impersonal. Many children and young people are kept from contact with death by well-meaning parents and adults.

When Mark's grandmother was dying of cancer, Mark was not allowed to visit her in the hospital. His parents felt that it would upset him to see her so wasted away, frail, and in constant pain. So although Mark had been very close to his grandmother and loved her a great deal, he was not given a chance to see her before she died.

Thus death has become remote, a subject that people don't talk about. It is seen as a rare, impersonal, almost abnormal event, rather than an integral part of life itself.

Death has become a taboo subject because it involves very private feelings and fears. In the past, when death was a part of family life, people could share their feelings and fears. This helped them learn to accept death as a part of life. Today, however, people tend to keep their fears and feelings about death to themselves.

After Alice's aunt died, Alice became very afraid and upset whenever death was mentioned. If a family member became ill, she worried that he or she might die. However, she didn't tell anyone about how frightened she was. It seemed shameful to admit to the others how she felt.

Most fears stem from the fact that death is final. It is a plain, stark fact—death is the loss of a human being. You cannot replace that loss. Instead, you must adjust to it. Healthy adjustment to death is only possible when

*Death has become an impersonal event because more and more deaths occur in hospitals.*

you can talk to others about your feelings. People need to be able to share their memories to overcome the pain that death brings.

**287**

Unit 4: Family Relationships

## experiences in human relations

### CONTACT WITH DEATH

Americans are both surrounded by and isolated from death. On one hand, newspapers, television, and radio report deaths from accidents, illness, murder, famine, flood, and war. However, most people have little if any personal contact with death. This experience will help you consider the contact you and your classmates have had with death.

Each of the questions below has two or more possible answers given in parentheses following the question. On a separate piece of paper, write the answer to each question which best describes your situation or feelings. Do not put your name on your paper.

• Have you ever seen a person die? (Yes, No)

• Have you ever seen a body before embalming? (Yes, No)

• Have you ever seen an embalmed body? (Yes, No)

• Is a member of your family, a close relative, or a very close friend dying of an illness at the present time? (Yes, No)

• When has a member of your family, a close relative, or a very close friend died? (Within the past year, Within the past two years, Within the past five years, Over five years ago, Never)

• When did you last attend a funeral or memorial service? (Within the past year, Within the past two years, Within the past five years, Over five years ago, Never)

• When you were a small child, how was death talked about in your family? (Openly, Guardedly, Among the adults, Not talked about, Cannot remember)

• How often have you been in a situation in which you seriously thought you might die? (Never, Once or twice, Several times, Many times)

When you have finished, look over your answers. How much personal contact with death have you had? How do you think this contact or lack of it has influenced you? Do your attitudes and values about death reflect the amount of contact you have had with death?

With your classmates, compile your answers to the questions to make a class profile of contact with death. Have most class members had contact with death? Or have most been shielded from such contact?

If you feel comfortable doing so, share with your classmates your experiences with death.

• • • • • • • • • • • • • • • • • •

### REACTIONS TO DEATH

In peacetime, two American families lose a family member through death every minute. The most common experience is the loss of the father bringing widowhood to the wife and mother. How do these families react to death?

There are as many reactions to death as there are individual people. When Mr. Carlin died, the reactions of the members of his family were varied. Mrs. Carlin was hysterical, crying and screaming until she had to be sedated by the doctor. Nineteen-year-old Julie Carlin was outwardly without emotion. She acted as if there were a wall between herself and others that shut out grief and pain. Twelve-year-old Nicky behaved as if nothing unusual had happened. It was as if he refused to think of the death of his father at all. Mr. Carlin's mother told everyone how much peace it brought her to know that her son now was living a life after death. She also talked about all of her son's good points, emphasizing what a perfect son, husband, and father he had been. Fifteen-year-old Toby Carlin was angry. He was angry at the doctors for being unable to save his father. He was angry at God for allowing his father to be killed in a car accident. Most of all, he was angry at his father for leaving him and the family alone.

All of the reactions of the Carlin family are perfectly normal. Some people may protest violently against death or resign themselves to it. Others become obsessed with the idea of death. Many people become totally disorganized for a period of time. On the other hand, others begin to work quietly and almost immediately to reshape their lives.

However people react to a death in the family, most reactions focus on either physical or emotional symptoms.

*People react in different ways to the death of someone they love.*

### Ch. 13: Family Breakdown—Death and Divorce

**Physical Reactions**

Most people are not prepared for the intensity of their reaction to death. The body reacts in its own way to the loss of a loved person. A common reaction is numbness. When Donna's mother died, Donna's whole body seemed numb. She felt as if pins stuck in her flesh wouldn't hurt because everything was so unfeeling.

Another common reaction is a pain and tightness in the throat. This is probably related to a person's holding back tears or having cried a great deal. Bill's brother Andrew died of an overdose of heroin. "I really didn't feel like crying," Bill relates. "But it felt as if all the tears in the world were pooled in my throat. It was so tight it was almost impossible to swallow. I felt as if I were choking."

Other people find it hard to eat and sleep. Mrs. Harris was never hungry after her elderly father died. Food neither sounded, smelled, nor tasted good. She also found she couldn't sleep. She would awaken at four and five in the morning, unable to go to sleep again. Her whole body felt restless and jittery.

On the other hand, some people react to death by becoming very tired. John's steady dating partner was killed in an automobile accident. He found himself so tired that he would sleep twelve to fourteen hours a night.

Many people describe a feeling of unreality. Mr. Ruiz felt as if there were a glass wall between himself and others. Nothing seemed real to him. He felt as if his body were taking part in a play. At the same time, his mind seemed disconnected from what was going on around him.

Many people become physically ill when someone they love dies. Their complaints may range from catching a cold to serious health problems such as a heart attack. The experience of death produces many physical

## Unit 4: Family Relationships

reactions in the survivors. Knowing that your body is likely to be affected can help you prepare for the possibility of meeting death in the future.

## experiences in human relations

### YOUR DEATH

Most people find the thought of their own death very frightening. As a result, the majority try to avoid thinking about the possibility of their death. Every person must eventually die. To avoid ever thinking about your own death is to avoid facing an event that ultimately must happen.

On a separate sheet of paper, write a statement of no more than 50 words about your death. If you cannot imagine your own death, write about why it is hard for you to think of your own death.

When you have finished, reread your statement. What emotions toward death does your statement reveal? Does anything surprise you about your statement? Did you find it easy or hard to write this statement? Why do you suppose it was easy or hard for you?

Now imagine you are a member of a newspaper staff. One day you are called on to write your own obituary notice. Use the following format. Try to be as objective as possible.

(Your name) _____, age _____, died yesterday from _____.

(He or She) is survived by _____.

At the time of death (he or she) was working on becoming _____.

(He or She) made contributions in the area of _____.

(He or She) will be honored for _____.

(He or She) always hoped to _____.

The body will be _____.

Does this notice give a good reflection of your life? Was the obituary easier or harder than writing about your death? What did you learn from this experience?

• • • • • • • • • • • • • • • • • • • • •

### Emotional Reactions

Just as people are not prepared for the physical responses of their bodies to death, they are also not prepared for the emotions which they feel. They are taken unaware by the stabbing pain, the sudden anger, the sense of the unfairness of life, and their feelings of relief, guilt, and gladness.

It is normal, universal, and natural to have strong feelings when someone important to you dies. How you handle these feelings is crucial in whether you can come to accept the death of the other. It can be psychologically harmful to hide and deny such feelings. Many of the feelings people have at death are not rational or logical. People need to be able to express such feelings to others without being afraid of being judged.

Many common emotions are associated with death. One of these is guilt. People always feel guilt at the death of someone they love. When Jeremy's father died of a heart attack, Jeremy was overcome with guilt. He felt that if he hadn't argued so much with his father, the heart attack might not have happened. He felt as if he should have taken an after-school job to help with the money problems the family had. He was overcome with guilt for asking his father for money and to borrow the car. Probably Jeremy's actions had nothing to do with his father's heart attack. However, it was natural and normal for him to feel guilt at his father's death.

Anger and hostility are other usual responses to death. Sally was very angry at the doctors after her twin sister died of kidney failure. She felt that if the doctors had known their medicine better, her sister would still be alive.

Other people feel anger against the dead person. Gloria Jefferson's husband died of carbon monoxide poisoning while he was repairing his car in a closed garage. Gloria was angry because he had been so careless as to run the car without opening the garage door. Her anger was directed at her husband for leaving her and their son alone.

A sense of relief and joy may also accompany the death of a loved person. Mr. Parks died after a long and painful bout with cancer. During his final days, he was in such pain that he moaned and thrashed about the hospital bed constantly. Don Parks found that he was overcome with relief when his father finally died. He said, "I was really glad when Dad died. How could I want him to stay alive longer and have to suffer that horrible pain? I certainly didn't want him to have to die. I know I'm going to miss him terribly. But after his cancer got so bad, I was glad to have it over."

Finally, fear and anxiety are common emotional reactions to death. People always have some fear of the different world they face when their lives change. Death in particular causes many people to feel insecure and fearful.

Tony Dalton confessed that he was very afraid when his wife died. "I thought I'd never be able to carry on," he says. "I had this big ball of fright in my stomach. How would I be able to go to work? What would happen to our kids? Who was going to manage everything? Of course, we managed in the best way we could. But it took a long time for me to stop being anxious about life."

Although the emotions described above are the most common ones, many people

**Ch. 13: Family Breakdown—Death and Divorce**

*At death, many people feel anger toward "fate," the medical personnel, other family members, or the dead person.*

experience other feelings. No matter what your feelings are at the death of another, you should feel free to experience them and talk about them with someone you trust. Only then can you overcome the grief that accompanies death.

Unit 4: Family Relationships

## TO SUM UP...

1. What are the two most common causes of family breakdown?
2. Describe how death was handled in the past in the United States.
3. Why has death become more impersonal today?
4. Why do people react differently to the death of someone important to them?
5. What are several common physical reactions to death?
6. List several emotions that people usually experience when a family member dies.
7. In what circumstances might relief be experienced at death?

### Grief

Grief is the pain, discomfort, and the mental and physical feelings that most persons feel following the death of a loved one. Thus *grief* is both the physical and emotional reaction that a person experiences to death. Whether grief begins at the moment of death or when it becomes obvious death will occur, people cope with it through the mourning process.

### Mourning Process

To mourn for a dead person is the process by which powerful emotions are brought under control. When the mourning process is successful, the dead person becomes a "living memory." That is, the surviving person can remember the other without feeling grief or loss.

There are three stages which make up the mourning process. The first stage is one of shock. This period of shock usually occurs between death and the final arrangements for the body. Friends and neighbors frequently gather around to provide support for the bereaved. During the shock period, the person often denies that the death has occurred. The shock also often brings protests about life's unfairness. Shock causes a variety of physical reactions. Some people may collapse physically while others have violent emotional outbursts. Some people withdraw from others. They seem almost dazed, not able to accept the fact of death.

Marcia couldn't believe that her father was dead. Her first reaction was that it couldn't be true. Her violent outburst of crying and screaming left her dazed and exhausted. She spent the next few days unable to eat—she felt as if her tight throat would choke her if she ate. Her friends and dating partner spent a lot of time giving her support and affection during her first shocked reaction to death.

The second stage of mourning is that of intense pain and feelings of loss. This aspect of mourning lasts anywhere up to two or three months in most people. This stage of mourning is often treated as a weakness or a self-indulgence. However, grief is a psychological need if the person is to make a healthy adjustment to death.

During this second stage of mourning, many physical symptoms occur. The bereaved person may withdraw attention from the world. He or she may exist in a dream world. Restless sleep is often disturbed by many vivid dreams. A weight loss may be the result of poor appetite. Many people feel their first emotional reactions of anger, guilt, or pain turn to despair and hopelessness.

After Bob Grier's funeral, his mother seemed to withdraw from her family for several weeks. She was tired and slept a lot, yet her sleep was broken by many dreams of Bob.

*During the mourning process, many people have dreams about the dead family member.*

She also had many nightmares from which she would awake crying. The loss of her young son sent her into a wave of despair and sadness.

The third and final stage of mourning is called resolution. It involves resolving all the emotional and physical reactions to grief. The person begins to pick up the threads of daily life again. Eating and sleeping habits return to normal.

This final process of grieving does not involve forgetting the dead person. Instead, the bereaved person takes memories and traits of the deceased and integrates these into his or her own personality. To complete the mourning process, memories of the deceased bring joy and pleasure rather than the pain of grief.

Mr. Albert began to recover from his grief when he could think about his wife without pain. He got pleasure from remembering how much they had loved each other. He became closer to his children, telling them stories about their mother and the practical jokes she had once loved to play. High points in Mrs. Albert's career as an editor became a particular source of pleasure to him. He often thought about the many people who would still have contact with her work. He finally began attending social events. In short, he began the process of living his normal life again.

## Anticipatory Grief

Although grief is considered a normal reaction to death, the mourning process can begin long before death occurs. Such mourning is called *anticipatory grief.* It most often occurs when a person has an illness which the family knows will lead to death. In effect, grief begins when the family discovers that one of them is going to die.

Family members normally go through several stages in working through anticipatory grief. Just as the first reaction to an unexpected death is shock and denial, so it is when a death verdict is announced. Anger is likely to be the next emotion experienced.

When the doctors told the Marshes that Sandy's leukemia was incurable, they

## Unit 4: Family Relationships

couldn't believe it. When Mr. Marsh finally realized that Sandy was going to die, he was furious. How could fate be so cruel? Why couldn't the doctors do anything to prevent Sandy's death? His first shouts and rage turned into a slow, burning anger directed against the doctors and his wife.

Next, family members begin mentally to prepare themselves for the upcoming death. The more grief that can be expressed before death, the more bearable it will be afterwards. During this stage, many of the physical reactions that were described earlier occur. Marna felt as if her eyes would be washed away from her tears. Everytime she thought of her father's dying, she would cry.

Finally, family members accept what is coming. If family members can work through these emotional stages before the actual death, their shock and grief at death will be lessened.

In anticipatory grief, the mourning process is longer, but the emotions and physical reactions are usually less intense. When death occurs suddenly, the reactions are more intense and shocking. However, grief usually lasts a shorter time. Thus sudden death results in overwhelming physical and emotional reactions. However, these reactions last only a few weeks or months. Anticipatory grief may not entail such strong reactions, but it may extend over a period of months or years.

### experiences in human relations

#### GRIEF

Human beings go through three stages in the mourning process. These three stages help resolve the grief and pain from the loss of something or someone important. Although this chapter has only discussed the grief that comes with death, grief can be caused by other losses. This experience will help you think about how you react to grief.

On a separate sheet of paper, describe the three most important losses you have ever had. These could be losses of people, possessions, hopes, or something else. Be brief and concrete in describing your losses.

In which of the three losses have you failed to complete your grief? Are you still in stage one or two of the mourning process for any of the three losses? In what ways does your grief still influence your life? Does it cripple your ability to enjoy life? What influence does this grief have on your relationships with others?

In which of your three losses have you completed your grief? How do you think you were able to do that? In what ways did completing your grief help you grow as a person? Can you see any benefits of having experienced grief and the mourning process?

### TO SUM UP...

1. What is grief?
2. What is the mourning process?
3. Describe the first stage of the mourning process.
4. Discuss characteristics of the second stage of mourning.
5. What is resolution?
6. When is mourning completed?
7. What is anticipatory grief?
8. List the stages in working through anticipatory grief.
9. Compare anticipatory grief and the grief that comes with sudden death.

## The Importance of Family

Family members can be the most important source of comfort for each other at the time of death. They can help each other express their deep emotions. In the safety and security of the family, members can reveal their feelings and thoughts about the death of one of them. This helps them work toward resolution, the third stage of the mourning process.

The chance to talk over experiences and activities shared with the lost person is available with other family members. After the death of their grandfather, Tom and Carol shared some of their memories of him. Tom remembered the time Grandpa had taken them to the zoo and Carol had gotten lost. Carol laughed over the "Bald Is Beautiful" bumper sticker which he had kept on his car. By sharing their memories of their grandfather, Tom and Carol were able to help each other in the mourning process.

Death leaves a vacant role in the family. Families have to alter their relationships to fill the roles of the missing person. Needs and responsibilities have to be reassigned. The support and love of a family makes these painful problems easier to handle.

Death is an experience in which family members can relate as persons to share grief and loss. By providing mutual support, strong family relationships make the process of adjusting to death easier.

## Arrangements at Death

Facing and adjusting to death is primarily an emotional experience. However, there are also many practical arrangements which must be made at the time of death. These arrangements often call for decisions when people are least able to make them. Pre-planning can lessen confusion when a death does occur in the family.

### Ch. 13: Family Breakdown—Death and Divorce

## Arrangements for the Body

Arrangements for the care of the body are the first pressing decisions to be faced after a death. The body is usually taken to a funeral home or mortuary. There the family's wishes are carried out.

The most common way to care for the body is *interment* or burial of the body underground or in a tomb. The body is placed in a casket and may be buried in a plot of ground purchased for that purpose. Or the body and casket can be placed in a *mausoleum,* a building containing vaults or tombs for burial.

Another method of caring for the body is cremation. In *cremation,* the body is reduced to ashes through intense heat. The ashes can be buried, scattered, or stored in an urn.

A less common method is donation of the body to science. Medical students and researchers learn more about health and disease from such gifts. Donors find satisfaction in knowing they can make a contribution

*The body is taken to a funeral home or mortuary for preparation for burial or cremation.*

## Unit 4: Family Relationships

even after death. Sometimes only body organs are donated for transplants and the body is buried or cremated.

The choice of the way to care for the body should be made before death. If burial is chosen, a plot should be available. When Mrs. Grange died, she had already arranged to be buried in a plot in the same cemetery as her husband. Mr. Zwicker had had his lawyer prepare a statement which said that he wished to be cremated after death. Thus, neither Mrs. Grange's children nor Mrs. Zwicker had to face the painful decision of how to take care of the body. Those decisions had been made before death.

If the body is to be buried, it is usually embalmed. *Embalming* replaces the fluids in the dead body with chemicals for disinfection and preservation. Thus embalming is needed to preserve the body if several days pass between death and interment or cremation.

A *funeral* is the ceremony and ritual honoring the deceased person. It is a public acknowledgment that death has occurred. The funeral helps the survivors to accept the finality of death and to mourn for their loved one.

The type of funeral chosen meets the needs of the family involved. Many funerals are held in places of worship. Others are held in the funeral home. Some families may choose not to have a ceremony at all. The funeral for Lew Sussman was held in the chapel of the funeral home. In contrast, when Mr. Forthun died, his family chose not to have any service. Instead, many of their friends and acquaintances visited them at home.

Services vary a great deal. Some funeral services include music, prayers, flowers, and a eulogy, a speech honoring the deceased. The body may be present and often the casket is open. Others are simple ceremonies in memory of the dead person. The style of the funeral service reflects the values of the family. Some people place great emphasis on having an elaborate and dignified funeral as a memorial to their loved one. Others prefer their private thoughts and memories in a simple tribute.

## experiences in human relations

### FUNERAL DECISIONS

There are many decisions to be made after the death of a family member. The method for disposing of the body is one important choice to be made. Another is the kind of funeral or memorial service desired. This experience will help you become more aware of the decisions which must be made after a death in the family.

Form a group with three or four of your classmates. Pretend that you are a family that has just lost one of its members to death. Your task in this experience is to make the decisions that the family must make about the body and the funeral.

First, decide what will be done with the body. Do you wish to bury or cremate the body? How soon will it be done? When you reach a decision on the body, plan a funeral service for the deceased. Where will it be? Will the body be there? The casket open or closed? Who will officiate? What kind of service will it be? What kind of music do you want, if any?

Did you find that it was easy to make choices in your group? Think how you might feel if one of your family members actually had died. How would that affect your ability to work and plan together? What advantages do you see for some pre-planning of arrangements before death actually occurs?

● ● ● ● ● ● ● ● ● ● ● ● ● ● ● ● ● ● ● ● ●

## The Survivors' Tasks

Along with the stress of the funeral and disposal of the body, business affairs must usually be handled.

The first task involves settling the deceased's affairs. A *will* is a legal document which states how the deceased's money and property are to be distributed. Was a will left? If so, who is the executor of that will? The *executor* administers the deceased's affairs and property. The executor collects the deceased's debts and pays them from the money available. In many cases, a lawyer is necessary to assist the executor.

Mr. Karnes was named as his brother's executor after his brother was killed in a construction accident. He paid his brother's debts and funeral expenses. He sold his brother's interest in the construction firm and invested the money for his widowed sister-in-law. He also handled the inheritance taxes she was required to pay.

If there is no will, the deceased is said to have died *intestate*. In that case, the property that is left will be divided according to the intestacy laws in the state in which the deceased lived.

In many families, there may not be any property or money to inherit or divide. However, it may be necessary to transfer the titles of cars or checking accounts the dead person owned.

If the dead family member had life insurance, the family will collect their payments from the insurance company. They may be required to submit a copy of the death certificate before they can receive the benefits.

Most survivors are eligible for a lump sum payment from Social Security. Minor children will receive Social Security payments if one of their parents dies. There may be veteran's benefits if the deceased was a member of the military. Many companies and unions have death or survivor's benefits.

Thus the remaining family members have to get in touch with a number of agencies soon after death. It is only through contact with insurance agents, the Social Security office, and other groups that the family will receive the financial aid due to them.

After Mr. Lordman's death, Mrs. Lordman spent about two weeks meeting with people about death benefits. She made arrangements to receive his company profit-sharing benefits. She also filed for veteran's benefits for herself and her children. Social Security paid her a lump sum death benefit. She also applied for monthly support payments for her children. In addition, she made arrangements

*Social Security is one of several agencies which may pay benefits after the death of a family member.*

## Unit 4: Family Relationships

to receive the money from Mr. Lordman's two life insurance policies.

Making arrangements after the death of a family member is never easy. It involves knowing whom to contact about what. It also means making decisions. Becoming aware of the choices you will face helps make the death of a loved one less confusing. Planning helps you cope with the practical details as well as the emotional losses which eventually come to everyone through death.

### TO SUM UP...

1. Describe the kinds of support family members can give each other when death occurs.
2. Why is decision making difficult at the time of death?
3. Describe the three main methods of caring for the body after death.
4. What is embalming? When is it used?
5. Why is a funeral service said to be "for the benefit of the survivors"?
6. Why should you have a will made? When should it be made? Why?
7. What is an executor and what does he or she do?
8. List several agencies that may provide financial benefits after the death of a family member.

### DIVORCE

The other main cause of family breakdown is the divorce of husband and wife. When death strikes a family member, the family is permanently diminished. The family member is gone forever. In divorce, the breakdown of the family opens the way for different and sometimes better family relationships.

Divorce is a particular kind of family breakdown. Family members may still visit after the divorce. An ex-husband or ex-wife is not suddenly a non-husband or non-wife. Parents do not become non-parents. A divorce aligns the family in a new and different manner. It does not mean the permanent end of these relationships.

### FREQUENCY OF DIVORCE

One hundred years ago, there was one divorce for every thirty-four marriages. Divorce was considered a sin against God. Many people thought it immoral and an indication of a weak or poor character.

Today, both the frequency of divorce and attitudes toward it have changed. Now, people are expected to grow and develop throughout their entire lives. They change their jobs and occupations. Many families move from one part of the country to another. These moves bring them into contact with new friends and acquaintances and promote new interests. As part of the expectation that people change as they grow, more people have come to accept the idea of divorce. When a marriage does not work out, most people believe that the partners should have another chance to start over.

As a result of these changing attitudes and beliefs, more people are getting divorced. Today, there is one divorce for every two new marriages. This rate of divorce is a symptom of both the failure of marriage and its success. People value a happy family life so highly that they are unwilling to live in an unhappy setting.

The emphasis on the quality of family life reflects the functions of the family discussed

**Ch. 13: Family Breakdown—Death and Divorce**

earlier in this book. When the major family functions were economic, educational, and religious, there was little call for divorce when affection was lacking. But as affection and adaption became more important, divorce became more common as families sought to fulfill these functions.

The rising divorce rate does not indicate that more marriages are unhappy today. It simply reflects the fact that people are less willing to live in unhappy marriages. Marriage and family life have become so important a source of emotional satisfaction that few people put up with a marriage that doesn't provide it. The high rate of divorce thus shows how much Americans expect of their marriage and family life.

Robyn and Les reflect these new attitudes. Talking about their divorce, Les says, "I suppose we could have stayed married. We really didn't have violent fights or anything like that. But we just didn't have much in common any more. The closeness between us was gone. We rarely talked over our problems, ideas, or beliefs. We both felt that there should be more to a marriage than we had. So we got a divorce."

On the other hand, the divorce rate shows that Americans have not yet learned how to create satisfying family life. Successful relationships do not just happen. They require trust, honesty, compromise, and good communication skills. The divorce rate shows that many families have not learned these skills in relating to others.

Roughly, half of all divorces take place within the first six years of marriage. Approximately half of these divorces are granted in the first two years of marriage. Thus most marriages that end in divorce do so fairly soon after the wedding. Couples recognize early that they have been mismatched. They find that their love and attraction for each

*Today, there is one divorce for every two new marriages.*

## Unit 4: Family Relationships

other is not enough to overcome differences in values, interests, and personality.

Carla says, "It took us about six months to discover that our marriage wasn't perfect. That first big glow of living together, having sex, and being married wore off and there wasn't anything else. A couple of months more and we were sure that we didn't want to stay married."

Once couples get past the first six years, divorce is most apt to occur when the children begin to leave home. Couples who feel that they have had a comfortable if not passionate marriage suddenly find that they no longer have much in common. Their parental roles helped give them a common interest, which held the marriage together. When the children leave, they no longer wish to remain married. Thus, recently, many marriages of twenty and more years have ended in divorce.

When Ray and Twyla's last child moved into his own apartment, they were lost at home. They no longer had any children at home to talk to and about. Neither was very interested in the other's activities. It was as if the bottom had suddenly dropped out of their marriage after twenty-three years.

## experiences in human relations

### ATTITUDES TOWARD DIVORCE

Divorce is basically a neutral event. It is a legal decree which ends a marriage and allows the partners to remarry. The attitudes and values people hold about divorce influence whether they look at divorce as a positive or a negative experience. This experience will help you think through some of your beliefs and attitudes toward divorce.

On a separate sheet of paper, write yes, no, or maybe for each of the following questions.

*Are You Someone Who. . .*

1. Believes children should always live with their mother after a divorce?
2. Can imagine getting a divorce some day?
3. Holds religious beliefs against divorce?
4. Thinks divorce can be an opportunity for growth?
5. Believes divorce is usually the fault of one partner?
6. Would have marriage counseling before deciding to divorce?
7. Feels divorce is always bad for children?
8. Thinks you would love your spouse forever?
9. Would feel badly if your parents divorced?
10. Believes good communication skills between partners can prevent divorce?
11. Could cope if your spouse wanted a divorce and you didn't?
12. Feels couples who divorce haven't tried very hard?
13. Would want to have custody of your children?
14. Could live an unhappy home life to avoid divorce?
15. Would be a difficult person to be married to?
16. Will probably make a bad first marriage?
17. Believes second marriages are happier than first?
18. Thinks children can benefit from divorce if it is handled correctly?
19. Could easily share and divide possessions if you and your partner divorced?

20. Would look forward to building new relationships after a divorce?

Look back over your answers. What do your answers tell you about your beliefs and attitudes toward divorce? Do you generally have a positive or a negative attitude toward divorce? How could your attitude help or hinder you in building a strong marriage? How would your beliefs influence your adjustment to divorce?

## TO SUM UP...

1. How does the family breakdown through death differ from that through divorce?
2. What was the frequency of divorce one hundred years ago?
3. What is the ratio of divorces to marriages today?
4. Why is the divorce rate both a signal of the failure and success of marriage?
5. How has the changing emphasis on the functions of the family influenced divorce?
6. During which years of marriage do most divorces occur?
7. Why are some marriages prone to divorce when the children leave home?

### Who Gets Divorced?

Divorce cuts across the entire population. Old people and young people get divorced. Divorce happens to people from cities and farms. People of all ethnic backgrounds and races are divorcing. There are, however, certain groups of people that are more likely to divorce than others.

**Ch. 13: Family Breakdown—Death and Divorce**

The largest group which is apt to divorce are those couples who marry while in their teens. The younger the partners, the more likely it is that the marriage will end in divorce. One-half of all teenage marriages end within five years. Marriages where the teenage bride is pregnant are the most fragile of all.

Jeff and Althea married while they were seniors in high school. They both worked part time and were able to manage financially by living with Jeff's mother. After graduation, they worked full time and were able to afford

*Marriages where the teenage bride is pregnant are very likely to end in divorce.*

## Unit 4: Family Relationships

an apartment of their own. Soon after they moved, they began to have a great deal of conflict. They fought over money, friends, sex, and whether and when to have children. It soon became clear that they held very different values about many topics. Their conflicts finally led them to divorce.

Judy and Will were married when she became pregnant. Will was forced to drop out of school to support his family. Judy stayed in school until after the baby was born, but then found herself too tired to manage school, part-time work, and the baby. Judy says, "I really thought Will and I loved each other. I wasn't too sorry when I got pregnant because I was sure we could make a good, loving life together. I was a fool—I imagined us with the baby in a home filled with love. Instead, all we do is fight. There's never enough money, even though Will works hard at his job. He hates being around here when the baby is upset. So when she fusses, he goes down to the bowling alley—which makes the money problem worse. I'm so tired, all I seem to be able to do is cry. Life seems too hard for much love now. We're in the midst of getting our divorce."

In general, those with less education and money divorce more often. Life without enough money is never easy. Lack of money often causes stresses and strains that lead to divorce. People with more education are more likely to earn enough to support their families.

Frequently, teenagers who marry have little education. This helps contribute to the instability of their marriages. Gene, who is twenty-five, never finished high school. He dropped out of school when he married and has spent the eight years since holding jobs which pay very little. They have often been boring and unpleasant, besides. Although his wife Nancy works, too, she didn't finish high school either. Thus she isn't able to earn much money. The lack of money makes their married life difficult.

Couples with mixed or no religious ties are more likely to divorce than couples with the same religous beliefs. Couples with strong, similar religious beliefs are most likely to have stable marriages. Elwin says, "We took our time in deciding to marry because our faith is important to us. Since it discourages divorce, we felt that we needed to be sure that our marriage would last. Even when we have problems relating to each other, our belief in the sanctity of marriage helps us work out our disagreements."

## experiences in human relations

### VALUES AND DIVORCE

People hold different values about divorce. Some people see divorce as a practical matter for getting out of a bad marriage. Others consider divorce a moral disaster showing poor character and lack of ethics. These various values reflect people's backgrounds, their experiences with divorce, the values their parents taught them, and their religious training. This experience will help you and your classmates better understand the variation in values about divorce.

Using masking tape, make a line about 9 meters [10 yards] long on your classroom floor. If your classroom has a long chalkboard, you may prefer to draw the line on the chalkboard. Imagine that the line represents all the possible values about divorce. On one end of the line place a sign that says "Steadfast Stacy—I would never get a divorce, no matter what the circumstances." At the opposite end of the line, place a sign that says "Many-marriage Martin—I sue for divorce after the first fight."

On an index card, briefly describe your position on divorce. Tell what circumstances would lead you to divorce. Then, find a place on the line which you feel represents your position. Your classmates will also find places on the line to reflect their values about divorce. Compare your ideas about divorce with those of the people standing next to you. You may find that you need to change positions. Keep comparing values until everyone in the class feels in the right place.

Look up and down the divorce line. Are most of you in one spot or are you evenly distributed up and down the line? Did any of your classmates choose to share the positions of Steadfast Stacy or Many-marriage Martin? Is your position similar to others in the class or are you in a minority position? How does that make you feel? What does this experience tell you about the values you and your classmates hold about divorce?

### TO SUM UP...

1. Which group of marriages are most prone to divorce? Why?

## DIVORCE PROCEDURES

*Divorce* is the process of changing the legal duties and rights of a man and a woman toward one another. Divorce is the legal action which ends a marriage. Getting the divorce decree is the last step in a choice-making process that lasts for an average of two years. This is because divorce is often preceded by a long time of conflict.

### Ch. 13: Family Breakdown—Death and Divorce

The procedure for divorce is set by the government in your state. There are two basic approaches to granting divorces. One approach is the adversary system; the other is the no-fault divorce.

### The Adversary System

In the *adversary system* of divorce, one partner must charge the other with some "marital crime." Thus one spouse is guilty of misconduct, while the other spouse is innocent. The particular "crimes" which can be the basis of divorce are called *grounds* for divorce. These are the reasons that state legislators think sufficient to dissolve the marriage. Most states accept adultery, mental or physical cruelty, impotence, desertion, and

*The adversary system of divorce calls for one "guilty" and one "innocent" partner.*

## Unit 4: Family Relationships

insanity. In the United States, over 40 grounds for divorce are used. Thus legal grounds for divorce vary a great deal from one state to another.

Cora talked to a lawyer after she and Dan decided to divorce. In her state, cruelty, desertion, adultery, and conviction of a crime were grounds for divorce. She chose to sue for divorce on grounds of cruelty.

In the adversary system, the spouse who brings the charges must not be guilty of the same charges. In addition, the partners are adversaries or opponents. Couples are not allowed to cooperate on the divorce agreement or grounds. If they do so, they are guilty of *collusion*. This can cause a judge to dismiss the case and refuse to grant the divorce.

Many people feel that the adversary system breeds hostility and bad feelings between divorcing couples. The grounds for divorce presented in court are rarely the reasons that the marriage failed. The fact that one partner is considered innocent and one guilty creates hard feelings. Besides, the guilty partner may suffer in the division of property or in child custody matters. Thus both partners fight to present the faults of the partner and their own virtues.

Martha and Judd had a very bitter divorce. They both wanted custody of their two children. During the legal proceedings, each charged the other with mental cruelty and adultery. They fought fiercely over the house and every other possession they had. By the time the divorce proceedings were complete, they hated each other.

### No-Fault Divorce

Recently, many states have moved to replace the adversary system. These states have gone to *"no-fault"* divorce proceedings. Marriages may thus be dissolved without proof that one spouse is guilty of any misconduct. California passed the first no-fault divorce law in 1970. Most other states have since revised their laws to allow for no-fault divorce.

In no-fault divorce, partners simply claim that the marriage relationship has broken down. A separation may be all the proof needed of such a breakdown. If two people cannot bear to live with one another, that in itself shows that a meaningful marriage no longer exists.

Joan and Karl decided to live in separate apartments after 18 months of marriage. They were unsure whether they wanted a divorce, but both felt they needed some time away from each other. After a year of living apart,

*In no-fault divorce, the judge grants the decree after a couple has shown that the relationship has broken down.*

## Ch. 13: Family Breakdown—Death and Divorce

they agreed that the marriage was broken. They then applied for a no-fault divorce on the basis of their separation.

The judge who hears a no-fault divorce case grants the divorce when satisfied that the husband and wife have reached an impasse. The judge hears evidence of cruelty, adultery, or drunkenness only when there is a battle over child custody. Such evidence is useful in deciding who is the better parent to rear the children.

No-fault divorce is considered an easy, fairly conflict-free method of divorce. "I couldn't believe how simple our divorce was," says Barbara. "We had some friends who got divorced several years ago before no-fault was allowed in our state. Their divorce was terrible. They fought over everything. They ended up hating each other, which was very hard on their children. In contrast, our no-fault divorce was very peaceful.

"We'd tried marriage counseling and had worked on improving our relationship. We finally just decided that we couldn't go on. We had several long sessions together trying to decide who would get what—it was very friendly. In fact, it was really funny in a way. We're always fought over money our whole married life. But we didn't then. We have joint custody of the children although they live with him during the school year. We easily agreed on how much child support I should pay. Our divorce went through without a hitch. As it turned out, we're much better friends now than we ever were when we were married. I really believe that the no-fault divorce helped us become friends rather than forcing us to be enemies."

The major problem so far with no-fault divorce is that fair property settlements are more difficult. The economically dependent spouse, which is most often the wife, has no bargaining power to get decent support and property settlements.

Where the adversary system is in effect, these wives often get more support if the husband wants to avoid a courtroom settlement by the judge. The "innocent" wife is in a position to get good settlements from a "guilty" husband.

Many wives who have been out of the labor market for many years have no job skills. Thus the money they can earn is not enough to maintain a household. However, after a no-fault divorce, they are expected to earn a living for themselves just as well as the ex-husbands do.

Ann Garrett was a financial victim of no-fault divorce. She had married right out of high school and had no work skills. During their marriage, their savings and home ownership were held in her husband's name. After the divorce, he was allowed to take his property, and she hers. Because she had never worked, she had no property. Thus, at age 40, she had to find a job but she had no job skills and no financial "nest-egg" to fall back on. In contrast, her husband had his well-paying job as a factory foreman plus their home and savings. It was no wonder that Ann felt that she had been cheated by her "no-fault" divorce.

## experiences in human relations

### DIVORCE LAWS

The laws governing divorce are set in each state. Therefore divorce laws in different states vary. This experience will help you become more familiar with the laws in your state.

## Unit 4: Family Relationships

For this experience, write a report describing the divorce laws in your state. You may be able to find books in the library which describe your state's laws. Lawyers, legal assistants, legal secretaries, and divorce or family court officials may also be able to provide you with information you need.

Find out whether your state uses the no-fault or the adversary system. If the adversary system is used, what grounds are considered justification for divorce? What evidence of marital breakdown will the court accept in no-fault systems?

How long does a person have to be a resident of your state in order to file for divorce? Is the divorce decree granted immediately, or does your state award an intermediate and then a final decree? What laws does your state have about property or child settlements? Include any other information that you can find that relates to the divorce laws in your state.

On the basis of the material you have gathered, do you think your state's divorce laws are good ones? Do you agree with the system used? Do you feel the grounds allowed are too strict or too lenient? How long a separation do you think indicates that a marriage has ended? Finish your report with some suggestions for improvements in your state's divorce laws.

### TO SUM UP...

1. What is divorce?
2. How is the procedure for divorce established?
3. Describe the adversary system.
4. What are grounds for divorce?
5. What is apt to happen if collusion occurs in a divorce case?
6. How does the adversary system cause bad feelings between divorcing partners?
7. What is no-fault divorce?
8. What are the grounds in no-fault divorce?
9. Describe the major problem with no-fault divorce.

*The economic divorce involves dividing the couple's property and money.*

### ASPECTS OF DIVORCE

Although divorce is defined as a legal process, it is actually more complex than that. People who divorce experience changes in six areas of their lives. The changes which occur in these overlapping areas make up the total divorce experience. These different aspects of divorce are emotional, legal, economic, parental, community, and psychological.

### The Emotional Divorce

The emotional divorce occurs when the partners decide that the marriage is hopeless.

Gone are the attraction and trust which once bound the partners together. The self-regard of each partner is no longer supported by love from the other. Both partners withhold their emotions from the relationship. In essence, the loving relationship that led the partners to marry is lost. Partners going through an emotional divorce usually feel hurt and angry.

The emotional divorce may occur a long time before the other aspects of divorce. In fact, in some marriages, an emotional divorce may occur, yet the partners do not get a divorce decree. However, in most cases, the emotional divorce is the first step in the divorce process.

Peter Ashe can tell you the exact day of his emotional divorce. "It was a Saturday," he says. "We had disagreed about something as usual. When I get mad, I clam up, and I was giving Mildred the silent treatment. All of a sudden I just decided that I didn't have to live like that. I didn't have to go through all the fights and silences. Just like that, I felt free of my love and fear and guilt. I knew that I was through trying to stay married. Soon after that we agreed and filed for divorce."

## The Legal Divorce

The legal divorce is simply the court decree. It does nothing more than allow the partners the freedom to remarry. The decree is the result of a process by which the state ends a marriage.

Because the work which the lawyer does to prepare for divorce court is complex, couples often feel bewildered by the legal process. They may feel that they lost control of the divorce when the lawyer began to work.

Art and Irene Cooper were granted a divorce decree after a ten-minute court appearance. Their lawyers presented the evidence of marriage breakdown to the judge as well as the property and child custody agreements. The judge found the papers in order and granted the decree promptly.

## The Economic Divorce

The state views each married couple as an economic unit. A divorce breaks up this economic partnership. The economic divorce is the process which divides the assets of the couple. This is the agreement of "who gets what." In many divorces, the amount of property is so small as to cause no dispute.

If alimony is to be paid, the amount and details are worked out in the economic divorce. Regardless of the financial status of the family, there is never enough money to suit both partners. Therefore the economic divorce often leaves partners with the feeling that they have been cheated.

When Corrine and Mac were divorced, she got the furniture and household goods as part of her settlement. Mac got the car. They split the $2000 savings account which they had. Mac agreed to pay Corrine $200 a month for either six months or until she found a job to support herself, whichever came first.

## The Parental Divorce

If a couple has children, part of the arrangements include the parental divorce. Taking care of the children often requires a complex agreement. Both parents have privileges and responsibilities toward the children. The parental divorce helps work out custody, the single-parent home, and visitation rights. *Visitation rights* specify the exact time when the child is allowed to be with the parent who does not have custody.

A couple may worry about the parental divorce. They may also feel guilty about the effects of the divorce on the children.

Doris was granted custody of the children when she and Allen divorced. Allen was

## Unit 4: Family Relationships

given visitation rights for each weekend and for a month each summer when the children would live with him. He was required to pay a certain amount of child support each month to help Doris care for the children.

## experiences in human relations

### ECONOMIC AND PARENTAL DIVORCE

The legal decree which ends a marriage is only one aspect of divorce. The breakdown of the economic partnership and the parental roles is often very difficult. This experience will help you realize some of the decisions which must be made in the economic and parental divorces.

Choose a partner. Imagine that you are a married couple who have decided to divorce after four years of marriage. You are the parents of a two-year-old child. The wife worked as a secretary before the birth of the baby, but has not held a job since. The husband sells appliances in a large retail department store. You own a three-year-old car, which is paid for. You live in a rented apartment, but have your own furniture. You have a $700 savings account.

Decide how you are going to divide your property. Who will get the car? Will one partner stay in the apartment you have been living in? Will that partner keep the furniture? Or will you divide the furniture to use in two apartments? Who will get the TV and the tape deck? How will you divide the savings account? If alimony is allowed in your state, who will get alimony? How much? How will it be paid?

Now, decide how you will handle the parental divorce. Who will have custody of your child? How much child support will the other parent pay? How often will the other parent visit? Will the child ever stay with the other parent?

Were you and your partner able to make these decisions easily? Do you think these would be easy choices if you were really in the middle of the divorce? What suggestions would you make so that couples could settle decisions like these in a friendly manner?

● ● ● ● ● ● ● ● ● ● ● ● ● ● ● ● ● ● ● ●

### The Community Divorce

Each married couple is part of a "community" of friends, colleagues, and acquaintances. Divorce may have a drastic effect on this community. Some friends no longer care to remain friendly after the divorce. Close friends may have taken "sides" during the conflict which led to the divorce. Thus, after the divorce, those friends will remain close to the partner they supported. Acquaintances and colleagues may ignore the divorced man or woman. Divorce may mean that a person has to begin again making friends and building relationships.

Many divorced people have angry feelings towards people they once considered friends. During and after the divorce, these "friends" did not offer support and friendship. Thus a divorce may show that the loyalty of some friends is rather weak.

Olivia tells about her experiences after her divorce. "I always thought I had a lot of friends," she says. "But after the divorce I discovered that many of the people I knew were Steve's business friends. Those people didn't want to be friendly with me— business required them to be Steve's friends. I also found that my neighbors weren't too friendly afterwards. I guess they thought maybe I would be after their husbands. At any rate, I

**Ch. 13: Family Breakdown—Death and Divorce**

problems—there's nobody to blame for your difficulties.

While most people feel afraid and lonely as they are learning to be themselves again, it is also a very liberating process. Being independent means that no one is blaming you for their problems. There is no one leaning on you and nobody to stop your growth as a person.

Roberto felt very lonely right after his divorce. He felt as if there were no one to help him meet life. He had depended on Lisa for so long that he felt incomplete without her. However, as he became more used to relying on himself, he began to enjoy the feeling of competence he felt. He had finally gotten his psychological divorce from his ex-wife.

## TO SUM UP...

1. When does an emotional divorce occur?
2. What feelings are partners likely to have during an emotional divorce?
3. What is the legal divorce? What does it do?
4. Describe the arrangements which may be part of the economic divorce.
5. What decisions must be made during the parental divorce?
6. Why does the parental divorce often cause worry and anxiety?
7. Describe what is meant by a community divorce.
8. What is a psychological divorce?

### Adjustment to Divorce

Because divorce is such a major change in the lives of all family members, it requires

*One aspect of divorce is learning to be an individual again.*

was snubbed and ignored by several neighbors that I had considered good friends."

### The Psychological Divorce

The psychological divorce is the process whereby people learn to think of themselves as individuals once more. When they marry, two persons become a couple. Many people become so used to thinking of themselves as half of a pair that it is very hard to return to being single. Becoming a strong, independent person requires developing new strengths and personality traits. It means learning to live without someone to lean on. As an individual, you have to learn to solve your own

309

## Unit 4: Family Relationships

many adjustments. Even when the divorce has been friendly and comes as a relief to everyone involved, changes in life style must still be made.

**Spouses**

Both the man and woman have to learn to adjust to living as a single person again. For most divorced couples, this means learning to live alone or learning to live as a single parent. There is no one in whom confide successes and failures. Being a single calls for the building of new friendships and interests.

Many wives in particular have a hard time adjusting after divorce. Those women who have centered their lives around their families may not have held jobs. In addition, many women enjoyed their identity as someone's wife. Divorce means that they need to respect themselves for their own accomplishments. In most cases after divorce, women need a job to support themselves. The change from homemaker to working woman may be difficult.

Katie had always enjoyed homemaking. She helped her husband in his work and felt as if she had contributed when he got a raise. After the divorce, she no longer could claim any status as "Harry's wife." Instead, she was just plain Katie, on her own. It was a long time before she could take pride in her own talents and skills.

Many divorced couples have financial problems. It costs a great deal more to have two homes than it does one. Larry and Rosa Craig found it difficult to make ends meet after their divorce. Both of them had worked before the divorce and they had managed to save some money. They thought money would not be a problem after the divorce. However, after each paid apartment rent and contributed toward the support of the child, there was little money for luxuries and treats. Both Larry and Rosa found they had to live very thrifty lives in order to balance their budgets.

The first few months following the divorce are the most difficult. There are so many adjustments and decisions to make about the new life. However, after a few months, most people come to appreciate and enjoy their new lives.

**Children**

Most people believe that divorce is bad for children. However, this stereotyped idea is not always so. Children in homes with lots of conflict often suffer more than children in divorced homes. Thus it may be that many children adjust better to divorce than they did to their former two-parent home.

A great deal depends on how the children viewed their parents' marriage before the divorce. Most children from openly unhappy homes feel that divorce is the best choice for everyone. However, children who believed their parents were happy are likely to be shocked by the divorce. They are apt to be so upset that they find adjustment hard.

Most children adjust to the divorce in the same way that their parents do. If the parents feel the divorce was a disaster, the children are likely to feel the same way.

Mrs. Ullman was divorced by her husband because he wished to marry another woman. As a result, she was very bitter over the divorce, feeling that it had ruined her life. She spent a lot of time crying and making plans for revenge on her ex-husband. Chris and Tina Ullman also believed that the divorce was a terrible thing. They hated their father for what he had done to their mother and themselves. Their attitude toward the divorce reflected their mother's.

On the other hand, if parents feel that divorce is the best solution for their marriage

### Ch. 13: Family Breakdown—Death and Divorce

*Children tend to react to a divorce in the same way as their parents. If parents feel the divorce is a positive step for them, the children will be apt to agree.*

problems, the children will probably agree. Cloris and Dirk Norris found that they had grown apart during their ten years of marriage. They divorced as good friends. Both were looking forward to new friends and experiences. Their children also adjusted easily to the divorce. They enjoyed having the parent they were with to themselves. They found that they had lots of new experiences as a result of the divorce. When Cloris married again, they enjoyed having two "fathers" whom they could love and rely on.

### Remarriage

Divorced people are rarely soured on marriage—just on *that* marriage. As a result, 80 percent of those who divorce eventually remarry. The main reason for remarriage is companionship. Partners also seek to meet emotional needs in a new marriage.

Jody Warren remarried about three years after the divorce. She says, "I really enjoyed being on my own after we divorced. I think in several ways I had things to prove to myself. But after a while, I found my life lacking. I wanted someone that I could trust and love completely. The intimacy that a good marriage brings was just not available to me as a single. So, I began to seriously think about marriage again."

If the first marriage produced children, remarriage creates new relationships. Blended families, which have stepparent-stepchild relationships, are discussed on page 272.

Some people feel that those who are divorced are poor risks for another marriage. However, the chance that a second marriage will end in divorce is only slightly higher for a young couple than the chance a first marriage will. Those middle-aged or older who remarry

Unit 4: Family Relationships

*Most people who remarry are usually happier in their second marriage than they were in their first.*

have less chance of a divorce than people their age in a first marriage.

Most people who divorce and remarry feel their second marriages are much better than their first. From the first marriage, they have usually learned something about marriage and what they need in a mate. Remarriage obviously takes place at an older age than first marriage. Thus the divorced person brings added maturity to a second marriage.

Bart tells about his marriages like this. "I was just too young when I first got married. I really had no idea what I needed in a wife. My first wife was a clinging kind of person who couldn't decide anything. After a couple of years of being married to her, I felt like I was being smothered. When I decided to remarry after the divorce, I knew that I needed a wife that could be independent. Shelli is just that, and we get along beautifully."

Remarriage for a divorced partner is the birth of a new family. Through divorce and remarriage, many people are able to live happy, satisfying lives. The attitudes and values people hold will determine whether they will be able to build new lives for themselves through divorce and remarriage.

## TO SUM UP...

1. Describe some of the adjustments ex-husbands and wives must make after divorce.

2. What are some of the factors which determine how children adjust to divorce?

3. When may divorce actually be better for children than marriage?

4. What percentage of divorced people remarry?

5. Why is a person's second marriage often much happier than the first?

## UNIT FIVE

*Relating to the Larger World*

Chapter 14. Relationships in Groups, 314
Chapter 15. Entering the World of Work, 338
Chapter 16. Careers in Working with Others, 361

# CHAPTER 14
## Relationships in Groups

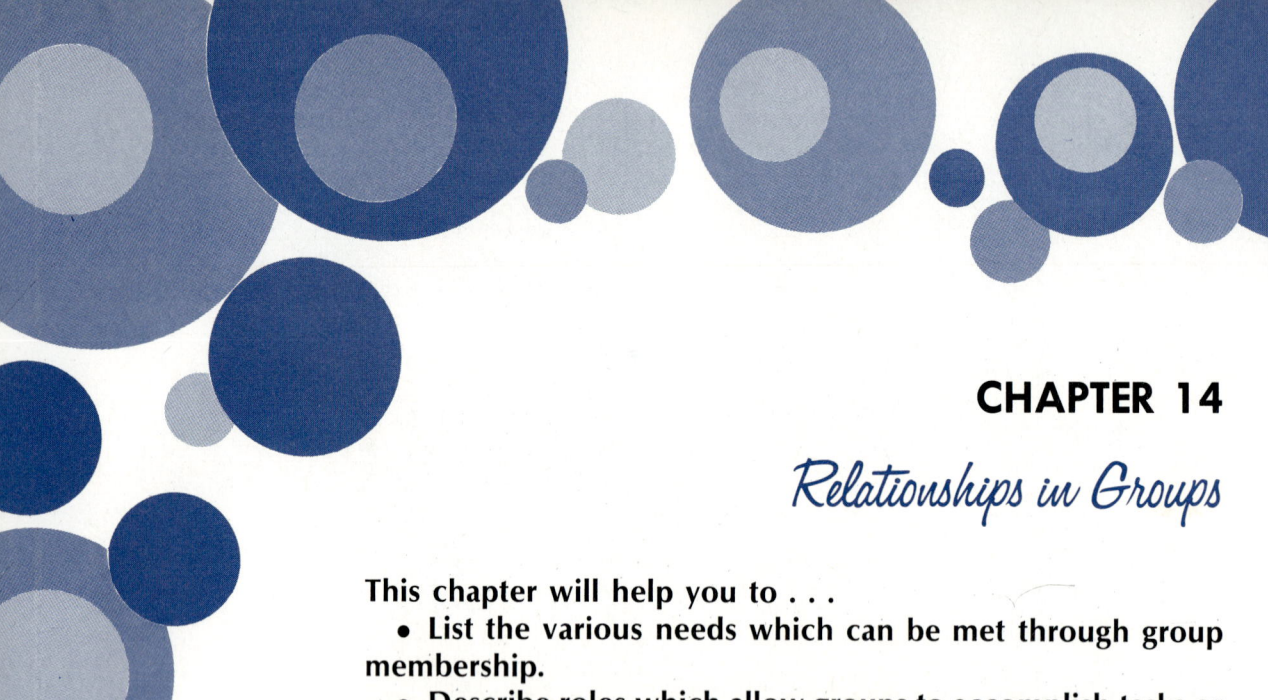

This chapter will help you to . . .
- List the various needs which can be met through group membership.
- Describe roles which allow groups to accomplish tasks or jobs.
- Identify several group-building and maintenance roles.
- Understand leadership traits and styles.
- Explain how group norms can affect conformity and cohesiveness.
- Describe personal growth which can occur through experiences in groups.

Group membership is part of living. Babies are born into a special kind of group called a family. Children play in groups with childhood friends. They attend schools where they are grouped into grades. Teenagers attend school and share leisure with groups of friends. Adults work in groups, play in groups, and belong to groups. Thus relationships in groups are an important part of everyday life.

A *group* is two or more persons who are interacting with each other. In a group, each person influences and is influenced by the others. Members of a group are aware that they have something in common.

Groups have a strong bearing on how people's lives are shaped. Most beliefs, values, feelings, and habits stem from experiences in groups. Of course, the first group to influence a child is the family. Other groups become important once the child begins to have contact with others.

Coming home from nursery school one day, four-year-old Tanya announced that she was not going to wear dresses any more. Her friends all wore jeans or pants and she wanted to dress like they did. Thus Tanya had her first contact with the influence of group values.

Ch. 14: Relationships in Groups

*The peer group is important to teenagers as they begin to become independent of parents.*

Groups continue to have a great deal of importance as a child grows up. Eric kept insisting that he wanted to go out for the basketball squad at his junior high school. He had never shown any interest in basketball before. When his parents asked him why, he replied, "Well, everyone I know is going out for basketball. If I don't, they won't be my friends anymore."

Teenagers are very open to the influence of groups. They are beginning to break away from their parents and assert their independence. Part of this bid for independence often pits the values of the group against the values of home.

Jeanne's group of friends decided that they were going to have marijuana at their next party. Jeanne knew her parents would be very upset if she smoked it. On the other hand, she could expect to be teased and ridiculed if she didn't smoke with the others. The fact that Jeanne smoked a marijuana cigarette at the party shows that the group had a strong influence on her behavior.

Adults also are open to the influence of the groups to which they belong. Adam spends a lot of his free time at the pool hall. His favorite group of buddies there enjoys auto racing. Because Adam wants to share the interests of his friends, he has become very interested in racing.

The work group to which a person belongs also can be important. Kathy's first job after graduation was on an assembly line. She wanted to do a good job and impress her boss. The first week, she often stayed at her station a few extra minutes after the coffee break bell rang. However, her co-workers left their stations as soon as the bell rang. Kathy could overhear them making comments about her failure to join them. She found that the others thought her snobbish and unfriendly because she didn't take her entire break with them. Kathy discovered that if she wanted to have friends on the job, she had to leave her station when the break began.

## MEETING NEEDS THROUGH GROUPS

Besides being influential, groups are able to fulfill many of the basic needs of members. The friendship and support of the group can allow people to meet their own needs. In addition, members may fulfill their needs through the actions of the group as a whole.

### Basic Needs

Chapter 3 discussed the fact that people have certain needs. The basic needs as described by Abraham Maslow are physical, safety, love, esteem, and self-actualization. Membership in groups can be crucial in helping people meet any or all of these needs.

Most people meet their physical needs through the family group. The Hillyer family provides for the physical needs of its members—shelter, food, and clothing. The sexual needs of Mr. and Mrs. Hillyer are met in the marriage relationship.

A health club is another type of group formed to meet physical needs. Arlene belongs to a club where she swims and uses the exercise room twice a week. She feels this helps keep her body healthy and strong.

Groups may help fill the need for safety in a variety of ways. Abe joined the union at his factory. He feels much safer and more secure now that he has the backing of a union. The union grievance procedures help insure that he won't lose his job unfairly.

Recently, the housing project in which Julie lived had a number of burglaries. The families on the tenth floor decided to do something to protect themselves, so they formed a Floor Association. Each night of the week, a different family served as floor patrol. They watched for strangers coming onto the floor and called the police when anything unusual seemed to be happening. Their nightly patrol helped prevent thefts on their floor.

The need to be with people, to give and receive affection, can only be met through group membership. Few people can be happy for long with only their own company. Groups provide a chance for people to gain affection and support from others.

Sue's group of friends is together almost every weekend. If one group member has special work to do, most of the other members pitch in to help. When Sue had to mow the lawn one Saturday, three friends came over to help. When they had finished, they went to the park for a softball game. Later that same day, the friends gathered at Doris's house for a party with their dates.

Many people help meet their need to belong through membership in organized groups. Millie and Ted belong to a square dance group which meets once a month. A pinochle club provides entertainment for Karen. Membership in a Bible study group gives Russ a feeling of belonging to a group whose members share spiritual beliefs.

Belonging to certain groups helps meet people's needs for esteem from others. Thirty-five people tried out for a place on the school cheerleading squad. When Larry made the squad, he became a member of an exclusive group. He felt as if his membership on the cheerleading squad was a position to be envied. Others looked up to him because he had been chosen.

**Ch. 14: Relationships in Groups**

reach self-actualization through his role in the play.

Thus, in many ways, groups help people meet their personal and individual needs. Groups can provide an atmosphere of security and stability which lets people grow individually and as group members.

## experiences in human relations

### GROUPS AT YOUR SCHOOL

Groups make up a large part of school life. Students attend classes in groups. They form friendship groups. Dating partners are two-person groups. Athletic teams, musical organizations, drama casts, and various clubs are groups which students can join. This experience will help you consider some of the needs which the groups at your school may fulfill.

Form a small working group with four or five of your classmates. Together, make a list of all the organized groups at your school. Do not include friendship groups or groups of dating partners. Be sure to include groups such as athletic teams, extracurricular clubs, bands, and choruses.

Next, consider the five levels of the hierarchy of needs. Which need or needs do you think each group on your list would meet? Some groups allow anyone interested to join them. Being chosen is the only way to join others. Would the selection process have anything to do with the needs a certain group might meet?

Now consider the purposes of the groups on your list. Which groups are information sharing or problem solving? Are any groups formed simply for enjoyment?

*Membership in certain groups brings prestige and esteem.*

Group membership can also help people achieve self-actualization. They can live up to their potential only with the help and support of others.

Andrew gave a superb performance as Sky Masterson in the musical *Guys and Dolls*. He acted and sang as he never had before in his life, using his talents to the utmost. However, he could never have given such a performance without the support of the other members in the cast. In this case, the play cast formed a group which allowed Andrew to

Unit 5: Relating to the Larger World

To which groups do you belong? Do you feel that your group memberships meet some of your needs? How did you decide which groups to join? Are you attracted to any other groups? What is keeping you from belonging to those groups?

• • • • • • • • • • • • • • • • • • • • • •

## Group Purposes

People can also meet their needs through the goals which groups have. Working through groups, people can accomplish what they cannot do alone. Thus they can further their own interests and meet their own needs through group action.

### Information Sharing

Some groups are formed for the purpose of sharing information. Classroom groups, for instance, band together to learn. When Corrine wanted to learn how to do simple maintenance on her car, she took an adult education course one night a week. The instructor and students worked together on their cars to learn how to care for them.

Jeff joined the Home Economics Related Occupations (HERO) chapter in his school. The chapter members planned programs so that they could learn more about getting and holding jobs.

When Annabelle reached voting age, she joined her county's Voter's League. The League gathered information on what the candidates believed. It also was able to provide information on bills in the state legislature so that members could write to their government officials. Annabelle felt that being a member of the Voter's League helped her be a good citizen. Her voting choices were based on information she received through her Voter's League membership.

### Enjoyment

Other groups are formed for the simple purpose of providing fun and entertainment to members. Most friendship groups give enjoyment to their members. When Gene is with his group of friends, he feels on top of the world. They spend a lot of time talking about and participating in sports. The group provides each member with the support and affection of the others. It also gives members a chance to enjoy their shared interest in sports.

Louise belongs to a music club at school. All of the members of this club enjoy classical music. At some meetings, they learn about classical composers and their works. However, the main purpose of the club is for members to enjoy listening to music together.

### Problem Solving

Finally, many groups are organized around solving problems. The family is a problem-solving group. The need for food, clothing, and shelter are "problems" which family members must solve in order to live comfortably. The family also works to solve personal and relationship problems.

When Don and Marie had their second child, their three-year-old son Chris was very jealous of the baby. Don and Marie worked to give Chris lots of love and attention. This finally helped to eliminate the poor behavior which was causing problems.

Many citizen's groups are formed to help solve problems. Avadner Washington believed that the city government should fund a child care center for the children of low-income mothers. Most of these mothers could not afford to pay the high fees charged at the private child care centers in town. Avadner began working with others on this project. Soon she had a group of twenty-five

## Ch. 14: Relationships in Groups

*Some groups are formed to provide members with fun and entertainment.*

people helping her. This group was able to put pressure on the city government. Finally, with the help of some revenue sharing money, the city opened the child care center which Avadner and her supporters worked to get.

Many groups may not fall naturally into these three categories. Some groups may be information sharing, problem solving, and enjoyment oriented. Most groups, however, are formed for one of these three purposes. If the group is able to achieve its purpose, its members are also likely to meet theirs.

### TO SUM UP...

1. Why are groups important in the lives of people?
2. Define a group.
3. Give examples of some ways a group may influence its members.
4. List the basic needs and explain how groups can help meet these needs.
5. What is an information-sharing group?
6. What are some examples of groups that are formed for enjoyment?
7. Discuss the kinds of problems that groups might work to solve.

## ROLES IN GROUPS

In order for groups to function, certain roles must be filled. These roles tend to fall into three general categories. First are those roles which are needed to get certain tasks done. Second, another series of roles helps build and maintain group feeling. Finally, the leadership role must be filled.

People who fill these roles are not limited to any one kind of role. The same person may be able to fill all three roles. On the other hand, each person may handle one function better than the other two. Personality traits and how a person relates to others are important in determining which roles that person assumes.

### Task Roles

People who take on the work of helping a group get a particular job done assume *task roles*. Those who take on task roles usually like "getting a job done." There are several specific roles involved under the overall heading of task roles.

#### Initiating

A person who takes an *initiating* role is one who suggests tasks or goals. If a group is

*One person in a group usually initiates "bright ideas" for the others to consider.*

without direction, the initiating person often is able to define the group's problem. In addition, once the problem has been outlined, the initiating person often suggests ideas for solving that problem.

Francie, a member of the flag drill team, performed the initiating role. Suggestions for developing new routines often came from her. Usually, she also had ideas which could be used to improve old routines.

## Information Seeking

The *information seeker* is the group member who requests facts. This person seeks out relevant information about some concern of the group. The information seeker often asks for suggestions and ideas.

The Student Council at Bridge High School was working to organize a Bike-a-thon. They hoped to earn enough money to buy a new trampoline for the school. Harry didn't make any suggestions as the group made plans. However, the questions he asked helped the others think of items they had overlooked. First, Harry wanted to know if and how student council members were going to staff the school activity booth to sign up others for the event. Later in the planning, Harry wondered if anyone had contacted the city street department to find out if the route they wanted would be all right. The subject of pledge cards was raised by Harry when the group was discussing getting pledges from parents, friends, and acquaintances. Harry's questions helped the group focus on issues they had neglected in their planning.

## Information Giving

The *information giver* is the person who has the facts to offer. He or she provides information about a group concern. Giving suggestions or ideas or stating beliefs are other task roles the information giver performs.

Tim is the information giver for his group of friends. The friends usually spend Friday evening together. They rely on Tim to have all the facts about the entertainment available in their town. He knows which movie is playing at which theatre at what time. The special activities at the town's three high schools are known to him. He also is aware of the kind of entertainment available at the local junior college. Because of the information which Tim provides, the group can choose their fun for Friday night knowing they have considered all the possible choices.

## Clarifying

The person who *clarifies* for the group works to clear up confusions. The person may interpret or reflect ideas and suggestions. Giving examples is another common clarifying response. The clarifier may indicate issues and choices before the group.

Rebecca and Alice were members of a group taking tennis lessons at the park district. After a lesson on the back stroke, Rebecca still did not understand how to position her feet while hitting the ball. Alice was able to show how the feet should be placed, thus clearing up Rebecca's confusion.

## Summarizing

The person who takes the *summarizing* role pulls together related ideas. The summarizer restates suggestions after the group has discussed them. Sometimes he or she offers a decision or choice for the group to accept or reject.

Clara was a member of a student group assigned to design and construct an exhibit for National Education Week. After listening to the group discuss various ideas, she said, "It seems to me that there are basically three ideas that have been mentioned. The first involves showing special projects and work that students in this school have done. Some of the work that has been mentioned in this area are the art collages, the science fair projects, the furniture made by the woodworking class, and the batiks the textiles classes made.

"The second main idea is to show what education could be like in the future. John mentioned the teaching machines and Kyle talked about learning at home through TV. The third idea is to show how education has changed over the years. Ruby was talking about using slates and going to school in one-room school houses for this idea." Thus Clara organized the random suggestions the group made. She summarized the choices the group could make.

## Consensus Testing

A person who takes on the role of *consensus testing* checks with the group to see how much agreement has been reached. The consensus taker tries to find out if the group agrees on a solution to a problem it faces.

Valerie, Donna, Kate, and Sonja sang in a barbershop quartet. They had been asked to sing for the athletic banquet at the high school, so they met to decide which songs to sing. After a lot of talk, Kate finally said, "OK, it sounds to me as if we agree. We'll sing this slow sweet song first. Then we'll sing the medley of patriotic songs. The third number will be the medley of popular songs we've worked up. As a finale, we'll do, 'For They Are Jolly Good Fellows.' Is that all right with everyone?" Kate tested the consensus or agreement of her group by outlining a program to the others.

Unit 5: Relating to the Larger World

## experiences in human relations

### YOUR GROUP ROLES

Each person tends to play certain roles in the groups to which he or she belongs. Some people play task roles. Others are more comfortable with group-building roles. This experience will help you discover which roles you are apt to play in groups.

Listed below are the various task and group-building roles discussed in this chapter. Copy the list of roles on a separate sheet of paper. Beside each role, draw a short line. On one end of the line place the number 1 and the word *poor*. At the other end of the line place the number 5 and the word *excellent*. Place the numbers 2, 3, and 4 evenly spaced between the 1 and 5.

Now, think about how you act in groups. Consider your family and friendship groups as well as other organized groups. Think about each role in turn. Place an X on the line to indicate how well you feel you perform that role.

When you have checked yourself on each role, look over your lists. Do you seem to do better at task roles or at group-building roles? Do you fill many or few roles in the groups to which you belong? How would you rate your contributions to the functioning of the groups to which you belong?

*Task Roles*
    Initiating
    Information Seeking
    Information Giving
    Clarifying
    Summarizing
    Consensus Testing

*Group-Building and Maintenance Roles*
    Encouraging
    Expressing Group Feelings
    Harmonizing
    Compromising
    Gate Keeping
    Standard Setting

### GROUP-BUILDING AND MAINTENANCE ROLES

A second series of roles help build and maintain group rapport. These *group-building roles* help group members feel comfortable together and help them enjoy being with each other. Skill in relating to others and in communication are needed to perform these roles.

**Encouraging**

The role of *encourager* is carried out by people who are friendly, warm, and responsive to others. An encouraging person accepts others and their ideas and work. The encourager is always ready and willing to give others a chance for recognition.

Jonas filled the role of encourager for the baseball team. He was friendly to everyone, and never criticized the other team members for poor play. When a team member made a good hit or fielded the ball well, Jonas responded with a compliment. The team members teased him about his positive attitude. In a friendly way, they nicknamed him "The Cheerleader."

**Expressing Group Feeling**

*Expressing the group's feelings* is a role taken by someone who isn't afraid to talk about emotions and feelings. This person senses the feelings and moods of the group members and is willing to talk about them.

This person also shares his or her own feelings with the other members of the group.

Irene was the stage manager for the spring production of the drama club. Somehow, she could sense the mood of the actors as they practiced their lines. When a scene or an act was over, her comments always seemed just right to the others. She might comment on the group's frustration, hope, excitement, enthusiasm, depression, or joy. Whatever the mood of the group, she was able to understand and explain it.

### Harmonizing

Some people are born peacemakers. They assume the *harmonizing* role in groups as they work to solve conflict. The harmonizers are able to reduce tension by "pouring oil on troubled waters." These people are able to help others in the group explore their differences constructively.

Duane was the harmonizer in the group of males who worked as busboys in a cafeteria. When others argued over who should clear a certain table, Duane could resolve the disagreement and get the table cleared. When two of the others almost got into a fist fight over a female they both liked, Duane was able to prevent the clash. Through his skill in peacemaking, Duane kept the group almost free of conflict.

### Compromising

Another role to help build and keep group rapport is that of the *compromiser*. This means admitting error and being willing to "give" a little bit. The compromiser is flexible and will move from his or her first position. Some people also have skill in helping others compromise. A compromiser is able to find a middle ground that is attractive to others who hold different ideas.

*Some people are able to encourage others to perform to the best of their abilities.*

Carol served as a compromiser in her group of friends. Norma and Arden both initiated ideas, but they rarely liked the same suggestion. Carol usually was able to suggest a

Unit 5: Relating to the Larger World

*The standard setter in a group helps the members set standards for the group to achieve.*

compromise that suited both of them. For example, when six friends decided to go shopping, Norma wanted to go downtown, while Arden thought a shopping mall would be better. Carol was able to suggest that they might go downtown first, then go to the mall on their way home. Her suggestion was adopted by the group.

## Gate Keeping

Another role in groups is that of *gate keeping*. The gate keeper helps keep communication flowing between all group members. This person helps everyone participate in the group discussion or activity. The gate keeper often suggests ways members can best discuss the problems of the group.

Rich acted as a gate keeper for his literature discussion group. If one member of the group didn't add anything, Rich would often ask what he or she thought about the topic. Sometimes talk would get confused and people would interrupt each other. Rich would then mention a way to proceed so that everyone could have a chance. Sometimes he would suggest that they go around the circle and each talk in turn. At other times, he would act as a moderator, helping keep order.

## Setting Standards

In a group, one person usually sets the standards for all to achieve. The *standard setter* helps the group express what the goals are. Evaluating whether or not the group met its goals is another role often filled by the standard setter.

Darcy served as a standard setter when the young people's group at her church planned a fund drive for UNICEF. She suggested that the group should be able to raise $200 through selling greeting cards produced by UNICEF. She gave group members quotas and later checked to see whether each person had sold their allotment. Through her work in checking up and encouraging, the group was able to meet its goal.

## experiences in human relations

### OBSERVING GROUP ROLES

For this experience, you will need to observe a group in action. You may choose to do this experience at a meeting of a group to which you belong. You may prefer to do it during a class, family, or friendship group discussion.

On a separate piece of paper, copy the list of task and group-building roles discussed in this chapter. List the roles one under the other along the left side of your paper. Be sure to leave plenty of space next to each role to write people's names.

Now, listen carefully to the conversation of the group you have chosen. Anytime you hear someone taking one of the roles you have listed on your paper, place his or her name beside the role. Continue to do this throughout the entire discussion or conversation.

When the discussion is over, look at your sheet. Were you able to pick out examples of all the roles you had listed? Did any one person seem to dominate a particular role? Did anyone fill several roles? Were task roles or group-building roles more common? What kind of a discussion was the group having? Was it just a casual conversation or was it problem solving or information sharing? How did this influence which roles were filled? What did you learn from this experience about group roles?

**Ch. 14: Relationships in Groups**

### TO SUM UP...

1. List the three main types of roles to be filled in groups.
2. What influences the role or roles a person may play in a group?
3. Briefly describe the six group task roles.
4. What characteristics do people who perform group-building roles need to have?
5. What are the differences and similarities of the harmonizing and compromising roles? The encouraging and standard-setting roles?

### LEADERSHIP ROLES

A *leader* is a person who has some power and authority over group members. Most groups have a formal or an informal leader, although leadership sometimes shifts from one person to another. Leaders can either be appointed or they can emerge from the group.

Jana has been selected by the band director to fill the position of student band leader. Because she was not chosen by her peers, her ability to provide leadership depends on how well she can fill task and group-building roles.

Sam was selected as captain of the basketball squad by the team members. He emerged from the group as a leader. The others recognized his leadership ability by choosing him captain.

It seems to be almost impossible to be a leader in both task and group-building functions at the same time. The leader in group-building and maintenance roles must like others in the group and must be liked in return.

In contrast, the leader who specializes in task roles must remain aloof. The leader must not become so attached to the others that he or she can't use power over them. The use of leadership power is often needed to get group members to complete a task.

A person is usually not as good in one type of role as in the other. A personality which can perform the group-building roles well is not apt to have as much ability in the task roles. Likewise, people who do the task roles well often are unable to maintain the strong relationships needed for the group-building roles.

James was the captain of the defensive platoon on the football team. He often made the other squad members angry or upset with his orders and comments. However, the squad led their conference in defense, mostly due to James' ability to see what defensive plays should be used. Tom, on the other hand, worked to build and keep the relationships strong on the squad. His ability to relate to the others helped them cope with James' manner. Tom was the group-building leader and his ability to build good group feeling was as important as James' football skills.

Some leaders have a knack for controlling and dispelling conflict. Others have a knack for forcing the group to accomplish its task. It usually takes both kinds of leaders to make a strong, efficient group.

## Leadership Traits

Group leaders tend to share certain traits. First, most leaders are intelligent. They have the ability to deal with many situations and problems. Such leaders can see relationships and reach sound conclusions. Intelligent group members seem to be more active in the workings of the group and participate more in group activities. Thus they are more likely to emerge as leaders.

Steve became the leader of a group of students who were preparing a report on drug use in the community. His intelligence led him to make suggestions about how they could gather information. His ideas about putting the material into their report helped convince the others that he would be the best leader the group could have.

The intelligence that leads to good grades is not the only kind of intelligence that makes a good leader, however. Marsha was the percussionist in the rock band at her school. She became the leader of the group because of her musical intelligence. This included not only superb musical skills, but also an ability to sense what music was right for which occasion.

Most group leaders have a sense of responsibility. They are in control of themselves and work to keep the group together. Such leaders have integrity and are able to rely on themselves. They are likely to have a positive self-concept, with ability to control and discipline themselves to achieve goals.

Flexibility is another trait good leaders have. They are able to adjust to changes and help other group members do so, too. When the routing procedures were changed in the typing pool, Gloria was eager to try the new method. She was quick to see its advantages. When others complained that the new method was confusing, Gloria helped them adjust to the new requirements. Her ability to change when necessary helped the others adjust.

Most good leaders have empathy. They have insight into the feelings of others. When Norman's relay team was beaten for the county championship, he recognized how disappointed the others were. He was able to overcome his own disappointment and help console the others.

Finally, all leaders have some desire to be a leader. People who become leaders have the wish to assert themselves. They want to influence or have power over others. What separates those who lead from others who also have leadership traits? The motive to become a leader. Barb is an intelligent, flexible, and responsible member of the Drama Guild, skilled at making scenery and sewing costumes. She has been asked to be Stage Manager for several different plays. Each time she refuses, but always stresses her willingness to help whoever is chosen. Although Barb has the traits of a leader, she lacks the wish to be one.

## Styles of Leadership

People lead others in many ways. Their styles of leadership reflect their different personalities. However, most leaders are either autocratic or democratic. These two styles of leadership reflect, in part, whether the leader is best at task or group-building roles.

The *autocratic leader* is likely to be firm, demanding, and directive. He or she is not apt to accept the ideas of others. Instead, this kind of leader uses power to force others to carry out his or her ideas.

Groups led by autocratic leaders are very efficient. They perform tasks quickly and well. The leader tells each group member what to do and how.

Relationships are often unhappy under an autocratic leader. Group members resent being told when to do what. They dislike always having to obey orders from the "boss." Satisfaction within the group is often low.

Ruth is maintenance floor supervisor in a hospital. She tells the employees who work for her where to work. Usually she assigns each employee to work alone. Each job has a set routine in which it is to be done. Ruth checks up on the others to be sure they are working as she orders. Ruth's sparkling clean floor is the best maintained in the hospital. Jobs are done promptly and always on time. Ruth's boss considers her a superior manager.

However, those people who work for Ruth don't like her. They feel they could set their own work routines. They would like to alternate or share work sometimes. Her employees quit frequently or request transfers to other floors. Most of them hate working for Ruth.

*People who become leaders have a strong desire to assume the leadership role.*

### Unit 5: Relating to the Larger World

Ruth is a typical, if extreme, autocratic leader. She is outstanding on task roles, but is unable to build group feeling. She sees herself as the boss, a person whom the others should obey.

In contrast, the *democratic leader* encourages group members to help make group decisions. This kind of leader draws ideas and suggestions from group members and urges them to participate in matters that concern them. The democratic leader often tries to play down the leadership role in the group. The leader may provide information, materials, and facilities for the group, but does not direct group action.

Because the democratic leader does not direct group activity, these groups often are not very productive. Group members feel free to do their tasks in their own way. As a result, tasks are often not done well or consistently.

However, group relationships are usually good under a democratic leader. There is frequent, friendly, confiding conversation. The leader stays on the same level as the others, joking and laughing with them. Thus the democratic leader is often a good leader of group-building and maintaining functions.

Mr. Darrien was a history teacher who used democratic methods in his classroom. He let his students have some say in choosing subject matter to study, and in suggesting class activities and projects. The atmosphere in his classes was friendly, with lots of talking and joking. Most of his students enjoyed being in his classes for he was a popular teacher.

However, at times the history suffered. His classes were often only half through the book when the school year ended. Students usually had less knowledge of history than students of other teachers. In Mr. Darrien's classes, the task of learning history often seemed less important than working together on interesting projects and activities.

## experiences in human relations

### GROUP LEADERS

Every group has a leader or several leaders. Most leaders share several personality traits. In general, leaders tend to stress either task or group-building roles. It is almost impossible for one leader to be equally talented in both kinds of roles. This experience will help you think about the kind of leadership you enjoy and respond to best.

Think about the groups to which you belong. Include groups at home, school, church, or work. Who is the leader of each group? What kind of traits does each leader have? Which leaders have an autocratic style of leadership? Which have a democratic style? Look over the list of group roles again. Do the leaders of your groups stress task or group-building roles? Can you pick out individual roles at which each leader is especially skilled?

Now consider how effective each leader is. Which leaders do you consider very good at leadership? Which traits and style do they have? Do you respond best to autocratic or democratic leaders? Which groups do you enjoy most? Do you think the style of the leader affects your response to the group?

Are you a leader in any group? What leadership traits do you have? Are you an autocratic or a democratic leader? How satisfied are your group members with your leadership?

### TO SUM UP...

1. What is a group leader?
2. Why do people find it hard to be

leaders in task and group-building roles at the same time?

3. Describe personality traits which most leaders possess.

4. What trait separates leaders from other group members who may also be qualified for leadership?

5. Compare and contrast democratic and autocratic styles of leadership.

6. What is the relationship between group satisfaction and leadership style?

## GROUP NORMS

A group *norm* is a group standard. It is a "rule" that is accepted at least to some degree by most members of the group. Norms are guidelines that define the kind of relationships a group has. They also dictate the group's attitudes toward tasks of the group. Finally, norms define what kind of conduct or behavior is accepted by the group.

Most group norms are informal—they are not spelled out directly. Instead, the norms of a group are given by example. Regardless of the kind of group, members are expected to follow certain ground rules or patterns of behavior.

Patrice is a member of the Ballet Club at school. In this group, events start on time. People who come in late are given disapproving looks. Group norms dictate that members must be on time to keep the approval of others.

In contast, Patrice is also a member of a woodworking club. In this group, no one arrives on time. Meetings begin anywhere from fifteen minutes to one-half hour after the announced time.

Most teenage friendship groups have norms about appearance and clothing. Todd's friends all wear denim pants and jackets. One day, Todd's mother tried to get him to wear a sweater vest to school. Todd refused because he knew his friends would disapprove of the vest. The norms of his group forbid him to wear anything different.

In much the same way, all the girls in Betty's group wear their hair long. When Betty had hers cut very short, she found that her friends disapproved. Because she broke the group norm for long hair, she isn't accepted as willingly as before.

Work groups often have norms which influence members' attitudes toward work. Some groups are proud of their ability to get work done. Other groups may put more emphasis on getting along with each other.

Judy's first job was in an office. She was amazed at how much talking the other bookkeepers did and how little work they seemed to do. The group norm dictated that group members talked and socialized rather than worked. Later, Judy was transferred to another office where the group norm was toward accomplishment. The others were friendly, but didn't gossip or talk much. Instead, they worked hard and were proud of the amount of work they accomplished.

Athletic teams often show different norms about winning. Lee's swim team concentrates on winning swimming meets. They train hard and work together to win as many events as they can. The group norm on Lee's team is winning.

In contrast, Will is a member of the golf squad. While members of the squad enjoy winning, they enjoy just playing golf even more. They joke around together and have fun during their practices. However, they seldom win tournaments. The norm for this group is having a good time rather than winning at the expense of fun.

Unit 5: Relating to the Larger World

*Cooperation is a norm in this group of employees. They work together to finish their jobs quickly and well.*

## CONFORMITY

Group norms tend to produce conformity. When group members obey the norm, they act alike or *conform* to the norm. To some extent, groups require some conformity in order to do the tasks they face.

For example, Mark works with a group on an assembly line. Unless all group members conform and report to work at a certain time, no one on the line can work. Each person must conform so the group can turn out a finished product.

When the band marches in a parade, all band members are expected to conform by wearing their uniforms. They would present an unattractive appearance if they all wore different outfits. Thus conformity is needed for the band to make a good appearance.

Some conformity is needed for groups to be able to function well. However, conformity has a negative side. Sometimes people conform just for the sake of being like others. By conforming, they may compromise their own ideas of what is right or wrong. Some people are afraid of being different. To avoid standing out, they conform to group norms.

Wilma was interested in attending a symphony concert, so she tried to get several friends to go with her. Since they preferred rock music, they teased and laughed at her for having such a different interest. They called Wilma old fashioned and peculiar for enjoying symphonic music. Their scorn was so frightening to Wilma that she decided not to attend the concert. Wilma gave up her interest in the concert to conform to the musical ideas of her group of friends.

People with low self-esteem are especially apt to conform in order not to be different. Because they have little confidence in their own ideas, they are willing to do what others tell them to do. Joe had a very poor self-concept. At the start of his junior year, he became friends with a group of males whom he admired a great deal. He felt very proud to have become a member of the group. After about a month, he found that the group members cheated during exams by passing answers to each other. One day Dale, another group member, tried to copy Joe's answers during a math test. Joe didn't want to let Dale copy. However, because he felt unworthy of being Dale's friend, he didn't want to refuse. By letting Dale copy his answers, he was conforming to the group's norm that cheating was all right. He gave up his own personal belief that cheating was dishonest because he wanted to belong.

## COHESIVENESS

Another trait which relates to group norms is cohesiveness. *Cohesiveness* is the feeling of togetherness that members have toward each other and toward the group as a whole. Cohesiveness is shown by a member's sense of identification with the group. If members are strongly attracted to the group, the cohesiveness is high.

Florence and three other friends have formed a cohesive group. They all admire and respect each other and enjoy each other's company. They call themselves "The Quartet" and spend most of their free time together. Members of The Quartet tend to ignore others who are not in their group. Their main interest is in keeping their group strong and cohesive.

In groups that are not very cohesive, membership may change often. Group members may put other priorities before the group. Conflict may be common because members don't care whether the group is maintained or not.

In general, cohesive groups are more satisfactory to members, who gain satisfaction from the sense of togetherness. In addition, cohesive groups are often better able to accomplish tasks which they are assigned.

Bruce works in a nursery after school. The four workers who help care for the trees, bushes, and plants consider themselves a team. They are a cohesive group. Their teamwork allows them to help each other get chores done. Because they cooperate, they are able to complete their work quickly and well. All four members of this group gain a lot of satisfaction from their relationship.

When cohesiveness is high, there is greater pressure to uphold the group's norms. Each person in the group feels an obligation to the others. Thus each person is more willing to abide by the "rules" of the group.

Hal is editor of the school newspaper. The staff has become very close and cohesive through their work together. One issue of the paper carried an article containing gossip about several students and teachers. Because the staff is such a closely knit one, Hal felt pressure not to tell the newspaper adviser

*Conformity can prevent people from expressing their own tastes and ideas.*

## Unit 5: Relating to the Larger World

who had written the article. The cohesiveness of the group reinforced the norm of not telling on each other. In a less cohesive group, Hal probably would not have hesitated to name the author of the article.

### TO SUM UP...

1. What is a group norm?
2. How do norms influence group behavior?
3. Describe the relationship between conformity and group norms.
4. List advantages and disadvantages of group conformity.
5. Define cohesiveness.
6. What are advantages in group cohesiveness?

## GROUP COMMUNICATION

Communication is important between people who relate to each other. It is also very vital in group relationships. The more members in a group, the harder it is to have good communication.

### Patterns of Communication

Groups communicate in many ways. Some patterns of communication reflect the leadership style used in the group. Other patterns are chosen to help with task or group-building roles. People's happiness with a group is influenced by the pattern used. The most common patterns of communication are: all channels, circle, chain, Y, and wheel.

### All Channels

The all-channels pattern is the most open and democratic of all patterns. It allows each person in the group to communicate with all others. No single person controls the mes-

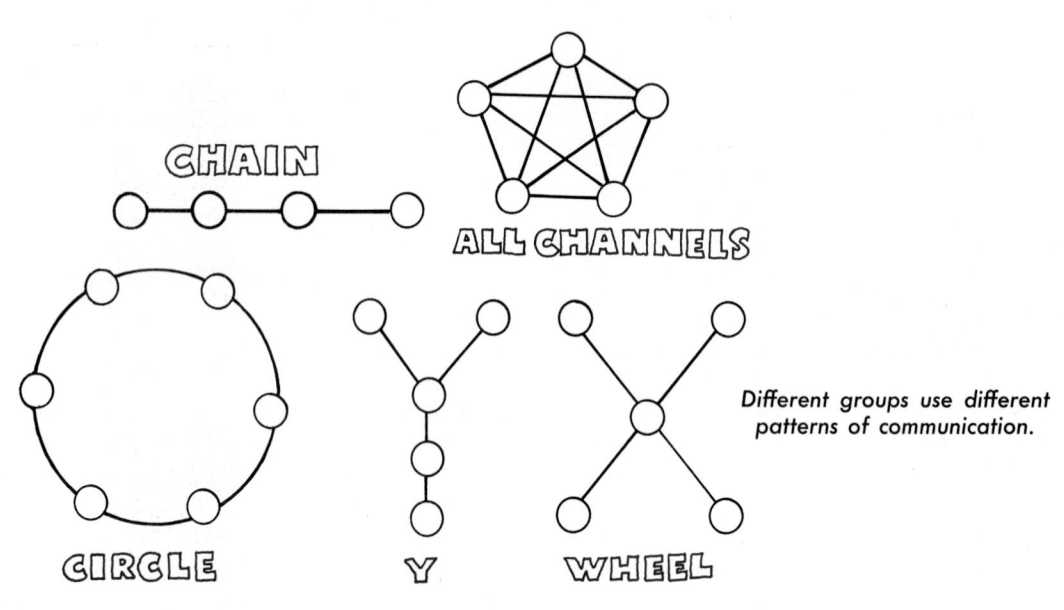

*Different groups use different patterns of communication.*

sages sent and received since all group members have contact with each other. Most informal groups use all-channels communication.

Sally's special friends use the all-channels pattern. When they are together, the conversation flows among all group members. No one feels left out—in fact, their communication pattern helps increase group cohesiveness. Satisfaction is usually high when a group uses the all-channels pattern of communication.

### Circle

In the circle pattern, messages go from one group member to another around a circle. Groups which use the circle pattern of communication often have no strong leader. They are active and unorganized, but the group relationships are enjoyed by members.

Barney's friendship group communicates like this. Each person passes on information and talks to others in a circular method.

### Chain

In the chain pattern, one person starts the message. The message is passed to another person and so on down a line. Messages can come back along the chain in the same way. The chain pattern usually is satisfactory to people in it.

This communication pattern is used to tell Claudine's mother about school events. The principal announces to the teachers that an event will be held. The homeroom teacher tells Claudine, who then relays the message about the event to her mother.

### Y

The Y pattern includes at least five people. Three or more people are in a short chain pattern representing the tail of the Y. When the message reaches the person at the center of the Y, that person then informs two others. The Y pattern is more structured than the chain or circle because the person in the center controls the messages.

The members of Luke's basketball team tend to use the Y pattern of communication. Jules, one forward, talks to Paul, the other forward. Paul talks to Scott, the center. Scott, in turn, usually talks to both of the guards, Quinn and Luke. In addition to playing center on the team, Scott is also in the center of the group's Y communication pattern.

### Wheel

The wheel is an even more centralized pattern. The group leader holds a middle position, communicating with other group members in turn. These group members are compared to spokes on a wheel. Groups with wheel patterns are apt to be good at problem solving and task accomplishment.

The wheel pattern of communication is used in Martha's job at the nursing home. She and the other aides each receive their instructions from their boss. They don't have a chance to become friendly with each other. Each aide communicates only with the boss, who forms the center of the wheel.

As a rule, people in the center of a pattern are satisfied with the pattern. Those on the outside of the pattern are often unhappy with the group's communication. When a pattern is centralized, leadership tends to be autocratic. Leadership is more democratic when patterns are open.

## Nonverbal Communication

Nonverbal communication is as common in groups as it is between individuals. When a group is seated, the place each person chooses sends a nonverbal message. If a group is seated around on oblong table, those people at the ends and in the center of the sides

*The ends and side center positions at a rectangular table are usually taken by group leaders or those who talk a lot.*

expect to talk more. The talkers choose the more central seats so that they will be able to see all of the others. These central seats are often chosen by the leader of the group.

When the Future Homemakers of America officers meet, the President, Rosie, sits at the end of the table. Norine, the treasurer, always talks a lot. She usually chooses a seat in the center of the table side. The officers leave the other end of the table for their chapter adviser. Tina, the secretary, rarely says anything during meetings. Typically, she chooses a seat at one end of the table side.

Seating patterns affect communication in another way. Two people seated side by side tend to talk less than those seated across from each other. Communication also is better when people feel separated by a comfortable amount of space. When group members are too close or too far away from each other, communication is hindered.

Nonverbal communication tells how cohesive the group is. If the group is a cohesive one, members will be relaxed when together. There will be a great deal of eye contact between members. The space between people will be small and people will seem to lean toward each other.

When a group is not cohesive, members are stiff and unrelaxed. They avoid each other's eyes and maintain a larger distance between each other. Members will appear to lean away from each other rather than to lean toward one another.

## experiences in human relations

### COMMUNICATION IN GROUPS

This experience will help you become more aware of how groups communicate.

You and your classmates should divide into two equal groups. One group sits in a small inner circle. The other group sits in an outer circle around the inner circle. The outer circle will be observers during the first part of the experience.

If you are in the inner circle, begin a discussion with the others about what traits a group leader should possess. As you talk, the outer circle listens and analyzes the discussion. Who talks in the inner circle? How long do they talk? Whom do people look at when they talk? Do they look at others who support them? At the group leader (if there is one)? Or do they look at the group as a whole?

Who talks after whom? Who interrupts whom? Are all members of the group participating? If not, why not? Do people seem to be listening to each other? What communication pattern does the group seem to be using? Do you notice any nonverbal messages being passed?

After the group has talked for about ten minutes, the discussion stops. The outer group then reports their observations of the inner group's communication. After the outer group has reacted to what the inner group did, the groups change positions. The outer group becomes the inner group that carries on a discussion. The inner group becomes the observing outer group. After ten minutes of discussion by the new inner group, the new outer group reports on the communication of the inner group.

## TO SUM UP...

1. Why is communication important in a group?
2. Describe five patterns of group communication.
3. What types of patterns are usually used by autocratic leaders? By democratic ones?
4. What nonverbal messages are sent by a group member's choice of a seat?

### Ch. 14: Relationships in Groups

5. Describe nonverbal messages which indicate that a group is cohesive. Not cohesive.

## GROWING THROUGH GROUP MEMBERSHIP

Group membership is one way for individuals to grow as persons. Learning to interact in a group can be a very exciting experience. The stimulation of other group members can help each person learn new skills in relating to others.

Being a member of a group can help people learn to work with other people. Working on a project alone is quite different from working with others. You must be able to communicate with the others, compromise if needed, get the job done, and yet enjoy your companionship with the others. Many people never learn to work with groups. They miss out on many rewarding experiences by choosing always to work alone.

Tansy, Patty, and Amelia were working together on a patchwork quilt. They had to decide how and when to cut the squares. They disagreed over how the squares were to be sewn together. Planning was needed to find time to work on the quilt. When the quilt was finished, the three felt as if it had been well worth while. Their quilt was very attractive and each girl had learned to work better with others to achieve a goal.

Group membership helps people learn to accept authority. Although many people like to be independent, there are times when everyone must accept authority. Being in a group can help people learn to adjust when other people use power against them.

335

Unit 5: Relating to the Larger World

*The support of the group can help members learn to accept criticism gracefully.*

Rob had always found it hard to obey orders from someone else. He wanted to do things his own way. When he became a member of the football squad, he was quite unhappy at first. He didn't like being told when to do what. As the team began to improve, he found that he enjoyed being a part of the team effort. He could accept his assigned part because of the contribution it made toward the team's winning. Through his football experience, Rob began to change his attitude about authority figures.

The group setting is one way to learn to accept criticism gracefully. No one likes to be criticized, yet each person can improve in some ways. The security of the group can help people learn to accept feedback about their behavior. The group setting can also help people learn to give others constructive feedback.

When the play cast members were rehearsing, they were often criticized by the play director. Because all the cast members wanted to act their parts well, they accepted the director's comments. Each cast member knew that everyone else was criticized. If someone was given especially harsh criticism, the others were there to sympathize.

Conflict is a normal part of group membership. Even two people alone rarely get along perfectly all the time. A group has many more people who can come into conflict. If the group is to survive, the members must learn to handle conflict. If a positive approach is taken, conflict between members can result in creative solutions to problems.

Allen talks about the conflict in his group of friends. "I'm the kind of person that has always avoided conflict. I don't like arguments or fights. But you just can't get away from them when six guys are together so much. We try to solve all disagreements right away, so we don't carry resentment around with us. Sometimes we shout and rave, but then everyone has it out of his system and it's over. I feel that I've really learned a lot about how helpful conflict can be sometimes."

Finally, group members can learn to rely on others. People often try to do things themselves. They hesitate to ask others for help or support. However, help and support are an important part of group membership. Each person uses his or her talents to contribute to the group and to appreciate the contributions of others.

When Sue started work at the florist's shop, she felt very much alone. She was afraid the others would think her questions stupid. She worked in her corner, trying to do everything herself. As she became acquainted, she discovered that the others were willing to help. When she felt comfortable, she began asking questions. The answers and suggestions she received helped her to create beautiful floral arrangements. The group of employees was able to provide a strong, stable group that each member could rely on.

Group membership is a part of everyone's way of life. Each person can learn new skills in relating to others in groups. Making the most of your experiences in groups can help you to grow as a person and as a group member.

## experiences in human relations

### GROWTH IN GROUPS

People can learn or improve their skills in relationships as members of groups. Some groups are better than others in helping members grow. This experience will help you consider whether a group to which you belong provides a setting for growth.

Choose a group to which you belong. Use the following rating scale in judging your group.

1. Excellent
2. Superior
3. Average
4. Fair
5. Poor

Using this scale, rate your group on the eight statements given below.

1. All members are involved in group projects and activities.
2. Group members are eager to develop new interests and have new experiences.
3. Group members accept a variety of values and ideas.
4. Many members have a chance to assume leadership roles.
5. Warmth, acceptance, and trust are found among group members.
6. Group communication involves all members in a free-flowing exchange of ideas and information.
7. Conflict in the group is resolved with respect for the ideas and feelings of all members.
8. Group members give each other support and help in many situations.

Add your eight ratings together and divide the sum by eight. This is your group's average rating. The lower the number, the more group members are apt to grow because of their membership. The higher numbers indicate that the group promotes little growth in its members.

Try to get some other members of your group to rate the group. Compare your answers with theirs. Did you agree on your group's strong points and weak points? Were your overall ratings similar? How could you help improve your group?

### TO SUM UP...

1. What relationship skills are needed in doing a project with others?
2. Why is acceptance of authority necessary at times?
3. How can group membership help members learn to accept criticism?
4. Describe opportunities for growth that groups provide to members.

## CHAPTER 15

*Entering the World of Work*

This chapter will help you to...
- Understand reasons why people work.
- Identify traits which help people fill work roles successfully.
- Recognize the importance of relationships on the job.
- Explain the characteristics and effects of work groups.
- Describe job expectations held by employers and workers.

Most people enter the world of work at some point in their lives. During a working lifetime, an average person spends at least one-third of his or her waking hours at paid employment.

Work is important because it involves so much of a person's life. Although work may take place during certain hours at a certain place, its influence is felt in all areas of life. The amount of money earned on the job determines in part the type of life style a family can afford. When Dirk Watson was promoted, he received a large raise in salary. With the increased money, he and his wife bought some new furniture that they had been unable to buy before. They also found that they were able to hire a babysitter and go out more often.

People's self-images are influenced by the kinds of jobs they hold and by how well they can perform their jobs. Annette was delighted when she was hired to be an assistant buyer in the appliance section of a large department store. It made her feel good about herself to know that she had been chosen over 33 other applicants for the job. Thus her self-image was made more positive.

However, Annette found it hard to adjust during her first few weeks on the job. There were many details to learn and she sometimes had trouble remembering them all. Her first solo buying trip resulted in stock that didn't sell. The department ended up selling it at a loss. The problems Annette had in learning her new job affected her self-image in a negative way. She became less confident about herself and her abilities.

Feelings about the job have a direct effect on the feelings people have in their out-of-work lives. When Mary closes a real estate

*A worker who has had a good day on the job brings those feelings home with him.*

sale and receives her commission, she is excited and cheerful. Around home she is happy and bubbly. However, when she hasn't made any sales for a while, she tends to be depressed. This leads to cross and grouchy behavior toward her family. Mary's feelings about what happens on the job affect how she feels at home.

Because work plays such a major role in people's lives, knowing *how* to work is important. However, simply having some work skills is not enough. Work is basically a social situation. A person works for and with other people. Between 5 and 15 percent of the people who lose their jobs do so because they do not have the job skills needed. The other 85 to 95 percent lose their jobs for one of two reasons. Some have personality traits which interfere with their work. The rest lose their jobs because they are not able to relate to the other people around them. Many people are simply not aware of the many personal traits and relationship skills that a worker needs.

Learning to work effectively with others calls for an entire range of relationship skills. Most of the ideas and skills which have been discussed in this book can be applied to the work setting. Workers must know themselves and how to perform their roles as workers. They must know how to relate to others whom they meet on the job. Cooperation with co-workers and supervisors is crucial in holding a job. Learning to resolve conflict with others can be as important on the job as it is with family and friends.

Your needs, values, and personality traits will influence your success as a worker. Your ideas about work as well as your experiences

## Unit 5: Relating to the Larger World

have shaped the attitudes and values you now hold about it. If your attitudes and values toward work allow you to make full use of your relationship skills, you are most apt to be a successful worker.

## experiences in human relations

### WORK IN EVERYDAY LIFE

Work influences just about all aspects of everyday life. Your life style, feelings, and values are influenced by your work (if you hold a job). They are also influenced by the jobs held by other members of your family.

For one week, take an "outsider's" view of your life. Try to look at yourself in an objective, detached way. Keep a journal of all the ways in which work influences your life.

How does the amount of money (or lack of it) from work affect your life? Does it influence your eating habits, where you live, your clothing, recreation, and the transportation you have?

How does work affect your schedule? Do you eat or sleep at certain times because of work commitments?

Look at the feelings and emotions work rouses in you. How do you feel before you go to work? When you come home? How are these feelings expressed? How do these feelings affect others? In general, does work make you happier or unhappier? If you are unemployed or looking for work, how does this affect you?

What values do you associate with work? Is work something that is important in life? Is it something that you avoid, if possible?

After you have kept your record for a week, read over what you have written. Does work have a large or small influence on you? Are there any areas of your life that are not influenced by work? What did you learn from this experience?

● ● ● ● ● ● ● ● ● ● ● ● ● ● ● ● ● ● ●

### WHY WORK?

Why do people work? You are likely to answer that question by saying that they need money. However, this answer does not tell the whole story. It does not explain why people who have enough money for their needs keep working. Nor does it explain why some people work at poorly paid jobs when they qualify for higher-paying ones. Finally, it doesn't explain why some people work at volunteer jobs without pay.

During the 1950's, studies of workers showed that the amount of salary they made was most important in rating a job. The higher the salary, the better the job.

In today's world, attitudes are changing. People now expect to meet some of their psychological needs through work. Recent studies have shown that a chance for advancement, satisfaction from the job itself, and relationships on the job all rank higher than salary as desired job traits.

### HIERARCHY OF NEEDS

Several times during this book, the hierarchy of needs has been discussed. Almost all human behavior is concerned in some way with meeting needs. Work behavior is very vital to meeting needs all through the hierarchy.

You will recall that physical needs and safety needs are the two lowest needs on the hierarchy. Money earned on the job is used to help meet these needs. Art Draper's salary pays for food, clothing, and shelter to meet his family's physical needs. The money that

### Ch. 15: Entering the World of Work

important place where belonging needs can be met. Some people enjoy belonging to a small work group, while others meet needs through affiliation with a certain company or profession.

Larry Wills feels a strong sense of belonging to his work group. He and four other men work on the loading dock of a manufacturing plant. Larry says, "You know, it is sort of funny because the five of us really aren't much alike. But after you've sweated in the sun together and frozen in sleet storms, you really feel as if you belong together. We're a real team—and our work record shows it, too."

Lucie Bennett is a lawyer who works for the law firm of Kieren and Fromm. She is proud to tell others where she works. As an employee, she feels a part of important work. Her sense of belonging is directed to the company, rather than to a small work group.

Esteem needs can also be met in the work situation. Toni Lopez felt good about herself when she got her first after-school job. Her family didn't have much money, so when she earned her own spending money, it helped relieve the family budget. Having a job helped her feel that she was an important, contributing family member. It allowed Toni to meet her need for self-esteem.

Holding certain jobs can bring esteem from others. Leslie Mondale had long admired Mr. Appleton, the shop foreman. When Mr. Appleton retired, Leslie applied for and got the promotion to foreman. The status and responsibility that went with his new job brought him respect and esteem from those who worked with him.

Finally, work can help a person reach the top of the needs hierarchy. When work calls for the use of all the potential and talents a person has, it helps him or her grow to self-actualization.

*Holding a responsible job helps a worker's self-esteem and brings respect and esteem from others.*

Art has saved helps him feel safe and secure against crisis or money problems that may come in the future. His salary pays the insurance premiums that financially protect his house, car, and health.

The love and belonging needs come next on the hierarchy. Because work involves being with others in so many cases, it is an

Unit 5: Relating to the Larger World

*Some people find intrinsic values in their work.*

Peter Grebbs is an architect. About a year ago, he was given the chance to design a shopping mall. He still talks about his experience. "I wasn't really sure I could handle the job," he says. "I think I worked harder on it than on anything I've ever done. Yet it was a challenge—an exciting job—I had to use everything I'd ever learned. They're about to start construction soon. I'm looking forward to seeing my plans carried out."

Sandra Henry teaches emotionally disturbed children. She feels that it takes all of her skill and talent as a teacher to help her students learn and grow. Her belief that her own growth as a person depends on that of her students causes her to work long and hard at teaching. Thus she is able to self-actualize by making full use of her teaching abilities.

Simply holding a job does not automatically mean that all needs on the hierarchy will be met. Instead, the kind of job and the personality of the worker determine what needs will be met. A job that helps one worker meet belonging and esteem needs may only meet the physical needs of another worker. What may be challenging for one person may be boring for another.

It appears that people who work in low-paying jobs that do not require much skill tend to have only their lower-level needs met through work. Sara has worked on an assembly line since high school graduation. Some days she feels as if she will burst out screaming from boredom. The only thing she likes about her job is the money that she earns. Sara's job provides her money for meeting her physical and safety needs. A group of special friends helps meet her needs for belonging. Her skill and devotion to racquet ball help her meet her needs for esteem and self-actualization. She is the current women's singles champion at her racquet ball club. Sara is like many others who hold jobs that provide little challenge or stimulation. Her higher needs are met through her activities outside of work.

In jobs which require more skill and which pay more, people are more apt to meet higher needs through work. Martin Grey, a doctor, is wrapped up in his work. He spends up to sixteen hours a day seeing patients and working at the hospital. Because his job meets so many of his needs, he does not feel his schedule is too taxing. Instead, the challenge and excitement of the work meets his higher needs.

Meeting needs is an important part of why people work. In a survey taken recently, people were asked whether they would continue to work if they suddenly inherited a fortune. Almost two-thirds of the people said they would want to keep working. When asked why, some replied that they enjoyed being with and working with others on the job. Others said that they would miss the challenge and satisfaction of work. These answers show that people work for reasons other than the money they earn.

### VALUES OF WORK

Another way to look at why people work is through the idea of intrinsic and extrinsic values. *Intrinsic values* are those found in the work itself. Satisfaction with a job comes from the doing of the job.

Renee is a social worker who finds a great deal of satisfaction in helping her clients. Because one of Rob's favorite activities is tinkering with cars, his job as a mechanic brings him much enjoyment. Jilda works as a computer programmer. She can become completely absorbed in planning programs which are needed by her employers. Each of these workers finds joy and satisfaction in the actual doing of their jobs. In other words, their work has intrinsic value for them.

In contrast are *extrinsic work values*—work is done for something other than the pleasure of doing it. Betty works as a house painter for the money she earns. Mark is a teacher who likes his job only because he enjoys having the free summers for travel. Although Brian doesn't particularly like being outside every summer day, the admiration that his life guard job brings from his friends makes it all seem worthwhile. A job with a major airlines lets Norine fly without cost when she wishes to take trips. Her work is boring but the chance to travel cheaply makes the job a desirable one for her.

All of these people keep or like their jobs because of something outside the job itself. Rather than enjoying what they do for itself, they enjoy the extrinsic values. The rewards for holding the job come from outside of the job itself.

Most jobs bring a combination of intrinsic and extrinsic values to the worker. Extrinsic values can be very attractive to job holders. However, people who gain intrinsic satisfaction from their jobs tend to be more satisfied and happier in their work.

## experiences in human relations

### WHY DO PEOPLE WORK?

People work for a variety of reasons. However, many of these reasons are not immediately obvious to either the worker or others. This experience will help you explore the attitudes people hold about why they work.

Talk to at least ten workers. Try to choose people who hold a wide variety of jobs and who are of different ages. First, ask the subjects why they work. Next, ask them if they would keep on working if they were to inherit a million dollars. If they say that they would keep on working, inquire why. If they would not keep working, ask what they would do instead.

When you have talked with the subjects, compile their answers. How many of them said they worked only for money? Did some of them say they would keep working even if they inherited money? What did the others say they would do instead of working? Did differences in age and type of job held make any difference in the answers people gave?

Why do *you* think the people whom you interviewed worked? Do you think they recognized the wide variety of reasons that people work? Explain.

Unit 5: Relating to the Larger World

## TO SUM UP...

1. Describe some of the ways that work influences people's lives.
2. What job trait was most important to workers during the 1950's?
3. What are some traits which help bring job satisfaction to present-day workers?
4. How can work help a person meet needs found on the hierarchy of needs?
5. What do people do who cannot meet many of their needs on the job?
6. Compare and contrast intrinsic and extrinsic work values.

## WORK ROLES

Every member of a firm holds a position. An office may have a receptionist, a file clerk, several typists and secretaries, and a manager. Other departments have other types of positions. For each position there is a work role.

You will recall from Chapter 9 that a role is a part you act out in your relationships with others. In a work setting, a role also includes the behavior that is typical or expected of the people holding a particular job. The work role may include the work that is done. For example, Jennie is a secretary. Her tasks include typing and dictation. She refuses to do any filing because she says that is Carol's job as file clerk. Jennie doesn't see her work role as helping Carol with the filing.

The work role often includes ideas about how a person is supposed to behave toward people in other positions. The other stockroom workers were shocked when they heard John swearing at the supervisor. Many of the others complained about the supervisor behind his back. However, they felt it was not acceptable for John to be openly hostile to the boss.

Another aspect of the work role may be the clothes or the uniforms worn. When Terri was hired as a grocery store check out cashier, she was told that she must wear a two-piece pants suit uniform while on duty. Clark works as a painter's assistant. Although there is no uniform for his job, he is expected to wear old clothes that will not be damaged by paint spatters.

The life style outside of work is sometimes influenced by certain work roles. Gloria Jarmond is the art director of an advertising agency. Her boss makes it clear that she is expected to do some kind of volunteer work. The company feels it is important that employees contribute to the community. Gloria's work with a 4-H club takes a great deal of her free time and influences her out-of-work life style.

Finally, work roles may call for the worker to hold certain attitudes and beliefs. Marsha Rivers was elected a representative of her union. Her job was to serve as a link to the company management. The union members expected her to support them at all times. However, Marsha often found herself agreeing with management when she was required to argue the union side of the issue. She could not fulfill her role as a union official because it required her to hold certain attitudes about both the union members and management. When the next union elections were held, Marsha asked not to be re-elected.

### Role Conflict

Role conflict occurs on the job just as it does in any setting where people fill roles. Role conflict may occur on the job when two people or groups expect different behavior from the worker. For example, Ellen feels trapped between what her boss expects and

*Strikes and other union activities sometimes cause role conflict for workers.*

what the others in the typing pool expect her to do. Her boss gives her more work than most of the others have. In order to get her work done, she has little time to visit or chat with the others. She frequently takes shorter breaks to have time to finish. The others in the pool are less pressed by work and have more time to socialize. They try to convince Ellen that she works too hard and that her boss is too demanding. As a result, Ellen is very unhappy with her job. Her typing accuracy has gone down so that it takes even longer to finish projects. People who experience a lot of role conflict on the job often simply quit rather than live with the stress. Although Ellen hasn't resigned yet, she has been thinking of doing so.

Another kind of role conflict may occur in situations where a union and management are in disagreement. When the nurses at Johns Hospital went on strike, Mike Terrill didn't know what to do. His union leaders demanded that he join the strike, which was called to get higher wages. However, Mike felt that as a nurse he had a responsibility to his patients. His role as a union member during the strike conflicted with his idea of the role a nurse should play in patient care.

Role conflict may occur between the demands of the company and those of clients. Ruthie worked as a salesclerk in a boutique. Over a period of a year, she became acquainted with a customer who bought many garments from her. This woman also suggested to many of her friends that they purchase items from Ruthie. Therefore Ruthie felt very grateful to her "special" customer. One day this customer came in and returned a dress which obviously had been worn. The shop rule was that any garment that had been worn could not be returned. Ruthie was torn between her loyalty to a regular customer and to the boutique owner. Ruthie refused to accept the dress, which made the customer quite angry. As a result, she never returned to the shop again.

Role conflict is apt to be related to low levels of job satisfaction. The worker in role conflict often becomes inefficient on the job and tries to avoid those who are causing the conflict.

### Filling the Work Role

Every work role has some requirements which a worker must fill in order to keep that job. Some people are more successful than others in performing the work role. Laura

Unit 5: Relating to the Larger World

never seems to be able to keep any job for long. She was fired from several jobs and quit others. She has failed to learn to fill the work role well enough to keep the jobs she obtains.

Certain traits help people fill the work role. These traits appear to be developed during the early school years. Thus those who are able to fill work roles well have learned through their school experiences how to do certain activities. Others who do not fill work roles well appear not to have developed such skills.

A good worker must know how to concentrate on a task for extended periods of time. Hattie has good powers of concentration. When she is involved in working on a project, she doesn't even hear others talking to her. She learned this while doing her homework in the bedroom she shared with her sister. On the job, she can concentrate on her work even though people at desks around her are talking or typing.

Another work skill involves learning to cope with people in authority. Tom was always in trouble in school for talking back to the teachers. After he quit school, he found that he could not hold a job very long. When he became angry, he would talk back to his boss, who would fire him. People in authority are not always right. However, a person with good work skills knows when to yield to those with power. Talking back to a teacher or a boss at the wrong time and place usually leads to trouble. A calm manner and quiet statements will help create a setting where the no-lose method of solving problems can be used.

Learning the value of cooperation and competition with peers is a useful work skill. Cooperation is the only way to get work done in some settings. On the other hand, competition is just as useful at other times. Knowing when to cooperate and when it is all right to compete is the mark of a good worker.

Lorna has always tried to be best at whatever she does. She wants to win when she plays games. In school, she always tried to get the highest grades. A small magazine employs her as a copy writer. She considers all the other copy writers as competitors and tries to do better than they. During one rush project, she finished her assignments early while several other writers were slower. As the project deadline came near, Lorna was asked to help some of the others. She refused, saying that she had done her share and that it wasn't her job to help others who couldn't get their own work done. Her lack of cooperation was reported to the personnel office. Lorna was passed over for promotion because she was unwilling to cooperate with the others.

Finally, a good worker has learned that hard work is usually rewarded in some positive way. The worker also learns that not working brings either no reward or punishment. In school, teachers try to teach this by awarding good grades for achievement and poor grades for non-achievement. On the job, good work may lead to promotion or a raise in pay. Poor work can lead to the loss of the job. A person with good work skills wants to do well. The worker tries to do the job to the best of his or her ability. A willingness to work hard for some kind of reward is the mark of good work skills.

## experiences in human relations

### WORK ROLES

Being able to fill a work role well involves having certain job skills. It also calls for certain personality traits and the ability to get along with others. This experience will help you to see what specific aspects of work roles employers emphasize.

Read the want ads in one day's paper. Keep a count of how many ads request workers with specific work skills. Another count should show how many ads want workers with certain personality traits or relationship skills. Also count how many ads ask for both items.

When you have finished reading the want ads, look at your three figures. How many ads asked for only work skills? Only personal traits or relationship skills? Both? Share your findings with your classmates. Listen as they report what they discovered.

Only 5 to 15 percent of people who lose their jobs do so because of the lack of work skills. Did your findings reflect this fact? How would employers be able to check on how well a person could fill the work role? If you were applying for any of the jobs you read about, how would you show that you had the desired skills?

## RELATIONSHIPS ON THE JOB

Because most jobs involve working with others, building relationships on the job is crucial in several ways. Employers want workers who can get along with and cooperate with others. Workers are more satisfied with jobs if they like being with their co-workers. Good relationships on the job increase the workers' abilities to do their tasks well. They also help prevent conflict, which might interfere with the work output.

### SUPERVISOR RELATIONSHIPS

Relationships between the supervisor and the worker are formed around power and authority. When someone pays your salary, you, as a worker, always have some kind of authority over you. Your direct supervisor may not actually be the person who pays you. However, your boss's reports can influence those who employ you. Therefore building a good relationship with a supervisor is needed to make a job satisfying.

## TO SUM UP...

1. What is a work role?
2. Describe some aspects of work roles.
3. Identify an example of a role conflict at work.
4. What is the usual outcome when a worker experiences severe role conflict?
5. List some of the traits a good worker uses in filling work roles.

*Good relationships at work help people be more satisfied with their jobs.*

## Unit 5: Relating to the Larger World

*Facing common problems in similar work helps people form cohesive work groups.*

People react differently to authority. Some people have great respect for tradition. They submit to those with power and take orders well. They feel that a person in a job with authority should be obeyed. These people tend to work well under leadership from others.

Roger worked for a printing company. As a typesetter, he followed directions and did his work well. Because he always followed his boss's orders, he was considered a good worker.

In contrast, Tony was not good in following the directions of his supervisor. He had always rebelled against authority even as a child. On the job, he often did the opposite of what was requested. He was popular among his fellow workers, but was fired from his job because he could not get along with his boss.

Most workers learn to have some balance between the two extremes. They need enough acceptance of authority to carry out orders. However, they also need some bit of rebelliousness to see that what the boss says may not always be right. What was done last year may be out of date. A tactful suggestion may show initiative and motivation.

Most workers hope that their supervisors will be sympathetic with their problems. They expect to get good help or assistance in solving such problems. On the other hand, they do not want the supervisor to check them too closely. Most people want to feel that their boss trusts them to do a job without constant supervision.

The spinning machine workers in a textiles plant felt that their supervisor, Mrs. Sampson, was the best in the company. She had once worked on a spinning machine herself so she understood their jobs. She was always willing to help when problems arose, but she did not constantly watch the workers as they did their jobs.

A supervisor serves in the same kind of leadership role that group leaders do. Many successful supervisors first showed their leadership skills while a member of a work group. Because of their leadership ability, they were later promoted to supervisory jobs.

The supervisor has two main tasks. The first is to see that the work is done properly. Thus the supervisor must be concerned with the task functions of the working group. Second, the supervisor must look after the welfare of the group members. Keeping up worker job satisfaction is part of the group-building role of a supervisor.

As a sales manager, Margie Owens supervises ten traveling salespeople. As part of her task functions, she plans the work to be done. She schedules the salespeople with customers and makes sure that supplies are available.

She trains new employees. Checking the work that has been done and giving the salespeople feedback on their performance is a major part of her job. Margie motivates the workers to maintain high sales levels.

Jonathon Barker is foreman of the night maintenance crew at a chemical plant. He is especially skilled at group-building tasks, and gives high priority to the needs of the workers. A personal interest in each employee helps build friendly, supportive ties in the group. When mistakes are made, he helps cope with the results and works to insure that they won't happen again. He praises those workers who do their jobs well. Solving conflicts which arise between two or more workers is another of his skills. The workers whom he supervises feel that he has their interests at heart. His concern for their welfare helps keep them satisfied with their jobs.

As discussed in Chapter 14, good group leaders can combine task and group-building functions. So, too, do good work supervisors. They are able to use explanation and persuasion rather than just giving orders. They also allow workers to share in decisions that affect them. The good supervisor persuades the group to set high targets and to work for these goals without needing further supervisory pressure. A supervisor with these skills helps keep production high and workers satisfied. That is the result for which all supervisors strive.

## RELATIONSHIPS WITH OTHER WORKERS

In working with others, people build relationships and form groups. Work groups are different from other kinds of groups in one respect. They are formed so people can work together to do certain tasks. As a result, the relationships in the group are influenced by the task that is to be done.

The size of the work group is important in job performance and satisfaction. Groups of five to ten people do better at most tasks. When groups become larger, they tend to break down into informal subgroups. For example, a work group of 15 may actually be two small groups, one with seven workers and one with eight. If the two small groups are unable to work well together, job performance may go down.

Small groups tend to be closely knit with strong relationships. Therefore, workers usually are more satisfied when the work group has five or six members. As a result, small work groups have less absenteeism and less labor turnover than larger work groups.

## Cohesiveness in Work Groups

In Chapter 14 cohesiveness was defined as the feeling of togetherness that group members have toward each other and toward the group as a whole. Cohesiveness in work groups develops in several ways. People who work in the same room or in one area in a large room tend to form a group. If the people who are close together do the same or similar work, they are apt to build close ties. They are faced by the same problems and thus can help each other in many ways.

Vanity worked as a dispatcher for a fleet of taxi cabs. She became friends with the four other dispatchers who worked with her. Their common problems in scheduling taxis to customers helped them build up rapport and a feeling of being a group.

Cohesiveness is greater in groups where members share similar traits. Likenesses in age, roles, family background, and attitudes toward work help build group feeling.

Otto worked with a group of young men at a local car wash. They were all students who worked after school and on weekends. They liked to work rapidly to finish a car so that they would have a chance to talk before another car came through the line. Because they were similar in many ways, they were able to build strong group feelings.

If communication in a work group is good, the group is more apt to be cohesive. A noisy work setting cuts down or eliminates talk between people. This often prevents group feeling from forming.

Betsy worked in a newspaper plant. The noise of the presses made it hard to talk to the other workers. Although Betsy would have liked to have been friendly with the others, she never seemed to have a chance. The noise prevented the communication which could have built group cohesion.

The ability of co-workers to build strong work groups helps keep them happy. Workers are more satisfied on jobs where they feel a part of a cohesive work group. In a cohesive group, members are more apt to cooperate with each other. They have an increased ability to meet some of their belonging needs on the job. Workers resign or are fired less frequently when they have strong relationships with their co-workers.

## Advantages and Disadvantages of Work Groups

Being a part of a group of co-workers has a number of advantages and disadvantages for the worker. When the worker is learning a new job, having others around often causes nervousness. Chris was hired as a file clerk in an insurance firm. The complex filing system used by the company required all her attention as she learned to do her job. She was nervous, afraid that she would file information incorrectly so that others would be unable to find it when it was needed. When the other office workers were around, she became even more nervous and found it hard to concentrate on her work.

However, as workers learn their job skills, they come to enjoy the presence of others. When the task is familiar and routine, efficiency is usually increased by the presence of others.

Ellis was a plumber. Once he had studied the drawings and plans for a job, he liked to talk with others as he worked. The work seemed to go faster when he had someone with whom to interact.

The effect of work groups is very important when the work itself is boring and monotonous. For some workers the boring work may be offset by the pleasure that comes from being a part of a congenial work group. The social life around the job can give the satisfactions that are lacking in the job itself.

Keith works in a factory doing routine assembly line work. He finds the work boring but not unpleasant. His main pleasure comes from his relationships with others on the line. They talk and chat as they work. Practical jokes are common and Keith enjoys his reputation as a joker. Lunch time card games among the workers are a high point of the day. The cohesive work group to which Keith belongs affects his attitude toward his job. He is happy with the job because of the satisfaction the social relationships bring him.

On the other hand, the group can also affect workers in another way. If a strong work group has developed, a member may feel disloyal in leaving that group for promotion. Ralph had worked with the same construction crew for four years. They had become an efficient, smooth-working team. Then Ralph was given the chance to take a manager's job in the firm's headquarters. The decision was very hard for Ralph to make. He felt as if he were deserting the buddies with whom he worked so well. On the other hand, the new position offered more salary and chances for advancement. He took the new job, but found that his old crew members were resentful and unfriendly. They felt that his new job made Ralph "better than they were." Thus, while a strong work group can make a bad job bearable, it can also put pressure on members to remain. It may be very hard to leave a strong working group, even though it means advancement and a better job.

## experiences in human relations

### ON THE JOB

It is often difficult to think about what the world of work is like when you are sitting in the classroom. This experience will give you a small taste of what work can be like.

For this experience, you and your classmates will operate a Gadget Factory. This factory has an assembly line which produces "gadgets"—a chain of three linked paper clips. For your factory you will need about 600 paper clips, 100 envelopes, 2 pencils, and 50 rubber bands.

Along a table or counter, set up the gadget assembly line. The first person in line is the gadget assembler, whose job it is to link the three paper clips together. Next on the line is the packer, who places two gadgets in an envelope and passes it on to the labeler. The labeler marks the filled envelope with the word "Gadget." Next comes the inspector, who checks each envelope to make sure that it holds two correctly made gadgets. The inspector initials the checked envelope and passes it on to the bander. The bander joins together ten inspected packages with a rubber band. Also needed is a supervisor who is responsible for the entire assembly line operation.

Choose a work role on the assembly line. Others in the class will fill in the other roles. Those who choose not to work can observe the work habits and roles of those on the line. Operate the line for 15 minutes or until the stock of paper clips is gone.

When you have finished, talk about the experience. How did you feel working on the line? How would you feel after eight hours, or five days, or one year of making gadgets? Do you feel that gadget makers would be satisfied with their jobs?

What personality traits or relationship skills did you use during work on the line? Did you observe any traits or skills in your co-workers?

Was there a lot of talk and social activity during the work? Was the social life on the job able to make up for the dullness of the work? Did the workers cooperate well? How might lack of cooperation have effected the line?

What suggestions could you make to increase satisfaction from work such as this, which is basically dull and boring?

### TO SUM UP...

1. Why is an ability to get along with others important on the job?
2. Why is the relationship between worker and supervisor prone to conflict?
3. What kind of balance do most people take in their attitudes toward their supervisors?
4. List the two main tasks of a supervisor.
5. Why is the size of the work group important?
6. How is cohesiveness developed in work groups?
7. Describe the effects the work group has on its members.

Unit 5: Relating to the Larger World

## JOB EXPECTATIONS

When a worker takes a job, he or she has certain expectations about that job. The employer also expects certain qualities from the employee. If the work relationship is to prosper, both sides must benefit. Much job dissatisfaction results because the worker or the boss did not meet the expectations of the other.

### EMPLOYER EXPECTATIONS

An employer hires a worker to contribute skill or effort on the job. Employers must produce goods or services at a profit in order to stay in business. Workers must help in that effort or they are not worth their pay.

Most employers look for nine basic traits in the workers they hire. These traits are: basic skills, cooperation, loyalty, integrity, motivation, initiative, performance, communication, and appropriate appearance.

The emphasis put on each trait differs according to the kind of job. Cooperation is crucial to workers on an assembly line. A traveling salesperson has no co-workers with whom to cooperate on a daily basis. Appearance is probably more vital for a nurse than for a janitor. Thus employers will stress these traits differently. However, the more of these traits you possess, the more likely you are to be a good employee.

### Basic Skills

Most jobs require some basic skills. In order to get a job as a key punch operator, Rodney had to show that he was able to operate the key punch. Karen was hired to make deliveries for a dental laboratory. In order to get the job, she had to show her driver's license as proof that she had the skills to drive a car to make deliveries.

Some companies provide on-the-job training. Craig had never used a cash register when he was hired to work at the counter of a fast food restaurant. He was taught this basic skill on the job. However, the more basic work skills you have, the better chance you stand of getting the job you want.

### Cooperation

*Cooperation*—being able to work with others for the good of the company—is a trait all employers want. Grace and Jeanne were typists who found that their work was better when they cooperated. After typing their own work, each read the other's to see if there were mistakes. As Grace explained, "When I've typed a letter, I often don't see the mistakes because I know what the letter says. But I can see the mistakes in Jeanne's letters bet-

*A good worker is able to cooperate with others to get the job done well.*

ter than she can. By reading each other's work, we can correct the errors before we give it to our bosses. Helping each other lets us turn out perfect work."

Cooperation means using your talents for the good of your work group, whether or not you always get credit for your work. Cooperating with others helps build a team spirit that employers desire.

## Loyalty

Being loyal to a company means more than just lip service. *Loyalty* means having pride in the firm and respecting it and its products or services. Considering the interests of the company as well as your own is part of being loyal.

Shane McCaw sold pet food to grocery stores. She truly believed that her company's cat and dog foods were better than any other on the market. Her belief in the quality of the product she sold convinced many grocers to buy from her. The company that hired Shane recognized and rewarded Shane's loyalty through regular raises in pay.

In some cases, loyalty also involves questions of company security. When Bill Thompson was hired as a costing clerk, he was told that he was not to discuss his work off the job. The costs he worked with were used in preparing construction bids for his company. If other firms got information about Bill's projects, they might be able to make lower bids. This would mean the loss of projects worth millions of dollars for Bill's firm. Bill showed his loyalty to the firm by not discussing the projects on which he worked.

## Integrity

Many employers consider *integrity*—honesty and truthfulness—to be essential traits in a worker. All workers make mistakes. However, being honest about the mistakes you make is the mark of a good worker. Trying to hide a mistake is a serious offense on most jobs.

A worker with integrity is honest with the boss and co-workers. Employers seek those who do not try to pass blame on to others and who will learn from mistakes.

Sonja was the supervisor on the food service line in a big industrial plant. One day during the rush of the noon hour, she noticed that one cooler seemed to be turned off. She meant to ask one of the line workers to check it, but in the hurry, she forgot. It turned out that the cooler had broken down and all the food in it spoiled. Although the cooler was the responsibility of one of her workers, it was Sonja's job as supervisor to oversee the equipment. Therefore, when she was required to account for the waste, she took the responsibility for failing to check the cooler. Afterwards, she made it a part of her daily routine to check all the coolers that were used to store food.

## Motivation

*Motivation* simply means that you want to do the job. It is a desire to take action and accept challenge. It means you are willing to work hard but that you enjoy it. An enthusiastic and eager worker has a positive outlook on the job.

Carolyn Young wanted to hire a child care aide for the nursery school she ran. She talked with several people about the job, and finally chose Tracy Markus. As she said, "Tracy didn't have as many qualifications as some of the others. But I could tell as I talked with her that she really wanted *this* job. Some of the others seemed to be looking for any job that would pay the bills. But I wanted a worker who was excited about what goes on at the school. Tracy seemed ready to pitch in and help wherever she could."

**Unit 5: Relating to the Larger World**

*Workers who show initiative may have ideas for improving company procedures and policies.*

## Initiative

To show *initiative* means to be able to work on your own. Bosses like workers who can go ahead and complete their work. Good workers do not have to be told when to do what. They learn to use their skills to do the job.

Most jobs offer many chances for workers to use their talents. How you take advantage of your chances tells your boss how much initiative you have. People with initiative show interest in their work, in improving their skills, and in the company itself.

Derrick Mazza works as a stock clerk in a discount store. He has suggested several ways that the stock room could be better organized. In order to qualify for a higher-paying position in the company, he has been going to school at night. Derrick's boss says that Derrick shows more initiative than all the other stock clerks put together.

## Performance

Employers look for workers who can get the job done. They want workers who will do their jobs whether or not their bosses are around. The less supervision a person needs, the more he or she is worth to the firm.

People who perform their jobs well are dependable. Employers know they can rely on such workers to do their jobs properly. A dependable employee does the job as directed, whether or not others are taking shortcuts.

Joe works in a factory which makes electronic calculators. He tries to fit the parts together perfectly on each calculator he handles. He knows that other workers become careless when they see that the quality control supervisor is not checking their lines. However, Joe prides himself on being able to perform his job whether he is being checked or not.

### Communication

Chapter 7 was devoted to communicating with others. Employers want workers who can use the communication skills discussed in that chapter. A worker must be able to talk so that others will understand what is needed or wanted. Some jobs require that workers be able to write well.

All employers seek workers who will listen. A worker must be able to understand instructions or else to ask questions until he or she does understand.

Rosa always listened carefully when Mrs. Fritz gave the group of nurses aides their instructions each morning. She found that she could serve the patients better when she listened attentively. When her mind wandered, she usually didn't know what care she was supposed to give. Listening skills were important in helping Rosa work efficiently.

### Appropriate Appearance

People wear clothes which express their personalities. However, job requirements often dictate that certain clothing or hair styles are most appropriate. A worker should look like a worker to the employer. A horse trainer would not wear a business suit and tie to work. Jeans and a tee shirt would not be a suitable work outfit for a nurse. Workers represent their companies in the eyes of the world. Therefore it may be important to dress to please your employer.

Gene is expected to wear a tie and jacket in his job as a salesman in a men's store. Iris is required to tie back her long hair while she works with food in the ice cream parlor. Her uniform gives her the neat trim look that the company wants.

## experiences in human relations

### HOW WOULD YOU RATE?

Being successful on the job is the result of a number of personal traits. Some of these involve work skills and knowledge. Others relate to how well a worker gets along with people. This experience gives you a chance to think about how you would measure up to what an employer expects from a worker.

Listed below are several categories in which employees judge their workers. How well would you perform in each? If you hold a part-time job, rate yourself on that job. If not, choose an imaginary job you would like to have. How well would you be able to do it?

*Basic Skills:* How much do you know about the job? Do you have the basic skills needed to perform the work? Do you often need help? Do you have enough skill so that you are able to help others?

*Cooperation:* Do you always cooperate in your dealings with others? Do you cooperate

Unit 5: Relating to the Larger World

only when it suits you? Or are you unwilling to cooperate with others?

*Loyalty:* Do you have pride in your company? Do you respect the work that your firm does? Are you able to keep secrets that may involve company security? When you make choices about work, do you consider the company as well as yourself?

*Integrity:* Are you honest on the job? Do you own up to mistakes that you have made? Do you try to place blame on others? Do you take company supplies for your own personal use? Are you truthful when your supervisor requests information from you?

*Motivation:* Do you really want to do your job? Do you care about whether it is done well or not? Are you willing to work hard? Are you enthusiastic about your work?

*Initiative:* Do you have exceptional drive and ambition? Do you work to just do an acceptable job? Or are you completely lacking in energy and "get-up-and-go"? Can you work on your own without supervision?

*Performance:* Are you able to do your job as it should be done? Are you usually dependable? Can an employer count on you to do your job how and when you should? Or do you sometimes not complete your responsibilities?

*Communication:* Can you express yourself to others so that they understand your meaning? Do your communications sometimes leave a situation more confused than before? Do you listen when others talk to you about your job?

*Appropriate Appearance:* Do you look like a worker on the job? Is your clothing appropriate for the work you do? Do you conform to the company dress code if there is one? Or do you wear what you want even though there are rules against it?

Of the traits listed above, which do you feel is your strongest point? Your weakest? Do you feel that your traits will help you be successful on the job? If not, what could you do to improve your chances to do a job well?

● ● ● ● ● ● ● ● ● ● ● ● ● ● ● ● ● ● ●

## Worker Expectations

While employers expect certain traits in the workers they hire, the workers have expectations, too. Most young people seem to have at least six requirements in the work they desire. They want an adequate salary, meaningful work, challenging work, respect for their own individuality, the satisfaction of association, and a chance for advancement.

### Adequate Salary

The salary you receive as pay is for the contribution you make to your company. The company is paying for your skills and talents. A job with an adequate salary helps you feel good about your work. A poor salary can make a worker feel resentful toward the employer. It can also cause a worker to have a poor self-image.

What an adequate salary is depends on a number of factors. Salaries tend to increase as the worker has more skills and talents to offer. Thus what may be a high salary for a waitress may be a low salary for a computer programmer.

People also vary in their life styles, which influences their need for money. Freida and Dixie earn the same amount of money. Freida lives with her parents, spends a modest amount on clothing, and carries lunches from home. She saves a great deal of her salary and has enough money for special outings when she wishes. In contrast, Dixie never seems to have enough money. She is always borrowing the last few days before pay day. Dixie has her own apartment and spends a great deal of money on clothes. She enjoys eating lunch in

*Workers want to hold jobs that they feel are worthwhile and meaningful.*

fancy restaurants. What Freida considers a very adequate salary for her life style is inadequate for Dixie's way of life.

There are a number of questions you may want to consider in thinking about the value of money. Just how important is money to you? How much money is enough? Would you take a boring high-paying job rather than a more interesting, lower-paying one?

Rick was lucky enough to have two job offers made to him. One was to work in the public library after school, shelving books and doing some clerical work. The other job would be to work part time at the land fill. This job paid almost $1.50 more per hour than the one at the library. However, work at the land fill would be outdoors during the winter, and it would be dirty. Rick could make more money at the land fill, but the work would be less pleasant. After much thought, he took the job at the land fill. The pay was important to him because he was trying to save money to attend college.

### Meaningful Work

Workers want to feel that the work they do is meaningful, either to themselves or to others. Most people get satisfaction from doing something worthwhile.

Usually, all jobs are meaningful in some way to the overall operation of the company. A company would not waste money hiring a worker to fill an unneeded position. Sometimes, however, workers are unaware of the importance of what they do.

Carlos worked part time in the mail room of a hospital. The work was boring and he often felt that there was no meaning in sorting the mail. Then Carlos's father was in the hospital for surgery. Carlos saw how much pleasure his father received from cards mailed by friends and relatives. Carlos began to see that his job in the mail room *was* important—it helped patients keep up their morale while in the hospital. As Carlos changed his attitude toward the mail the patients received, his work became more meaningful to him.

### Challenging Work

People usually become bored easily so they seek change, variety, and something new. Thus most workers want challenging work that requires some effort. A job that calls for

Unit 5: Relating to the Larger World

*How workers use their work skills, personality traits, and relationship skills determines their success on the job.*

the same activity hour after hour soon becomes boring.

Making work a challenge is a major problem in many jobs. Work on an assembly line or in other automated businesses can be very boring. A bored worker is often not a good worker. Most jobs have at least some boring aspects. However, most people want the chance to use their creativity and talent to make their jobs interesting.

One of the reasons Maria Coates enjoys teaching is that it is never the same. She says, "I know some teachers who think that you do the same thing over and over. It is true that I teach reading, math, social studies, and penmanship every day. But it certainly isn't boring! We cover different subject matter in lots of various ways. It is really a challenge to me to involve my students in learning. I can use all my teaching skills to make my classroom an exciting and interesting place for all of us."

**Respect for Individuality**

Each worker wants to be respected as a person. Workers are not simply robots—they are people filling the work role. As such, they want to be treated as people with their own individuality. They do not want to be taken for granted on the job. They want their own achievements to be recognized.

Fred feels that his job allows him freedom to be himself. His firm permits workers to have flexible hours. This means that Fred can come in and work eight hours any time between 6:30 a.m. and 7:30 p.m. as long as he is there from 10:00 a.m. until 2:00 p.m. He is not criticized because of his long hair. Fred's supervisor is willing to listen to suggestions and complaints. The supervisor's attention assures Fred that he is considered a valued worker.

**Satisfaction of Association**

Most people want to work with others whom they can like and respect. As mentioned earlier, many people meet needs for belonging and love through work. Being able to feel close to your co-workers makes you

Ch. 15: Entering the World of Work

feel a part of the team. Your association with other workers thus brings you satisfaction.

Patrice is a teller in a bank. She has enjoyed working with the other tellers from the beginning. The entire group works hard, yet has a lot of fun kidding and teasing each other. The group cooperates and gives each other support and help. Patrice comments, "I really like the people I work with. My job is nothing fantastic, although it is interesting. If I couldn't get along with the others, I would quit because I know I could earn more money somewhere else. But I wouldn't dream of leaving my friends. The satisfaction I get from being with them makes this a super job as far as I'm concerned."

**Chances for Advancement**

Most new workers have to prove themselves on the job. Promotions and advancement do not come easily. However, the majority of workers want a chance to move up when they have shown that they can handle their jobs.

Arnold recently became an electrician's apprentice. He feels one of the biggest advantages of his new job is the many chances offered to improve and advance. Once he finishes his apprenticeship, the union has a program set up for regular advancement in the trade.

## experiences in human relations

### YOUR WORK EXPECTATIONS

This chapter discussed six of the job characteristics which people feel help them to be happy at work. These appear to be major sources of job satisfaction. However, for some people, other job traits are important, too. This experience will help you think about the satisfactions you expect from a job.

Copy each of the following list of job traits on separate, small index cards. You do not need to copy the brief definitions following each trait. Note that this list contains the six traits discussed in this chapter plus others which workers have said are also important.

- Adequate Salary—the pay you receive for the work that is done.
- Meaningful Work—the feeling of accomplishment you get from doing something worthwhile.
- Challenging Work—the chance to do something that makes use of your talents and skills.
- Respect for Individuality—being treated as an individual who is valued on the job.
- Satisfaction of Association—having good relationships with co-workers.
- Chances for Advancement—being able to look ahead to possible promotion.
- Activity on the Job—being able to keep busy all the time.
- A Chance to be Creative—being able to use your own methods of doing the job.
- A Chance to be Independent—being able to work alone to do your job.
- Good Working Conditions—having pleasant physical surroundings on the job.
- A Chance for Recognition—being able to get public praise for the job you do.
- Secure Work—knowing that your job will give you steady employment.
- Varied Work—a chance to do many different tasks while on the job.

Pick out the one card which lists the one trait you feel is most important to you in being happy with a job. Choose the card with the second most important trait and place it behind the first card you chose. Continue selecting

### Unit 5: Relating to the Larger World

cards until you have them all arranged in their order of importance to you.

What does this tell you about the kind of job you would like? Are any traits important to you not included on the cards? Where would you place them in your rank ordering of the cards? What traits are so important that you would not accept a job that did not have them? Which traits would you easily give up in order to obtain a job?

What did you learn about yourself from this experience?

### TO SUM UP...

1. Why do both employer and employee need to benefit from the work situation?

2. Why are different traits emphasized by different employers?

3. List and describe the qualities most employers seek in their workers.

4. Identify the job characteristics that most people desire for job satisfactions.

# CHAPTER 16

## Careers in Working with Others

This chapter will help you to . . .
- Consider factors in choosing a career.
- Define career clusters and ladders.
- Identify and describe various careers in service industries.

Most jobs and careers involve relationships with other people. Even jobs where people work alone require some contact with others. The watch-repair person must meet and talk with customers in order to have watches to repair. The scientist who spends hours over laboratory instruments interacts with workers and colleagues.

While just about all jobs involve contact with others, many careers are based on working with other people. If you enjoy being with others, relating to them, and helping them, you may wish to choose a career in working with others.

### CHOOSING A CAREER

Choosing a career can be a long and unsettling experience. There are over 30,000 jobs to choose from in the working world. It is no wonder that some people are confused when making career plans.

When Kent was a senior in high school, he began to worry about his future. He had no idea what he wished to do with his life. His parents wanted him to go to college and his grades were good enough for him to be accepted. However, he didn't know whether or not college would be the right choice for him.

Venetia was confused about the kind of career she wanted, too. Because her family couldn't afford college, she needed to start to work right after high school graduation. She hoped to find a job and later try to attend vocational school at night to train for a better position. However, she couldn't decide what her interests were.

Men and women spend most of their adult years employed. Not long ago, many women left the labor market upon marriage and never returned. Today, the average woman is employed outside the home for at least twenty-five years, even if she remains at home while her children are growing up.

People are spending up to fifty or more years of their lives working. Thus the choice of a job or career that is satisfying and enjoyable is important. When people are happy in their jobs, they are usually successful.

*People spend up to fifty years of their lives working at a job or career.*

How can you make the important decisions about your career? Choosing a career that is right for you involves looking at two areas. First, you need to study yourself. What are your interests, abilities, and values? What talents or traits do you have that might qualify you for certain types of jobs? Do you have traits that make you unsuitable for some jobs?

Second, you need to study different work roles and job requirements. By careful observation and reading, you will be better able to see where you can contribute the most and be the happiest.

The following questions are important to keep in mind when thinking about your life's work.

- Is this the kind of job you'd like to do?
- Do you have or can you get the education and qualifications which the job demands?
- Are you the kind of person who could succeed in this job?

Randy thought long and hard when he was trying to make plans for his life after high school. A shy person, he had always gotten along well with children. He was reliable and dependable and he felt that he could be responsible for caring for groups of children. A high school child development course made him realize what a challenge it was to help children grow and develop as people.

Randy considered a number of careers and jobs which would bring him into contact with children. Jobs which might let him express his interest in sports also attracted him. Randy was able to get a job as a leader's aide in his city's park and recreation office. There he helped plan and organize activities for children in both summer and winter. The work was so rewarding that he began saving money and making plans to attend college to become a recreation leader.

Paula went through much the same kind of decision-making process as Randy. However, Paula was a very different kind of person, so her thinking was much different. While Paula was good at working with her hands, she tended to have trouble relating to other people. She liked being outdoors and grew irritable when she was inside too long. Since she had no experience in working with animals or plants, she was unable to find jobs in those areas. She finally found a job with the city traffic control department. It didn't take her long to discover that she liked checking parking meters and helping direct traffic flow at peak periods. Her uniform helped her feel more secure in her dealings with others. Soon she found herself building good working relationships with others. Paula's personality characteristics fit the needs of the job she held, which made her a contented employee.

Your efforts in finding a job to suit your personality depend on whether you can assess your talents and find a place where you can use your skills. Everyone has unique abilities that can be developed in some way to make a contribution to others. Knowing yourself and your interests is the first step in choosing a career.

## experiences in human relations

### PERSONALITY TRAITS

The first step in making career decisions is to assess your strengths, weaknesses, and personality traits. This experience will help you become more aware of the traits you have which might be needed on the job.

First, think about your mental traits. How good are your grades? What are your hobbies? What do you do in your leisure time? Could any of these interests be used in some kind of career?

Now, think about your social traits. Do you prefer being in a group or alone? Do you like to see new places and meet new people? Are you happy when you can talk someone else into agreeing with your opinions? Do you care what other people think?

Your physical traits may be very important on the job. Is your health generally good? Do you have good physical endurance? Would you be strong enough to do manual labor? Do you have any physical handicaps which would make some jobs impossible for you?

Finally, what kind of character traits do you possess? Are you ambitious? How do you work under pressure? Are you patient and sympathetic in helping others? Would you rather discover new ideas yourself or have your work laid out for you?

Think back over your answers to the above questions. In which traits are you strongest? Weakest? How would your combination of traits influence how successful you might be at certain careers? Will your traits allow you to gain more education if that is required for a certain job? What kind of job do you think you are best suited for?

### TO SUM UP...

1. Why is choosing a career such an important decision?
2. What are two aspects of career choice that need thought before you make a decision about a job or career?
3. What questions should you ask yourself in thinking about specific jobs?

### CAREER CLUSTERS AND LADDERS

Certain groups of jobs are called *career clusters*. Jobs or careers within a cluster share

## Unit 5: Relating to the Larger World

general characteristics or traits. Several jobs in a cluster may call for the same or similar work skills. Knowledge or information about a certain subject may be basic to all jobs in another career cluster. The United States Office of Education has identified 15 major career clusters. These are:

- Agri-Business and Natural Resources
- Business and Office
- Communication and Media
- Construction
- Consumer and Homemaking Education
- Environment
- Fine Arts and Humanities
- Health
- Hospitality and Recreation
- Manufacturing
- Marine Science
- Marketing and Distribution
- Personal Services
- Public Service
- Transportation

Within a cluster, certain groups of jobs can be placed on an imaginary career ladder. At the bottom of the ladder are those jobs which require little if any skill or education. These are called *entry-level jobs*. Each rung up the ladder requires more ability, experience, and/or education. The jobs at the top of the career ladder require the most ability, experience, and education.

## experiences in human relations

### ENTRY-LEVEL JOBS

Entry-level jobs are those that require little, if any, skill or education. Workers in these jobs do not need experience or special talents. High school drop-outs or graduates often have no special work skills. Therefore they are hired to fill entry-level jobs. This experience will help give you some idea of the entry-level jobs which are available in your community.

Talk with at least five people who each work for different employers. Ask them to tell you about the kinds of work that people with no skills are hired to do. Make a list of the entry-level jobs at each place of work.

Later, in your classroom, tell the others what you discovered about entry-level jobs. Listen as they report their findings. Make one central list which gives all the entry-level jobs class members report.

Look at the jobs given on your classroom list. Which jobs do you think you would enjoy? Would you be happy doing one of these jobs your whole life? Do you have any skills which would qualify you for a job better than those listed? If not, how could you develop such skills?

● ● ● ● ● ● ● ● ● ● ● ● ● ● ● ● ●

As you go further up the career ladder, the jobs are generally more interesting, challenging, and better paid. Thus when you are considering a career or a career cluster, it is important to look at the career ladders in that cluster. How far do the ladders go? Are the ladders dead ends? How much education will you need to progress up the ladders? Looking at the career ladders in your field can help you consider further career advancement.

David was taking a Home Economics Related Occupations course in food service. He worked after school as a busboy at a French restaurant. David enjoyed the elegant surroundings at the restaurant. However, the fast food restaurants where two of his friends worked did not appeal to him. He felt that a career in an elegant restaurant would be more enjoyable and worthwhile.

**Ch. 16: Careers in Working with Others**

*Entry-level jobs on the career ladder require little skill or experience.*

He made an appointment to talk to Mrs. Carlino, the manager. Although David was interested in the restaurant business, he wanted to find out about the chances for advancement before making a decision. Mrs. Carlino told him that clearing tables as a busboy was the first step on the career ladder in food service. The next step for him would be to work as a waiter. A further promotion would be to wait at banquets and special group parties. The next step up the ladder would be as the restaurant host, welcoming guests and supervising the waiters, waitresses, and busboys.

The final step into the managerial role would be to serve as an assistant manager and then be promoted to be manager. Mrs. Carlino explained to David that there were no formal educational requirements to be a restaurant manager. However, she advised him that some background in business and personnel courses was needed to run a successful and profitable restaurant.

The career ladder in the child care occupations begins on the lowest rung with a child care aide. Patty took such a job at a child care center when she graduated from high school. She worked with the children under the supervision of a child care leader, Mrs. Thornton. To qualify for her position, Mrs. Thornton had taken a two-year child care course at the local community college. Mrs. Thornton's supervisor was the child development teacher, Mr. Drake. He planned the activities each day and helped the leaders and aides work with the children. Mr. Drake had a college degree in child development from the state university. Finally, Mrs. Comstock, the center director, was responsible for the business and the personnel of the center. Mrs. Comstock had several years of experience in working in child care centers. In addition, she held both

Unit 5: Relating to the Larger World

*Seven out of ten workers in the United States are employed in service industries.*

a bachelor's and a master's degree in child development. Thus, the child care center where Patty worked had employees who filled all the positions on the career ladder in child care.

Many people choose to work in an entry-level position to see whether the career cluster will really suit their needs. Norine thought that she might like to be a surgeon. She worked two summers as a nurses' aide at the hospital. Her experience there convinced her that she would not like the life of a doctor. Instead, she decided that she would enjoy the career of physical therapist more. Therefore, when she graduated from high school, she planned a college major in physical therapy.

Volunteer work is another way to discover if a career cluster would suit your interests. Bob Tolliver spent several hours a week answering the phone for his city's Hot Line. The Hot Line was set up so people with problems could call and talk with a sympathetic listener. Hot Line workers were often able to suggest where callers could receive help for their problems. Bob felt that by talking with people who had problems, he was helping others. His volunteer work convinced him that a career in working to help others would be interesting and rewarding.

As you look at career clusters, it may be difficult to figure out just how the career ladders in that cluster work. However, identifying career ladders will help you to see just how far you can rise with your education and skills. It will help you determine how much education you will need to get the job that is your goal.

## experiences in human relations

### A CAREER FOR YOU

No one can know exactly what a certain job or career will be like until he or she has experienced it. However, learning about the career can help you decide whether it might be right for you.

Choose a career or career cluster that interests you. First, go to the library or the counseling office and locate materials about that career. Job encyclopedias may give you some ideas about the job you have chosen. Special articles and pamphlets will help you learn other details about the career.

If possible, talk to someone who is in the career you have chosen. Find out the advantages and disadvantages of that career. What does your subject like and dislike about the job? What kind of education is required? Experience? What are the possibilities for advancement? What kind of salary could you expect?

What is it like to be a person on the job you have chosen? Would you work with people or with objects? Is the job setting noisy or quiet? Would you work at night or in the day? Does work in this career require a special uniform?

From your reading and talking with someone on the job, try to prepare a career ladder of opportunities. What are the entry-level jobs in the field? What would it take to gain promotion up the ladder?

How well do you think this job would suit you? Would the interests and abilities you identified in the experience on Personality Traits (page 363) be useful in this job? Would you be willing and able to get the education and experience needed for the job? Do you think this would be the right job for you?

### TO SUM UP...

1. What is a career cluster?
2. Identify some career clusters.
3. Describe a career ladder.
4. What are entry-level jobs?
5. How can people move up a career ladder?

### CAREERS IN SERVICE INDUSTRIES

In general, businesses are divided into two categories—they provide either goods or services. Those that produce goods make objects such as furniture, cars, silverware, or dog collars. All items that people purchase and use are made by goods-producing industries.

Service industries *do* things for people rather than *make* things for them. The service industries include health care, repair services, education, maintenance, and government.

Fifty years ago, only three out of every ten workers were employed by service industries. Today, almost seven out of every ten workers are involved in service to others. Thus, over the last fifty years, the largest growth in job openings has been in the area of the service industries. It appears that this trend will continue. As a result, people who want to serve

## Unit 5: Relating to the Larger World

and work with others will be needed to fill jobs in the service industries.

Many who work in service industries don't work directly with other people. However, a large percentage of the jobs available involve contact and interaction with others.

This chapter describes a number of careers involved in working with people. Many of the jobs described require a four-year college degree, called a bachelor's degree. Some require more study for a master's or a doctor's degree. Lower on the career ladders are positions for technicians, assistants, or aides that do not require more than a high school degree. If you do not plan to go to college, you may wish to consider a career ladder where a college degree is not essential for promotion.

There are few, if any, careers where the only requirement is ability to relate well to others. Most of the careers described below require some specific skills which are used in relating to others. For example, Mr. Kline is a teacher. Part of his skill in teaching comes from his ability to relate to students. However, he has to have subject matter and teaching skills in order to teach well. Thus for Mr. Kline, teaching is a way of relating to others by using his teaching knowledge and skills.

Carla Butler works with people selling insurance. She feels that her job is very important for she helps protect families from the financial hardships of crisis and disaster. Part of her success as a salesperson is her ability to relate well to others. At the same time, she has a vast knowledge of many kinds of insurance policies. She uses her skill in relating to people to learn what kinds of policies would best meet their particular needs. Her ability to get along with others would not get her very far without her knowledge and experience in insurance.

Thus in order to make a success in working in one of the service professions, people must have some skills and knowledge as well as an ability to work well with others. Just liking to work with people is not enough. You will need to develop skills and knowledge in an area which you enjoy in order to succeed in a career of working with others.

## HELPING PEOPLE UNDERSTAND EACH OTHER

There are a number of careers that involve helping people understand themselves and others.

### Social Worker

The social worker tries to help people overcome personal and social handicaps. Clients may be out of work or ill or they may have poor housing, little or no money, or other physical, mental, and emotional handicaps. Social workers work either on single cases, with groups, or through community organizations. The type of work the social worker does depends on the agency which employs him or her.

Lynn Wilson is a certified social worker. This means that she holds a master's degree in social work and has had two years of supervised training. She directs the program of an agency which works with migrant farm workers. She and her staff help individuals and families who are having problems. The agency staff plan recreation and classes for the children of the migrant workers. They are also trying to build community support to improve the poor housing in the migrant camps.

Lynn is the only certified social worker in her agency. Leo Juarez, who is her assistant, has a college degree in psychology. Several of the other employees who serve as case aides have had a year or two of college. However, all of them are able to understand the problems the migrant workers face. They are tolerant, patient, flexible, and truly like people.

**Social Service Workers**

Many people who are not qualified to be social workers work in the social services. They may serve as welfare case workers, program leaders for Scouting, YMCA's or YWCA's, or counselors in rape crisis centers. Other people work in traveler's aide, food stamp programs, or family planning clinics.

Jorine Adair went to a community college for two years, majoring in general studies. She had no desire to work for a bachelor's degree. Graduate school to become a social worker also did not appeal to her. She wanted to work with people and was happy to find a job in a Family Services Center. When families came to the Center for help, she held the first interviews with them. On the basis of her reports, the social workers and psychologists could then better plan help for the families.

**Psychologists**

Another group of people who help others learn to understand themselves are psychologists. These people hold doctor's degrees in psychology. They may use their knowledge in several ways.

Clinical psychology is concerned with helping disturbed people. Dr. Gene Brown works with patients in a mental hospital. Some clinical psychologists specialize in helping disturbed children. They may work with one patient at a time, although many have found they get good results treating patients in groups.

Psychiatrists are medical doctors who have done advanced work in mental health and illness. Their work is quite like that of the clinical psychologist. They tend to work with those who are mentally ill or disturbed.

Counseling psychologists work with normal people who have problems that they cannot face alone. These persons are not mentally or emotionally ill. However, they are upset, anxious, or struggling with some conflict. The counseling pscyhologist works in preventing mental health breakdowns.

Some psychologists work in schools. Dr. Louise Norton works with a large school district as a psychologist. She tests pupils who may be exceptional. She also counsels and works with students who have learning or behavior problems.

**Counselors**

Counselors work with people to help them with problems. You probably know the guidance counselor at your school. Guidance programs in schools aim to help each student grow toward maturity and adulthood. Coun-

*Many people are helped by social service workers who run agencies such as this Crisis Center.*

**Unit 5: Relating to the Larger World**

*This marriage counselor works with couples to help improve the marriage relationship.*

selors try to help students adjust as they enter and attend school. Testing is often a large part of the school counselor's job. They help students plan their courses of study. They may also help students find colleges, vocational schools, or training programs that meet the student's needs.

Another type of counseling is done by the vocational counselor. Many guidance counselors in schools also serve as vocational counselors. Vocational counselors are also found in employment agencies. They work to match people's skills with the jobs that are available. Vocational counselors are skilled in giving tests which reveal people's occupational strengths and interests.

Marsha Graham works as a vocational counselor in a large high school. Her job is to help students choose careers that match their interests and abilities. She talks with students, gives vocational tests, and provides students with information about careers. She suggests courses that students can take while they are in high school to learn more about careers in which they are interested.

Counseling is done in many other settings than in schools. Counseling psychologists help people cope with their problems as described above. Social service workers often counsel their clients or those who come to their agency for help. Many religious leaders counsel members of their church or synagogue.

One kind of counseling that has gained prominence in recent years is that of marriage counseling. Most marriage counselors have master's or doctor's degrees. Many religious leaders also do a great deal of marriage counseling. Only those people who have a good knowledge of how marriage relationships work have the skill to be good counselors. Many states do not have laws licensing marriage counseling. Thus, in some states, people may call themselves marriage counselors with little or no formal training or experience.

Most of the careers described above call for a college degree and many call for graduate school. There are not very many jobs on the lower rungs of the career ladders in these fields. Therefore, if you are planning a career in social work, counseling, or as a psychologist, you should count on going to college and graduate school.

## TO SUM UP...

1. What are the two general categories of industry?
2. How has the percentage of workers in the two types of industries changed over the last fifty years?
3. Why is skill in relating to others not enough to get and hold jobs in working with others?
4. What does a social worker do?
5. Describe the difference between social workers and those in social service work.
6. What education must psychologists have?
7. Identify different types of counselors. How do their duties differ?

## TENDING THE ILL, OLD, OR HANDICAPPED

Health care is an important career cluster which contains a wide range of jobs. Most of these jobs involve working directly with people who are ill, old, or handicapped. The health field offers exciting careers in helping others have fuller, healthier lives.

### Physicians

Probably the first person that comes to mind when careers in health are mentioned is the physician. The physician is on the top rung of the career ladder through his or her long education and training. As a doctor, Willa Hughes diagnoses and treats diseases and disorders of the body. Dr. Hughes works in general practice, although some doctors choose to specialize in surgery or other aspects of medicine.

Becoming a doctor is a long, expensive process. The doctor must graduate from college and medical school. A licensing examination is the next hurdle, then one to six years treating patients under the direction of other doctors. Only then is the doctor ready to set up an individual practice.

### Nurses

Other members of the health care team are nurses. They tend the sick and injured in homes, hospitals, clinics, schools, and industries. They work under the supervision of physicians in patient care.

Registered nurses can go through either a diploma or a degree program. Those who want a college degree can attend college and nurses' training at the same time. After four years, these students have a bachelor of science degree in nursing.

Diploma programs are run by hospitals and independent schools. These programs usually last from one to three years. Although fully qualifying students as nurses, a diploma program does not award a college degree. Nurses from diploma programs may find that advancement is slower than that of nurses from degree programs.

Often people want to become nurses, but are not able to enter a program to become a registered nurse. Many of these people choose to become practical nurses. In some states, such nurses are called licensed vocational nurses. These nurses work under the guidance of registered nurses and physicians. They keep checks on temperature and blood pressure readings, and give drugs and medicines. They also care for the comfort, cleanliness, and hygiene of the patient.

Licensed practical nurses are graduates of one-year courses in practical nursing. These

## Unit 5: Relating to the Larger World

*Massage by physical therapists helps build muscles, relieve pain, and improve circulation.*

courses combine classroom teaching and on-the-job training.

Jerry Stein's high school grades were not high enough for him to be admitted to nursing school. Therefore he entered the Vocational Nursing Program at the Area Technical School. After a year of study, he became a licensed vocational nurse. A job in a local nursing home gave him a chance to put his skills to use helping patients.

Finally, there are many entry-level jobs in the nursing field. Such jobs include hospital attendants, nursing aides, and orderlies. These people do many unskilled jobs such as bathing patients, running errands, and delivering messages. Such workers may also move equipment, set up rooms, and do cleaning and sanitation duties.

### Physical and Occupational Therapists

Physical therapists work with doctors to help ill or injured people regain use of their bodies. The therapist gives exercises designed to correct muscle ailments.

Patients who have had strokes or heart attacks, who have suffered polio, or who have injuries from accidents are often given physical therapy. Treatment may include massage to build muscles, relieve pain, or improve body tone. Heat treatments also may be given.

Most physical therapists are hired by hospitals. However, some work in doctor's offices or in rehabilitation centers. Others work in city health programs, in crippled children's clinics, or in the Armed Forces.

Becoming a physical therapist calls for a college degree. Often some advanced training is needed. Calm emotions, a wish to help others who can't help themselves, and good health are needed traits for those who hope to enter this field.

Occupational therapists chose and direct educational, vocational, and recreational programs to help disabled patients. "Curing by doing" has long been a form of treatment for patients. This kind of therapist works to build patients' physical, mental, or emotional health. Boredom is often a problem in a long illness. Therapists plan projects to hold the interest of patients. They also work to help patients become self-sufficient again. Such therapists work to help patients get well. They are also interested in teaching job skills, if possible.

Robert Hill works as an occupational therapist in a hospital. In the course of his work with patients, he has taught weaving, clay modeling, leather work, and jewelry making. His favorites are woodcraft, photography, and metalworking. He often has to study and learn new skills so that he can help patients with interests in areas where he knows little or nothing. One patient who had lost both legs in an auto accident was taught typing while in therapy. Her new skill helped her earn her living in a job where two legs weren't needed.

The occupational therapist needs a college degree. A clinical training period of nine to ten months is also required for professional registration.

**Dental Workers**

Another area of health care is dentistry. Dentists help people maintain healthy mouths through extracting, filling, cleaning, or replacing teeth. They also treat diseases of the gum and mouth and make and fit false teeth.

Dentists attend dental school for at least four years. Those who enter specialized fields study an extra two to three years. Scientific ability and skilled, steady hands are important to a dentist.

Many dentists employ hygienists who clean teeth and give flouride treatments. They also take X rays and assist the dentist where needed. Hygienists are licensed after graduation from hygienist school, which usually requires two years of study.

Dental assistants serve as general aides to dentists. They seat and prepare patients for dental work, get out the proper tools the dentist needs, and often act as chairside assistants. Many dental assistants go through one year of special training. This training qualifies them to give the dentist more assistance with patients. However, many dental assistants have no prior training before taking the job. The dentist then trains the assistant in his or her office procedures.

Rosemary Quinn was hired as a dental assistant and receptionist. She made appointments and greeted patients as they arrived. She seated patients in the dental chairs and got out the equipment the dentist would need. Her skill in making people feel at ease helped many nervous patients relax before their dental work.

**Rehabilitation Counselors**

Another type of career is that of the rehabilitation counselor, who works with socially, physically, or mentally handicapped people. Counselors usually work in a state rehabilitation agency or in institutional settings. They work closely with handicapped persons. Their aim is to help handicapped people become at least partly or totally self-sufficient.

Beth Marks is a rehabilitation counselor. When clients come to her for help, she first has them take a physical examination. When Wayne Garrett came to the center, he had lost his right arm in an accident. Mrs. Marks made the arrangements for him to be fitted with an artificial arm. Then together, Mrs. Marks and Wayne carefully looked at what kind of work he might be able to do. Wayne took several tests which showed that he had an interest and flair for sales work. Wayne decided that he would like to sell real estate. A special course in real estate and a car with modified controls started Wayne on his new career.

Other clients Mrs. Marks works with are so disabled that they may not be able to enter the normal working world. Sometimes handicapped persons are placed in sheltered workshop settings. There, they work under con-

*Rehabilitation counselors are helping this homemaker learn to use her kitchen from a wheelchair.*

stant supervision. They do simple work for which they are paid a small wage.

A rehabilitation counselor may work with halfway houses. Patients who are discharged from mental hospitals or paroled from prison live in a sheltered setting before they face the world on their own. The counselor can help such people learn to cope with the everyday problems of living.

Most rehabilitation counselors have master's degrees. Many of the aides who work in rehabilitation centers, sheltered workshops, and halfway houses do not have or need such advanced training.

**Jobs with the Elderly**

Some people choose careers helping the aged live full, rich lives. Many cities or counties have Councils on Aging where the elderly are helped with their problems. Helen Walters works for the local Council on Aging, where she runs a Food for Folks program. This project takes hot meals to elderly people unable to prepare food for themselves.

Mike Lozar works in a nursing home, planning activities and services for patients. Because the elderly are often lonely, he plans entertainment, games, and tournaments for the nursing home members. He has two aides who help write letters, read, or simply listen to those who need or wish such assistance.

Many of the jobs which involve working with the aged have no specific training or experience standards. They call for an ability to appreciate and relate to old people. As science continues to prolong lives, more and more people will be employed in giving support services to the aged.

## experiences in human relations

### HUMAN RELATIONS SKILLS

Being able to get along well with others is an important part of any job. It is essential in a career which involves working with other people.

Talk with at least five people who work with others. You may talk to teachers, sales personnel, recreation leaders, nurses, police officers, social workers, or religious leaders. Ask them, in relation to their jobs, how important it is to be able to get along with others. Which do they think more important—relationship or job skills? Are there any relationship skills or personality traits that seem most important to them? How important is communication? The ability to build trust into a relationship? Honesty? Empathy? Cooperation?

Summarize what your five subjects have told you and prepare an oral report. Share your findings with your classmates. Listen as they tell about their interviews. Did many people give the same responses? What skills or traits seemed to be the most important? What did you learn from this experience?

## TO SUM UP...

1. What is the purpose of a career in health care?
2. Identify some steps on the career ladder in nursing.
3. Describe what physical and occupational therapists do.
4. What are some positions open in the field of dental work?
5. What are rehabilitation counselors and what do they do?
6. Why are jobs in working with elderly people likely to become more important in the years ahead?

## HELPING PEOPLE LEARN

In the United States, the law requires that all children attend school. Thus, everyone has some contact with teaching and teachers. Teaching is the largest profession in this country.

The teaching profession covers a wide variety of jobs and positions. Teachers may teach in public or private schools with different age students. They may be administrators, supervisors, or consultants. They may work in government offices or in private agencies with educational programs. But regardless of the setting, teachers work to improve the lives of others through education and training.

### Elementary Educators

The first six to eight years of school are taught by persons trained in elementary education. Children learn reading, math, social studies, writing, art, music, and many other subjects. The teacher must know about a wide range of subject matter. In larger schools, teachers with special training in art, music, and physical education may teach these subjects.

State laws require teachers to be certified after completing a college degree in education. One certification requirement is a time of supervised classroom teaching, often called student teaching.

Beyond the training needed, a teacher must like children. An ability to relate to children and to be at ease with them is necessary.

John Doakes is an excellent third-grade teacher. He is a patient and understanding man who sees and likes his students as persons. He wins the respect of his pupils early each year through his quiet authority. However, it is his zest for learning which makes him such an outstanding teacher. He inspires his students to learn and to work on projects which he designs to meet their individual needs.

### Secondary Educators

Secondary school teachers instruct junior or senior high school students. At this level, the teacher concentrates on certain subject matter which is taught to several classes. Usually teachers are certified to teach only in

*This teachers' aide is giving individual attention to children who need extra help in reading.*

specific subject matter areas. For example, Martin Zanther received certification to teach vocational agriculture when he graduated from college. He was not qualified to teach other subject matter areas.

**Teachers' Aides**

While teaching jobs require college education, many school districts hire teachers' aides. A high school diploma is usually all that is required for a teachers' aide. Such aides work under the direction of teachers, and help in classroom management. Most aides work in elementary schools, but some school districts have hired them in secondary schools.

Tessie Bennett is a teachers' aide at West Side School. In the mornings, she works with Mrs. Anfield, a first-grade teacher. Afternoons are spent with Miss Purcell in the other first-grade class. Her tasks include taking attendance, and collecting money for lunches, milk, and books. She keeps track of those children who receive free lunches. In addition, she listens to individual children read and helps those who are behind catch up. Checking papers is a frequent chore. Mrs. Bennett graduated from high school but never attended college. She has held three secretarial jobs, but says, "I never really enjoyed working in an office at all. This job just suits me perfectly. You do different things each day so it isn't dull. And I really feel like I'm doing something worthwhile when I help the children."

**College and University Educators**

Teaching jobs are also found in colleges and universities. Such teachers are required to hold master's and/or doctor's degrees. Their teaching is usually in a certain subject matter.

In many cases, college teachers have less contact with their students than do other teachers. Classes can be large lecture sessions where teachers have little chance to talk personally with students.

Many colleges place a great deal of stress on faculty research projects. Designing these projects, carrying them out, and writing reports about the results take a great deal of time. These activities may cut out the chance to build close relationships with students.

Many college teachers are able to find time to build close ties with their students. However, teachers who enjoy building close relationships with students may find more satisfaction teaching in another type of school.

**Educators Outside Schools**

Teaching positions are not limited to the school setting. Ray Corrie teaches piano and organ lessons. Sherrie Udall is a yoga, relaxation, and meditation teacher. Anthea Gilbert is a home economist with the Cooperative Extension Service who teaches homemakers through informal meetings and lessons. Swimming and diving are taught at the YMCA by Andrew Glass. Other people teach pottery, television repair, modern dance, ballet, and voice.

Teaching jobs such as those described above do not always have college educational requirements. If you are skilled in some subject and are interested in teaching your skill to others, you may wish to teach privately. Some vocational or technical schools hire teachers who have specialized skills but no formal training as educators.

Peter White was an experienced auto mechanic. He had attended several schools to learn his trade, but he had never gone to college. The Central State Vocational School hired him to teach in the auto mechanics program. Although he was not a certified teacher, he got the job because of his training and skill in mechanics.

**Librarians**

Librarians work with people outside of schools to help them learn. The modern library contains books, pamphlets, magazines, and newspapers. It may also have art objects and tape and phonograph recordings to check out. The library may sponsor lectures, puppet shows, and story hours for children. Library employees have many chances to work with and teach people in a nonschool setting.

Librarians hold master's degrees in library science. However, libraries hire workers and clerks who may need only a high school degree. Most of these workers have many chances to meet and interact with library patrons. The work calls for a wide knowledge of the resources of the library. Also needed are an outgoing personality and a real interest in people.

Jim Sumlar was hired as a circulation clerk at the branch library in his neighborhood. He checked books in and out and made friends with regular patrons. His knowledge of the library's resources made him effective when he was asked for help.

There are many kinds of libraries in which jobs can be found. Most people are familiar with public and school libraries. In addition, libraries can be found in hospitals, military bases, and research facilities. Those who enjoy books, reading, and people may find a career in library work right for them.

### TO SUM UP...

1. What is the largest profession in this country?

2. Describe the educational requirements to become a teacher.

3. What is the main difference in approach between elementary and secondary education?

4. What are teachers' aides?

5. Why is it difficult for college or university teachers to build strong relationships with students?

6. List some opportunities for out-of-school educators.

7. Why is a librarian considered an educator?

Unit 5: Relating to the Larger World

## ORGANIZING ACTIVITIES FOR PEOPLE

A final group of careers in working with people has wide variety. This group involves organizing activities and dealing with people. It ranges from careers as religious leaders to ones as sales clerks.

### Recreation

Recreation leaders help people enjoy and use their leisure time well. People of all ages have and will have more and more leisure time. The typical worker has over 4,000 free hours a year. It appears that in the future leisure activities will replace work as the central life interest of a large number of people.

Recreation leaders are hired by park districts and voluntary agencies. They direct programs at playgrounds and at recreation, community, and rehabilitation centers. Leaders have a college degree with study in recreation and/or physical education. However, many programs hire high school graduates to work with a recreation leader.

Many people feel that a recreation leader mainly works with sports. It is true that sports are a large part of any program. This is because of the well-being they bring participants. However, most programs also have arts, crafts, music, dance, and drama.

Sonja Ruiz worked for the city park board. She was involved in many different activities. She organized an egg roll, a bike rodeo, and a track meet for 8-to-10-year-olds during one week. She taught tennis and gymnastics. She filled in part time as a life guard at one of the swimming pools. An arts and crafts show that she organized was the grand finale of a three-week day camp, where children learned to make a variety of items. Sonja's enthusiasm and love of people makes her a success at her job.

### Management and Personnel

Management is needed in any organization where one person directs another. Business and government have grown steadily larger in this country. Thus management personnel are required to coordinate the efforts of thousands of workers.

Management is the art of getting things done through other people. Most managers work with groups of others who require leadership and direction. In one sense, managers are group leaders on the job. Successful man-

*Recreation leaders organize activities for the constructive use of leisure time.*

agers tend to be good at task roles. However, they are most successful when they can also promote group-building and growth.

Although upper-level managers tend to have college degrees, many lower-level managers do not. Some two-year community colleges have management programs. In other cases, companies prefer to train their managers themselves.

Manda Blakely went to college for a year. She was unhappy with her program, so she found a job as a management trainee with a department store chain. During her six months of management training, she learned about all aspects of the store's operation. After her training, she supervised a staff of clerks and stock personnel. Her ability to get along with the others helped win their respect. She had a knack for respecting her staff as persons, yet inspiring them to peak performance. Her personal traits helped her become a good manager.

Personnel work is closely related to management. Nothing is more vital to the success of an organization than the people who work in it. Who those people are and how well they are able to do their jobs depends in part on the personnel manager.

Although all organizations are different, most personnel workers hire, transfer, and fire others. Many company training programs are run by the personnel department. Employee benefit programs and counseling are done by personnel. Finally, in many companies, personnel workers handle union-management relations.

Again, many people without college degrees work in the field of personnel. However, the top positions are usually held by those who have college degrees. One of the most important requirements is that personnel workers must be highly capable of understanding others. This helps them decide how

*Americans eat over one-fourth of their meals away from home.*

each person's talents and abilities can best be used to meet the goals of the organization.

### Food Service

Over 25 percent of all the food consumed in the United States is eaten away from home. Restaurants, cafeterias, snack bars, fast food restaurants, and automats serve food. Hospitals, schools, dormitories, sanitariums, and industrial plants may make food available to workers and others. The food service industry hires millions of workers to feed its customers.

**Unit 5: Relating to the Larger World**

At the top of the career ladder in food service are the managers who are responsible for the overall operation of the facilities. Many managers own the establishments. Maria Grier owns and manages a restaurant, The Fatted Calf. Some managers are hired to run establishments for others. Tom Lorenzo manages the employee snack shop in the local computer factory. He is hired by the company to serve the employees good food at low prices.

Managers organize and direct the work of food service employees. In addition, they plan menus and purchase food and equipment. Many managers handle the financial aspects of the food service business.

A large part of the manager's work is with customers. The manager creates a friendly atmosphere, taking suggestions and handling complaints.

The manager must be familiar with all aspects of food service work. Many managers began their careers as waiters, assistant cooks, or busgirls or boys. In addition to knowing the work involved, the manager must have some business training. The manager must be prepared to live his or her personal life around the needs and hours of the business.

Training requirements differ among food service businesses. In many cases, no set standards exist. However, many restaurants now seek people with college courses in restaurant management. Vocational or technical school graduates from food service programs also have an employment advantage. The National Restaurant Association has a program to train potential managers.

Mid-level on the food service career ladder are the positions of waiter and waitress. The kinds of tasks they perform depend in large part on the type of food service business in which they work. Taking orders for and serving food and beverages are common to all waiter or waitress jobs. These workers also make out customers' food checks. In small restaurants, they may serve as cashier, clear and clean tables, or prepare salads and beverages. Some waiters and waitresses replenish supplies and clean equipment.

Josie works after school as a waitress in a sandwich shop. The food is good and customers expect and receive fast service. Josie is quick and has a good memory, which makes her a favorite among steady customers. Her friendly smile and manner help make her a good waitress. When business is slack, Josie refills the napkin holders and the salt, pepper, and sugar containers. When work is slow she also cleans the pie display case.

In small cafes, diners, sandwich shops, and fast food businesses, efficiency is stressed. The customer is to be served swiftly with little luxury and ceremony.

In large restaurants where dining is more formal, emphasis may be on luxury and relaxation. Food service workers see that customers find dining pleasurable. In this type of restaurant, there may be captains, hostesses, and busboys and girls to assist the waiters and waitresses.

Most employers prefer to hire waiters and waitresses who have finished high school. However, non-graduates are sometimes hired.

Regardless of the type of food service business, waiters and waitresses need to have patience and the desire to please and to be of service to the public. Skill in relating to others helps make customers feel welcome and sets the stage for enjoyable dining.

In some cases, serving as a waiter or waitress may be an entry-level job in food service. In larger, more formal restaurants, the entry-level jobs are those clearing tables and doing miscellaneous chores. Many of these entry-level jobs do not require meeting the public.

However, many people who have begun as busboys or girls have used their skill in meeting all types of people to move up the career ladder.

## Religion

Religious leaders, regardless of their faith, attend to the spiritual and moral needs of the members of their organization. They also have an interest in the welfare and educational needs of their groups.

*Religious leaders spend a great deal of time in personal counseling.*

Religious leaders interpret their faith and beliefs to their followers. They perform services and ceremonies to pass on the spiritual guidelines of their faith.

In addition, personal counseling is one of the most important responsibilities of the leaders of all denominations. They counsel people of all ages about the entire range of human problems. Religious leaders organize activities for children, couples, teenagers, singles, and the elderly. These activities bring people with common spiritual beliefs together for study and enjoyment.

To be religious leaders, people must feel deeply that God's will for them is full-time religious service. Persons who enter religious work feel that their faith compels them to serve others as they serve God. While religious leaders must have a strong relationship with their god, they also must be able to relate to people. Through their work with people, they interpret religious ideals and values. Thus a person with strong religious values and an ability to understand and relate to others might find satisfaction in a career as a religious leader.

Louella Morgan had always held strong religious beliefs. As a high school student, she spent most of her free time in church work. During college, she decided to become a minister in her denomination. After graduating from college, she entered the seminary. Her ordination as a minister occurred when she graduated from the seminary. For her first pastoral post, she served as assistant minister in a large inner city church. Besides her normal pastoral duties, she was very interested in organizing activities for the many elderly people who lived in the neighborhood. Gradually, she was able to bring many of them into the life of the church. She felt that her career helped interpret God's word to others. Her ability to build relationships, to

### Unit 5: Relating to the Larger World

listen, and to give feedback and comfort made her a successful minister.

## Sales

Factories which produce goods require some means to get them to the consumers who want them. People with careers in sales make it possible for products to move from factories to the purchasers.

Careers in sales cover a wide variety of activities and products. Door-to-door salespeople sell everything from cosmetics to magazines. Life insurance, stocks and bonds, and real estate are sold by sales personnel. Manufacturers have salespeople who sell their goods to retail stores. Finally, over 60 percent of all sales positions are in retail sales—direct sales to customers in stores. Salespeople sell everything from alarm clocks to candy to postage meters.

The level of knowledge and skill required in the sales field depends on the kind of position held. Keith is a clerk in a discount store. He needs some skill in operating a cash register and handling money. Samual Keyes is an electronics salesperson who sells American-made computers to overseas governments. Thus he must have a great deal of highly technical knowledge and skills.

Regardless of the type of sales work, the salesperson must have poise and an attractive personality. Also needed are an ability to meet and work with strangers and a sincere desire to serve others. Successful sales personnel depend on their skill in relating to others to make sales and to bring customers back for sales in the future.

Jobs in sales offer good chances for promotion. A college degree increases a person's chances to advance. However, sales personnel without a college background can build successful careers through hard work and through skill in relating to others.

Sharon Percival is a salesperson for an automobile dealer. She feels that the cars she sells are excellent products. Therefore her enthusiasm helps convince customers to purchase cars from her. In addition, she has learned to point out the features of a car that will appeal specifically to each customer. When a customer is interested in economy and pollution control devices, she stresses these features. Engineering appeals to others while some are more attracted to appearance and handling. Another part of Sharon's job is arranging financing and insurance for the cars her customers purchase.

Les Anthony is a wholesale salesperson who works for a large cleaning products manufacturer. He calls on store managers who might be interested in selling the products his firm makes. During his calls, he points out new products that the company is marketing, often bringing samples of the products. Les works with his customers to set up advertising in their stores to draw attention to the products he sells. With regular customers, Les checks stock, writes up orders, and arranges delivery of his products. Les sometimes entertains customers at lunch or in the evening to build good will.

Margie Lee is a sales clerk in a department store. When she was first hired, she worked in a stockroom as a clerk. She also helped to set up displays of merchandise. After some experience, she was promoted to sales in the children's clothing department. She enjoys working with parents who are shopping for clothing for their children.

These examples are only a few of the many opportunities available for persons interested in a career in sales.

## Hotels and Motels

Another area which provides a wide range of jobs working with people is the operation

## Ch. 16: Careers in Working with Others

of hotels and motels. Such establishments provide rooms and meals for travelers or permanent guests. Small motels may provide only guest rooms and baths. Large hotels may have dining rooms; convention, conference, and banquet rooms; and exhibit areas. They may also have magazine stands, drug stores, beauty and barber shops, retail shops, and boutiques.

Hotels are most often found downtown near the business center of a city or town. Motels are usually near highways on the outskirts of towns or cities. Resort hotels cater to vacationers, conventions, and sales meetings.

Hotels and motels are operated twenty-four hours a day for the comfort, protection, and needs of guests. People choosing a career in hotels or motels should be prepared to work a variety of shifts.

The manager has overall responsibility for running the hotel or motel profitably. The manager is also in charge of providing the best possible services and comfort for guests. In small hotels or motels, the manager may also be the owner. A successful manager must be able to handle many business matters. He or she must also be able to relate well to guests and employees. The more at ease the manager is with people, the more likely he or she is to succeed. A lot of patience and tact as well as a sense of humor are needed personality traits.

Rosita and Neil Evans own and manage a small motel. They enjoy meeting people from all over the country who stay with them. Rosita handles the financial aspects of the business while Neil welcomes and chats with guests. Together they run a profitable business which lets them meet many interesting people.

Managers in large motel or hotel chains may be required to have a college degree in hotel administration. Some two-year colleges offer training in hotel or motel management. In smaller motels and hotels, managers may be advanced from within the staff. A high school degree plus on-the-job training may be all that is needed to become a manager. Alert, hard-working employees have many chances for promotion.

Below the management level are a number of jobs which allow employees to work with people. Bellmen or women, busboys or girls, and desk and reservation clerks are needed for the smooth operation of the business. Hotels and motels hire many people who work behind the scenes but who do not meet the public. Starting in such a job may lead to promotion which will allow a person to use his or her skills in relating to others.

*Careers in sales involve selling a great variety of products.*

Unit 5: Relating to the Larger World

**Other Careers**

The careers described above are merely a small sample of the many jobs available in working with people. There are many others.

In the area of law enforcement, police officers work with others to uphold the law. Lawyers consult with clients and act on their behalf.

Barbers and beauticians use their skills in personal care as well as their skills in relationships to please clients. Flight attendants serve airlines customers on trips from one city or country to another. Public relations and advertising jobs involve working with clients. Such careers offer a chance to do meaningful work while relating to other people.

fourths of all Americans will work in jobs that did not exist in 1975.

Therefore, making plans for the future requires that you consider long-range possibilities in the career cluster that interests you. How can you prepare yourself for changes that may occur? Will you be ready if your job becomes obsolete?

The average twenty-year-old will change jobs six or seven times during his or her lifetime. Some of these changes will be advancement in a chosen career. However, others will be required because the old job will no longer exist.

Education beyond high school is one way that people can prepare themselves for job

## TO SUM UP...

1. Describe some activities which a recreation leader may direct or organize.
2. Why are careers in management and personnel needed?
3. Describe various jobs on the career ladder in food service.
4. What is the special trait needed by religious leaders?
5. Why are there so many different types of jobs in sales work?
6. Identify personal traits a successful sales person must have.
7. Describe what is involved in careers in hotel or motel work.

## PLANNING FOR THE FUTURE

Today in the United States, 25 percent of the workers are in jobs that did not exist five years ago. It is estimated that by 1990, three-

*Careers in working with others offer variety, challenge, and chances to meet new and interesting people.*

changes. Vocational training and college education both give a student flexibility, which is an advantage in getting and keeping a job. In addition, education beyond high school is a help when transfers or changes in jobs are made.

An ability to get along well with people is a big advantage in retaining a job. Those people who have skill in working with others will be kept when some workers are being fired or laid off. Being successful in service careers demands that you have good communications skills. You need to be able to build strong relationships. The ability to be honest, trustworthy, and responsible are traits that you need to possess. Such characteristics will help you be successful in carrying out your plans for the future.

## experiences in human relations

### A RESOURCE FILE

There are many hundreds of jobs which involve working with people. This experience will help you become aware of the broad scope of careers in this area.

With your classmates, prepare a resource file. You may wish to keep the material you collect in a drawer or on a shelf. Try to find pamphlets and articles describing jobs which involve working with people.

The library or counseling office may have extra copies of pamphlets describing jobs which could be included in your resource file. Newspapers are good sources of possible articles. They often carry articles which describe careers or jobs in which people work with others.

Many magazines have articles about people and their careers in working with others. If you cannot get a copy of the magazine for your file, try to copy the article. Be sure to note where the article was found. The *Reader's Guide To Periodical Literature* can help you locate articles. The *Guide* is found in libraries and lists the titles of articles found in many magazines. You can look up topics related to careers in working with people.

When you have finished your file, think about what it contains. Do you have articles describing a wide variety of jobs? How could the file be used by someone who was interested in a career in working with others?

### TO SUM UP...

1. What are some ways that you can prepare yourself for a future job that does not exist today?

2. How many times are you likely to change jobs in your lifetime?

# Index

## A

Abilities, 44, 45
Abstinence (sexual behavior), 99
Abuse
 child, 195, 196
 drug, 82
Acceptance, seeking, 113
Accepting others, 133-135
Accepting self, 43, 52, 53
Adjustment to divorce, 309-311
Acquaintances, relationships with, 111
Active listening, 154
Adaptation, function of family, 218, 219
Addiction, drug, 82, 83
Advancement on job, 359
Adversary system of divorce, 303, 304
Affection
 function of family, 217
 in relationships, 123
Alcohol, 85-87
All-channels pattern of communication, 332, 333
Amphetamines, 88
Anticipatory grief, 293, 294
Appearance, on the job, 355
Arguments, how to settle, 197-203
Arrangements at death, 295-298
Aspects of self-concept, 32-35
Attraction, in conjugal love, 243
Authority, accepting, 335
Autocratic leader, 327
Automobile accidents and alcohol, 86

## B

Bagging (conflict style), 197, 198
Balancing needs, 54
Barbiturates
 See depressants
Basic skills for job, 352
Benefits
 from relationships, 124, 125
 of communication, 163, 164
Blaming (communication pattern), 145
Blended families, 272, 273

Blow up (conflict style), 197
Body bubbles, 161-163
Body language, 157-160
Boundaries, family, 221-223
Bragging, 37
Breakdown of traditional roles, 178-181
Brother-sister relationships
 See sibling relationships
Burial urn, 295
Business relationships, 114

## C

Cancer and smoking, 85
Career, choosing, 361-363
Career clusters, 363-367
Career ladders, 364-367
Careers in
 counseling, 369-371
 dental work, 373
 education, 375-377
 food service, 379-381
 hotel work, 382, 383
 library, 377
 management, 378, 379
 medicine, 371, 372
 motel work, 382, 383
 occupational therapy, 372, 373
 personnel, 378, 379
 physical therapy, 372
 psychiatry, 369
 recreation, 378
 rehabilitation counseling, 373, 374
 religion, 381, 382
 sales, 382
 social service work, 369
 social work, 368
 working with elderly, 374
Ceremony, marriage, 255
Chain pattern of communication, 333
Challenging work, 357, 358
Changes
 at home, 185-187
 fast pace of, 12-18
 in life styles, 258-260

386

# Index

on the job, 183, 184
social, 182, 183
Changing marriage styles, 266-278
Changing role expectations, 181
Changing subject (in defending self), 37
Characteristics of
  self-accepting people, 42, 43
  self-actualizing people, 52-58
Child abuse, 195, 196
Child-parent relationship, 224-227
Childless marriages, 270, 271
Children
  adjustment to divorce, 310, 311
  relationship with parents, 224-227
Choices, to solve problems, 61
Choosing
  a career, 361-363
  a dating partner, 247-253
  options, 62, 63
  values, 72
Chosen roles, 169, 170
Cigarettes, 84, 85
Circle pattern of communication, 333
Cirrhosis of liver, 86
Clarifying role, 321
Cliché conversation, 140
Cocaine, 88
Cohesiveness
  in a group, 331, 332
  in work groups, 349, 350
College education, career in, 376, 377
Collusion in divorce, 304
Communal living, 279-285
Communication
  group, 332-335
  importance of, 136-139
  in family, 228
  in solving conflict, 205, 206
  nonverbal, 157-163
  nonverbal in groups, 333-335
  on the job, 355
  patterns of, 144-148
  skills, learning, 148-157
  verbal, 139-143
Community divorce, 308, 309
Companionship, in conjugal love, 244
Compromise, in a quarrel, 202
Compromising roles, 323, 324
Computing (communication pattern), 145, 146
Concern, in conjugal love, 244
Conflict

and divorce, 303, 304
general discussion, 189-194
how to handle, 194-208
in communes, 281, 282
in families, 229
in groups, 336
in work roles, 344, 345
role, 175-177
solving, 194-208
styles, 194-197
Conformity, in a group, 330, 331
Conjugal love, 242
Consensus-testing role, 321
Constructive communication, 137, 138
Constructive results of conflict, 191-194
Context (in communication), 150
Contract marriages, 266-270
Cooperation
  learning, 335
  on the job, 352, 353
Counselor, career as, 369-371
Cremation, 295
Crisis, family, 230-235
Criticism, 37, 336

### D

Dangers of
  alcohol, 86, 87
  depressants, 88
  hallucinogens, 92, 93
  heroin, 90, 91
  LSD, 92, 93
  marijuana, 93
  smoking, 85
  stimulants, 89, 90
Dating, 245-253
Dating exclusively, 253
Dating partners, relationships with, 111
Death, 286-297
Decision making
  about drugs, 96-99
  about sex, 103-106
  process, 60-64
Defending the self, 37, 38
Defenses, to protect self, 37, 38
Delirium tremens, 87
Democratic leader, 328
Dental worker, career as, 373
Depressants, 87, 88
Destructive communication, 137, 138

**387**

## Index

Destructive results of conflict, 191, 192
Development of self, 26-29
Diets, use of drugs, 89
Differences
    emotional, 25
    intellectual, 24, 25
    physical, 24
    social, 25, 26
Disagreements
    how to settle, 197-203
    on the job, 345
Distracting (communication pattern), 146
Divorce, 298-312
Divorce procedures, 303, 304
Divorce rate, 299
Double standards (sexual behavior), 99, 100
Driving and drinking alcohol, 86
Drug abuse, 82
Drug addiction, 82, 83
Drug misuse, 82
Drug use, 82, 94-96
Drugs, 80-98

### E

Economic divorce, 307
Economic functions of families, 212, 213
Education
    careers in, 375-378
    changes in, 14, 15
Educational function of family, 214, 215
Effects of
    alcohol, 85, 86
    depressants, 87
    hallucinogens, 92
    heroin, 90
    LSD, 92
    marijuana, 93
    nicotine, 85
    stimulants, 88
Elderly, careers with, 374
Elementary education, career in, 375
Embalming, 296
Emotional differences, 25
Emotional divorce, 306, 307
Emotional intimacy, 119
Emotional needs, meeting, 112, 113
Emotional reactions to death, 290, 291
Empathy, in conjugal love, 243, 244
Employee expectations, 356-359
Employer expectations, 352-356

Encouraging roles, 322
Engagement, 254, 255
Enjoyment (group purpose), 318
Enrichment, 113, 114
Entry-level jobs, 364
Escape, related to drug use, 96
Esteem needs, 48, 316
Executor of will, 297
Expectations
    marital, 268-270
    work, 352-360
Experiences, kinds, 56-58
Exploitation, 124, 145
Exploring values, 76-79
Expressing group feelings, 322, 323
Extrinsic values, 66, 67
Extrinsic work values, 343

### F

Family
    blended, 272, 273
    effect on self-concept, 31, 32
    forming own, 245-257
    functions of, 212-219
    general discussion, 210, 211
    importance at death, 295
    influence on drug use, 95
    influence on self-development, 26-28
    influence on values, 69, 70
    relationships with, 110, 224-230
Family boundaries, 221-223
Family crisis, 230-235
Family rhythm, 221
Family style, 219-223
Family tempo, 221
Family themes, 220, 221
Feedback, 155, 156
Feelings, sharing, 141
Fight, learning how, 197-203
Food service, careers in, 379-381
Frequency of divorce, 298-301
Friends, relationships with, 110
Funeral arrangements, 295-298

### G

Gate-keeping roles, 324
Given roles, 168
Going steady, 253
Grief, 292-294

# Index

Grounds for divorce, 303, 304
Group-building and maintenance roles, 322-325
Group communications, 332-335
Group marriage, 276, 277
Group norms, 329-332
Group roles, 319-329
Groups
  general discussion, 314-316
  purposes of, 318, 319

## H

Habits, 56
Hallucinogens, 92, 93
Handling conflict, 194-208
Harmonizing roles, 323
Health
  and sexual responsibility, 103
  effects of drugs on, 84-93
Health care, as a career, 371-375
Heroin, 90, 91
Hierarchy of needs
  general discussion, 49-52
  on the job, 340-343
Home, changes in, 12-14, 185-187
Homogamy, in dating, 245
Honeymoon, 255, 256
Hotels, careers in, 382, 383

## I

Ideal mate, 248, 249
Ideas, sharing, 140
"I-messages", 150-152
Individuality, respect for, 258
Infatuation, 240, 241
Influence of values, 67-69
Information-giving role, 320, 321
Information-seeking role, 320
Information sharing (group purpose), 318
Integrity on the job, 353
Intellectual differences, 24, 25
Intellectual intimacy, 118
Interment, 295
Intestate, 297
Initiating role, 319, 320
Initiative, on the job, 353
Intimacy ladder, 118-121
Intimate distance, 160
Intrinsic values, 66, 67
Intrinsic work values, 343

## J

Job
  changes in, 183, 184
  expectations, 352-360
  relationships, 347-352
  requirements, 345, 346

## K

Kinds of
  drugs, 84-94
  families, 210, 211
  life styles, 219-223
  relationships, 108-111

## L

Leader, 325
Leadership, 325-329
Learned roles, 168, 169
Learning
  communication skills, 148-157
  self-acceptance, 40-43
  to fight, 197-203
Legal divorce, 307
Leveling (communication pattern), 146, 147
Levels of verbal communication, 139-143
Librarian, careers as, 377
Life styles, 219-223, 258, 259
Listening skills, 152, 153
Living together, 278, 279
Loneliness, caused by change, 18, 19
Love, 237-245
Love needs, 47, 48, 316
Loyalty on the job, 353
LSD, 92, 93

## M

Maintenance roles, in groups, 322-325
Malnutrition, 90
Management, careers in, 378, 379
Marijuana, 93
Marriage, 255-257
Marriage contracts, 266-270
Marriage, reasons for, 236, 237
Marriage styles, changing, 266-278
Masks, to protect self, 35, 36
Maslow, Abraham, 45, 49
Mate, ideal, 248, 249

## Index

Mausoleum, 295
Meaningful work, 357
Mental addiction to drugs, 82, 83
Misuse, drug, 82
Motels, careers in, 382, 383
Motivation, on the job, 353
Mourning, 292, 293
Mutual dependancy, 115

### N

Narcotics, 90-92
Nearness, in dating, 248
Needs, basic
  fulfillment, 115
  hierarchy of, 49-52
  meeting, 45-52, 316
Negative self-concept
  and drug use, 94, 95
  developing, 30-40
  in relationships, 125-127
New experiences, 56
Nicotine, 84, 85
No-fault divorce, 304-306
No-lose method of arguing, 203-208
Nonverbal communication
  general discussion, 157-163
  in groups, 333-335
Nurse, career as, 371, 372

### O

Occupational therapist, career as, 372, 373
Office of Education, U.S., 364
Open marriage, 274-276
Opium, 90
Options in decision making, 61, 62

### P

Pace, family life, 221
Parental divorce, 307, 308
Passive listening, 154
Parents, relationship with children, 224-227
Patterns of communication
  among individuals, 144-148
  in groups, 332, 333
Peak communication, 142, 143
Peak experiences, 57, 58

Peer pressure and drug use, 95
Peers
  influence on self-development, 28, 29
  influence on values, 70
  related to drug use, 95
  relationships with on the job, 349
Perceptions of others, 133-135
Perfectionism, 37
Performance, on the job, 353, 354
Permissiveness with affection (sexual behavior), 100
Permissiveness without affection (sexual behavior), 100
Person-to-person relationship, 131-135
Personal distance, 160
Personal growth through groups, 335-337
Personnel, careers in, 378, 379
Physical addiction to drugs, 82
Physical differences, 24
Physical intimacy, 118
Physical needs, 45, 46, 316
Physical reactions to death, 289, 290
Physical therapist, career as, 372
Physical violence, 195, 196
Physician, career as, 371
Placating (communication pattern), 145
Positive self-concept
  developing, 30-40
  in relationships, 125-127
Post-addiction symptoms, 91
Power conflict, 130, 131
Power in relationships, 127-131
Pregnancy
  effect of smoking, 85
  responsibilities of, 103
Premarital sex, 99-101
Principle of least interest, 129
Problems
  agreeing on, 197, 198
  defining, 61
  solving (as a group purpose), 318, 319
Procreation, function of family, 217
Propinquity, in dating, 248
Protecting self-concept, 34-40
Protection, function of family, 213, 214
Psychological divorce, 309
Psychologist, career as, 369
Public distance, 161
Punishment, in relationships, 123, 124
Purposes
  of group, 318, 319
  of relationship, 111-115

# Index

## Q

Quarrels, how to settle, 197–203

## R

Rapport, 115
Reactions to death, 288–291
Reasons for
  divorce, 301–303
  drug use, 94, 96
Recreation, career in, 378
Recreational function of family, 215
Rehabilitation counselor, career as, 373, 374
Reiss, Ira, 99
Relating to world, 54
Relationship skills, learning, 20, 21
Relationship wheel, 115–118
Relationships
  characteristics of, 121–131
  developing, 115–121
  family, 224–230
  in open marriage, 272–275
  kinds, 108–111
  on the job, 347–352
  parent-child, 224–227
  person-to-person, 131–135
  purposes of, 111–115
  siblings, 227, 228
  stress caused by change, 18–20
Religion, careers in, 381, 382
Religious function of family, 216, 217
Remarriage, 311, 312
Renewable marriages, 267
Reporting facts, 140
Requirements, job, 345, 346
Respect for individuality, 358
Responsibility for decisions, 63, 64
Reward, 123, 124
Rhythm, family, 221
Risks of communication, 163, 164
Role conflict, 175–177, 344, 345
Role expectations, 171, 181
Role relationships, 165, 166
Roles
  advantages of, 170–172
  disadvantages of, 172–175
  group-building and maintenance, 322–325
  in groups, 319–329
  kinds, 165–170
  related to self, 187, 188
  sex, 177–187
  task, 319–322
  work, 344–347
Romantic love, 241, 242

## S

Safety needs, 46, 316
Salary, 356, 357
Sales, careers in, 382
Satir, Virginia, 148
Satisfaction, with job, 358, 359
Secondary educator, career as, 375, 376
Sedatives
  *See depressants*
Self
  and roles, 187, 188
  development of, 26–29
  differences in, 24–26
Self-acceptance, 52, 53
Self-acceptance, learning, 40–43
Self-accepting individual, characteristics of, 42, 43
Self-actualization, 317
Self-actualization needs, 49
Self-actualizing people, characteristics of, 52–58
Self-concept
  and drug use, 94, 95
  general discussion, 29–40
  in relationships, 125–127
Self-revelation, 115
Service industries, careers in, 367–384
Setting-standards roles, 324, 325
Sex roles, 177–187
Sexual responsibilities, 101–103
Sharing feelings, 141
Sharing ideas, 140
Sibling relationships, 227, 228
Silence (as defense), 37
Silent treatment (conflict style), 197
Single parents, 263–265
Singlehood, 260–262
Sister-brother relationships
  *See sibling relationships*
Smoking, 84, 85
Social changes, 182, 183
Social differences, 25, 26
Social distance, 160, 161
Social service worker, career as, 369

391

## Index

Social worker, career as, 368, 369
Society, changes in, 15-18
Sources of values, 69-72
Space relationships, 160-163
Spouses, adjustment to divorce, 310
Standard-setting roles, 324, 325
Standards, group, 329-332
Steady dating, 253
Stereotyping, 173, 174
Stimulants, 88-90
Stress caused by change, 18-20
Style
    conflict, 194-197
    family, 219-223
    leadership, 327, 328
Summarizing role, 321
Supervisor relationships, 347, 348
Surgeon General, warning on cigarettes, 84

### T

Talents, 44, 45
Task roles in groups, 319-322
Teachers' aide, career as, 376
Tempo, family, 221
Tolerance, drug, 82
Traditional roles, breakdown of, 178-181
Tranquilizers
    See depressants
Trust, 121-123

### U

University education, career as, 376, 377
United States Office of Education career clusters, 364

### V

Value indicators, 75

Values
    and drug use, 97, 98
    and sex, 104
    choosing, 74
    exploring, 76-79
    general discussion, 65-72
    influence on life style, 73-75
    of work, 343
Valuing process, 72-76
Verbal communication, levels of, 139-143
Visitation rights, 307
Volunteer work, 366

### W

Wheel pattern of communication, 333
Will, 297
Withdrawal (conflict style), 196, 197
Withdrawal from
    alcohol, 86, 87
    drug addiction, 82
    hallucinogens, 92
    heroin, 91
    LSD, 92
    smoking, 85
    stimulants, 89
Work
    changes in, 15
    general discussion, 338, 339
    reasons for, 340-343
Work expectations, 352-360
Work groups, 347-351
Work relationships, 347-352
Work roles, 344-347

### Y

Y pattern of communication, 333